Southern Exposure

D1568922

Other books by Stetson Kennedy

Palmetto Country, American Folkways Series edited by
Erskine Caldwell (New York: Duell, Sloan & Pearce,
1941; reprinted Tallahassee: Florida A & M University
Press, 1989).
The Klan Unmasked (London: Arco 1954, as *I Rode
with the Ku Klux Klan*; Paris: Morgan, 1958; reprinted
Boca Raton: Florida Atlantic University Press, 1990).
Jim Crow Guide, Collection Les Temps Modernes edited
by Jean-Paul Sartre (Paris: Julliard, 1955; London:
Lawrence & Wishart, 1959; reprinted Boca Raton:
Florida Atlantic University Press, 1990).

SOUTHERN EXPOSURE

Stetson Kennedy

Florida Atlantic University Press
Boca Raton

Library of Congress Cataloging-in-Publication Data

Kennedy, Stetson.
    Southern exposure / Stetson Kennedy.
       p.   cm. — (A Florida sand dollar book)
    Originally published: Garden City, N.Y. : Doubleday, 1946.
    Includes index.
    ISBN 0-8130-1078-0 (acid-free paper)
    1. Southern States—Politics and government—1865-1950.
    2. Southern States—Social conditions. I. Title. II. Series.
    F215.K33   1991
    975′.04—dc20   91-11664
                                                    CIP

The Florida Atlantic University Press is a member of the
University Presses of Florida, the scholarly publishing agency of
the State University System of Florida. Books are selected for
publication by faculty editorial commmittees at each of Florida's
nine public universities: Florida A & M University (Tallahassee),
Florida Atlantic University (Boca Raton), Florida International
University (Miami), Florida State University (Tallahassee),
University of Central Florida (Orlando), University of Florida
(Gainesville), University of North Florida (Jacksonville),
University of South Florida (Tampa), and University of West
Florida (Pensacola).

Orders for books published by all member presses should be
addressed to University Presses of Florida, 15 Northwest 15th
Street, Gainesville, FL 32611.

To all who strive for a new South for all.

THANKS: to my wife, Edith, without whose untiring assistance *Southern Exposure* would not have been written; to my son Loren, whose first sentence was "Go write the book"; to Marjorie Arnette, without whose generous research aid it would have lacked much of its comprehension; to Bucklin Moon and Paul Hollister, Jr., for patient editorial guidance; to Arnold Forster and Alex Miller for their splendid cooperation; and to all the others who have helped in one way or another.

ADDENDUM: This is the last of the quadruplets to which I gave birth at mid-century to be born again under the umbrella of the University Presses of Florida, and for their prenatal blessings I wish to thank Dr. Raymond Mohl of Florida Atlantic University, Dr. Patricia Waterman of the University of South Florida, Dr. Ann Henderson of the Florida Endowment for the Humanities, Horace and Jody Glass of the *Mandarin Advertiser*, and my wife of these many years, Joyce Ann.

Southern Exposure *does not pretend to present a complete or al-together pleasing view of the South. Some Defender-of-the-South has observed, "It is possible to become so concerned over the plight of the sharecropper as to forget how the good earth smells at dawn," et cetera. I know this to be true from personal experience. But it seems to me that the sharecropper's plight deserves priority over the earth's smell. Perhaps one reason why I have written this book is to enable me to inhale the South's varied smells with a clear conscience. No one could appreciate moon-light and magnolias more than I; but the South has had more than its share of literature on that theme, and under the circum-stances, I for one am not inclined to provide more. Suffice it to say that I am attached to my birthplace and home; I like much of what the South is, and still more of what it is to be. . . .*

Stetson Kennedy

CONTENTS

3. The Road Ahead

THE HEAT'S ON!

When *Southern Exposure* first appeared in 1946, my Aunt Lizzie said that I couldn't be expected to understand the problem of the South (blacks), having been born and raised in Florida.

I didn't argue with Aunt Lizzie then, and there is scarcely any need to do so now that she and the Jim Crow prototype of apartheid have both passed away. By and large, my family, region, and nation cast off the ugly integument with what grace they could muster, and I am proud of them.

Occasionally, however, I still receive an anonymous poison pen letter from some next-of-kin, addressed to "Mr. BLACKsheep." And when a photograph appeared recently in the local paper, showing me and my cat looking over some of my books, some kissin' cousin called to say, "Thank God it was a cat!"

So, as we all know, much remains to be done.

The global holocaust that was World War II left virtually every place on earth "standing at a crossroads," and the American South was no exception. And as the South went, so would go the nation. This was because there had been no truly free elections in the South for generations, thanks to such institutionalized frauds as the poll tax and white primary, which kept masses of people— white and black—from voting. Thus the small manipulated electorate was able to send back, term after term, the same old racist, feudalist, reactionary demagogues to House and Senate, where, by virtue of seniority, they controlled key committees and literally "ruled the roost."

Most of the research that went into *Southern Exposure* was carried out during World War II under the working title "The Four Freedoms Down South." Some few may yet recall that it was President Franklin D. Roosevelt who hit upon "The Four Freedoms" as the Allies' war aims. As would seem to be the fate of almost all war aims, all thought of The Four Freedoms vanished with the victory parades. At the considerable risk of being cited for disturbing the unholy peace that now prevails, I will cite them here and now: Freedom of Speech, Freedom of Religion, and Freedom from Want and Fear—not just for the victors, but for all the world!

Since the American South was as short on some of these items as anybody else, it occurred to me, when a childhood back injury kept me out of the armed services, that the patriotic thing for me to do would be to write "The Four Freedoms Down South," in the hope that thereby we would not be overlooked in any postwar dispensation.

And so I did. In that self-appointed task I was far from being alone. Throughout the war, everybody who was anybody (or thought they were)—popes, prelates, potentates, presidents, union bosses, chamber of commerce heads, storefront preachers, journalists even—felt constrained to set forth their visions of "The World We Fight For." The sky was the limit—"jobs and homes for all," "garden cities of tomorrow," you name it. Nothing seemed out of reach.

I clipped and saved every vision that came to hand, little suspecting it would prove to be nothing but ephemera that would vanish on the winds of peace and business as usual. About the only survivor was a fragment from a wartime ditty:

> There'll be bluebirds over,
> The white cliffs of Dover,
> Tomorrow when the world is free.

A couple of decades later I bundled it all up, the whole comprising several cubic feet, and sent it to the New York Public Library. It soon came back, collect, with an indignant note: "We have no room for such stuff. In future query before sending anything." Happily, the millions worldwide who gave their lives for The Cause will never know.

The untimely consignment of The Four Freedoms to limbo meant that I had to reorganize my manuscript and find a new title before submitting it to a publisher. "Southern Exposure" came to me in the middle of the night, and I leapt out of bed to jot it down.

All over that postwar world—the questions of "Germany Over All" and Japanese Pan-Asianism having been settled for the time being—peoples were locked in a struggle to throw off colonial, feudal, and royal yokes in favor of democracy. While the American South was not ruled by any visible royalty, the earmarks of colonialism, feudalism, and racism were all too apparent.

The South had been designated one of the major hunger areas of the world. Its energies were sapped by pellagra, malaria, dengue, and hookworm; most of the people who tilled the land were themselves landless; feudalism lingered on in the form of sharecropping, tenant farming, peonage, and the commissary system; extractive industries, absentee ownership, discriminatory freight rates, regional and racial wage differentials conspired to keep it in poverty; and illiteracy doomed it to skill-lessness and ignorance. This is not to say that the fish weren't biting good or that we didn't have some fun; but the fact remains that we were a Third World region and didn't even know it.

In rewriting my manuscript I essayed to throw down a gauntlet not only to apartheid and white supremacy but to the entire state of affairs. Consequently, when I finally put it in the mail to Doubleday & Company, it dealt with a lot more freedoms than four. Soon I received a telegram, which I, before opening it, thought must be an acceptance. What it said was, "ATTORNEYS SAY EVERYTHING IN IT LIBELOUS. COME AT ONCE WITH FULL DOCUMENTATION."

In short order I arrived at the Wall Street offices of Doubleday's law firm, briefcases bulging, to be greeted by a bellow: "Whadaya mean, calling Prentis a fascist? He's a friend of mine! We play golf every weekend!"

Although I succeeded not at all in placating the attorneys, who strongly urged Doubleday not to publish, they did so without changing a word, and no libel suits were ever filed. "When *you* got through documenting them, I guess they figured the best thing to do was stand mute," a relieved Doubleday editor said to me at the time.*

The appearance of *Southern Exposure* rattled the cages of the white supremacists no end. As in all my writing, I was hoping not so much for literary laurels as societal impact, and all the indications were that the book was on target and on time.

In many instances, regular book reviewers were brushed aside as governors, publishers, and editors took it upon themselves to take up the cudgels in support of the challenges it made. It was the reaction of The Enemy, however, that was most gratifying to me. Mississippi's Senator Theodore Bilbo, for example, the ranking racist of them all, called a press conference around the hospital bed where he was being prepped for surgery for cancer of the throat. Waving copies of my *Southern Exposure* and Lillian Smith's *Color Blind*, he avowed that they were bent upon destroying all that the South held dear.† He much preferred, he went on to say, the vertical throat-cutting style of his surgeons to our horizontal one.

Those were the days when the CIO's "Operation Dixie" announced that it was coming South to "organize the unorganized," black and white in the same union, and the KKK responded, "We shall fight horror with horror!" Highlander Folk School was training folks to do the job that had to be done, and the Southern Conference for Human Welfare, wrecking bars in hand, was probing for cracks in the Jim Crow wall.

I was in there pitching with all such forces for progress. And in

---

*My collection of original documentary hate sheets and related materials accumulated in the course of my infiltration of the KKK and other racist-terrorist groups was conveyed to the Schomburg Center for the Study of Black Culture at the New York Public Library in 1948. The collection is available on microfilm (four reels, comprised of 3,625 frames). The more extensive "Stetson Kennedy Papers" (6.6 lineal feet) reflect the broader scope of my life's work and are accessible at the Southern Labor History Archive, Georgia State University, Atlanta.

†For an assessment of the impact of these two books on precipitating the struggle against segregation and racism, see William Beyer's doctoral dissertation "Searching for Common Ground, 1940–49," University of Minnesota, 1988. The magazine *Common Ground*, published by the Common Council on American Unity headed by novelist Pearl Buck and edited by Margaret Anderson, printed chapters from both books.

1950 when George Smathers defeated Florida Senator Claude Pepper in the Democratic primary by distributing a photograph of him emerging from a black church in California, and referring to him as "Red Pepper" and a "thespian," I announced as a color-blind write-in candidate on a platform of "total equality." For my pains I was arrested at the polls and threatened with lynching by the deputy en route to St. Augustine jail. But Clifford Durr at the Federal Communications Commission had upheld my demand for equal radio time, so my reward was sitting in jookjoints and watching the faces of the good ole boys when my spot announcements came on. They got the message, but you would have thought it was Doomsday.

Thereafter (1952) I went to Geneva to testify before a United Nations committee about forced labor in America. I remained overseas for the next eight years, traveling on four continents and getting my *Jim Crow Guide* and *The Klan Unmasked* published in a score of languages, all with a view to giving our dearly beloved Uncle Sam a hotfoot on the subject of apartheid.

My unstated goal in writing *Southern Exposure* had been to "soften up the South for righteousness"; but righteousness, when it finally came, was due not so much to white repentance as to black insistence. The prescription I so fondly recommended in my book was for working folks to arm themselves with a ballot in one hand and union card in the other and then march together toward an unsegregated, democratic, prosperous Southland. But it didn't work out quite that way.

It was blacks themselves who seized the initiative, and when they took to the streets organized labor was not all that prominent among the whites who joined them. And, remarkably, it was not the legislative or executive branch of government that was the first to respond but the judicial.

When the marching began and the first decision was handed down, I decided to go home and be in on the kill. As a reporter and columnist for the black *Pittsburgh Courier*, I followed in the footsteps of Martin Luther King from Albany to Selma to Ole Miss and had a little to do with bringing him to St. Augustine, where the final nails were driven into the coffin of James Crow, Esq.

Not everyone who devotes a lifetime to a cause is privileged to see it come to fruition, and it is good to live in a South and America that are not nearly so hateful as they were. Back then, I tried to tell my white southern compatriots that desegregation would not hurt and that they would feel better about themselves when it was over. And obviously they do.

I remember that while the plaudits of nonsouthern reviewers of *Southern Exposure* were heartening, I was put out when a note of self-righteousness crept in—so much so that one day at Doubleday I muttered a threat to write a sequel, "Northern Exposure," They sat me down in a chair and hurried off to draw up a contract, but I was obliged to confess that the problems confronting the rest of the country were too overwhelming for me to tackle at that juncture. A half century later, they are all the more so.

I might be tempted to say, however, that there is yet need for a *Southern Exposure II*, were it not for the fact that a namesake magazine is being published in Durham, North Carolina, and valiantly carrying the standard forward.

While regionalism remains a valid approach to certain problems, the nationalization and universalization of many another has become a fact of life—so much so that global regionalism has become the one that makes the most sense. (It was this realization, and his acting upon it, that got Martin Luther King killed.)

The overriding need at this late hour, as I see it, is for someone (else) to write a "Global Exposure" focusing on the incipient greenhouse effect that threatens to do us all in. Or does it? Perhaps the colored races will be able to stand the heat, and only we palefaces will have to get off the map.

Stetson Kennedy
Beluthahatchee, Florida
October 1990

1. The Problem of the South

THE SQUALID SOUTH

Problem I, Section I

"We of the North have been too long deceived by the surface charm of the South, by the sincere friendliness and hospitality of the Southern people, which is a thin crust over the treacherous economic and social quicksand that engulfs the mass of the Southern population," newsman Leeds Moberly has written.

"The condition of too many people in the South is deplorable, degrading, destructive of the decencies which men expect from American civilization," replied the Raleigh (N.C.) *News and Observer*. "But history shows and God knows that not all the blame for that condition is Southern . . . There are bad men in the South, blind men, ruthless men, greedy men. But the South has no monopoly on them."

It so happens that there is truth in both of the foregoing observations. The South *is* a quagmire which threatens to engulf the entire nation, but much of the responsibility for the South's sad condition lies outside the region. At the same time there is no denying that the South is hypersensitive to criticism which emanates from the outside, and professional Defenders-of-the-South never fail to take advantage of every opportunity to aggravate this unfortunate psychopathic condition. The South's paranoia dates from its "whupping" in the Civil War and has not improved much since.

Typically symptomatic of this was the reaction which followed the remark by Frances Perkins (while she was Secretary of Labor) that "A social revolution would take place if shoes were put on the people of the South."

"Why, even the mules of the South wear shoes!" indignantly rejoined Senator Joshua Bailey of North Carolina.

"There is a considerable colored population in the South who would regard it as a distinct punishment to be required to wear shoes," added Senator Duncan Fletcher of Florida.

"Miss Perkins' ideas of the South are probably derived from having seen an 'Uncle Tom' show, from what she has been told by professional agitators, and from reading some of the metropolitan newspapers," concluded a Southern editor.

But the hottest reception of all was rendered the epochal *Report on the Economic Condition of the South,* prepared for President Roosevelt by the National Emergency Council in 1938. The remarks of H. Bond Bliss in the Miami *Herald* were typical:

> Another group will set out to investigate the South and find out what is wrong with it. The South was not aware that it was in serious shape. Thought it was doing nicely. That is compared to most of the country. But President Roosevelt thinks differently. Declared it was the "Number 1 economic problem." That it unbalanced the nation. Not the budget.
>
> So the Southerners will be investigated; their doors opened, inquiries made on grits and grunts and pay. The truth is that the North is jealous of the South, of its conservative independence, its rising economic status. The North is a bit afraid. It wants to see what can be done. Not to save the South. But the North. From Southern competition.

In seeking to misinterpret the President's *Report* as a sample of damnyankee meddlesomeness, reactionary Southern papers blithely ignored the fact—clearly set forth in the *Report's* preface—that it was prepared under the editorship of Dr. Clark Foreman in collaboration with one of the most competent advisory committees of Southerners ever assembled. Among them were Dr. Frank P. Graham, president of the University of North Carolina, Dr. B. F. Ashe, president of the University of Miami, Barry Bingham, publisher of the Louisville *Courier-Journal,* and nineteen others, including manufacturers, chamber-of-commerce men, and labor leaders.

Needless to say, the common people of the South do not need to be convinced of the accuracy of the President's *Report;* to them the statistics therein represent the hard facts of their daily lives. They, more than anyone else, know that Roosevelt was right when, geographically speaking, he said that the South was the nation's economic problem number one.

Anyone who has been in the South, and who is not physically or willfully blind, will have no difficulty transposing the figures on life in the South into the peculiarly Southern shapes of hunger and pain. Others may find faithful reproductions in such books as *You Have Seen Their Faces* (Viking), and *These Are Our Lives* (Chapel Hill).

In addition to the President's *Report,* we now have the *Report* of the Southeastern Regional Planning Commission, based largely upon the 1940 Census. Like the President's *Report* before it, this later study speaks with a bona fide Southern accent, the Southeastern Regional Planning Commission being composed of members appointed by the governors of the seven Southeastern states of Alabama, Florida, Georgia, Mississippi, North Carolina, South Carolina, and Tennessee. Figures hereafter cited from the President's *Report* are for the entire South, embracing the additional states of Virginia, Kentucky, Louisiana, Arkansas, Texas, and Oklahoma.

No Ready-Made Money

The South has been the poorest region in America ever since its rulers chose the devastation of civil war to evolutionary progress; today the richest Southern state is poorer in per capita income than the poorest state outside the South.

In 1940 the Southeast's per capita income was only $309 as compared to $573 for the nation. While the region had 14 per cent of the nation's population, it had only 11.5 per cent of the country's wage earners, and they received only 7.3 per cent of the national wage total. Nearly 45 per cent of the region's people were farmers, and their average cash income was only $607 as compared to the average national farm income of $1,370.

Even in the boom year of 1929—when folks were eating high

off the hog—Southern farm people had an average gross income of only $186 a year as compared to $528 for farmers elsewhere. Out of that $186 the Southern farmer had to pay all his operating expenses—so it is no wonder that such items as automobiles, radios, and books are relative rarities in the rural Southland.

"For more than half of the South's farm families—the 53 per cent who are tenants without land of their own—incomes are far lower," says the President's *Report.* "Many thousands of them are living in poverty comparable to that of the poorest peasants in Europe. A recent study of Southern cotton plantations indicated that the average tenant family received an income of only $73 per person for a year's work. Earnings of share-croppers ranged from $38 to $87 per person. An income of $38 annually means only a little more than 10 cents a day. A study of Southern farm-operating white families not receiving relief or other assistance showed that those whose incomes averaged $390 spent annually only $49 on food, $31 on clothing, $12 for medical care, $2 on education, $1 on reading, and $1 on recreation.

"The South's industrial wages, like its farm income, are the lowest in the United States. In 1937 common labor in 20 important industries got 16 cents an hour less than laborers in other sections. A recent survey of the South disclosed that the average annual wage in industry was only $865 while in the remaining states it averaged $1,219." Significantly, at the same time it was found that the *profits* of Southern textile mills were higher than those in the North.

The South's great poverty is further revealed by the fact that the assessed value of its taxable property in 1935 was only $463 per person, compared to an average of $1,370 in nine Northeastern states. Furthermore, the South's banks in 1937 had only 6 per cent of the national total of savings deposits, although the region had 28 per cent of the country's people. State and local governments in the South collected only $28.88 per person in 1936, while in the nation as a whole the amount was $51.54. Two years earlier, federal income-tax collections in the South averaged only $1.28 per capita.

"So much of the profit from Southern industries goes to outside financiers," says the President's *Report,* "that the South has piled its tax burden on the backs of those least able to pay, in the form of sales taxes. In every Southern state but one, 59 per cent of the revenue is raised by sales taxes. The efforts of Southern communities to increase their revenues and to spread the tax burden more fairly have been impeded by the vigorous opposition of interests outside the region which control much of the South's wealth. Many Southern towns have found that industries which are not willing to pay their fair share of the cost of public services likewise are not willing to pay fair wages, and so add little to the community's wealth."

Thus the South has learned the painful lesson that industrialization, for which it has yearned so long, provides no magic formula for prosperity, but like agriculture, has problems of its own requiring public planning and regulation.

The War for the Four Freedoms gave some impetus to the South's rate of industrialization, but not nearly so much as was desirable, with shipyards and training centers comprising the major developments. During the first stages of the war the South's share in war contracts amounted to only 10 per cent of the total. In some measure this was due to the South's lack of investment capital and the reluctance of outside industry to expand Southward. But as H. Clarence Nixon pointed out, it was likewise true that "This region could not forthwith take on a big job of producing fine, high-quality instruments of warfare, because it lacked the organization, the technology, the machine tools, and the highly trained personnel required. In spite of significant gains in the period between the two wars, Southern manufacturing was far below the national level." Even by the war's end none of the nation's thirty great industrial zones were in the South.

Evidence of the South's disadvantaged wartime position was found by the U. S. Chamber of Commerce in a survey in which only 27 per cent of the South's people—the lowest proportion in the nation—said they were better off in 1942 than in 1941. Moreover, while 56 per cent of America's people were found to be saving money, only 45 per cent of the South's people were able to do so. A *Fortune* magazine survey in 1943 found that the median monthly earning in the South had risen to $103 per month—but in the rest of the country, excluding the Northeast, it was $151. For Negroes in the South and Southwest the median was less than $50 per month, while Negroes in the rest of the country had a median of $92.

Grits without Gravy

"Southern people need food," says the President's *Report*. "The all too common diet in the rural South of fat back, corn bread, and molasses, with its resulting pellagra and other dietary diseases, is not dictated by taste alone." Pellagra, the nutritive deficiency (starvation) disease, caused *deaths* at the rate of .65 per 10,000 population in the Southeast in 1940, as compared to the national rate of .16. Alabama's rate was highest—.87.

"Considering farm operators, sharecroppers, and Negroes combined, the rural Southeast ranks far below the North and West in nutritional practices," states the Planning *Report*. "At comparable levels of income, sharecroppers have less satisfactory diets than do farm operators. About one half of the Negro families of the Southeast have poor diets. Nutrients frequently absent from farm operators' diets in the Southeast are certain of the basic vitamins, i.e., vitamins A, C, B, and G. Lack of these vitamins, occurring day after day, has been described as 'hidden hunger,' which is manifest in chronic fatigue, slow thinking, nervous disorders, and digestive disturbances and has been described by well-fed Southerners as 'general triflingness.' "

Even when judged by the imperfect standard of national consumption, the South has a deficit of 121,000,000 gallons of milk, 70,000,000 dozen eggs, 18,000,000 purebred cattle, and so forth.

Of special benefit to the undernourished South was the U. S. Department of Agriculture's food-stamp plan, whereby persons certified as being unable to afford an adequate diet were granted, on the basis of family need, stamps with which they could purchase from their grocer whatever foods were designated as "surplus," such as fresh vegetables, pork, butter, eggs, dried beans, flour, and so forth. The stamps were then redeemed at face value by the U. S. Treasury. This stamp-plan method of increasing the food-purchasing power of persons with sub-subsistence diets gave a boost not only to farmers, but to wholesalers and retailers as well, and thus met with the enthusiastic approval of nearly everyone. Similarly, the cotton-stamp plan proved to be a boon to the South, enabling those who raise and process cotton, among others, to clothe themselves with it more adequately.

Another program launched by the Roosevelt Administration which has succeeded in establishing a greater measure of freedom from want of food is the free hot school lunch agency. Before this plan was instituted, the Department of Agriculture found that 9,000,000 American youngsters were not getting even one square meal a day. By 1941, 5,000,000 of them were benefiting from the program, and 4,000,000 were fed in the relatively prosperous year of 1942. To the South, with more underfed children than any other region, the hot lunches, inexpensive but nourishing, have been a boon indeed. The heartening record of health, scholastic, and personality improvements which have stemmed directly from these lunches is one of the most moving documents in existence.

Lethal Statistics

> *The South is the No. 1 health problem of the nation.*—
> DR. THOMAS PARRAN, Director U. S. Public Health Service

Hand in hand with undernourishment goes disease—nowhere is there a vicious circle more vicious than the misery-go-round of poverty and sickness. First poverty causes people to lose their health; then ill-health prevents them from overcoming poverty. And so the wheel of misfortune goes around and around . . . and when it will stop depends upon what people do about it, together.

The poor Southerner has been scrawny, puny, and ailing from

way back. He has been reduced to this state not only by his lack of good and sufficient food but also by his lack of adequate clothing and housing. And then there are the related factors of ignorance of hygiene, sanitation, nutrition. Too, there is the excessive humidity of many areas, the warm climate conducive to microscopic growth, and the mushrooming of cities. All things considered, it would be surprising if the poor Southerner were not in that well-known foul shape.

And foul it is. The death rate for the nine South Atlantic states rose 7.3 per cent in a single recent year—an insurance company reports—while in no other region did it rise more than 4.8 per cent, and in some sections it declined.

Mother and child have less chance of survival in the South than anywhere else in the country. In 1939 the maternity death rate (per 10,000 live births) was 56.16 in the Southeast, compared to 40.39 in the nation. Florida's rate was highest: 65.27. Similarly, the Southeast's infant death rate (per 1,000 live births) was 58.6, compared to 48 for the nation. In 1937 stillbirths throughout the South ranged from a rate of 52 to 68, while the national rate was only 29.9.

When the National Youth Administration surveyed the health of its employees, it found that Southern youth exceeded the national rates for hookworm, venereal diseases, heart trouble, faulty blood pressure, and so forth.

The relatively poorer health of the relatively poorer Negroes finds expression in a life expectancy of only 45 years, as compared to 59 years for whites. In other words, to be born black in America is to be sentenced to die 14 years sooner than your white contemporaries. The Negro death rate is 32 per cent higher than the white (in 1925 it was 62.5 per cent higher); total daily sickness among Negroes is 43 per cent higher than among whites; the incidence of tuberculosis among Negroes is more than two and a half times higher than among Southern whites and five times as high as Northern whites. Moreover, the Negro maternity death rate is three times as high as the white rate, and the Negro infant mortality rate is two thirds higher than the white. Those are but a few of the hazards incurred by being born black in a white man's country.

Chief subverter of the South's health is malaria. In 1940 the Southeast's death rate from this disease (per 10,000) was .45, compared to .11 for the nation. The rates of Mississippi, Alabama, and South Carolina were highest—.80, .72, .62. Worse yet, 39 of the Southeast's counties had rates of 2 or more. On the basis of $10,000 as the value of a human life, malaria cost the South $39,500,000 in 1936 alone. More than 90 per cent of the national incidence of five or six million cases of malaria annually occurs in the South. At the minimum out-of-pocket expenditure of $40 per case, the annual cost of the South's 5,400,000 cases is $216,000,000. In addition, the disease reduces the South's industrial output approximately one third.

Pneumonia and influenza combined in 1940 to cause a death rate of 9 per 10,000 in the Southeast, as compared to 7.03 in the nation. Tennessee and South Carolina had the highest rates, 10.32 and 10.22. Furthermore, 217 of the region's counties had rates of 10 or more, and 42 counties had rates of 15 or higher.

The Southeast's death rate from tuberculosis per 10,000 population in 1940 was 5.35, compared to the national rate of 4.99. Tennessee again was high with a rate of 7.58, while 110 Southeastern counties also had rates of 7 or more.

Syphilis caused a death rate of 1.85 per 10,000 in the Southeast in 1940, while the national rate was 1.44. Florida had the highest rate, 2.65, and 76 Southeastern counties had rates of 3 or higher. Selective-service figures on the first two million draftees also gave Florida the highest incidence: 53.3 per 1,000 whites, 405.9 per 1,000 Negroes. Since it is estimated that gonorrhea is five or six times as prevalent as syphilis, its incidence among Florida Negroes would appear to be something like 2,200 cases per 1,000 persons.

So much for the South's priorities on disease. The question is: What is being done about it? The answer is: Damned little. It is an inhuman truth that more attention has been given to the conservation of such resources as soil, water, forests, minerals, and even wild life than has been given to the preservation of human life and health.

In 1942, 204 of the Southeast's counties—nearly a third of

the total—neither had full-time public-health departments nor were included in consolidated full-time health districts. Georgia was worst-off in this respect, with two thirds of its counties lacking full-time health service; and more than half of Florida's counties were likewise deficient. Even of those Southeastern counties which had full-time health service, more than half had 2 or less health-service employees for every 10,000 persons in the population; while only 6 per cent had more than 4 employees per 10,000 population. Total receipts for public-health services in 83 per cent of the counties were less than 71 cents per capita, and more than 40 per cent of the counties took in less than 40 cents per capita per year. Altogether, public-health expenditures in the region in 1941 amounted to only 7 per cent of the national total—to provide for 14 per cent of the country's people.

"Obviously most of the health departments in the region are without adequate personnel to carry on an effective health program," concludes the Planning *Report*. The need is greatest in the thinly populated rural counties, and the most immediately available solution for them would seem to be consolidation into health districts.

Another aspect of the South's lack of medical service is the region's wholly inadequate number of physicians. With its 14 per cent of the nation's people, the Southeast in 1940 had but 9 per cent of the nation's physicians to serve them. In 80 per cent of the region's counties there was but one physician for every 1,112 people.

Still another index to the region's lack of health facilities is the fact that in 1939 it had but 11.5 per cent of the nation's hospitals to accommodate its 14 per cent of the nation's people. Even more indicative of the inadequacy of the region's hospital facilities is the fact that it had only 5.57 hospital beds for every 1,000 people, while the nation had 9.74. Furthermore, 41 per cent of the region's counties had less than 3 beds for every 1,000 people, while less than 1 per cent of the counties had as many as 5 beds per 1,000 persons.

To add tragedy to tragedy, even these hospital beds are not fully occupied—not because Southerners shouldn't be in them, but because they can't pay the price. In part this is due to the fact that a greater proportion of the Southeast's hospitals are under private control than are those throughout America. More than half of the region's counties had no general hospitals in 1941.

Be It Ever So Humble

Although the family has been relieved of many of its responsibilities by the public school (and has defaulted on much of the remainder) it nevertheless continues to be the center around which life in America grows. This being true, the house must be regarded as the seedbed. By the same token, the South's role as cradle to the nation makes Southern housing a matter of vital national concern.

As the President's *Report* points out, "The effects of bad housing can be measured directly in the general welfare. It lessens industrial efficiency, encourages inferior citizenship, lowers the standard of family life, and deprives people of reasonable comfort. There are also direct relationships between poor housing and poor health, and between poor housing and crime."

Franklin D. Roosevelt was the first American President to shoulder the government's responsibility for improving the lot of the "one third of the nation that is ill-fed, ill-clothed, and ill-housed." In the South, however, the burden is even heavier. "By the most conservative estimates," says the President's *Report,* "four million Southern families should be rehoused." This is one half of all the families in the South.

Inasmuch as two thirds of the Southeast's dwelling units are rural, their condition warrants first attention. "Houses in the rural South are the oldest, have the lowest value, and have the greatest need of repairs of any farmhouses in the United States," says the President's *Report.* "More than half of them are unpainted and more than a third do not have screens to keep out mosquitoes and flies. Hookworm infection and consequent anemia have flourished as a result of soil pollution. Contaminated milk and contaminated water, frequently found, cause typhoid fever, which is becoming a widespread rural disease in the South."

"The story of rural housing in the Southeast is a familiar one," adds the Planning *Report*. "Many thousands of families live in unpainted shacks in an advanced stage of dilapidation, with daylight visible through walls, roof, and floor. Water is drawn from a shallow, often polluted well or carried from the nearest 'branch.' Privies are usually open to flies and animals and frequently afford no semblance of privacy. About a fifth of the families are without privies. The cabins usually contain either two or three rooms, occasionally one or four. The families living in them are often extremely large. In some areas, the windows are without glass; solid wooden shutters are closed to keep out rain or cold."

Statistics reveal that the Southeastern rural housing situation is so bad as to be almost incredible. In 1935, 85 per cent of the region's farmhouses lacked inside water. Alabama, Mississippi, Georgia, and Tennessee had the astonishing percentages of 97, 95, 94, and 92 of their farmhouses without inside water. In other respects, the farmhouses of the region measured up as follows: without bathtubs, 94.1 per cent; without electricity, 92 per cent; without indoor flush toilets, 95 per cent.

To some extent the South's poor rural housing may be attributed to the enormous increase in farm tenancy since 1900 (there were 774,000 tenant farmers in the Southeast in 1940, almost half of them Negroes). With a third of the tenant farmers on the move every year, little or nothing is done by either the landlord or tenant to improve the latter's housing. The net result is that while the average Southern farmhouse is worth $650, the tenant farmer's house is worth but $350.

There was a time—not so very long ago—when the America that is not included in New York City fancied that it had no slums merely because it had no six-story tenements. Now, says the Planning *Report,* the United States realizes that it has "the largest per capita acreage of urban blight of any nation in the Western World."

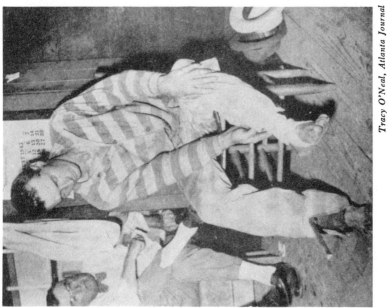

Tracy O'Neal, Atlanta Journal

*Poor whites fare somewhat better under "the law."
This man cut his tendons to avoid road-gang lash*

INS

*"A nigger's got just two chances in the South—
slim, and none at all"*

The Negro is taught early to grin and bear it——

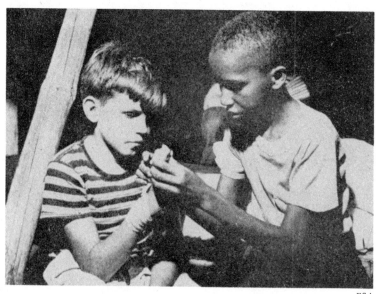

FSA

——but prejudice is made, not born

Ben Shahn, FSA

From the cradle to the grave—insecurity

Russell Lee, FSA

Got the Eviction Blues

TVA transforms poverty into plenty

and the new South looks ahead

"The type of slum most usual in Southern towns consists of antiquated, poorly built rental quarters for working people," adds the President's *Report*. "The rows of wooden houses without any modern improvements, without proper sanitary facilities, and often without running water, are usually in congested areas and in the least desirable locations. Often they are next to mills or mines where the tenants work, or in low swampy land subject to floods and no good for anything else. They are usually far removed from playgrounds and other recreation areas. The Southern slum has often been built to be a slum. It is simply a convenient barracks for a supply of cheap labor."

While the Southeast's urban housing is not generally so bad as the rural, it is bad enough. Studies of the region's urban housing in 1934–36 revealed the situation to be as follows: lacking indoor flush toilet, 32 per cent; lacking bathing equipment, 41 per cent; lacking electric or gas lighting, 25 per cent; lacking running water, 13 per cent; congested occupancy, 9 per cent; requiring major repairs, 20 per cent.

During the South's period of almost purely agrarian development (and prior to the spread of tenancy), its farm folk tended to stay put, on or near the place of their birth. At that time home ownership was the ideal housing goal. But with the appearance of commercial and industrial occupations, as well as the vast mechanized "factory-in-the-field" plantations—all of which require more or less mobile labor—home ownership became an encumbrance, not to say an impossibility, and the demand for rental housing increased apace. But private enterprise responded not at all to the need for rural rental housing, and urban rental units were for the most part merely improvised out of old dwellings. New construction, both for rent and for sale, has been largely confined to a price range well beyond the reach of that half of the South's population which needs new housing most.

Man and Land

My father—a merchant by trade but an agrarian (from Bulloch County, Georgia) at heart—has always said that Southerners have been in double-trouble ever since they began to get their food out of paper sacks instead of out of the soil. After intensive research, the U. S. Government has finally reached the same conclusion.

The Southland's pioneers were able to achieve a modicum of self-sustenance by planting a variety of garden crops and acquiring a cow, some hogs, and a flock of chickens. Such a modest farm establishment was—and is—capable of providing a substantial diet; but that does not mean that it can provide an adequate standard of living. While man may be able to live by bread alone, it is no fun.

Anything less than 100 acres is generally regarded as inadequate to provide an adequate farm family income; yet 80 per cent of all the farms in the Southeast are smaller than this. Consequently these land-hungry farmers are impelled to plant all the acreage at their disposal to some cash crop, without regard for the need for crop rotation, and even at the expense of a garden plot. In this ruinous procedure—whose appalling results in malnutrition and pellagra have been noted—the tenants and sharecroppers are generally encouraged by their landlords and creditors.

In the beginning the small farmer in the South had to compete with the big plantation system operated by Negro slave labor. After Emancipation the plantation system continued to operate with theoretically free Negro and white tenant farmers and sharecroppers. But continuous overconcentration on the money crops of cotton and tobacco has consistently brought bankruptcy to Southern agriculture in general and to small farmers in particular.

One result of this has been a progressive increase in farm tenancy, which rose from 25 per cent of all farmers in 1880 to

42 per cent in 1935. About two thirds of all the tenants and croppers in the United States are in the South, where two thirds of them are white and one third are Negro. However, the relatively disadvantaged status of the Negroes is revealed by the fact that about four fifths of all Negro farm operators are tenants or croppers. Of the South's non-landowning farmers, about half are tenants and half are croppers, with a great deal of interchange between categories, as well as to the status of farm laborer.

In every respect the economic and social condition of the cropper is worse than that of the tenant. But whether the payment to the landlord be in cash or a share of the crop, 60 per cent of the South's farmers pay from a fourth to a half of what they produce as rent. In addition, a large proportion of Southern farmers must go into debt for their family's subsistence while making a crop, as well as for fertilizer, seed, and other supplies. "For these advances they rely on loans from merchants or landlords," reports the President's Committee on Farm Tenancy, "for which they pay a combination of interest and 'time' prices frequently equivalent to 30 per cent or more on the face value of the loan." There is still truth in Louis XIV's assertion that "Credit supports agriculture as the rope supports the hanged."

There is, no doubt, something to be said for the dire effects of this primitive system on the landlord, who must exact high rents and interest to cover the losses frequently involved. It is impossible, however, to go along with Southern columnist John Temple Graves when he says that "The sharecropper relation is more liberal for the tenant and more illiberal for the landlord than any other known form of tenancy. Instead of the South *admitting* that it is the home of the sharecropper, it might *boast* of it." While the cropper is nothing for anyone to boast about, it is true that the grossly inefficient arrangement is costly to all concerned.

Both man and land have been sadly eroded by the system. "About 61 per cent of all the land that is badly eroded in the U. S. is in the Southern cotton belt," the Department of Agriculture reports. "In these same Southern states twenty-two millions of acres of formerly fertile soil are ruined beyond immediate repair. An expanse as large as South Carolina has been washed away. Another area the size of Oklahoma and Alabama has been seriously damaged." Because of this, the South spends $161,000,000 a year for fertilizer, while all the rest of the country uses only half as much.

The bulk of the blame for the plight of Southern agriculture must be attributed to King Cotton's Old Deal, whose anarchic administration is fully exposed in Charles S. Johnson's *Statistical Atlas of Southern Counties* (University of North Carolina Press). Based largely on the 1930 Census, the *Atlas* covers all 1,104 counties of the 13 Southern states. Cotton was found to be the basic crop in half of the South's counties; 15 per cent of them had some other crop specialty; only 12.6 per cent were self-sufficing; 10.2 per cent were predominantly non-farm; only 8.5 per cent were grain-livestock-dairying counties, and only 3.4 per cent concentrated on raising vegetables and fruit.

"In the cotton counties definite characteristics mark off the group from other counties," the *Atlas* states. "In 63.3 per cent of the cotton counties, cotton was the only important crop raised. Only 12.1 per cent of the other farm counties were devoted to a single crop.

"Counties which raise cotton are dominated by it socially as well as economically. Traditionally, cotton and the plantation system have gone hand in hand . . . The statistical characteristics of the cotton counties reflect the continued existence of the plantation system: a large, untrained, Negro laboring force, few industrial non-farm occupations, low per capita incomes, a great gulf between the white-owning and white tenant population and between the white and Negro population, and rigid enforcement of racial restrictions.

"In 81.3 per cent of the cotton counties more than half the farm operators were tenants. The median per cent of tenancy was 65.7 for cotton counties, and about half this for the other farm counties.

"Changes are already making themselves felt within the cotton economy. The tenant farmer is being replaced, particularly in the newer cotton areas of Texas and Arkansas, by hired farm labor working on mechanized farms. This implies a consolidation of small operating units into agricultural 'factories.' "

The trend toward vast mechanized "factories-in-the-fields" continued at an accelerated pace during the decade from 1930 to 1940. While family-size farms decreased greatly, large farms of 1,000 acres or more increased from 28 per cent to 34 per cent. However, the old cropper-tenant system still predominates, maintaining its strongest strangle hold on the delta lands of Louisiana, Mississippi, and Arkansas, where it encompasses 85 per cent of all farmland.

Nevertheless, the appearance of "factories-in-the-fields" presages a technological revolution in Southern agriculture comparable in scope with that wrought by the cotton gin. Whereas the decadent plantation system calls for the settlement of a tenant or cropper family on every twenty or so acres, the new mechanized plantations can hire, as needed, one tractor driver to do the work formerly done by twelve or fourteen families—and the entire proceeds of the crop goes to the landowner. In such manner the tenants and croppers, as they say, are literally being "tractored off the land."

Ruthlessly the relationship between man and land—already highly precarious under cropper-tenant tenure—is being severed by the machines. As one Arkansas traveler complains, "Now we got to till the land of some man we don't even know." Mechanization is rapidly converting croppers and tenants into a mass of uprooted, homeless, voteless, poverty-stricken migratory farm workers whose yearly earnings have averaged only $250.

By 1940 the number of farm laborers in America had risen to 3,191,000. Each year between one and two million of them— men, women, and children—wander over the country looking for work, under conditions dramatically portrayed in John Steinbeck's *Grapes of Wrath* and more statistically stated in Carey McWilliams's *Factories in the Fields*. That the problem is of special concern to the South is indicated by the fact that nearly half of the migratory workers who entered California came from Arkansas, Missouri, Texas, and Oklahoma.

The policy of the owners of the "factories-in-the-fields," as confirmed by congressional investigation, is to "hire and fire." All manners of inducements are offered, through newspapers, handbills, and billboards, to attract farm labor when it is needed;

and then when the work is done law officers have frequently been prevailed upon to eject the workers from the community in order to avoid charity bills. In addition, the planters, through the officers, have viciously opposed every effort of the farm workers to organize, bargain collectively, or strike for their rights. As one deputy testified to the Senate Civil Liberties Committee, the big planters gave him to understand that his job was to "see to it that law and order be maintained and that the cannery operate."

THE NEW ORDER OF SLAVOCRACY

The South did not get to be the nation's economic problem No. 1 as a result of any deficiency in human or natural resources. It has the stuff—material and human—from which prosperity is made. The South has produced abundantly, but the bulk of its produce has been siphoned off by a few, leaving little or nothing for the many who produced it. Hence the problem of the South.

Prior to the Civil War, the despoilers of the South were the small class of slave-driving large planters. Since the Civil War, the parasites who have enriched themselves beyond measure through the impoverishment of the South's people are predominantly corporate interests, the main body of them being situated outside the South, with tentacles sucking at the region through Southern "representatives." Then, too, the South is not without its indigenous exploiters.

And so the story of the South, like the story of most other regions, is the old, old story, not yet ended, of the people's struggle for the right to enjoy the riches of their land and the fruits of their labor.

In common with the rest of America, the South was largely settled by folk who came to the brave New World in search of freedom. But while most of them found religious and political freedom in appreciable measure, their economic opportunities have been relentlessly circumscribed by a transplanted system of exploitation quite as oppressive as the counterpart left behind in the Old World.

The Negro slavery which formed the basis of the South's ante-bellum economy represented the ultimate in the exploitation of man by man on the American continent. Not only the Negroes were exploited by chattel slavery; the great mass of non-slave-owning Southern whites was forced into the intolerable position of competing with slave labor. Altogether the system was so profitable to its proprietors that it was only natural for them to plunge the nation into the Civil War in a violent attempt to maintain it.

Mercenary considerations have ever been uppermost in determining attitudes toward slavery. The Treaty of Utrecht in 1713 resulted in a monopoly of the slave trade by Great Britain, which became a major source of revenue to the Crown, and consequently King George frustrated all legislative attempts to abolish the traffic. Came the American Revolution, and the first draft of the Declaration of Independence, beginning with the proposition that all men are created equal, continued with this scorching indictment of the King:

> He has waged war against human nature itself, violating its most sacred Rights of Life and Liberty in the persons of distant people who never offended him, captivating and carrying them into slavery in another hemisphere, or to incur miserable death in the transportation thither. This piratical warfare, the opprobrium of infidel powers, is the warfare of the Christian King of Great Britain. He has prostituted his negative for suppressing every legislative attempt to prohibit or restrain an execrable commerce, determined to keep open a market where men should be bought and sold.

But even then slavery had fastened its grip upon the South to such an extent that the above condemnation of slavery was, at the insistence of Southern signatories, stricken from the document.

Slavery did not become really unpopular in the North until industrialization set in with its requirement of skilled labor; moreover, Northern industry was not unaware of the advantage to itself of freeing the Negroes and introducing them into the competitive labor market. In the South, slavery did not become widespread until the invention of the cotton gin paved the way for large plantations. But slave breeding had no sooner become profitable than the Southern states began to oppose further importation of slaves. On the other hand, New England manufacturers opposed cessation of the trade because they were producing the rum which was shipped to Africa and exchanged for Negroes.

Secession finally came when the Southern planters realized that Northern industrialists had deprived them of the control they had long exercised over Congress. Also making for secession was the fact that Southerners were indebted to Northerners to the extent of two hundred million to four hundred million dollars. One of the first acts of the seceding states was to repudiate these debts, thus winning the support of a large number of Southern planters and merchants.

Even after some states had seceded, Congress revealed its willingness to accept slavery permanently by adopting a joint resolution endorsing a constitutional amendment to prohibit any future constitutional abrogation of established slavery. That the South did not secede primarily to maintain slavery was also made evident when the Confederate cabinet, in a bid for British support, proposed the abolition of slavery. As for the Emancipation Proclamation which came in the middle of the conflict, it was primarily intended as a war measure to weaken the South.

The defeat of the Confederacy in 1865, and the subsequent adoption of the Thirteenth Amendment abolishing slavery, the Fourteenth Amendment establishing the citizenship of Negroes, and the Fifteenth Amendment guaranteeing the right to vote marked a tenuous dividing line in the history of the South. Obviously the old order of slavocracy had to be altered somewhat. The problem confronting the slavocrats was how to establish a new order which would be as profitable to them as had been the old. Their whispered battle cry became, "Chattel slavery is dead; long live wage slavery!"

All that was necessary to make wage slavery secure was to frustrate every tendency of the part of the South's working people to unite, economically or politically. The simplest way to accomplish this was to drive a wedge along racial lines. And so the decrepit war-torn institution of white supremacy was given a face lifting. Negro disfranchisement and Jim Crowism were to supplant the foundation of chattel slavery which had been washed away by the tide of war.

A good deal of the substance of chattel slavery was salvaged and made part and parcel of the new order, however.

"The big gun fired on Saturday, and meant that the Yankees had come and the slaves was free," said ex-slave Margaret Nickerson. "Niggers came out of the woods from all directions. The next day Mr. Carr got us all together and read a paper to us that didn't none of us understand except that it meant we was free. Then he said that them what would stay and harvest the cotton and corn would be given the net proceeds. Them what did found out that the net proceeds wasn't nothing but the stalks." Some slaveholders who were not under the immediate surveillance of federal troops were not so subtle; they actually held Negroes in slavery until after the crops had been harvested.

The manner in which labor contracts between Negro workers and white planters were used to establish a modified form of slavery was brought out by a former slave named Robert Meacham, in testimony to the Joint Congressional Committee Investigating the Condition of Affairs in the Late Insurrectionary States.

"There has been a great deal of difficulty in regard to labor contracts," Meacham told the committee. "The farmers draw up the contracts and read them to the colored people, but the colored people are generally uneducated and when a contract says this or that they hardly know what it means. When the farmers advance supplies, they get a lien on whatever portion of the crop is supposed to go to the workers. They also provide that if the colored people violate any of the articles of the agreement they are to be turned off and get nothing. The slightest insult, as the planters call it, is sufficient to turn the workers off. This takes place mostly in August and September, after the crops have been laid by."

The Freedmen's Bureau undertook to supervise the drawing and fulfillment of labor contracts, but the states soon devised laws whereunder the Negro who failed to perform as agreed was liable to arrest, whereas the planter who violated a contract was liable only to civil suit by the Negro (a practical farce then as now).

The provisional governors of the erstwhile Confederate states —elected by Southern whites who could take the ironclad oath of not having supported the Confederacy—lost no time in informing the Negroes that they should not take literally the wartime promise of "40 acres and a mule." The slavocrats were determined to keep the Negroes in the status of landless laborers. As former slave Emanuel Fortune told the Investigating Committee: "They will not sell us land. They will sell our people a lot now and then, but nothing of any importance."

In short order the slavocrats also devised "legal" means of practically re-enslaving the Negroes. One of the first steps of the legislatures was to adopt an annual $3 per capita tax; Negroes who failed to pay it were arrested, and assigned to work for the planters who paid their fines. Another method of virtual enslavement was the enactment of comprehensive vagrancy laws under which "idle" Negroes could be arrested, and, through the convict lease system, farmed out to planters, lumber, turpentine, and phosphate operators. Interestingly enough, these vagrancy laws were copied almost verbatim from the statute books of New England, where they were directed against poor whites. The Florida statute (enacted in 1868, amended in 1905 and 1907) is typical:

> Rogues and vagabonds, idle or dissolute persons who go about begging, common gamblers, persons who use juggling, or unlawful games or plays, common pipers and fiddlers, common drunkards, common night walkers, thieves, pilferers, traders in stolen property, lewd, wanton and lascivious persons, keepers of gambling places, common railers and brawlers, persons who neglect their calling or employment, or are without reasonably continuous employment or regular income and who have not sufficient property to sustain them and misspend what they earn without providing for themselves or the support of their families, persons wandering or strolling around from place to place without any lawful purpose or object, habitual loafers, idle and disorderly persons, persons neglecting all lawful business and habitually spending their time by frequenting houses of ill fame, gaming houses or tippling shops, persons able to work but habitually living upon the earnings of their wives or minor children, and all able bodied male persons over

the age of 18 years who are without means of support and remain in idleness, shall be deemed vagrants and upon conviction shall be subject to penalty.

But despite all the post Civil War devices for controlling and
exploiting Negroes, Negroes as such were free to come and go
as they pleased until one or more of the devices was applied to
them as individuals. This revolutionary change wrought by the
Civil War naturally rankled the overlords of the South (as it still
does today). Their inability to any longer control the movements
of Negroes gave rise to such as this in the Madison (Fla.) *Recorder:*

> For several weeks a steady exodus of Negroes has been going
> on from every county in Middle Florida, and it has at last
> reached such serious proportions as to cause serious inconven-
> ience to farmers, and a positive damage to the planting inter-
> ests of this section. Not one farmer in ten has, or can procure,
> hands enough to pitch a full crop. If the Negroes were going
> to benefit themselves by their change of place, we could under-
> stand their motive in immigrating, but as the large majority
> are going to East and South Florida, where very little corn
> and no cotton is raised, and where the demand for their labor,
> except on the railroads, must be limited, we confess our in-
> ability to perceive wherein they will better themselves.

When such persuasion proved unavailing, the *Recorder* could
think of nothing better than to refute its previous editorial by
saying:

> A great many Negroes have left this county during the past
> six months, but we are happy to say that the labor interests of
> the county have not been materially affected by the exodus.
> With rare exceptions, the Negroes who have taken their de-
> parture were an idle, thriftless, and vicious set, and as a prom-
> inent citizen remarked a few days ago, the "county has had a
> happy deliverance," for in the main those who have sought
> new fields to prey upon were sore-eyes in this community. But
> few of the sensible, honest, and thrifty Negroes have been en-
> ticed from their old homes in Jefferson.

While the efforts to peonize Negroes ranged from the vicious
to the ridiculous, the slavocracy was above all determined to deny
Negroes the vote. Even when President Johnson enfranchised
those Southern whites who would take the ironclad oath of not

having supported the Confederacy, those whites elected constitutional conventions which repealed the ordinances of secession
and ratified the Thirteenth Amendment abolishing slavery, but
at the same time resolved that "neither the white man nor the
black is prepared for the radical change" of allowing Negroes to
vote.

Needless to say, before the Civil War "free persons of color"
had not been allowed to vote. And yet the Southern states had
been allowed to count three fifths of their four million slaves in
computing the number of representatives the whites could elect
to Congress. Inasmuch as Emancipation did not carry with it the
right to vote, its effect was to add still further to the disproportionate congressional strength of Southern whites by rendering
Negroes whole persons in the population.

This situation gave the Democratic party, dominated by Southern planters, some hope of recapturing control of Congress from
the Republican party, dominated by Northern industrialists. One
economic issue at stake was whether the industrialists could enact
high protective tariffs for their products or the planters establish
free trade with cotton as king. The Republicans realized that their
only hope was to enfranchise the Negro and enlist his vote in
behalf of his "liberators," and the Democrats were equally aware
that their only hope was to keep the Negro voteless.

The first maneuver of the Republicans was to refuse to seat the
Representatives which Southern whites elected to Congress, on
the ground that they were "not representative of their constituents." Congress then proceeded to enfranchise Negroes through
passage of the Civil Rights Act of 1866, over President Johnson's
veto. Later the same year the Act was translated into the Fourteenth Amendment.

With the exception of Tennessee, no Southern state would at
first ratify this amendment. This gave the Republicans an opportunity to create a wave of "moral indignation" throughout the
North, though the role that selfish considerations played in this
was revealed when, at the same time, such solid Republican states
as Connecticut, Ohio, Kansas, and Minnesota rejected referendum proposals to enfranchise Negroes within their own borders.

The South's defiant refusal to endorse the Fourteenth Amendment paved the way for passage of the Congressional Reconstruction Acts of 1867. The existing governments of the Southern states were declared to be dissolved, and the South was divided into five military districts under the command of five United States Army generals. Elections were then scheduled in which the Negroes were to be permitted to vote for the first time, with order at the polls being maintained by United States troops. With the Negro's participation in the elections thus assured, a feverish campaign was begun by both parties to secure his vote.

The Republicans, being in control of Congress, had the advantage of administering the Reconstruction program. The principal agency with which they sought to win the Negro's support was the Freedmen's Bureau—an organization which has been maligned by Southern whites in proportion to the security it afforded the Negroes. The Bureau supplied needy freedmen with food and clothing, supervised labor contracts, established loan banks, sometimes exercised its prerogative to conduct courts to hear cases involving Negroes, and contributed substantially to Negro education through state, private, and religious schools, as well as some schools of its own.

With the Freedmen's Bureau to provide for the Negroes' basic material needs, the Republicans undertook to organize them in a political body known as the Lincoln Brotherhood. Leadership for the Brotherhood—necessarily a highly secretive society—was largely provided by white carpetbaggers whose aim was to make their Negro followers "just voters" so that they themselves could do the officeholding.

In a desperate countereffort to obtain the Negro vote for themselves, the Democrats went so far as to employ Negroes to speak for them. One such Negro speaker, William Marvin, traveled about urging his people: "Do not break with the Southern white man; do not be made tools to be used when wanted and then cast aside. I say to you to keep away from the secret societies. Let politics alone." The Negroes listened respectfully to this propaganda and then passed resolutions that "We cherish no ill-will against our former masters, but the loving people of the North deserve our thanks for our freedom; we resolve, therefore, to identify ourselves with the Republican party."

In due time, however, the Negroes awoke to the design of their carpetbagger leaders and consequently began to insist upon full political rights and the nomination of Negroes for political candidacy. When the carpetbaggers refused to accede to this demand, the Negroes organized a "radical" Republican group known as the Loyal League, which soon became a powerful rival of the more conservative Lincoln Brotherhood. Besides advocating full political rights for Negroes, the League insisted that the old promise to break up the large plantations and give every man "40 acres and a mule" should be kept.

Needless to say, the appearance of these Negro political societies struck fear in the hearts of the propertied Southern gentry (as they would today). When it became evident that the Negroes were not to be cajoled or threatened out of their votes, the planters resorted to more forcible means of persuasion by organizing a secret society of their own under the misnomer of the "Constitutional League." This terrorist organization was a forerunner of the Klan and was soon absorbed by it.

The state governments elected under congressional Reconstruction were comprised of three elements: the Democratic party, dominated by white planters who wanted to re-establish slavery by means of vagrancy laws and other provisions of the Black Codes; the conservative Republicans, dominated by white carpetbaggers whose aim was generally to further their own personal interests and those of Northern industrialists by harnessing the Negro vote within the Lincoln Brotherhood; and the "radical" Republicans, organized in the Loyal League of Negroes who, together with the poor whites, wanted genuine political democracy.

When these three groups came to grips in the constitutional conventions and legislatures, the carpetbaggers often posed backstage as bulwarks against "black radicalism." With each showdown on the Negroes' right to hold office, the carpetbaggers almost invariably deserted their Negro followers to form a coalition with the Democrats. In this way the planters succeeded in forcing the adoption of new state constitutions providing that no man could be elected to the higher state offices unless he had been a citizen for a prescribed number of years. This, of course, barred former slaves from such offices.

It was not until 1870 that the Fifteenth Amendment was adopted, providing that "The right of the citizens of the United States to vote shall not be denied or abridged by the United States or by any state on account of race, color, or previous condition of servitude."

There have been so many horror stories told about Negro rape and rampage during Reconstruction that the truth would seem to be in order.

While the Civil War was still in progress, the planters' propaganda story (accepted by many Northerners as well as Southerners) that enlisting Negroes in the Federal Army would result in unspeakable atrocities, was disproved by events. A Confederate observer, on hand at the federal occupation of Jacksonville, Florida, when some troops engaged in rioting, reported, "It gives me great pleasure to state that the Negro troops took no part in this vandalism, and were merely silent spectators at a sad spectacle."

When David S. Walker, a white Southerner, was elected the first Reconstruction governor of Florida, he declared in his inaugural address: "I think we are bound by every consideration of duty to make these people [the Negroes] as enlightened, prosperous, and happy as their new situation will admit. They have been faithful to us. Not one instance of insult, outrage, or indignity has ever come to my knowledge. They have remained at home and made provision for us, not only in peace but in war. We ought to protect them in all their rights, both personal and property, as much as we do our whites."

Then when the Florida legislature opened for the first time with Negro delegates included, a white reporter wrote, "Now I have never been known as a Negro-worshiper, but I must say I do not see any cause for alarm or want of intelligence in their faces or conversation. Fifteen of them are former slaves, well-bred gentlemen, and eloquent speakers."

It goes without saying that Reconstruction politics were neither altogether good nor altogether bad. Apparently there was even more incompetency, graft, and corruption then than now; but the pertinent truth is that the Negroes' participation in politics was not the cause of it. On the contrary, with but few exceptions, the records of the Negro legislators were exemplary. They generally took no part in the "plundering," and often appointed "smelling committees" to locate the sources of the carpetbaggers' sudden wealth. They took a genuine interest in promoting the general welfare, and displayed exceptional honesty in voting on every issue according to their convictions. For these reasons those Negroes who were elected to the United States Congress gave little satisfaction to the Republican industrialists of the North.

What with the surviving tradition of interracial etiquette under slavery, it would have probably been possible to give Jim Crow his new post-bellum lease on life without resort to terrorism. Not so with the denial of political rights to Negroes, however; the natural corollary to Negro emancipation was Negro enfranchisement. But the tottering slavocracy knew that it could not tolerate political democracy, because economic democracy would have ensued. And so the slavocrats called into being the Ku Klux Klan to serve as midwife to the new order of wage slavery based on white supremacy—a new order conceived in tyranny and dedicated to the proposition that all working men were created to be exploited.

This birth of damnation was quite painful. The Negroes were determined to have the full fruits of freedom, and there was substantial sentiment in Congress, and among the non-Southern public, and in the army of occupation, that the Negroes should not be cheated of their "hard-boughten" citizenship. Even more significantly, the South's poor whites and Negroes lost no time in uniting their strength to advance their common cause of democracy; and this co-operation found both economic and political expression.

All this the Klan had to contend with. As imperial wizard William Joseph Simmons said when he reincarnated the Klan, "When the roar of guns ceased and the smoke of battle lifted from the South in 1865 it meant the end of the War Between the States, but it marked the beginning of a new battle for the South."

The Reconstruction Klan was nothing more nor less than an underground terrorist army engaged in treasonable conspiracy and rebellion against the United States Government. This is frankly admitted by *KKK* (a recent volume endorsed by the Klan): "As the South had been defeated on the battlefields and was absolutely bankrupt after Appomattox, the Southern people were not in a position to start another armed rebellion—but the organization of the Ku Klux Klan was undoubtedly a form of rebellion."

The Southern slavocracy had abandoned all hope of secession and slavery, but it was determined to establish as close an approximation of slavery as possible. To accomplish this the armies of the Confederacy simply changed from gray uniforms to white ones and from open to guerrilla warfare.

The Klan was founded at Pulaski, Tennessee, in 1865 by six Confederate veterans. The name Ku Klux was derived by a phonetic corruption of the Greek work *kuklos,* meaning circle, and "Klan" was probably suggested by the Scottish clans, whose custom of summoning members to war by means of a messenger bearing a fiery cross was also adopted by the KKK. During the first two years of its existence the Klan spread phenomenally all over the South, and when the first klonvokation was called in 1867 there were already five thousand local units in operation. These united to form an "Invisible Empire" whose territorial subdivisions—realms, provinces, and klantons—were organized and operated on a military basis.

"The Klan played an important part in politics," *KKK* admits, "and its members intimidated the negroes and kept them from the polls. Often men in large numbers, who were thought to be Klansmen, attended the polls, and, heavily armed, by a threatening attitude prevented the negroes from ·electing their candidates. There were many affrays at the polls, and the Ku Kluxers, as well as other Southern men, used the six-shooter and the shotgun as a method of direct persuasion. They were thus able to convince the negro that it was not wise for the black race to participate in political affairs."

In an effort to cope with the Klan rebellion, the Reconstruction governments of Tennessee, Alabama, Mississippi, and other Southern states passed laws providing stiff sentences. To this the Klan responded defiantly. In an interview published in the Cin-

cinnati *Commercial* in 1868, Wizard Nathan Bedford Forrest declared:

"The Klan is a protective, political, military organization. I am opposed to negro suffrage under any and all circumstances . . . If the militia are called out, we can only look upon it as a declaration of war. In all the Southern states there are about 550,000 Klansmen. I think I could raise 40,000 men in five days, ready for the field. If the militia goes to hunting down and shooting these men, there will be war, and a bloodier one than we have ever witnessed. I have no powder to burn killing negroes. I intend to kill the radicals. In each voting precinct we have a captain who is required to make out a list of all the radicals who are known, of both colors. Their houses are picketed, and when the fight comes not one of them would get out of the country alive."

In short order the Klan established a veritable reign of terror. Violence was most prevalent in the Black Belt counties where Negroes presented a threat to white majorities at the polls. An ex-slave named Emanuel Fortune told the Investigating Committee: "I left Jackson County because there got to be such a state of lawlessness and outrage that I expected that my life was in danger at all times; in fact, I got, indirectly, information very often that I would be missing someday and no one would know where I was, on account of my being a leading man in politics.

"They always speak very bitterly against Negroes voting. They say, 'The damned Republicans has put niggers to rule us and we will not suffer it'; 'Intelligence shall rule the country instead of the majority'; and 'This is a white man's government and colored men have no rights that white men are bound to respect.' We are told that all colored people who vote are going to starve next year. We have got to go to the merchants and have advances of meat and corn."

"Fifty or a hundred colored folks were mistreated by shooting at them and trying to cut their throats," testified Henry Reed, another ex-slave. "In going to church at night they would stand behind a tree and shoot your brains out. Ah, gentlemen, it was as terrible a place as ever there was in this world!"

This sort of "mistreatment" led President Grant in 1870 to send a special message to Congress declaring that "the free exercise of the franchise has by violence and intimidation been denied to citizens in several of the states lately in rebellion." With his message he sent a documented report of some five thousand cases of Klan floggings, lynchings, and other overt acts of violence. Thereupon the Joint Congressional Committee to Investigate the Condition of Affairs in the Late Insurrectionary States was appointed to conduct hearings throughout the South. The Committee compiled thirteen volumes of sensational testimony. Out of the investigation came a report that "revolutionary conditions" existed as a result of "a Southern conspiracy against Constitutional law and the Negro race. The Ku Klux Klan does exist and it has a political purpose which it seeks to carry out by murders, whippings, intimidation, and violence."

On the heels of this investigation Congress passed the Enforcement Act of 1870 to implement the 14th and 15th Amendments. Then came the "Ku Klux Act" of 1871 which recognized a state of Klan-wrought insurrection in the South and authorized the President to suspend the writ of habeas corpus in order to cope with it. (Finally the provisions of these Acts were incorporated in the Civil Rights Act of 1875; but by 1894 virtually all of them had been held invalid by the Supreme Court because they went beyond enforcement of the Constitutional Amendments. In 1909, however, the tenable sections were incorporated in the U.S. Criminal Code chapter entitled "Offenses Against Elective Franchise and Civil Rights of Citizens," which protects the constitutional rights of citizens from infringement by either officials or private individuals.)

The election of 1876 was recognized by all factions as the showdown. Democrats openly threatened that they "would carry the election or kill the last damned Republican in the South." The Klan brought its intensive campaign of terrorism to a whirlwind climax. Shipments of arms hurriedly dispatched to military units were confiscated by Klansmen who had been tipped off by railroad officials. On election day the locations of many polling places were suddenly changed without notice in an effort to lose the Negroes. The whites appeared with rifles in hand and turned away prospective Negro voters. Many Negroes who sought to vote under escort of United States marshals were shot, and the marshals with them.

Out of the election came claims of both Democratic and Republican victory, with both parties claiming four of the Southern states. A congressional commission was appointed to investigate, and wholesale evidence of intimidation and fraud was found. Finally there was a deal whereby the Republican Hayes was awarded the presidency, with the agreement on his part to withdraw Federal troops from the South.

In addition, the decision in the Southern state elections was given to the Democratic candidates, and the Southern whites were jubilant. The election has ever since been hailed as marking the return of "Democratic home rule." The former Republican governor of Florida observed, "The newspapers tell that the Republican party is now dead in Arkansas as in Mississippi, Alabama, and Georgia. The white Republicans have been forced to leave those states, and the Negroes are woefully different in self-reliance."

Completely disillusioned by the repeated betrayals of some of their white "friends" and the failure of the federal government to protect them in the exercise of their constitutional rights, the Negroes tried to make the best of the bad situation. "We are aware that recently a political revolution has taken place throughout the South," resolved a Negro conference in 1877, "and it is our hope that now the race issue in politics with all its accompanying evils will pass away and that intelligence and integrity will now dominate without regard to color and previous conditions."

This proved to be wishful thinking. The complete effectiveness of Klan terror in the absence of Federal troops was brought out by the further testimony of Emanuel Fortune to the Congressional Committee: "Captain Dickinson said to me a year ago, 'Fortune, you could go back to Jackson County and live if you would; you would not be hurt.' I said, 'Could I go back there and be a free man, to use freedom of speech and act in politics as any man would want with his own people—could I do that?' He said, 'No, you could not—you would have to abandon all that if you went back.' "

Of course the Southern press lent full support to the new order. Typical of the journalistic endorsements given the Klan was the following editorial from the Gainesville (Fla.) *Weekly Bee* in 1882:

> In Jefferson County a goodly number of colored Republicans own property and pay taxes, and as representatives of that class deemed it necessary to vent their spleen against certain Democrats by having them indicted in the U. S. Court for alleged political offences, the Commissioners [Klansmen] concluded that they would call upon the colored taxpayers to assist in defraying the cost of the music by which their white fellow citizens were dancing before the court. They [the Negroes] accordingly made an appropriation [were robbed] of $500 for said music. Some folk are disgruntled over the conduct of these Commissioners, but in the language of Tweed, "What are they going to do about it?" It is certainly one way to check political persecution.

When the Klan had succeeded in driving the Negroes from the polls it realized that to perpetuate the situation would require a continuing program of subversive terrorism. It was also realized that such a long-range program would be most likely to endure if it could be conducted by the police and courts behind a pseudo-legal cloak of law and order, with intimidation being accomplished insofar as possible by implied threat rather than overt action. By keeping state and local government in the hands of Klansmen and fellow travelers, white supremacy could be given a "legal" status which would in time acquire the coercive force of tradition.

It was with this in view (as well as the prospect of federal prosecution for treason) that Grand Wizard Forrest issued a proclamation: "The Invisible Empire has accomplished the purpose for which it was organized . . . Therefore the grand wizard, being invested with power to determine questions of paramount importance, now declares the Invisible Empire and all subdivisions thereof dissolved and disbanded forever."

The book *KKK* admits that "some of the klans obeyed this proclamation and some did not." For a time autonomous Klan activity actually increased, with Klansmen in some instances engaging militiamen in pitched battles. A good deal of this Ku-Kluxery was conducted under new names, such as the Knights of the White Camellia, Constitutional Union Guards, White League, White Brotherhood, Council of Safety, '76 Association, Pale

Faces, White Line, and Rifle Clubs. "After 1868," says *KKK,* "all these organizations, including the Klan, were societies of armed whites actually struggling for control of government in the South and for white supremacy."

It was not long, however, before the burden of enforcing white supremacy was assumed by officers of the law; and it was this second change of uniform by the erstwhile Confederates that gradually brought about the virtual dissolution of the Klan which the wizard's edict had failed to achieve.

It is significant that no wave of "moral indignation" swept the North upon the final establishment of white supremacy through Klan terror. The Constitutional grant of civil and political rights to Negroes was thus revealed to have been in large part inspired by the desire of Northern industrialists to harness the Negro vote. When the Negro citizen's integrity and democratic instincts proved beyond corruption, those who had emancipated and en-franchised him abandoned him to the Klan, which forced him back into an economic, political, and civic quagmire in some re-spects worse than his former status as chattel.

The North not only acquiesced in this counterrevolution (which meant that the North won the war but lost much of the peace by default). Some Northern spokesmen actually championed the new order of white supremacy. For example, O. M. Crosby wrote: "Between 1865 and 1876 the former slaves worked faith-fully in the plantation of politics; but at the latter date a second emancipation changed their status slightly. Since then they have been working somewhat more and voting rather less, and are doing vastly better in all important respects. The future fortunes of the negroes are largely in the hands of the controlling race, and they themselves will probably have little to do in shaping it; and doubtless the less they have to do with it the better."

It did not take Southern employers long to recognize that their new order of wage slavery had a number of advantages over the old order of chattel slavery. As Edward King reported in *The Great South,* "The captain of the Oklawaha River steamer *Marion* expressed himself better satisfied with free than slave labor; thought it released employers like himself from a great many obli-gations." Bearing out this appraisal, an Alabama planter of that day said, "It's a great relief not to be responsible for them. We pay them from $10 to $16 a month, but we keep a store and most of the money comes back to us on Saturday nights."

It was unfortunate that the Civil War was required to bring home this lesson. Had the Southern exploiting class been more literate and less adamant, they might have seen the light and made the transition without bloodshed, for the London *Economist* had pointed out as early as 1853:

> Slaves are costly instruments of production, and the commodities which they raise must be sold to procure their clothing and subsistence. A slave population hampers its owners in more ways than one, and there is some reason to believe that the low price at which slave-raised produce is sold, is the consequence of the necessity which the slave owner is under to sell in order to maintain his people.
>
> The responsibility of the employer of free labor is at an end when he has paid the covenanted wages; and his greater advantage in dealing with the general market is exemplified in that *there are more fortunes made by the employers of free labor than by slave owners.* The Astors, the Girards, and the Longworths are the millionaires of the States, as the Rothschilds, the Lloyds, and the Barings are the millionaires of the world—not the slave owners, however wealthy, of Carolina, Cuba, or Brazil.

The realities of the new order of wage slavery were clearly seen in 1868 by William Sylvis, president of the National Labor Union. "No man in America rejoiced more than I at the downfall of Negro slavery," he said. "But when the shackles fell from the limbs of those four million blacks, it did not make them free men; it simply transferred them from one condition of slavery to another . . . We are all now one family of slaves together . . ."

THE PERVERSION OF POPULISM

After snatching away the ten-year-old Reconstruction-born democracy of the South, the region's overlords sought to sugarcoat the new order of slavocracy with visions of a "New South" of prosperity based upon industrialization. Leading press agent for this mirage was Henry Woodfin Grady, editor of the Atlanta *Constitution,* whose "New South" address before the New England Society made a tremendous hit with Northern financiers. It called for Northern capital to tap with railroads the raw materials of the South, Northern capital to build Southern factories, protective tariffs—and perpetual racial segregation.

The capital was forthcoming, the railroads snaked southward, factories arose, and Southern industry and commerce boomed. But while the "New South" had a way of paying handsome dividends to Northern capital and its Southern representatives, Southern labor received only starvation wages. Outstanding critic of the "New South" was Georgia's Thomas E. Watson. For the "Southern apologists of the capitalist masters with their glib editorials" he had only contempt. "You teach me nothing whatever when you tell me that the people have built more railroads, raised more cotton, manufactured more cloth," he said. "To all your bombast upon *that* subject I will answer by the query: who got the increased wealth after it was made? . . .

"Just as the English maintain their conquest of India by taking into copartnership with themselves a certain percentage of Hindus," he continued, "so the North holds the South in subjugation by enlisting Southern capitalists and politicians. They put their money into our daily papers; they subsidize such organs as *The Manufacturers' Record;* they buy up our railroads; they capitalize our mills; they finance our street railways; they supply our banks; —always taking Southern men in with them to a certain extent, and they appoint some of our politicians to good positions. United themselves, the Northern capitalists divide the Southerners, and thus rule and despoil the South."

While the bulk of Southern opposition to such predatory industrialization came from the small dirt farmers, tenants, share-croppers, and wageworkers, those big planters who had not become merchants or stockholders in industry were similarly threatened with serfdom. The railroads symbolized the "foreign" exploitation of the South, and their spokesmen sought to discredit attacks upon them as attacks on private property. "Better shake the pillars of property than the pillars of liberty!" thundered Georgia's Bob Toombs in reply. "The great question is shall Georgia govern the corporations or the corporations govern Georgia? Choose ye this day whom ye shall serve!"

In due time control of the Democratic party passed from the hands of the planter class to the agents of the "New South." At the same time the dissatisfaction of the plain people with their lot in the "New South" began to take organized political form. To discourage all thought of revolt and independent political action, it was cried that anything but all-out support for the straight Democratic ticket was treason to the white race. Furthermore, Independents were accused of trying to "Africanize" the South.

"As there is some talk of an Independent movement in Florida politics," the Gainesville *Weekly Bee* observed in 1882, "we would like some friend to tell us just what an Independent is. We could name several who would probably like to *lead* an Independent movement, but the trouble seems to be a scarcity of followers."

As a matter of fact, the proprietors of the "New South" were highly alarmed by the rapidly growing spirit of revolt. By 1875 the National Grange, which originated among the rebellious farmers of the West, had acquired substantial membership in the South. After that the Grange was succeeded by the Farmers' Alliance, which spread like wildfire among the South's impoverished farm folk. During the eighties, when the expanding capitalism of the North made the most of the "New South," every effort on the part of the Farmers' Alliance to liberalize the Democratic party failed.

It remained for the acute depression of 1887–88 to unleash the forces of rebellion against predatory capitalism. "The farmer has about reached the end of his row," reported the *Southern Alliance Farmer* in 1891. "The lowest price that cotton has reached in a third of a century" prevailed, and "hundreds of men will be turned out of house and home, or forced to become hirelings and tenants in the fields they once owned. . . . The doors of every courthouse in Georgia are placarded with the announcements of [sheriffs'] sales. . . . The roads are full of negroes begging homes."

In the South's urban slums conditions were at least as bad as on the farms. The Atlanta *Journal,* describing the workers' quarters at the Exposition Mills in 1892 (where a decade earlier Henry Grady had hailed the coming of the "New South"), said, "Famine and pestilence are today making worse ravages than among the serfs of Russia." Mill workers were paid "the magnificent sum of 36 cents a day for their labor, and . . . the average wage found in the factory district is 9 cents a head divided among the members of the family." Bodies of the dead went long unburied. The *Journal* went on to describe "rooms wherein eight and ten members of one family are stricken down, where pneumonia and measles are attacking their emaciated bodies; where there is no sanitation, no help or protection from the city, no medicine, no food, no fire, no nurse—nothing but torturing hunger and death."

The depression had the effect of stimulating not only the Farmers' Alliance but also the organization of industrial labor. The Knights of Labor, forced to operate underground for the first decade after its founding in 1869, came out into the open and took in 800,000 members. The well-nigh general sentiment in favor of vigorous trust-busting was also to be found among small businessmen.

As the Farmers' Alliance grew in strength, Democratic organs sought to lead it away from its "wild-men" leaders. Typical of these bids was the following report in the Quincy (Fla.) *Herald:*

> On December 1 (1890) the Farmers' Alliance and Indus-
> trial Union Exposition will open its doors to the world at
> Ocala, signalizing the most auspicious event in the history of
> the state. It is estimated that 50,000 strangers will visit this
> exposition, drawn from every state in the Union by a meeting
> fraught with intense and vital purport, sounding the tocsin
> that will vibrate from continent to continent and awaken the
> slumbering yeomanry by the million, and with hooks of steel
> link them as one in the battle for succor and relief from the
> burdens that weigh upon the struggling husbandmen.

When, however, the Ocala convention came close to launching a political party to represent farmers and workers, the Democratic press promptly changed its tune. "The Alliance is becoming a political machine," they wailed, and charged it with advocating "paternalism, communism, and downright socialism." Actually, the Ocala platform adopted by the convention called for public ownership of the railroads and various other "radical" reforms. The Ocala platform—like the Populist party which arose to champion it—placed great faith in such monetary panaceas as a subtreasury system. The purpose of these was to bring about inflation for the benefit of debtors—a category into which most farmers had by then been forced.

The Alliancemen from the West were quick to break away from the Republican party, but those in the South had to be weaned away from lily-white Democracy. It was in 1890 that Tom Watson founded his *People's Party Paper,* and the party itself emerged the following year with Watson leading Western congressmen who had endorsed the Alliance platform; and in 1892 it took the field in the South. Under the leadership of men like Watson and "Pitchfork" Ben Tillman of South Carolina, the Populist movement proved to be one of the most significant in the South's history and deserves the close scrutiny of every serious student of the region. For our purposes here, the typical experiences of Watson must suffice (for a full-length portrait see Woodward's *Tom Watson—Agrarian Rebel*).

Unlike the West, the South had to predicate its Populism on interracial co-operation. Watson, speaking as Populist leader in

Congress, had this to say about relations between the white man and Negro: "Now the People's party says to these two men, 'You are kept apart that you may separately be fleeced of your earnings. You are made to hate each other because upon that hatred is rested the keystone of the arch of financial despotism which enslaves you both. You are deceived and blinded that you may not see how this race antagonism perpetuates a monetary system which beggars both.' "

Watson insisted on "political equality," asserting that "the accident of color can make no difference in the interests of farmers, croppers, and laborers." "What is the use," he asked, "of educating these people [the Negroes] as citizens if they are never to exercise the rights of citizens?" And when South Carolina in 1895 altered its constitution to disfranchise Negroes, Watson protested: "All this reactionary legislation is wrong. . . . Old-fashioned democracy taught us that a man who fought the battles of his country, and paid the taxes of his government, should have a vote in the choosing of rulers and making of the laws."

Watson also opposed the convict lease system (most oppressive to Negroes) and declared that an aim of the Populist party should be "to make lynch law odious to the people." He nominated a Negro to serve on the executive committee of the party, as "a man worthy to be on the executive committee of this or any other party."

In the election of 1892, when Watson was running as Populist candidate for Congress, one of his most active supporters was a young Negro preacher named H. S. Doyle. Despite numerous threats on his life, Doyle delivered sixty-three speeches in Watson's behalf. On one occasion, when lynching seemed imminent, Doyle fled to Watson for protection. Watson took him in, sent out riders for assistance. During that night and the next day fully two thousand armed white Populists came roaring into town in answer to the call. Led by a Populist sheriff, they marched to the courthouse to be jointly addressed by Watson and Doyle.

"We are determined," said Watson, "in this free country that the humblest white or black man that wants to talk our doctrine shall do it, and the man doesn't live who shall touch a hair of his head, without fighting every man in the People's party!"

Needless to say, the spectacle of armed whites turning out en masse to protect the right of a Negro to make a political speech caused quite a stir in the South's conservative circles. "Watson has gone mad!" was the theme of the Democratic press.

Ministers of the gospel were employed to proclaim that Populism meant "negro supremacy, mongrelism, and the destruction of the Saxon womanhood of our wives and daughters." One Democratic candidate denounced his Populist opponent as a "preacher of atheism, sympathizer of bloody-handed anarchy, shameless defamer of our spotless, pure, and peerless Southern womanhood." The' Democratic press followed through: "The chief of the Third party in Georgia is a Republican and an infidel. He believes neither in Democracy nor our God. Populism is the work of selfish and designing men who prefer, like Satan, to rule in hell rather than serve in heaven. . . . Come back, brethren, come back!"

When the brethren refused to re-enter the Democratic fold to be sheared as of yore, enticements were offered. On one occasion, for instance, Watson was speaking before a predominantly Negro audience at Sparta, Georgia. Suddenly a Democratic band blared out from a near-by grove and a Democratic horseman rode up.

"A free dinner for everybody!" he cried. "You're all invited down to the barbecue, white and colored!"

"You may have the trees," Watson replied, "but we have the men; and these men are not going to be enticed away from free, fair discussion of these great public questions by any amount of barbecued beef!" Sure enough, his ranks held firm, and when the speaking was done they even remained to escort him back to his lodging.

It was also common for merchants and other creditors to refuse to extend credit to anyone who would not disclaim all sympathy for the People's party. During the campaign of 1892 the county Democratic chairman at Washington, Georgia, issued a circular "To the Democratic Farmers and Employers of Labor," in which he warned of the danger of a Populist victory and said:

> This danger, however, can be overcome by the absolute control which you yet exercise over your property. It is absolutely necessary that you should bring to bear the power which

THE PERVERSION OF POPULISM

your situation gives over tenants, laborers, and croppers. . . .
The success of the Populists . . . means regulation or control
of rents, wages of labor, regulation of hours of work, and at
certain seasons of the year strikes. . . . The peace, prosperity,
and happiness of yourselves and your friends depends on your
prompt, vigorous, and determined efforts to control those who
are to such a large extent dependent upon you.

On Election Day that year one Dan Bowles, a white Democrat,
was herding fifty Negroes to the polls at Augusta, Georgia. The
procession was met by a group of Populists, one of whom, Isaac
Horton, a Negro, sought to disengage another Negro from the
Democratic line-up. A free-for-all fight ensued, during which
Bowles shot and killed Horton. The jury's verdict: "Justifiable
homicide."

Similarly, in Elbert County, Georgia, a group of white and
Negro Populists en route to the polls together was intercepted by
Democratic planter B. H. Head. He recognized among the Negro
Populists a number "who had once lived with him and bore the
name of Head." In an effort to dissuade them from voting Populist, Head struck one elderly Negro with a wagon standard. When
the Negro's son struck back, Head went home for a shotgun with
which he proceeded to shoot two of the Negroes. Another white
Democrat present drew a pistol and shot three more Negroes.

Similar violence characterized the elections in which Populists
participated in many parts of the country, with the Populists actually being driven from the polls in some places.

"If the law cannot protect us, we will protect ourselves with
Winchesters!" one Populist wrote Watson. The whole temper of
the times was supercharged by a popular determination to bring
about change—peaceably, if possible, but forcibly, if necessary.
One Populist paper, *The Revolution,* bore on its masthead the
legend: *"Not a Revolt; It's a Revolution!"—Thomas E. Watson.*
Another, *The Farmers' Light,* declared: "There is no wiping out
the fact that this is a revolution, and it depends upon the enemy
whether it shall be a peaceful or a bloody one. To be candid about
the matter, we believe it will be the latter."

The rise and fall of the People's party, including its prenatal
and senile stages, occupied most of the four decades from 1870

until 1910. A great many of its difficulties and setbacks were attributable to the reluctance of Southern Populists to break with the lily-white Democratic party, and the eagerness with which these same Populists abandoned their platform and entered into fusionist compromises with the Democrats.

In the presidential campaign of 1892 the Populists were led to believe that if they would endorse William Jennings Bryan ("The Commoner" and free-silver advocate), Tom Watson would be chosen as his running mate on the Democratic ticket. This agreement, if any, was not kept; but Watson ran for the presidency and carried five states, the Populist vote totaling 1,550,000.

A breakdown of the South-West alliance threw Populism for a loss in 1896, and the Spanish-American War which was precipitated in 1898 weakened the movement still further by diverting attention from the need for domestic reforms. By 1904 Populism was able to score only a slight comeback, with Watson polling 117,000 votes for the presidency—which was more than double the Populist vote in 1900. But the South went solidly Democratic, and Watson was indignant. "You did not care to know anything about the platform, you didn't read it, you simply wanted to know if it was labeled 'Democratic,'" he accused his constitutents. "Whether Peruna, or applejack, or champagne, or cider, it did not matter what, you put the dear old jug up to your lips and just drank it down all the same."

The election evidently represented the last straw which broke the back of Watson the Populist, leaving Watson the demagogue. As early as 1902 he had observed, "The argument against the independent political movement in the South may be boiled down to one word—nigger." Later, in comparing himself with William Jennings Bryan, he said, "His field was the plastic, restless, growing West; mine was the hidebound, rock-ribbed Bourbon South. Besides, Bryan had *no everlasting and overshadowing Negro Question to hamper and handicap his progress:* I HAD."

And so Watson concluded that his only hope for a return to political power was to make Southern Populism even more lily-white than the Democratic party. He took his stand shortly after the 1904 election: "In Georgia they do not dare to disfranchise the Negro because the men who control the Democratic machine in Georgia know that a majority of the whites are against them. They need the Negro to beat us with." And he added, "The white people dare not revolt [against the Democratic machine] so long as they can be intimidated by the fear of the Negro vote." Consequently, Watson proffered Populist support to any anti-machine Democrat who would advocate "a change in our constitution which will perpetuate white supremacy in Georgia."

Hoke Smith accepted the offer and was elected with Watson's support. "Everybody knew that the Disfranchisement issue was the cause of our success," Watson wrote. And while the Hoke Smith regime—in which Watson was the ex-officio power—enacted a great many Populist reforms, it also adopted a constitutional amendment setting forth literacy requirements for voters, which Watson was assured would disfranchise 95 per cent of the Negroes in the state. Every other Southern state had already taken this step backward.

Another result of the reckless use of racism in the campaign to elect Hoke Smith was the Atlanta race riot of 1906, which broke out a few days after the election and raged for four days. In addition to Watson's unequaled demagoguery, the Atlanta *Journal* had pointed out day after day, in bold-faced capitals, that Hoke Smith favored "THE ELIMINATION OF THE NEGRO FROM POLITICS . . . BY LEGAL AND CONSTITUTIONAL METHODS . . . WITHOUT DISFRANCHISING A SINGLE WHITE MAN." In addition, the *Journal* printed such inflammatory editorials as this:

> Political equality being thus preached to the negro in the ring papers and on the stump, what wonder that he makes no distinction between political and social equality. He grows more bumptious on the street, more impudent in his dealings with white men; and then, when he cannot achieve social equality as he wishes, with the instinct of the barbarian to destroy what he cannot attain to, he lies in wait, as that dastardly brute did yesterday near this city, and assaults the fair young girlhood of the South. . . . It is time for those who know the perils of the negro problem to stand together with deep resolve that political power shall never give the negro encouragement in his foul dreams of a mixture of races.

The same sort of thing appeared in other Atlanta papers, which were as much concerned with rivalry among themselves as with the outcome of the election. The riot which they and Watson incited saw mobs of rowdy whites hunting down and shooting hundreds of Negro men and women on the streets, and all manner of arson, looting, and brutality went unrestrained and unpunished.

The following year Watson was advocating, in his *Jeffersonian* magazine, a policy of repression of Negroes so severe that "the great mass of the negroes would reconcile themselves to a condition of recognized peasantry—a laboring class . . ." He who had once branded the "negro domination" bugaboo as the "stock-in-trade" of Southern demagoguery now wrote of the "HIDEOUS, OMINOUS, NATIONAL MENACE of negro domination," and asserted that "there is no equality of sexes or races." In an editorial entitled "The Ungrateful Negro," attacking Booker T. Washington, he asked, "What does Civilization owe the Negro? Nothing! *Nothing!* NOTHING!" The piece was more widely published throughout the South than anything else he had written.

Needless to say, Watson's reversal of position on the Negro question caused great consternation among Populists and other progressives elsewhere in the country; it served, in fact, to snap the tenuous links which the People's party had formed between Southern agrarianism and national progressivism.

It is significant that Watson did not stop with turning anti-Negro; once embarked upon the path of the demagogue, he went all the way. His anti-Semitic tirades in connection with the Leo Frank case brought on reincarnation of the Klan and were at least as violent as his attacks upon Negroes. So, too, were his diatribes against Catholics. "I have forced the popery issue into Georgia politics," he boasted, "to the consternation of the old-line politicians."

The justified regionalism which he had once employed with such telling effect against Northern exploitation was now perverted into a petty sectionalism and appeal to prejudice. Reviving the Cause of the Confederacy, Watson wrote, "We are quite sincere in saying, as we have done before, that it would have been far better for the South had the Confederacy succeeded." The day would come, said he, "when the Union will be split into four grand divisions, and this hemisphere will be the happier for it."

The People's party in the South was doomed to disintegration when its leaders set about purging it of Negroes in an effort to convert it into a lily-white People's party. Lincoln once said, "Those who deny freedom to others do not deserve it for themselves, and under a just God they shall not have it." And so there was a certain grim justice when the white Populists who conspired with the Democratic plutocracy to disfranchise the Negroes were themselves disfranchised by the poll tax, which the plutocracy then imposed on all poor folk, white and colored alike.

Where is the People's party now? Its foundation, the Farmers' Alliance, is no more. The National Farmers Union—logical successor to the Alliance—is making rapid headway in other parts of the country but has just begun serious attempts to organize the South. Southern labor, on the other hand, is a far more important factor and is much better organized than it was during the Populist era. Future hope for a people's party in the South—whether a new party or a renovated one—must most likely depend upon the prior unionization of the region's farmers, the further unionization of its labor, and a coalition of the two.

But the history of the People's party contains many lessons for today and tomorrow. Besides bringing about numerous salutary reforms—regionally and nationally, directly and indirectly, contemporaneously and subsequently—Populism proved something of prime importance to the South. It proved that the plain people of the South—whites and Negroes, farmers and laborers—can work together in the same economic and political organizations and co-operate with similar coalitions nationally for the betterment of all. In other words, Populism proved what Reconstruction indicated: that democracy can work in the South. As Dr. George S. Mitchell, of the Southern Regional Council, has said, democracy is not so much a form of government as it is a kind of people. Populism proved that the plain people of the South do have—suppressed though it is—the stuff democracy is made of.

FREEDOM ROAD—CLOSED

And so the problem of the South today—with its denial of economic, political, and racial democracy—has been handed down to us directly from that post-Civil War birth of damnation. Because the United States reneged on its obligations to the freedmen, because it made a soft peace with the Southern slavocracy, not only Southern Negroes but Southern whites and all Americans are suffering under the yoke; for the Southern slavocracy not only rules the South; it has long been in the congressional saddle, sawing savagely on the reins to hold back the nation.

But those who suffer most under the new order of slavocracy are those Southerners who are actually held in involuntary servitude. In probing further the problem of the South, these peons are certainly entitled to prime consideration.

Testifying to the existence of the old-yet-new slavocracy we have none other than the Georgia Baptists, who are well known for taking their text directly from the record. Recently in convention assembled these deeply Southern folk said: "Peonage or debt slavery has by no means disappeared from our land. There are more white people involved in this diabolical practice than there were slaveholders. There are more Negroes held by these debt-slavers than were actually owned as slaves before the War Between the States. The method is the only thing which has changed."

The method of enslavement to which the Georgia Baptists refer is the company commissary system of getting workers in debt and then applying intimidation or force to make them work indefinitely against their will to liquidate the debt.

For an authoritative description of the commissary system we can turn to the *Congressional Record*. Speaking a few years ago on the subject of "The Company Store," Representative Luecke of Michigan said:

> At the outset I wish to say that this is not a condition which can be applied to any particular section of the country. To the contrary, it is very much a national affair. . . . Company stores are found in every nation, and in England are known as "tommy shops." The American worker refers to them as "gyp-me stores," "pluck-me stores," "gyp-joints," and "robber-saries."
>
> In the early days when industry had to go into the undeveloped sections of the Nation it was necessary to have a commissary. As time went on and the company became established, abuses crept in . . . The issuance of company scrip is one of the evils which is an offspring of the company store. In some places the company issues scrip between paydays and this scrip is discounted for cash. The discount ranges all the way from 5 to 25 per cent. The worker takes this scrip and cashes it at the company store at a discount. There are communities in which the independent merchants cash this scrip also, and, of course, make a handsome profit.
>
> The pay of these workers, mostly unskilled, is so small that it does not provide for independence, and trading at the company store is an economic necessity with them. The news report which I had the pleasure—or displeasure—to read said, "I have found hundreds of men in the sawmill industry who haven't seen any money for years." Reading on, in another report I find this choice bit of information: "In one plant it was claimed by the laborers that there were three workers who had not received any cash in the last fifteen years. One case was encountered in which the company had not even gone through the formality of having a cash payday in the last two years."
>
> That the company store must be a profitable venture is made plain in the report of a certain company to a House committee. . . . There are practically no losses from bad debts, which are a considerable item in the accounts of retail merchants. . . . The operating expenses of company stores are also much less than independents. . . . The prices at company stores range all the way from 10 per cent to 37 per cent higher.

These workers mainly live on flour, potatoes, corn meal, and sugar. All other purchases, such as rice, canned vegetables, bacon, ham, eggs, and milk, average less than 1 per cent of their purchases. Fresh meat and fruits are unheard of.

In the South the company commissary system of peonage is most prevalent in the work camps of the turpentine, lumber, and mining industries, and the cotton plantations.

One case came to my attention when I visited a Florida turpentine camp in 1941. A Negro boy told of getting sick and arranging with his Negro landlady not to pay rent until he went back to work. After three months he was able to return to his job, but instead of wages at the end of the first week he received a bill for fifty dollars back rent. Rather than pay the bill, he decided he would "work it out with the county." Sure enough, he was arrested and sentenced to three months on the chain gang. The phonographic recording I made of his story is in the Library of Congress. My opportunity to make the record came when the camp owner was called away to the telephone to give the sheriff a description of "a nigger who pulled out without paying his debts." The camp Big House, incidentally, resembled an arsenal, complete with side arms, shotguns, and high-caliber "riot guns."

A few weeks prior to my visit to this camp, a research worker came away from it with these notes:

> One time a Negro hand left the camp owing the company $129. The sheriff had all the roads guarded and nobody was allowed to leave. . . . The Klan paraded last night over in ——. There is a grave not far from here of a hand they beat to death.

As a welfare worker once said to me, "Any Negro who is foolish enough to go to work in a turpentine camp is simply signing away his birthright." What this implies has been described by a turpentine foreman as follows: "The supreme authority in the camp is the foreman. To the niggers he is the law, judge, jury, and executioner. He even ranks ahead of God to them. Most camps are so deep in the woods that, outside of murder, officers usually leave it up to the foreman to make and enforce his own laws." The real dictators, it need hardly be pointed out, are the camp owners, who as often as not are corporations, many of them situated in the

North. They not only run the camps to suit themselves—they sometimes act as though they were beyond the pale of federal law. FBI agents who have entered turpentine camps in search of evidence of peonage have actually been jailed for trespassing.

What might well be taken as the attitude of the turpentine industry is to be found in a recent report issued by the University of Florida's Bureau of Economic and Business Research:

> The negroes are a shiftless class and it is estimated that three fourths of them are constantly in debt. The practice of cash advances to them is vicious, as the losses from unpaid accounts is enormous. Without any notice, they frequently leave one operator and go to work for another, usually leaving an unpaid account behind. Some operators will pay the moving expenses of a negro's family in order to obtain another workman. Recommendations for the industry: (1) When a negro leaves a still, or applies for a job at another still, have the operator give his name and description to a central agency. In this way a full check on the whereabouts of negro workers would be kept. (2) Having a gentlemen's agreement between operators not to hire runaway workers of other operators without their consent.

Not only do turpentine operators frequently pay the moving expenses of Negroes in order to obtain new workers; some operators—as well as some planters—are also willing to "buy a debt," which, as they say, is tantamount to "buying a nigger." The procedure is simply for them to pay a Negro's debt at his old place of employment and put him to work for them. That is one way, at least, in which Negro peons can change masters.

From time to time the Southern slavocrats have resorted to wholesale peonage on a community-wide or county-wide basis. ". . . in the South the police stage a sort of roundup during the cotton-picking season," stated a recent report of the American Civil Liberties Union. "Sometimes the victims are given the choice of picking cotton at the prevailing wages, which are generally bottom prices, or of going to the county farm."

This is indeed an annual occurrence in many parts of the South. One violent instance took place in 1937 in Warren County, Georgia. This is a typical Black Belt county: 65 per cent Negro, 97 per cent of cultivated lands devoted to cotton, 81 per cent of all the farmers are tenants or sharecroppers, only 4.6 per cent of the Negroes are full owners, 20 per cent of the Negroes illiterate, 3 out of every 100 persons subscribe to a daily paper, et cetera.

The value of all crops raised in Warren County was approximately one and a quarter million dollars. When the mass enslavement came out into the open, most planters were paying Negro cotton pickers thirty cents per hundred pounds, which meant that the average picker could earn fifty cents per day.

According to Sheriff G. P. Hogan, planters from neighboring Glascock County came to Warren County and offered the pickers "75 cents a hundred and a drink of liquor in the morning and evening" if they would move over to Glascock to pick. "Our farmers just put a stop to it," said Sheriff Hogan. "There was no trouble, although some of them carried guns and fired them into the air. They told the pickers there was plenty of cotton to pick in Warren County, and asked them to stay home and pick it. The pickers decided to stay."

Actually, what happened was this: On September 13 an armed mob of whites entered Warrenton, the county seat, and milled about the square discharging weapons. A truck driver from Glascock County was seized, threatened with an ax handle, and warned to stop trying to recruit Negro labor and to get out of the county. The mob then proceeded to enter many business establishments and ordered all Negroes to leave their jobs and go into the fields and pick cotton. A bootblack who objected was beaten. Then the mob invaded the Negro district, firing into the air and into Negro homes, and shouting orders for the Negroes to get into the cotton fields. Domestic servants took refuge in the closets of their white employers, and Negro children hid in the cemetery. The mob patrolled the highways for days to prevent the exit of Negroes or the entrance of anyone to recruit Negro labor to be used outside the county. The "law," as aforesaid, condoned the entire proceedings.

Ofttimes the techniques of enforcing peonage bear a striking resemblance to those ordinarily associated with chattel slavery. For example, in 1939 a sawmill operator of Lauderdale County,

Mississippi, was convicted for apprehending a Negro and returning him at gun point to work out a twenty-dollar debt; at night he shackled the Negro into bed with a log chain around his neck. It should not be supposed that the only perpetrators of peonage are die-hard Southern slavocrats back in the hinterlands. One of the most notorious cases of peonage in recent years involved the potent United States Sugar Corporation, a large operator in the Everglades cane fields. The corporation was indicted in 1942 by a federal grand jury, and the district attorney charged that Negro workers, recruited in Southern states and transported free to the sugar plantations, were notified upon arrival that they were in debt to the corporation for the cost of their transportation. If they attempted to escape before discharging the debt, he added, they were apprehended and returned to the plantation. Sheriff Jeff Wiggins of Glades County was also indicted for removing inmates from the county jail and forcing them to work on his own farm without pay.

An interesting case of peonage on a cotton plantation came to light in 1944, when a Negro peon escaped from the 2,000-acre Cross County, Arkansas, farm of Albert S. Johnson. The Negro charged that Johnson was holding eleven persons in peonage, including four white women and a white man. In the trial of Johnson which ensued, United States Attorney Sam Rorex accused Johnson of depriving the victims of their food- and shoe-ration books, forcing them to trade at the plantation commissary, refusing to accept payment of debts in cash, forcing them to work out all debts, and beating a seventeen-year-old white girl because she tried to attend school during the cotton-chopping season. Witnesses testified that they had been intimidated by beatings and by Johnson's arsenal of weapons, which included revolvers, a rifle, and brass knuckles.

A Negro named Clyde Miller said, "The way I came to work for him was one day when he picked me up along the road and told me to come to his place. He put me to plowing. I didn't owe him anything. He just said he needed a young boy to work for him." After working two weeks without being paid any money, Miller "borrowed" four dollars from Johnson and made his departure. A week later Johnson came for him at church with a rifle and ordered him to "get back to work or I'll kill you!" A straw boss on the plantation struck Miller. The doctor's bill was four dollars, which Miller's mother offered to pay Johnson, but he said, "I don't need your money; I'd rather have him work." Altogether Miller worked two and a half months, was paid no money but allowed to "borrow" ten dollars.

Deputy Sheriff Claude Holt testified that he had once been called out to a highway near Johnson's plantation, where he found Johnson had shot a hole in the tire of a truck which was trying to carry off one of his peons, a Negro girl named Essie Lee Wright. Johnson told the deputy, "My rifle is still loaded," and, "I'm ready to use it again if I have to."

One of the Negro peons, William "Preacher" Reddick, testified, "My house was so bad it snowed in on us. We had pneumonia. My baby died." But when he said something about moving, Johnson told him, "Preacher, you talk about moving. You can't move! I'll kill you!" On the witness stand Reddick's testimony varied from what he had previously told the FBI, and under cross-examination he revealed that Johnson had persuaded him to testify falsely by promising to provide him food, clothing, and money "so long as I have a dollar." To this Reddick added, "White folks, I hate to say this, but I'm just naturally scared of all white folks. I would tell them anything."

Upon the advice of his attorney—who had been unaware of Johnson's attempt to bribe witnesses—Johnson then pled guilty to the charges of holding two of the Negroes in peonage. He was sentenced to two and a half years, and the Government dismissed the other charges, including an OPA charge that he had hoarded sixteen hundred pounds of sugar.

More often than not, attempts to influence witnesses in peonage cases take the form of brutality rather than bribery. For instance, in a 1943 peonage trial at Tampa, Florida, Melissa Williams, the principal witness, was beaten by police "for resisting arrest."

One of the most complete exposés of the scope and character of slavery in the South today came in 1939 with the escape of six Negro peons from a plantation in Georgia. The Negroes made their way to Chicago, where their reports of the owner's cruelty evoked national indignation. The owner, accompanied by a deputy sheriff and an attorney, went to Chicago with extradition papers for three of the Negroes, who were jailed for a month but released after a hearing at which their extradition was refused. One of the Negroes testified: "I worked on the plantation for twenty-two years—from 1916 to 1938. During this time me and my family never received more than ten dollars a year in wages. Every year, when settling-up time came, Mr. —— would say that we owed him money and that we'd have to stay to work it out. We worked day in and day out from sunup to sundown, and we was always hungry.

"Every two weeks Mr. —— rationed out sowbelly and beans. There was never enough food given out to last for the whole two weeks, so we generally had nothing to eat for two or three days before the supplies were issued. Sometimes our poor white neighbors would slip us a little food so we wouldn't have to work on empty stomachs.

"I wore overalls, summer and winter. Mr. —— gave me two pair each year, and the new pair was handed out when the old ones were so worn out that they were falling off of me like the old rags you put on a scarecrow. I wanted to send my children to school, but Mr. —— told me, 'They don't need no goddamn schoolin'! Niggers and mules was made to work!' So my children only received about one month's schoolin' each year. Whenever they were needed in the fields, Mr. —— took them out of school and told them to 'git that cotton chopped!'

"In 1923 I got tired of working for nothin' and ran off to Atlanta. But Mr. —— had me brought back and put on the chain gang until I agreed to work for him again. Then in 1939 he beat me over the head with a pistol and threatened to send me to jail because I didn't work fast enough to suit him."

When this Negro made good his escape to Chicago, Mr. —— went to see his wife and, waving an iron poker over her head, said, "If you don't tell me where that triflin' nigger has gone I'll knock your damn brains out!"

Another of the refugees from peonage said that Mr. —— had sold him a cow on credit in 1927 and told him that he could work it out. When he ran away after nine years of work, the cow

debt was still unliquidated, according to Mr. ——'s computa-
tions. A twenty-four-year-old runaway reported that "When I
received my first check from the AAA, Mr. —— took me in his
car to get it cashed. On the way back he made me give the money
to him, letting me keep twenty-five cents." Another Negro said
that in 1933 a cousin in Chicago sent him thirty-five dollars to
aid him to escape, but Mr. —— opened the letter and took the
money order.

A nineteen-year-old Negro boy testified that he had been given
about seventy-five lashes with a leather strap for allegedly stealing corn. Another Negro was beaten all over his body with a
pistol. On another occasion Mr. —— knocked a Negro down with
a wagon standard, and when his son ran to help his father, Mr.
—— shot the boy in the groin. Then he had both Negroes sent to
the chain gang.

One of the women who escaped declared, "Many's the time
I've wanted milk for my little baby and I would stand there by
the dog troughs watching the dogs lap it up. The dogs had their
own special cook and were fed lamb chops, while we were so
skinny that our ribs stuck out from under our clothes."

An adept at the old technique of divide and rule, Mr. ——
habitually warned his Negro peons, "Stay away from them poor
white trash—they're one-gallus men and ain't as good as you."
At the same time he told his white sharecroppers, "Stay away
from them niggers—I give 'em sowbelly and leather and make
'em like it."

As an outcome of such evidence *presented* to the U. S. Department of Justice, Mr. —— was finally indicted in 1941.

The War for the Four Freedoms gave wage slavers a new
weapon with which to peonize Negroes: the Selective Service
Act. Of course there is nothing whatever wrong with the principle
of work-or-fight in wartime, *provided* it is applied equitably
through national legislation. But the way the United States went
severally about it was all wrong.

The Southern states were by no means the only offenders; for
instance, Maryland went so far as to enact a work-or-fight statute

under which workers were sometimes paroled into the custody of their employers. South Carolina also adopted a work-or-fight law, and many Southern governors, mayors, and sheriffs took it upon themselves to issue "decrees" and "edicts" to the same effect. Some of these may have been prompted by patriotism, but in practice they all served the abominable purpose of giving fascist-minded employers a weapon with which to force Negroes to work involuntarily for wages lower than they could otherwise have commanded.

To create public sentiment in favor of this procedure, a deliberate and vicious propaganda campaign was launched by some of the employer interests who stood to profit thereby. By blaming the Roosevelt Administration for the wages being paid Negroes under Civil Service and government war contracts, these employers combined an economic drive for lower wages with a political attack upon Roosevelt. The daily press played a prominent part in disseminating this propaganda, as per the following unsigned story in the Miami *Herald*:

> Uncle Jim had been working for Mr. Jones for years but quit and took a government job. He worked several months, met Jones on the street, and his old boss said, "Uncle Jim, is everything all right with you on that government job?"
>
> "Yassuh, boss; plenty good," Uncle Jim replied.
>
> "I suppose," Jones said, "you're buying war bonds every week."
>
> "No suh," said Uncle Jim. "Ah ain't bought none. When a government'll pay a old colored man like me fifty dollars a week, Ah ain't got no confidence in it."

On top of such as that, the political demagogues provided many a spoken word to further the cause of cheap Negro labor. For example, Millard B. Conklin, a "white supremacy" opponent of Senator Claude Pepper in the 1944 Florida primary, declared in a radio address that he stood for postwar homes dominated by the housewife and not by the servant. Along this same lowly line, I was told in many parts of the South by highly indignant white housewives how they had sought in vain to employ Negro women as servants, only to be met with the reply, "I'm lookin' for somebody to come work for me!"

That this sort of "atrocity" story was not without its effect on the total attitude of Southern whites toward Negroes was indicated by the remark made to me by one white Southerner: "When the war's over we oughta take all the Germans, Japs, Wops, Jews, and every nigger who's worked for the government and pen 'em all up behind electrified barbed wire and keep 'em there!"

The history of work-or-fight in Florida is most illuminating. In January of 1945, Governor Millard Caldwell sent a letter to all sheriffs in the state, calling upon them to "use their good offices" to eliminate idleness. John Ford, executive secretary of the Florida Farm Bureau Federation (who also took an active part in promoting Florida's "Christian American" amendment aimed against union security), lost no time in proclaiming that "This is not simply a work-or-fight order. It is in effect a work-forty-hours-a-week-or-fight order." He further ventured to say that the edict also applied to all those "who fail to work satisfactorily."

At St. Augustine, Sheriff Jurant T. Shepherd asked for "the co-operation of citizens in turning in to the sheriff's office the names of persons who should be working and are loafing instead." He complained, moreover, that "there are people, mostly colored, who nightly patronize jook joints and are in no condition the next day to do an honest day's work." Needless to say, only Negro jooks were raided in pursuance of this line of thought, while white jooks—particularly those in the night-club and hotel class—went unscathed.

In Tampa certain shipbuilding contractors were active in prodding the sheriff to enforce the order. G. D. Rogers, Negro insurance man, asked, "What we want to know is whether this order will mean an unemployed Negro carpenter, plumber, brick mason, or other mechanic will be arrested and made to go to work as a common laborer because Negroes are not permitted to work at skilled trades in the war plants here?"

The work-or-fight edict was also perverted notoriously at Fort Lauderdale, Florida, where it was enforced by Sheriff Walter Clark. During February and March of 1944 alone, 49 Negroes were arrested "for vagrancy" and fined from $20 to $35 each without trials. (Under Florida law sheriffs receive all of the fines they collect up to $5,000 per year, 60 per cent of the next $3,000 assessed in fines, and 30 per cent of the next $2,000—which means that a sheriff, especially in the less-populous counties, has to do a lot of fining to make his maximum salary of $7,500.)

One of the Fort Lauderdale cases is especially significant. A bean grower of Oakland Park, a suburb of Fort Lauderdale, prevailed upon a group of eight Negro men and six women to come to his farm to pick beans at a certain price, based upon the assurance that it was a "first picking." Upon arrival the Negroes found the beans had already been picked over and that it would not be worth while for them to pick at the price stipulated. When they prepared to foot it back to town they were warned that if they tried to leave they would be shot—and thus they were held until "the law" took over. In other parts of Florida substantially this same procedure was used to force Negroes to work against their will on Saturdays (no overtime pay, of course).

In Miami (the Nation's Playground) the following story appeared in the Miami *Herald* in 1943:

Work or Fight, Negroes Told

Loafing days for able-bodied male Miami negroes are over and they must "work or fight," it was decreed Thursday by the county's chief law-enforcement officers. The decision was reached at a conference attended by Sheriff D. C. Coleman, Crimes Court Judge N. Vernon Hawthorne, County Solicitor Robert R. Taylor, and assistant solicitors Clenn C. Mincer, Albert D. Hubbard, and Andrew Healy.

"Report after report has reached me, draft boards and the sheriff's department, that it is practically impossible to employ a negro man except for a few hours work—enough for him to earn the price of a bottle of shine and a package of cigarets," Taylor explained.

A general county-wide roundup of all unemployed negro males in selective service ages will be made. Each will be examined for venereal disease. Those infected will be jailed for the cure. Those free from infection will be interrogated under oath, in court, as to their draft status. The information elicited will be handed over to draft boards. As soon as those jailed for venereal treatment have been cured, they too will be reported to their draft boards for appropriate action.

Shortly afterward the Miami *Herald* reported:

Police Push Work-or-Fight Drive Here

Acting on the complaint that scores of males loitering in the negro section derided offers of work, patrol cars converged on N.W. Third Avenue and 14th Street Tuesday morning to find the corners deserted. The complaint was made by Mrs. Briggs Branning, assistant to Mrs. C. H. Reeder, general salvage chairman of the Dade County Defense Council.

Needing men to help salvage scrap, Mrs. Branning offered several groups of negroes $3 per day. All of them refused her offer, declaring that they would not take less than $5. When several of the men became impertinent Mrs. Branning threatened to call police. Police Chief H. Leslie Quigg dispatched six patrol cars to the negro section where not a man was found loitering. While there police raided a suspected gambling house. Ten men were arrested and charged with vagrancy and gambling. In touring the negro section police picked up three men later in the day and charged them with vagrancy.

The raid Tuesday was in keeping with the police policy laid down two weeks ago by county and city prosecutors that negroes must either "work or fight." At that time police arrested twoscore men.

A familiar institution in areas which have been a haven for the indigent, particularly Florida and California, is the "Hobo Express." Law officers serve as the conductors, taking persons charged with vagrancy to the county line and dumping them there with a warning not to return; there the accused are often met by law officers of the adjoining county, who in turn transport them to some other county; and so the "Hobo Express" wends its way until the accused somehow manage to escape the custody of "the law."

In carrying the "Hobo Express" to its logical destination, California sought to prohibit pauperous migrants from entering the state, but the United States Supreme Court, in *Edwards v. California* (1941), put a stop to it (at least legally). The majority of the Court based their opinion on the commerce clause of the Constitution, but four of the justices were also of the opinion that such discrimination was also a violation of the rights of national citizenship as guaranteed by the Constitution and Fourteenth Amendment.

As Mr. Justice Jackson put it, "We should say now, and in no uncertain terms, that a man's mere property status, without more, cannot be used by a state to test, qualify, or limit his rights as a citizen of the United States . . . The mere state of being without funds is a neutral fact—constitutionally an irrelevance, like race, creed, or color."

But those who are still taken for a ride on the "Hobo Express" cannot hitchhike the long way to the United States Supreme Court to have their constitutional rights as American citizens reasserted. And so the "Hobo Express" keeps chugging along as though there were no such things as the Constitution, Supreme Court, and Department of Justice.

"Why don't you leave and get out of it?" a Negro peon at Louisville, Georgia, was asked.

"Because," said he, "the onliest way out is to die out. If anybody tries to leave any other way, the boss man sends the sheriff after him and has him put on the chain gang."

Under the circumstances, the Negro peon must be forgiven for this conclusion. To swear out a warrant against his master *might* result in a conviction; but it would almost certainly require that the Negro move to some other locale.

One of the greatest obstacles in the way of overthrowing peonage is the reluctance of lily-white Southern juries to return convictions. For an authoritative description of how this works I am indebted to a venerable Florida attorney who conducted the defense of nearly everyone who has been charged with peonage in that state. Not one of his clients was convicted.

"The last case I handled was a good example," he said. "It involved a turpentine operator—he knew he was guilty, and he was scared. But I told him he didn't have a thing to worry about. I went ahead and did what I always do in peonage cases: get the jury panel and pick my jury. When I got through picking I let the defense rest right there. The government presented its evidence, and there was a ton of it; but I knew my jury. My client was sweating when the jury went out, but, sure enough, they brought in a verdict of 'not guilty.' Afterward one of the jurymen told me, 'Why, we couldn't convict the Old Man for *peonage* just because he had to whip a few vagabond niggers to keep 'em from runnin' out on their debts!' "

In some Southern states there are, in addition to the vagrancy laws, statutes and ordinances under which the enforcement of peonage is "legally" conducted. These laws provide that a person who accepts an advance of cash or other thing of value from an employer, and then fails to perform the labor for which it was made, is liable per se for fraud. The Georgia statute to this effect was declared unconstitutional by the Supreme Court in 1942. Florida had an almost identical statute, and in 1943 District Attorney Herbert S. Phillips warned in a news story headed *Overlapping Peonage Laws' Repeal Asked:*

> I have always understood that the statutes were enacted by the Florida and Georgia legislatures at the behest and for the benefit of turpentine operators, mill men, and small merchants who make advances to tenant farmers. As long as the statutes remain unrepealed, some justice of the peace or some employer may, if the occasion arises, institute proceedings under them, which very likely would result in somebody being prosecuted in the Federal courts on a peonage charge.

Sure enough, the Florida statute was invoked, and though no one was charged with peonage, the case was carried to the Supreme Court and the law declared unconstitutional. Emanuel Pollock had obtained five dollars from J. V. D'Albora as an advance against future wages for work he did not perform. Sentenced to sixty days, Pollock contested the law's constitutionality; his claim was upheld by the circuit court but denied by the Florida supreme court.

But in the end the U. S. Supreme Court declared: ". . . we are compelled to hold that the Florida act . . . by virtue of the Thirteenth Amendment and the Anti-Peonage Act of the United States is null and void . . . the state . . . must respect the constitutional and statutory command that it may not make a failure to labor in discharge of a debt any part of a crime. It may not directly or indirectly command involuntary servitude, even if it was voluntarily contracted for."

LAST HIRED, FIRST FIRED

The right to work for a living in the common occupations of
the community is the essence of the personal freedom and
opportunity that it was the purpose of the 14th Amendment
to secure . . . —U. S. SUPREME COURT.
A nigger's got just two chances in the South: slim, and none
at all.—FOLKSAY

Ever since the Negro's importation as a slave there has been
a nice division of labor along racial lines. To some extent the
Negro's lot in this respect was worsened by Emancipation; the
slaveowner had protected his investment by hiring poor whites to
do the most dangerous work, but such jobs were promptly forced
upon the Negroes as soon as they were freed.

The first separate occupational census of Negro workers, taken
in 1890, revealed that they were then confined almost entirely to
agricultural pursuits, domestic and personal services. Of the three
million Negro wage earners, nearly 60 per cent were in agriculture
and 30 per cent were in service jobs. At that time over 90 per cent
of the Nation's Negroes lived in the South. The majority of some
200,000 Negroes then in manufacturing and mechanical jobs
were unskilled and for the most part worked as railroad hands,
laborers in lumber and planing mills, iron and steel plants, and
tobacco factories. Skilled Negro workers were chiefly artisans—
carpenters, bricklayers, plasterers, and blacksmiths.

The decade from 1900 to 1910 marked the beginning of the
Negro's industrial advance, with the increase of Negroes in manufacturing and mechanical jobs reaching 100 per cent. Whereas
only one tenth of all Negro workers were in non-agricultural and

non-service occupations in 1890, by 1910 one fifth of all colored workers were engaged in mechanical and industrial jobs, trade and transportation, and professional work.

The advance of the Negro in industry reached a peak during World War I, when somewhere between 400,000 to 800,000 Southern Negroes migrated Northward, chiefly to Illinois, Pennsylvania, New Jersey, and Michigan, to take jobs in war industries. While most began as unskilled workers, there was considerable room for advancement.

By the time the 1920 Census was taken there were 965,804 Negroes in manufacturing and mechanical occupations and another 540,451 in trade and transportation; yet both figures represented a decline from the wartime peak, due to displacements by whites. More of the Negro's wartime gains were lost during the depression of 1920–21. Yet during the prosperity of the later twenties the Negroes were able, through their war-work experience, to regain and extend their foothold, so that by 1930 there were 14 per cent more Negroes in manufacturing and mechanical industries than in 1920. During the same decade Negro migration Northward involved 716,000, who settled chiefly in New York, Philadelphia, Pittsburgh, Chicago, and Detroit. By 1930, 60 per cent of the entire Negro population of the North resided in these cities.

In 1930 the division of labor along racial lines was revealed by these facts: 37 out of every 100,000 gainfully employed white people were lawyers, judges, and justices, but only 2 out of every 100,000 Negroes were in those professions; 35 out of every 100,000 whites were physicians and surgeons, while only 7 out of every 100,000 Negroes were in those professions; 940 out of every 10,000 whites were office workers, but only 70 out of every 10,000 Negroes. On the other hand, 2,870 out of every 10,000 Negroes were engaged in domestic and personal service, as compared to 760 out of every 10,000 whites; and 1,300 out of every 10,000 Negroes were tenant farmers and sharecroppers, compared to 460 out of every 10,000 whites.

The Depression of the thirties vastly accelerated the displacement of Negroes from jobs which had become more desirable either through technological improvements or increased wage scales. Negroes were squeezed out of their jobs as boilermakers, machinists, and in the building trades. On the railroads, the number of Negro firemen decreased to 2,500, as compared to 5,000 in 1910.

The Depression not only cost many Negroes their new jobs; desperate unemployed whites took from them such traditionally "Negro jobs" as waiters, bellmen, truck drivers, et cetera. This was the era during which the Blackshirts paraded Atlanta's streets bearing placards reading "No Jobs for Niggers Until Every White Man Has a Job!" In such fashion the Negro was shoved off the bottom rung of the job ladder.

Despite this—or perhaps because of it—Negro migration northward continued during the decade, until an estimated 317,000 had left the South. By 1940 only 77 per cent of all Negroes remained in the South, as compared to 90 per cent back in 1890; and the Negro population of cities increased 20 per cent. By 1940 New York State ranked ninth in Negro population—exceeding Tennessee, Florida, and Arkansas. Chicago has 335,000 Negroes —twice as many as any Southern city.

The job status of Negroes as revealed by the 1940 Census, at a time when the United States was embarking upon its national defense program, is worthy of special note. At that time Negroes constituted an even smaller proportion of all workers in mining, manufacturing, trade, and transportation than they had in 1910. In manufacturing alone the proportion was 5 per cent, as compared to 6 per cent in 1910.

While Negro men comprised only 10 per cent of the total male working population, they represented 60 per cent of all males in domestic service, 21 per cent of all male laborers, and 21 per cent of all farm laborers. Negro women formed 19 per cent of the total female working population, 47 per cent of all women employed in domestic service, and 27 per cent of all women laborers. In the white-collar field were six out of every fifteen whites, but only one out of every fifteen Negroes. There were only 4,000 Negro physicians and surgeons throughout the United States, and only 1,200 Negro lawyers.

Not even Pearl Harbor and the urgent threat to America's national security carried sufficient impact to open the doors of prejudice which barred Negroes from jobs in war industries. One month after the Japanese attack, more than half of the job openings listed with the U. S. Employment Service were still closed to Negroes as a matter of "industrial personnel policy."

This was in sharp contrast to the prevailing attitude on the fighting front, where, as one front-line fighter said to me, "When you looked around and saw a man in GI uniform, he looked damned good, no matter what the color of his skin."

Charles S. Johnson, in *A Preliminary Report on a Survey of Racial Tension Areas,* prepared for the Rosenwald Fund in November of 1942, said: "When placements through the U. S. Employment Service reached its highest peak, Negroes and other non-whites composed only 3 per cent of the placements in 20 large war industries, and they were less than 3 per cent of the referrals for pre-employment training courses. They are at present about 1 per cent of the total in these pre-employment and refresher courses. In one city . . . with two large shipbuilding concerns, there were nationwide requests for shipyard workers, in spite of the fact that the U. S. Employment Service reported 6,000 Negro workers available in the active file of the Service in that city."

A survey in 1942 indicated that the South, with roughly 80 per cent of the Negro population, was training only about 20 per cent of the Negro participants in the government's war industry training program, while the North, with only 20 per cent of the Negro population, was training 80 per cent of all Negro participants.

The same year, Robert C. Weaver, of the War Manpower Commission, reported that there were at least half a million Negro men and half a million Negro women workers who were still either unemployed or underemployed and were not being utilized in war production because of racial prejudice.

The textile industry provided one of the most inexcusable examples of prejudice-over-patriotism. Despite the existence of critical shortages of textile products for the armed forces throughout the war (MacArthur reported that a shortage of duck held up his advance in the Pacific), the textile industry on the whole refused to employ Negro workers. In 1940 only 26,000 of the

industry's 635,000 Southern workers were Negroes, and this proportion increased but little during the war.

"Such employers are protecting their prejudices at the cost of
production for victory," said War Manpower Commissioner Mc-
Nutt.

Despite all the evidence to the contrary, an amazing number
of Americans seem to think that this is indeed a land of equal
opportunity. When the National Opinion Research Center asked
in 1945, "Do you think Negroes have the same chance as white
people to make a good living in this country?" 66 per cent of the
Southern white respondents had the nerve to say yes, and 52
per cent of the whites in other sections professed to think so too.

BOOK LARNIN', IN BLACK AND WHITE

In order to discriminate against employees in general and Negro employees in particular, the Southern slavocracy has imposed a segregated and inferior school system on the region. This is absolutely essential to the maintenance of the disunity-cheapness of Southern labor, upon which the slavocracy grows fat. The slavocracy knows full well that if the South's children, white and black, were permitted to study in the same classrooms, its regime would not survive that generation.

And so it is not too surprising to find the slavocracy going off the deep end from time to time in its insistence upon segregated education—as, for instance, when the 1940 Mississippi senate, in providing for free textbooks, added a proviso that the books for Negro children be kept in separate warehouses.

Southerners of both races have always suffered from the denial of education opportunities. The highways, industrialization, radio, movies, and world wars have all sharpened the Southern appetite for knowledge and skills. Hence the attitude of the typical contemporary Southerner is: "I want my young-uns to get all the schoolin' they can; it's hard enough to make a livin' these days even if you got a education, much less without one."

One measure of the proximity of education to the frontier is the number of one-teacher schools yet extant in America. Such schools increased in number until sometime between 1914 and 1918, when a trend toward consolidation set in. But as of 1940 there were still 130,000 such institutions, although they were passing from the educational scene at the rate of nearly ten a day.

Needless to say, Negroes have more than their share of these primitive educational units. The exact proportion of Negro schools which employ only one teacher is 64 per cent, and 93 per cent of all Negro schools have three teachers or less. Viewed from another angle, 82 per cent of the Negroes' elementary schools, and 50 per cent of their high schools, are one- or two-teacher institutions. A 10-state study conducted in 1938 revealed that most of these solitary teachers were supposed to be giving instruction in eight grades.

One of the basic tasks of democratic public education is the eradication of illiteracy. Literacy has been brought to the South in good measure, though not yet in full measure. Negro illiteracy has been reduced from 95 per cent in 1865 to 10 per cent in 1940. While only one out of every seven Americans is still functionally illiterate, there are five Southern states where one out of every three persons is functionally illiterate. Of 750,000 illiterates rejected by the armed forces during World War II, 250,000 were Negroes; the ten most illiterate states were found to be Tennessee, Arkansas, Virginia, North Carolina, New Mexico, Alabama, Georgia, Mississippi, South Carolina, and Louisiana.

As of 1940, 60 per cent of the American people who were over twenty-five years of age had never gone beyond grammar school, and 4 per cent had never attended school at all. Of the 29 per cent who had attended high school, only 14 per cent had graduated; and of the 10 per cent who had enrolled in college, less than half had graduated. The average schooling for whites was 8.8 years, and for Negroes, 5.7 years.

The prevailing use of child labor in the South (agriculture is not embraced by the federal child-labor laws) is a major factor in reducing the effectiveness of Southern education. In many rural communities the school term is split and scheduled so that vacations fall during the planting and harvesting seasons when the children are needed to work on the farms. This might be all right were it not for the fact that most of these schools fall far below the standard length of annual school terms. In addition to such regularly scheduled closings, attendance in the South's rural schools is most irregular, due to the children being kept home to do "fair-weather work." These conditions are not due to any desire on the part of the parents to deny their children schooling, nor to exploit them, but rather to the virtual necessity of all able-bodied members of the Southern farm family working in order to eke a bare existence.

Of course there are many instances of unconscionable exploitation of child labor by employers. In 1945 an Alabama farmer was arrested and charged with causing the death of a six-year-old boy by giving him "several swallows of moonshine whisky." According to the county solicitor, the boy had gone to the farm along with his older brothers and sisters, who were hired to pick cotton. The planter produced a half-gallon fruit jar containing whisky and passed it around to the children. The youngster "took two or three swallows," and later consumed "an additional amount," finally becoming unconscious, and dying the next day without having regained consciousness. A doctor diagnosed the cause of death as "pneumonia induced by alcohol."

One by-product of child labor is the educational retardation of the South's children. Negroes suffer most, with something like 70 per cent of them being retarded from the first through the eleventh grades. In 1940 only 10.5 per cent of Negro students were in high school, as compared to 23.1 per cent of white students. Such retardation is often concluded by leaving school at an early age, frequently below the legally prescribed minimum, due to the desire to augment the family income to improve intolerable living conditions.

Once upon a time John C. Calhoun was wont to say, "Show me a nigger who can parse a Greek verb or do a problem in Euclid and I will admit he is a human being like unto ourselves." Were Calhoun alive today, he would be confronted by a host of Negroes who could not only meet these peculiar tests of first-class humanity but far surpass them in every field of endeavor.

The average white Southerner, however, has not yet acknowledged the Negro's apparent intellectual equality. I have heard it said, "A nigger's got no more use with schoolin' than he has with a airplane!" And, "If we're spendin' twelve cents a year on nigger education, that's just twelve cents throwed away!"

In seventeen states (Southern and border) plus the District of

Columbia, "separate-but-equal" schools for the races are required by law. And elsewhere many communities gerrymander their school districts in such manner as to result in separate schools for whites and Negroes.

Although the laws of the seventeen states provide that "separate-but-equal" provision be made for the education of the two races, the provisions actually made are separate-but-unequal. The original "justification" of this was the thoroughly undemocratic argument that Negroes were entitled to educational facilities only on the basis of their contribution through taxation. Here's how the Quincy (Fla.) *Herald* put it back in 1890:

> In view of the fact that the white people of this State pay about 93 per cent of the taxes . . . I am induced to ask the legislature to distribute the school fund in proportion to the taxes paid by each [race] . . . White children are often kept at home to perform such drudgery as is necessary to contribute their portion to the support of the family, while the fathers of these children are paying taxes to educate the negro who does not work but are almost constantly in school.

This argument is still in vogue. So, too, is the system itself. A few figures will suffice to demonstrate the gross inequality between white and Negro educational facilities.

In the seventeen states and District of Columbia which prescribe "separate-but-equal" education of the races, the average annual expenditure per white child as of 1940 was 212 per cent higher than the expenditure per Negro child. The average in dollars and cents was $58.69 per white child and only $18.82 per Negro child. Mississippi spent 606 per cent more per white child than it did per Negro child, or $52.01 as compared to $7.36. In Louisiana, "separate-but-equal" education meant 276 per cent more for white children than for Negro children, or $77.11 as compared to $20.49. South Carolina spent $57.33 per white child and only $15.42 per Negro child—a disparity of 272 per cent.

Such figures recall the words of Booker T. Washington, the pioneer Negro educator: "It is too great a compliment to the Negro to suppose he can learn seven times as easily as his white neighbor."

The investment in public-school property in fifteen Southern states is now about $1,089,942,000, or $123 per pupil, as contrasted with an investment of $242 per pupil in the United States as a whole. The value of school plant and equipment for each white pupil in the South is $157, and for each Negro pupil $37. In a number of Southern states the disparity between white and Negro educational facilities has actually increased through the years. This discrimination occurs in the first instance in the state legislatures which make the appropriations, and again in the expenditure of the funds allotted. This latter procedure was explained in a recent report by the Florida superintendent of public instruction, who declared that fifty-five of the state's sixty-seven counties had not spent on Negro schools the money which the state had granted them for that specific purpose.

He said: "In a few south Florida counties and most north Florida counties many negro schools are housed in churches, shacks, and lodges, and have no toilets, water supply, desks, blackboards, et cetera. Counties use these schools as a means to get state funds and yet these counties invest little or nothing to improve the means." In like vein, a Monroe County (Fla.) grand jury recently reported that Key West's Negro schools needed repairs "too numerous to mention," and contented itself with the recommendation that sanitary facilities be installed and benches be provided for the auditoriums. These Florida examples are not extraordinary; on the contrary, the typical Southern situation is worse. For example, the President's *Report on the Economic Condition of the South* reported that "There were actually 1,500 school centers in Mississippi without school buildings, requiring children to attend school in lodge halls, abandoned tenant houses, country churches, and, in some instances, even in cotton pens."

One result of the inequitable expenditure of school funds is a serious overcrowding of Negro schools. For example, in Atlanta there is such inadequate provision for Negro education that the children are forced to attend school in two shifts of three and one half hours each, instead of the six-and-one-half-hour daily sessions provided white children. Even under this arrangement the city's Negro teachers have an average pupil load of forty, as compared to twenty-nine for each white teacher.

Needless to say, educational discrimination is also reflected in

school libraries. The libraries of Southern white high schools average more than twice as many volumes as the Negro schools, and
there is an even greater discrepancy in quality.

Again, in the matter of transportation to schools, Negroes get
anything but "separate-but-equal" treatment. In 1930, ten Southern states transported 749,434 pupils at a total cost of $12,782,-
414. Less than 2 per cent of this sum was expended for the
transportation of Negro children.

The separate-but-unequal school system affects teachers as well
as students. In the seventeen lawfully segregated states in 1939–40
the average salary for white teachers was 74 per cent higher than
the average for Negroes, or $1,046 as compared to $601. In many
Southern states the differential was even greater. For example,
Mississippi paid her white teachers 234 per cent more than she
paid her Negro teachers, the averages being $776 and $232 per
year respectively. South Carolina paid white teachers an average
of $953 a year, while Negro teachers received only $371, the
difference being 157 per cent. In Louisiana the difference was
135 per cent, or $1,197 compared to $509. Georgia's white
teachers fared 129 per cent better than the Negroes, receiving
$924 as compared to $404. In Alabama and Arkansas, respectively, white teachers received 113 and 70 per cent more than the
Negroes. The combined average of white and Negro teachers'
salaries in the South was $917, which was 50 per cent below the
national average.

During the past few years there has been a Southwide drive for
elimination of the discriminatory racial differential in teachers'
salaries. Of course most of the lily-white administrators of the
prevailing system are inclined to argue, as did the Dade County
(Fla.) school board, that "Negro teachers are not paid less because of race discrimination but because white teachers are required to spend more for their education and have a higher scale
of living." In 1944, A. C. Flora, superintendent of public instruction in Columbia, S.C., added a new note when he testified that
teacher salary differentials were based upon the "greater avail-
ability" of Negro teachers. The fact is that many Southern school
boards deliberately employ Negro teachers who have only temporary teaching certificates or no certificates at all, simply because

they can be hired for less money than duly trained and certified teachers.

In this connection it is interesting to note that in a 1935 study of the economic status of white and Negro teachers in Florida, Dr. A. R. Meade found that the Negro teachers of the state spent an average of $141 for self-improvement, whereas the white teachers, despite their higher salaries, spent only $120.

North Carolina, by means of an equalization fund, has now provided nine-month school terms for both whites and Negroes in all counties, and in 1944 finally eliminated the racial differential in teachers' salaries. To accomplish this, North Carolina increased Negro salaries 46 per cent during the decade ending in 1940. Tennessee increased salaries for Negro teachers only 4 per cent during the decade. Oklahoma increased Negro salaries 92 per cent, to wipe out all but a 2-per-cent differential. On the other hand, the racial differential in Mississippi *increased* 66 per cent during the decade.

In virtually every Southern state Negro teachers have had to carry their fight against salary discrimination into the courts. In most cases the opposition has been bitter. A Charleston newspaper has actually suggested that if the drive for equalization of Negro salaries continues, all public education should be limited to the three Rs. This would of course reduce Negroes and poor whites to a state of semiliteracy, with the well-to-do paying for their children's education in private schools.

Backed up by a Supreme Court decision upholding their right to equal salaries (under the Fourteenth Amendment guarantee of equality before the law), the Negro teachers of the South have instituted numerous suits against school boards, demanding an end to the racial wage differential. The decisions in these cases, which are heard in the federal courts, have generally upheld the Supreme Court and Constitution, ordering the school boards to equalize salaries.

In an effort to circumvent this, many Southern school boards have hastily devised salary-classification schedules which, in addition to such tangibles as training, experience, and seniority, include such intangibles as "character, general appearance, personality, cultural background, caliber of college training, effectiveness, value to the system," et cetera. Ratings of "fair, good, very good, or excellent" under these headings are generally made on a point basis. The salary schedule makes no mention of race, and it is only coincidental that under it Negro teachers are given lower ratings, apologists for the system say. Unfortunately, some of these nicely drawn "non-discriminatory" schedules have been held valid by some federal courts. It is the old story of white supremacy circumventing the Constitution and Supreme Court through adoption of a legal subterfuge which, though valid on its face, is susceptible to discriminatory administration.

Occasionally a spokesman for the white supremacy tribe lets the cat out of the bag. For example, in 1944 a South Carolina senator said, "We can get around the matter of equalization of teacher salaries on the basis of the Re-Certification Plan." This particular plan incorporated a credit system based upon a nine months' school year (South Carolina Negro schools average only five months); the highest ratings were reserved for holders of master's degrees (unavailable to Negroes in South Carolina); the employment applications listed race, and salaries were to be set by the school district trustees.

A series of forthright decisions from the federal courts, looking beyond such loaded salary schedules to the discrimination inherent in their administration, and granting appropriate redress, can put an end to racial discrimination in teachers' salaries. Or the offending states may prefer to follow North Carolina's footsteps in voluntarily equalizing salaries.

Higher education in the South also lags far behind national standards. Here again it is poverty gnawing at the roots. The total endowments of all the colleges and universities in the South are less than the combined endowments of Yale and Harvard. There is no top-notch university in the region, although the best Negro universities are in the South. As for medical schools, the South does not even have facilities to educate sufficient doctors for its own needs.

While there is in each Southern state at least one college for whites which has the approval of the Association of American Universities, only one Southern public college for Negroes is thus accredited. Furthermore, in nine Southern states there is no public Negro college which has the approval of even a regional accrediting agency. Nor is this aspect of the picture improving much. While there was a 21-per-cent increase in the receipts of Negro colleges from public sources during the decade ending in 1940, there was during the same period a decrease of 147 per cent in their income from private sources.

Although most white Southerners will now concede that a little instruction in the three Rs is conducive to increased efficiency among Negroes as workers, there is still widespread sentiment that higher education (high school, college, et cetera) has an opposite effect, i.e., tends to create an antipathy among Negroes against manual labor, and hence should be denied them. And so the slave-day Negro folk song has by no means lost all its meaning:

> *White folks in the college,*
> *Niggers in the fiel';*
> *White folks learnin' the knowledge,*
> *Niggers learnin' to steal.*

Although at least one undergraduate college for Negroes is located in each of the Southern states, many of the fields of specialization available to white persons are not available to Negroes. Relatively little graduate work is accessible to Negroes, and professional offerings are virtually nonexistent in the Negro public colleges and are available in only a few of the private Negro colleges.

It is, of course, in the field of higher education that the dual racial educational system is most costly, working its greatest burden upon both whites and Negroes. It is simply impossible for the Southern states to maintain separate-but-equal white and Negro universities of accreditable quality. In recent years the number of Southern Negroes who have applied for admission to white universities, in states where the public Negro college fails to provide desired courses, has increased. In most cases, as in Florida in 1944, the states' attorneys general have ruled that the white university must admit qualified Negro applicants under such circumstances but that the university must also arrange for the Negro students' complete segregation, in compliance with state laws.

Where the Negro applicants are willing, nine states provide out-of-state scholarship aid for those who wish to pursue a field of specialization that is offered at the state's white university but which is not available at a state institution for Negroes. In practice this arrangement has been limited almost entirely to graduate and professional study.

Recently the U. S. Supreme Court, in the famous *Gaines case* versus the University of Missouri, ruled that if a qualified Negro applicant objects to being sent out of his own state for study which is available in his own state's white university, then he must be provided such instruction within his home state. This decision strikes a near-fatal blow at segregated higher education. For the Southern states' white universities to admit Negroes and at the same time to segregate them is well-nigh impossible. And so it appears likely that the contradictions and injustices inherent in the dual educational system will bring about its disintegration at the higher levels first.

Despite the finality of the Supreme Court's ruling, the inculcated white sentiment in the South against any modification of the segregated school system is still being exploited by politicians and the press. For instance, in 1944 the United Press carried a story with the lead, "The U. S. Office of Education today called on white educational institutions of the South to open their doors to Negro scholars." The Southern press generally waxed indignant. Said the Jackson (Miss.) *Daily News:* "Here's telling the responsible head of the U. S. Department of Education, whoever he may be, to go straight to hell. The South won't do it . . . not in this generation and never in the future while Anglo-Saxon blood continues to flow in our veins. Nobody but an ignorant fatheaded ass would propose such an unthinkable and impossible action."

It turned out that the U. S. Office of Education hadn't made such a recommendation, anyway. It had simply urged that Southern white colleges ". . . work out ways and means of making their facilities available to Negro scholars . . ." A subsequent explanation stated that the intent of this was that white institutions send visiting instructors to Negro colleges, lend them books, et cetera.

WHITE MAN'S COUNTRY

By this time it should be apparent that although every third person in the South is a Negro, the region is pre-eminently white man's country. The Negro has no effective voice in conducting its public affairs, either legislative, executive, judicial, or civil. His daily life is governed not only by discriminatory legal codes and even more discriminatory law enforcement, but also by the rigorous dictates of an interracial etiquette enforced by lynch law (for further details see the South or Charles S. Johnson's *Patterns of Negro Segregation*).

Comes now the question—if it has not long since—"Is the South insane?" The answer is a categorical "Yes"; and its insanity has infected the entire nation.

Addicted as it is to protestations of Christianity and Americanism, the white South has long been suffering the mental torment of the damned, trying to rationalize the irreconcilable contradiction between the Christian-American doctrine of the brotherhood of man and the unchristian and un-American systems of slavery and white supremacy. After generations of being thus "troubled in mind," the white South, in addition to becoming the nation's economic problem No. 1, has also become the nation's pathological problem No. 1.

It was the historical purpose of the Civil War to eliminate this contradiction in American society, but that aim was handed down to us for solution when the Reconstruction Klan was permitted to ask its initiates: "Do you believe that this should be a White Man's Country, and will you faithfully strive to maintain it as such?"

It is needless to attempt to say whether the philosophy or the system of white supremacy came first. To a considerable extent —as faithfully portrayed in Howard Fast's microcosmic *Freedom Road*—the system was established by Klan violence in the face of extensive white opposition. In time, however, the system inevitably gave rise to adherence to the philosophy, so that today we find not only the mind of the South, but also the mind of America, polluted with the poison of racism.

As was only to be expected, a cult of witch doctors has arisen to administer the poison and conduct the rites of white supremacy. No diagnosis of the problem of the South would be complete without close scrutiny of these pathological symptoms. It is therefore necessary to bring together some of the witch doctors in a symposium here—not to disseminate their dogma, but to identify and isolate it so that the specific antidote (which is truth) can be properly administered.

The keynote of the South's new order of slavocracy was sounded by Henry Woodfin Grady, orator and journalist from Georgia during the eighties, who laid this shaky cornerstone for the "New South" he envisaged: "The truth above all things, to be worn unsullied and sacred in your hearts, to be surrendered to no force, sold for no price, compromised in no necessity, but cherished and defended as the Covenant of your prosperity, and the pledge of peace to your children, is that the white race must forever dominate in the South, because it is the white race, and superior to that race by which its supremacy is threatened . . . What God hath separated let no man join together."

"The Anglo-Saxon is the typeman of history," said Imperial Wizard William Joseph Simmons upon reincarnating the Klan in 1915. "To him must yield the self-centered Hebrew, the cultured Greek, the virile Roman, the mystic Oriental. The psalmist must have had him in mind by poetic imagination when he struck his sounding harp and sang: 'O Lord: thou hast made him a little lower than the angels, and hast crowned him with glory and honor. Thou madest him to have dominion over the works of thy hands; thou hast put all things under his feet.' . . . An inevitable conflict between the white race and the colored races is indicated by the present unrest. This conflict will be Armageddon, unless the Anglo-Saxon, in unity with the Latin and Teutonic nations, takes the leadership of the world and shows to all that it has and will hold the world mastery forever."

"The first essential to the success of any nation, and particularly of any democracy, is a national unity of mind," added Imperial Wizard Hiram Evans in 1937. "Its citizens must be ONE PEOPLE . . . they must have common instincts and racial and national purpose. This great law is now so well understood that there is no need to prove it here. It follows that any class, race, or group of people which is permanently unassimilable to the spirit and purpose of the nation has no place in a democracy. The negro race is certainly unassimilable; no one can claim that more than a few blacks are fit.

"We should see in the negro a race even more diverse from ourselves than are the Chinese, with inferior intellect, inferior honesty, and greatly inferior industry. We should see a race childish, lethargic, superstitious, mentally arrested at a low level, hardly removed from a savagery that is near the lowest type known.

"The negro, so far in the future as human vision can pierce, must always remain a group *unable* to be a part of the American people. His racial inferiority has nothing to do with this fact; the unfitness applies equally to *all alien races* and justifies our attitude toward Chinese, Japanese, and Hindus. No matter how intelligent or how well educated he might be, the negro is and will always remain an *alien race,* diverse in instinct and mentality, unable to share our points of view or our national purpose, animated by interests hostile to ours and a ready ally for any national enemy—a great and incurable national weakness. Certainly there is no principle of democracy which forces its supporters to accept such a weakness!

"But this is not all. The fact remains that *the negro is inferior.* Anthropologists believe that his race is older than the white, yet its development is far less. An uncounted number of centuries must pass before the negro will—if ever he can—become in mentality and character the equal, as a race, of the whites. More than intelligence is involved—independence, self-reliance, trustworthiness, initiative—all the great traits of character which make for the success of men and races. No amount of education can ever make a white man out of a man of any other color.

"It is a law on this earth that races can never exist together in complete peace and friendship and certainly never in a state of equality. The only possible escape from either negro diversity or inferiority would be through amalgamation of the races. I think no sane man will offer as a solution of our problem that we should make America a nation of mulattoes!"

"I believe in white supremacy, and as long as I am in the Senate I expect to fight for white supremacy, because I can see that . . . if the amalgamation of whites and Negroes in this country is permitted, there will be a mongrel race, and there will come to pass the identical condition under which Egypt, India, and other civilizations decayed . . ." said Senator Ellender of Louisiana, filibustering in 1938 against the anti-lynching bill.

"I expect to give the Senate three opportunities to vote on this problem of intermarriage of whites and Negroes . . . I propose to ask for a yea-and-nay vote on that question also, so that every senator will have an opportunity of expressing himself . . . I can just imagine how politicians have influenced the members of colored societies within their wards to say, 'We is going to vote for Mr. So-and-So, because he is going to have this law that prohibits us from marrying with white people in Massachusetts taken off the books, so as to allow us colored people to marry white folks.'

"Why did not the Negroes progress and become more highly civilized in their homeland—Africa? Africa is a fine land. They had as fine a country to live in as we did. They had as fine a climate as ours. But they did not have the intellect which the white people have!

"I will now cite from a book written by Alfred P. Schultz entitled *Race or Mongrel?* '. . . The absorption of a race belonging to a different stock is usually followed by degeneration, thus all Hamitic-Semitic people decayed; the Jews developed . . .' I shall now read from a book entitled *White America* by Earnest Sevier Cox. '. . . The cultural debit of the colored peoples to the white race is such as to make the preservation of the white race a chief aim of the colored, if these latter but understood their indebtedness. The insane desire of the colored to blot out the color line and bridge the evolutionary chasm between the races by the process of interracial marriage ignores the fact that the white race as white is the source of progress. That the colored race should seek to "kill the goose that lays the golden egg" is further proof that their inferiority, demonstrated so clearly in cultural attainments, extends to their rationing processes in general . . .

" 'A race which has not shown creative genius may be assumed to be an unfit type so far as progress in civilization is concerned and is a matter of concern for the eugenist. Those who seek to maintain the white race in its purity within the United States are working in harmony with the ideals of eugenics. Asiatic exclusion and Negro repatriation are expressions of the eugenic ideal.' "

"If one believes in history before effeminate and fallacious ideologies, the recognition of the superiority of the Nordic and the Nordicized world is immediate," wrote William Blanchard of Miami, of the White Front. "A dangerous upsurge of democracy and self-determination throughout the world of color is robbing the Western World of some of its power, but we have not yet lived to see the end of white supremacy.

"It does not take half an eye to see that the negro is the most gross member of the human family. Only when beckoned or compelled by the alien race does he step forward. The rich dark continent will always remain the toy of conquerors until the master stoops so low as to share his blood with the slave.

"Instinctively the black knows that his only hope of advancement is to mate with an alien race. This lust for emergence is precisely what knots the lynching rope. Negro blood is prepotent, and whoever introduces it to the veins of the white race has committed the most indescribably filthy betrayal. Sand is made more tasty by sugar, but never sugar by sand.

"Man has nothing against the gorilla, but if he entrusts his fruitful garden to such a beast he is a very great fool. The white man is still not willing to seal the destiny of his magnificent race in mulatto wombs. The white woman, and she alone, is the bridge over which the white race must pass to what it aspires to be. When 'that bridge falls, white primacy will be but the rotting memory of a dead age.

"What is surprising is not that occasional violence has punctuated the history of the postwar South, but that every day has not provided its account of a bloody race war. The abolitionist crusade that has continued with unflagging vigor since 1865 does not augur well for a bloodless Southern drama. Yet the white Southerner is content to live in peace with his lowly black brother, so long as his supremacy remains unchallenged.

"Is this *just?* Is it fitting that men with white skins should demand supremacy over men with black skins and stand ready to enforce their dictatorship at any cost? Is it proper that the negro has neither political nor social rights in the land where he has labored and reared his sons since the earliest dawn of American civilization? Since America is alleged to be a democracy and the negro is rumored to possess a vote, is it just that the South's black majority not only does not rule but can claim no representation in Council, Legislature, or Congress? Yes, it is *just*—as it is and should be.

"When the Federal Government recognizes superior biological values and proceeds systematically to solve the South's problem by expatriation, birth control, and rigid segregation, the long race vigil will be over. But until then, the era of parliamentary bedlamism will see the negro attack the white woman and for his trouble be forthright hung . . . Against that bitter and inevitable fruit of abolition, mass miscegenation, the gallows must rear a somber head . . .

"Must the American white man accept the nigger as his equal by order of a brace of Jewish commissars? . . . That dusky race which enslaved was happy and lovable must today be recognized for the sullen revolutionary mass it is and be disciplined accordingly . . . Racial Nationalism demands that the negro be made a ward of the nation and governed by special codes befitting the dignity of a white state.

[The Racial Nationalist Program of the White Front includes the following:]

"Miscegnation made a felony.

"Segregation of the Jews.

"With the Nordic nations of South America, the United States must exercise a strict tutorship over the whole Latin-American domain.

"American participation in white control and regulation of the world of color."

In slightly less fascistic tone, Vance Muse, of the union-busting "Christian-American" front, warns that "From now on, white women and white men will be forced into organizations with black African apes whom they will have to call 'brother' or lose their jobs."

"No niggah's's good as a white man because the niggah's only a few shawt yere-ahs from cannibalism," says Gene Talmadge, too-often governor of Georgia. "For thousands of yere-ahs the niggah sat on the wealth of the world. Gold and diamonds and rubies and emeralds. And wha'd he do? Filed his teeth and ate his fellow man. And all this time the Caw-cas-yun race was a-fightin' and a-dyin' and a-buildin' civilizations. Wherever the white man plants his *feet,* there he rules or finds his grave."

"Three theories are widely held concerning the condition of the Negro in America," wrote W. T. Couch as director of the University of North Carolina Press. "There is one which says his condition has been produced by his inferiority. In this view, prejudice and the additional burdens placed on the Negro on account of prejudice are results, not causes. Those who hold this view ask why no Negro civilization of any importance has been developed in Africa, why there is so little intelligent interest among Negroes, even intellectuals, in what happens there. They insist that everything the Negro demands in America he could get for himself in Africa, if he only had the ability to get it.

"There is [a second] theory that the Negro's condition is produced by inferiority, but that this inferiority can be overcome, and the prejudice resulting from it can be cured . . . Why (those who hold this view ask) is superiority so much feared and hated today? . . . Further, they wish to know: Is there any sanity in the view now often stated that no one but a Fascist or Nazi can believe one people or race superior to another? . . .

"The South, those who hold this second view may say, places numerous unnecessary burdens on the Negro—burdens which should be removed. But this cannot be done all at once. And it must not be done in such manner as to weaken the barrier between the races. This barrier cannot be made completely effective—but the fact that some people may cross it in secret does not mean that the barrier ought to be torn down. The barrier may be a tremendous handicap on the Negro; but removing it would result in something worse . . ."

Quite often the white supremacists' insistence upon their supremacy assumes ridiculous as well as vicious proportions. For example, there was the spectacle some Southerners made of themselves when in 1944 (during the presidential campaign) Representative Bob Sikes of Florida "discovered" that the Army had purchased 55,000 copies of an illustrated and highly effective booklet entitled *The Races of Mankind* for use in orientation classes for officer candidates. This booklet, prepared by Dr. Gene Weltfish and Ruth Benedict of Columbia's department of anthropology, contained the following chart:

Median Scores on A.E.F. Intelligence Tests

Southern Whites
Mississippi	41.25
Kentucky	41.50
Arkansas	41.55

Northern Negroes
New York	45.02
Illinois	47.35
Ohio	49.50

Needless to say, anti-Roosevelt Southern congressmen and editors had a field day. Of course they had to ignore the fact that the table was surrounded with such statements as: "Everyone knows that Southerners are inborn equals to Northerners . . . The white race did badly where economic conditions were bad and schooling was not provided, and Negroes living under better conditions surpassed them. The differences did not arise because people were from the North or South, or because they were white or black, but because of differences in income, education, cultural advantages, and other opportunities."

But the ranting of reaction ran its course. "Of course it may not be possible to get President Roosevelt to sue for divorce, but if he is going to let people like his wife take a hand in running the Army there are plenty of things Congress can do to deter him," declared the Fort Myers (Fla.) *News-Press*. "If our Representatives in Congress have any respect for themselves and their constituents they will utterly destroy the crawling vermin who are responsible for things like this," said the Macon (Ga.) *Telegraph*. "If the Government has any surplus energy, it should be put into winning the war with the Axis, not into the crusade for social equality," concluded the Rome (Ga.) *News-Tribune*.

Some Southern congressmen were no more restrained. A subcommittee of the House military affairs committee headed by Representative Durham of North Carolina charged that the booklet was "inaccurate" and "filled with Communist propaganda." Chairman May (Ky.) threatened to "investigate" the War Department. As a result, the Army first limited the booklet to "off-duty discussion," and finally withdrew it altogether as "inadequate."

But not only the South has been polluted by the poisonous doctrine of white supremacy.

All America must share the shame of the Red Cross's medieval policy of first refusing to accept the blood of Negro donors, and then segregating it, for no scientific reason whatever. As the St. Louis *Post-Dispatch* pointed out, "Medical science is the authority for assurance that the dried plasma is the same for all people, that no characteristics of any kind could possibly be transmitted through its use in transfusions. Opposition to a universal blood bank, therefore, is based on ignorance and prejudice."

The extent to which such ignorance and prejudice does obtain in America was surveyed by the *Negro Digest* in 1945. To the question, "Are all men created equal?" the replies were in the following percentages (the polling included ten whites for every Negro):

	Yes	*No*	*Undecided*
North	79	11	10
West	82	9	9
South	61	24	15

Interestingly, there were variations when the question was put, "Are Negroes equal to whites?"

	Yes	*No*	*Undecided*
North	21	68	10
West	24	62	14
South	4	92	4

The fact that 61 per cent of the Southern respondents agreed that all men are created equal, and then only 4 per cent would admit that Negroes are equal to whites, is just one indication of the insanity produced by the Myth of the Master Race.

The extent to which prejudice obtains throughout the nation was also probed in 1943 by the research firm of Elmo Roper for *Fortune* magazine. "Are there any groups in this country who might be harmful to the future of the country unless curbed?" it asked. Of those queried, 16 per cent thought Negroes should be curbed, 14 per cent specified the Jews, 10 per cent said Bundists, and 9 per cent said Japanese. Apprehension, significantly, was highest in the upper-income brackets and in the New England and mountain states.

An earlier poll in 1942 found that when asked if they thought there were other groups of people who were trying to get ahead at the expense of people like themselves, 22 per cent named the Jews, 12 per cent said big businessmen (plus 4 per cent who said the rich), 9 per cent said labor, 6 per cent accused politicians, 4 per cent said black-market operators, and 3 per cent said Negroes. None of these figures, however, should be regarded as reflecting the full amount of prejudice in America. A great many people who hold prejudices do not like to admit as much, and this has been particularly true since the Nazis turned prejudice into world war.

It has been generally supposed that Nazi Germany sank lower than any other nation in giving official sanction to the Myth of the Master Race, but in reality the myth enjoys its greatest *legal* status in the United States of America. While the Nazis adopted all manner of legal restrictions against the economic, political, and civil rights of Jews (more or less rigorous than the South's restrictions on Negroes), they did not go so far as to prohibit intermarriage between Nordic Germans and Jews. On the other hand, thirty states of the United States (including all Southern states) have statutes which provide that "All marriages between white persons and persons of Negro descent are forever prohibited and shall be void always." As an added precaution, Arkansas proceeds to state that concubinage between whites and Negroes is likewise *verboten*. Florida, displaying a nice regard for the double standard, provides a $1,000 fine and three months' imprisonment for any white woman who has sexual intercourse with a Negro man, but makes no reference to such relations between white men and Negro women.

These statutes are embellished with many a frill and enforcement provision. Mississippi and Virginia provide that no whites and Negroes who intermarry outside the state can return. Georgia and Virginia require that marriage licenses state the persons' race and the race of their ancestors. North Carolina, South Carolina, Georgia, and Virginia make it a misdemeanor for anyone to issue a marriage license to a white-Negro couple; penalties range from fines of not less than $500 to imprisonment up to ten years.

To keep a double check on interracial marriage, Arkansas and Mississippi require that the persons' race be specified on bills of divorce. Georgia provides that the parents of children whose birth certificate shows mixed blood be prosecuted; officers failing to prosecute may be impeached. Maryland says that any white woman who has a child by a Negro or mulatto shall be punished. In Georgia, to accuse a white woman of having had sexual intercourse with a Negro is slander per se.

South Carolina and Texas prohibit the adoption of a white child by Negroes, and the latter state—just to be fair—likewise prohibits the adoption of a Negro child by whites. Mississippi—

always the whole hog in matters of racial prejudice—has a statute which reads "Any person guilty of presenting for public acceptance and circulation written matter in favor of social equality or intermarriage between Negroes and whites shall be guilty of a misdemeanor." (Author's note to the attorney general of Mississippi: see pages 326–55.)

In defining racial purity many American states also go further than did the Nazis. The infamous Nazi Laws of Nürnberg permitted cultural and spiritual "Nordification" of Germans with one Jewish grandparent, but the only hope for a child born of an Aryan German mother and a Jewish father was for the mother to formally swear that the child was not the issue of her Jewish husband, but of an adulterous liaison with an Aryan. The Nazi Civil Service Law of 1933 prescribed that no German could be considered a bona fide Aryan if he had more than one eighth Jewish blood (more than one Jewish great-grandparent).

But the Laws of Nürnberg had nothing on the laws of some American states. Long before the Nazis adopted the same formula in defiance of all the laws of biology, South Carolina and Maryland defined colored persons as "Any person possessing one eighth or more Negro blood." However, South Carolina went on to provide that children of mixed parentage having less than one eighth Negro blood are entitled to the rights of whites; but if full-blooded whites object to their attending white schools, the state is obligated to provide them separate schools, neither white nor colored.

Florida imposes the Jim Crow line against all persons having as much as one sixteenth Negro blood. Arkansas and Virginia have preferred to vest discretionary power in the duly delegated (white) officials via the definition: "Any person having any ascertainable Negro blood." In Texas and Tennessee, Negro blood does not have to be either ascertainable or in any specific proportion, as the laws read: "Any person of mixed blood descended from a Negro." Georgia—all-out for white supremacy—includes among "colored persons": "Any person having Negro, West Indian, Asiatic, or Indian blood, and all descendants."

This sort of thing would simply be ridiculous if such laws were obsolete, as they now are in Germany; but they are very much

alive and exert a profoundly repressive influence upon many
millions of Americans. Just how was brought out in sharp focus
by the following "human interest" item in the Miami *Herald,*
September 11, 1943:

> BABY'S RACE "CHANGED"
> BY CERTIFICATE SWITCH
> An interchange of birth certificates made Friday in state
> records officially switched a Miami baby's race from Caucasian
> to negro.
> The unusual quirk diverting the course of the 20-month-old
> girl's life was disclosed when the state registrar at Jacksonville
> directed the Miami office to substitute an adoption birth cer-
> tificate listing the names of negro foster parents for the original
> birth certificate which recorded the natural parents as of white
> lineage.
> On the face of these official records it appeared that a negro
> couple was adopting a white child.
> The child was born to a 20-year-old white mother in Jackson
> Memorial Hospital and kept for a year in a white family before
> its negroid characteristics became evident. The mother, months
> earlier, had been sent to a mental hospital.

Every day in the South babies are born of Negro mothers and
white fathers. These babies are registered as Negroes, of course,
according to the law. No one, including the white father, looks
upon the event as anything extraordinary. But when, as in this
rare case, a child is born to a white mother of a Negro father, the
whole horrendous system of white supremacy is brought out in
sharp relief.

At the stroke of a pen an infant human being is demoted from
a "superior" race to an "inferior" one, a fake label carrying with
it a real sentence to a life of Jim Crow. Her entire world is im-
measurably shrunken and circumscribed, including her opportunities for a career and even her choice of a husband.

As a Negro instead of a white person (i.e., confined to a
Negro's environment) she is in effect sentenced to die 14 years
sooner, suffer 43 per cent more daily sickness, be three times as
likely to die in giving birth, run five times the risk of contracting
tuberculosis, eight times the risk of contracting syphilis, et
cetera. If she continues to live in "The Anteroom to Heaven"
(Miami), it must be in a black ghetto. If she were to go swim-

ming in the surf she would be arrested, and she would suffer the
same fate if she failed to make good her departure from the
City of Miami Beach before the nocturnal curfew for Negroes.
Perhaps, unless white supremacy is disposed of, she might ultimately gain recognition as follows (standard model from Asheville [N.C.] *Citizen,* 1944):

> ". . . , age . . . , negro, who had been employed at the
> R. B. Dickinson home for more than 50 years, died yesterday.
> She was known to many persons throughout the South as
> "Aunt Lizzie," and was noted for her cooking and faithfulness
> to duty.

THE 7.7 DEMOCRACY OF THE SOUTH

Needless to say, the South is no more democratic politically than it is economically or racially. As everyone knows, those who own a region or nation inevitably control its political life. The "public" affairs of the South, therefore, are for the most part administered by politicians who primarily serve the owners—Southern and non-Southern, individual and corporate—of the South's natural and productive resources.

Various means are employed by this plutocracy to thwart Southern democracy. Chief among these is the poll tax, which is still levied as a prerequisite to voting by the seven states of Alabama, South Carolina, Virginia, Texas, Arkansas, Mississippi, and Tennessee. Secondly, there is the institution of the white Democratic primary which, despite court rulings, has until now deprived Negro Southerners of an effective vote in the eight states of Alabama, South Carolina, Arkansas, Mississippi, Georgia, Florida, Louisiana, and Texas. And then there are the many devious mechanical restrictions on voting which tend to subvert democracy.

For instance, there are the various literacy qualifications for voting, which require that a person be able to read or write any part of the Constitution, or else "give a reasonable interpretation of same." Various states, however, exempt from this requirement Confederate veterans and their "lawful descendants," owners of forty acres of land or $500 worth of other property, or "persons of good character who understand the duties of citizenship." Although the law provides for an appeal to the courts for persons denied registration, the election is generally over by the time a court decision can be had.

Many registrars, instead of running the risk of refusing to register Negroes, simply require them to stand in a Jim Crow line—and let them stand until they become discouraged and leave. Also, in small communities it is quite common to appoint white women as registrars, who operate from their parlors where Negroes dare not intrude.

Another burdensome restriction on democracy is the maze of specifications as to when a person may register. Very often the period is limited to a brief period remote from all elections so that interest in registration will be slight. Public notice of registration periods is often inadequate or entirely missing. Three of the five states which still require periodic re-registration are in the South; they are: South Carolina, Tennessee, and Louisiana. On the other hand, Texas and Arkansas go to the other extreme and do not require registration at all. Then, too, the residence requirements for voting are entirely too long for our modern mobile era.

Twenty-three states now have laws which require employers to give their workers time off to vote on election day; but only five of these are in the South: Arkansas, Kentucky, Missouri, Texas, and West Virginia.

The four Southern states of Virginia, Tennessee, Kentucky, and Oklahoma do not provide for primary runoffs between the winner and runner-up of the first primary when the winner fails to receive a plurality over the combined vote of all his opponents. This is an undemocratic situation, because in some cases the runner-up would draw enough of the votes of the low-vote candidates to win the nomination. Not having a primary runoff gives the political machines an advantage—which means it keeps democracy at a disadvantage.

And of course democracy is bound to be vulnerable in a region where ballot boxes often consist of such things as matchboxes, envelopes, cardboard cartons, and tobacco cans, such as the Senate Investigating Committee found in use in Arkansas in 1944.

The Plutocracy of Polltaxia

While it is not possible to compute the exact number of Southerners who are disfranchised by the poll tax, it is possible to
determine the approximate number who are kept from the polls
through the combined obstacles of the poll tax, white primary,
mechanical restrictions, et cetera.

In 1944 there were an estimated 14,500,000 potential voters
in the eight poll-tax states, but only 2,700,000, or 19 per cent,
of them paid their poll tax and voted. In contrast to this, 57
per cent of the potential voters in the free voting states took part
in the election. Assuming that Southerners as such do not harbor
some innate antipathy toward voting, we can only conclude that
5,500,000 Southerners—with a ratio of three whites to two
Negroes—were kept from voting by one and/or another of the
obstacles. Worse yet, this figure is for a wartime voting year when
the national vote was much smaller than it might otherwise have
been. Following the same procedure for arriving at the number of
sidetracked would-be voters in the poll-tax states, we find that in
1940 they numbered about 8,698,000 and that in 1942 they rose
to about 10,000,000.

Some have argued that in the Solid South the Democratic
primary provides the real contest and that it draws a heavier vote
than the general election. The latter half of this proposition is
incorrect. In 1944 the total primary vote in the eight poll-tax
states was 1,334,000, as compared to 2,767,500 votes cast in
the general election. In other words, the primary vote was less
than half the general election vote, or 7.7 per cent of the potential as compared to 19 per cent. It is also a significant fact that
of the 79 congressional districts in the eight poll-tax states 25 did
not conduct primaries in 1944, in 15 others the primary candidates had no opponents, and in 36 districts the Democratic
nominees were unopposed in the general election.

The breakdown of primary and general election votes in the

poll-tax states in 1944, as compared to the number of potential voters in each state, is shown in the following table:

ACTUAL AND POTENTIAL VOTES, POLL-TAX STATES, 1944

State	Potential Vote	Actual Vote Primary	Actual Vote General	Per Cent Voting Primary	Per Cent Voting General
Alabama	1,614,654	124,294	222,338	8	14
Arkansas	1,068,413	73,902	217,207	7	20
Georgia	2,025,310	249,651	274,374	12	14
Mississippi	1,185,822	36,343	152,712	3	13
So. Carolina	1,005,126	47,496[1]	100,862	5	10
Tennessee	1,795,774	194,904	398,622	11	22
Texas	4,123,814	578,069	1,058,419	14	26
Virginia	1,764,934	29,450[2]	342,980	1	19
Total Poll-tax States	14,549,289	1,334,109	2,767,514	7.7	19
Free Vote States	74,088,357		42,335,509		57

[1]No poll tax required for primary vote.
[2]Incomplete.

The amount of the poll tax ranges from $1 to $2 per year, but in Alabama, Mississippi, and Virginia it is cumulative for varying periods, the respective maximum charges being $36, $6, and $5.08. While these sums may seem negligible to some, to many a Southern wageworker and tiller of the soil (who sees but little cash money) such a tax is always burdensome and often prohibitive. A dollar is a lot of money to spend for a vote when a man's family is hungry, cold, and sick. It has been truthfully said: You can't have a right and tax it too.

During the 1943 filibuster in the House against the bill to abolish the poll tax as a prerequisite to voting for federal officials, a young navy man, Evan Owen Jones, Jr., mounted the railing surrounding the visitors' gallery and, interrupting the debate, demanded, "If a man doesn't have to pay tribute to fight, why should he be made to pay tribute to vote?"

There is, of course, no satisfactory answer to this question,

except that he should not. And though certain Southern Democratic congressmen, in collaboration with certain Northern Republicans, defeated the universal federal ballot for servicemen
(which would not have required payment of a poll tax), the
poll-tax state legislatures subsequently took steps to exempt their
2,300,000 servicemen from the tax. Also exempt are approximately one million overage persons.

In addition to the foregoing exemptions, various poll-tax
states exempt: women who don't vote (in practice this virtually
subverts the woman-suffrage amendment); Confederate veterans,
their wives and widows; veterans of World War I; active members of the National Guard and Naval Militia; the permanently
disabled whose taxable property does not exceed $500; the in-
sane; the deaf, dumb, and blind; persons maimed by loss of hand
or foot; persons incapable of earning a living; and Indians not
taxed.

No one would deny that these groups should not be required to
pay a poll tax for the privilege of voting—but who can say that
others are not also entitled to a tax-free vote? These mass exemptions from liability only accentuate the intrinsic discriminatory
nature of the poll tax. What is unjust for some must be unjust for
all. Moreover, such wholesale exemptions further discredit claims
that the poll tax has any real merit as a fiscal measure. The all-
time high percentage of a poll-tax state's revenue obtained from
this source was only 1.8 per cent, collected by Virginia in 1937.
Alabama, a more typical example, derives only .6 per cent of its
revenue from the poll tax.

Equally unsubstantiated is the allegation that the poll tax
makes an important contribution to education; in none of the
poll-tax states does the tax provide as much as 5 per cent of the
state's educational fund. As the Birmingham Teachers' Association resolved in 1945, "Although the revenue received from the
poll tax goes to education in Alabama, the oligarchic practice
should no longer be allowed to stifle the achievement for which
education exists—freedom to act wisely. It will mean more to
education in Alabama to have the citizens we have trained take
part in the settling of political questions than to receive the pit-
tance from the tax and then see the vital matters of the state

decided by only 10 to 30 per cent of the people, many of whom have been prodded by political leaders to dig up the price of the tax."

Actually the pretense that the poll tax substantially supports public education has degenerated into a complete farce. In 1943 Justice Neil, of the Tennessee supreme court, said, "The point is made that the revenue derived from poll taxes must be set aside as part of a sacred fund and shall not be diverted to any other purpose. . . . This is a pure fiction. It is a well-known fact that there has been no such fund in existence for more than fifty years."

Judicial recognition of the real nature of the poll tax has also been forthcoming from other poll-tax states. For example, the Supreme Court of Appeals in Virginia has held that the imposition of the poll tax was not intended primarily for the production of revenue but to limit the right of suffrage. Similarly, a subcommittee created by the Virginia Advisory Legislative Council (an official body created by the legislature) reported in 1941 that:

"The poll-tax requirement was introduced into the present [1902] constitution for the express purpose of serving as a restriction on the free exercise of the suffrage; and it continues beyond any reasonable doubt to constitute a restriction in practice. The most cursory study of the proceedings of the constitutional convention of 1901 will easily establish the frank intention of those who introduced the poll-tax stipulations into the constitution; the Supreme Court of Appeals has expressly declared that the primary purpose of the poll tax is to serve as a restriction on voting; and abundant statistics, to reproduce which would be a work of supererogation, prove in fact what everyone knows— that the legal restrictions on the suffrage operate effectively in practice."

That the poll tax is deliberately intended to be a means of disfranchisement rather than a fiscal measure or financial test is conclusively demonstrated by the fact that advance notice of its being due is seldom, if ever, given, either publicly or individually, and once the dead line for payment has passed, the state makes no effort to collect the tax. The constitutions of some of the states, as a matter of fact, expressly provide that "No criminal proceedings shall be allowed to enforce the collection of the poll tax." If the poll tax were a bona fide attempt to raise funds, there is no reason why it should not be collected—as is being done in North Carolina and twenty-three other states—without making denial of suffrage one of the penalties for non-payment.

At no time has the oligarchic function of the poll tax been more clearly revealed than in 1932, when Georgia, whose constitution since 1877 had required the payment of "all taxes" (including a poll tax) as a prerequisite to voting, suddenly amended the provision so as to merely require payment of "all poll taxes." The reason for this alteration is self-evident: the Depression had caused so many propertied persons to become tax-delinquent that the propertyless—who had only to pay the poll tax—were at a comparative advantage when it came to qualifying to vote. This situation being the reverse of that which the poll tax was intended to perpetuate, the propertied groups controlling Georgia politics lost no time in "fixing" the constitution.

With the electorate reduced by the poll tax to a very small percentage of the potential voters, correspondingly small sums are sufficient to corrupt it. Although most poll-tax states have laws against paying another person's poll tax, the penalties are ridiculously small. For example, a Virginian convicted of illegally paying thousands of poll taxes may be fined as little as five dollars. That political machines and corporate interests frequently purchase large blocks of poll-tax receipts for distribution to those who will promise to vote according to instruction is a matter of common knowledge.

A typical situation has been described by George C. Stoney, a Southern member of the "Suffrage in the South" survey conducted by the New School for Social Research. "Consider what happened in one north Alabama county in the winter of 1940," Mr. Stoney wrote. "Over $10,000 of the $25,000 collected for poll taxes was received on the very last day, and the bulk of it was paid not by the individuals whose names were put on the receipts but by lawyers acting as 'agents' for the same. Candidates on both sides had persuaded a good many people to sign up through lawyers actually acting as 'agents' for the candidates.

The money paid, ranging from $1.50 to $36 a person, was, of course, supplied by the candidates."

One of the best summations of the evils inherent in the poll tax has come from Barry Bingham of the Louisville *Courier-Journal*. He wrote: "The real opposition to repeal of the poll tax lies beneath the surface of most printed argument. It is lodged in the conviction of a small group of Southerners on the upper rungs of the economic ladder that they are more entitled to rule than the public at large. These people often have the sayings of Thomas Jefferson and the tenets of democracy hot in their mouths, yet they privately fear the dangerous experiment of a government that is really of, by, and for the people. They mistrust the motives of the man in the street, the man looking for a job, the man working another man's land. They cannot persuade themselves that these men are created equal to themselves. Down in their hearts they treasure a belief in Alexander Hamilton's extraordinary dictum that 'the public is a great beast.'

"The states with poll-tax suffrage have elected precious few men of outstanding ability to public office, and they have placed some of the most extreme demagogues the country has known in the seats of the mighty . . . Some of the cleverest demagogues the South has produced have succeeded in serving as agents of entrenched wealth while posing as the plainest and homeliest men of the people. Among the most useful servants that selfish interests in the South have enjoyed have been the red gallus boys from the poll-tax states. It is easy to understand why the states with poll-tax suffrage have lagged behind all others in social legislation. The people who want laws to protect labor, the tenant farmer, and the bottom income group from exploitation are seldom the people who can pay a poll tax.

"The system of poll-tax suffrage is a direct though unavowed flouting of the democratic process. It is easy for a man who owes his election to only 6 per cent of the people of his state to represent the interests of that 6 per cent to the exclusion of the other 94 per cent. Where the voting class is small it is naturally dominated by vested interests, whose greatest desire is to maintain the status quo and assure financial profits."

Popular opposition to the poll tax finally brought about its repeal in North Carolina in 1920, in Louisiana in 1934, Florida in 1937, and Georgia in 1945. But in the remaining seven poll-tax states the tax can only be repealed by amendment of the state constitutions, which requires a two-thirds (in some states a three-fifths) majority of the legislature and then approval by a majority of voters in the next election. The obstacles which stand in the way of poll-tax repeal by these states are formidable indeed.

In Tennessee the constitution makes the heads of the people "liable to" a poll tax of "not less than fifty cents nor more than one dollar." It remained for the legislature to enact a statute imposing a specific tax. In 1943 the legislature repealed the poll-tax statute, only to have the machine-packed State supreme court, in a three-to-two decision, hold the repealer invalid on the ground that "This constitutional mandate has been so 'welded into intimate and permanent union' with the statute that the two have become indivisible, and the statute may not now be divorced or destroyed."

Chief Justice Green, dissenting, said, "If a constitutional provision requires the support of a statute in order to operate, it cannot function when that support is withdrawn—when the statute is repealed. The legislature has power to repeal any statute unless restrained by some limitation of the constitution." Justice Neil, likewise dissenting, added, "We are here faced with the incongruity, if not absolute absurdity, of being called upon to yield obedience and *compel* obedience to a statute that has been repealed—such a thing is unknown to the history of English and American jurisprudence."

Legal action has been taken to determine whether or not the repealed Tennessee poll-tax statute can be enforced. Also, the state's 1945 legislature passed an amendment abolishing the constitutional reference to a poll tax; but this amendment must wait for approval by the legislature "next to be chosen," and subsequently by popular referendum.

In every case the majority demand for repeal has been bitterly opposed by the plutocracy which owes its position of power to the tax. The Gallup Poll, surveying in 1943, confined its query to "regular voters who have paid their poll taxes," but found that even among this elite group only 53 per cent were in favor of retaining the tax.

When Arkansas voted on the issue in 1938, every newspaper in the state, with one exception, fought against repeal with front-page editorials. Schoolteachers were given to understand that loss of the poll-tax revenue would mean salary cuts for them. The bogey of Negro political domination was inflated to startling proportions. And so the vote was two-to-one in favor of keeping the tax. Of course those who voted for the tax constituted only 4 per cent of Arkansas's population, while the tax kept its opponents away from the polls.

In South Carolina a poll-tax-repeal amendment was passed with only one dissenting vote in the 1945 senate, but was bottled up in the house.

In Alabama the 1945 house voted 70 to 27 against abolishing even the cumulative feature of the poll tax, despite the fact that Governor Nelson Sparks, Senator Lister Hill, Representatives Patrick, Sparkman, and Raines, and other Alabama leaders, favored abolition of the tax. Senator Hill boldly proclaimed that the poll tax in his state was the "most burdensome, restrictive, indefensible, and undemocratic" of them all, and Representative Patrick added that the tax is "perhaps the worst enemy to public schools existing in the South."

The nature of the opposition which brought such crushing defeat to the efforts to persuade Alabama to repeal her poll tax is indicative of what state actionists are up against. Leading the incitement of race prejudice in opposition to poll-tax repeal was *Alabama* magazine, whose largest advertisers include Coca-Cola, Alabama Power Company, DeBardeleben Coke & Coal, Alabama Mills, Monsanto Chemicals, Southern Bell & Telephone, Bama Mills, Birmingham Trust and Savings Company, et al.

Hugh Morrow, one of Birmingham's "Big Mule" industrialists, mistakenly reported to favor poll-tax repeal, replied, "I have never lined up against the white people of the Black Belt . . . I am not now, nor have I ever been, nor can I visualize that I shall in the future ever be, in favor of repeal of the poll tax." Similarly, S. Palmer Gaillard of Mobile declared that the real aim of those favoring poll-tax repeal was "nothing short of complete social equality (on the statute books), abolition of all race segregation, and a strong pressure to bring about interracial marriage."

Some of Alabama's politicos, like their prototypes who originally imposed the poll tax against Populism, brazenly stated that it was aimed at the poor white as well as the Negro. Said Gessner McCorvey, chairman of the Democratic party in Alabama, "A great many of the thriftless, shiftless, worthless type of people, both white and colored, fail to pay their poll tax, and by reason thereof, we have a more intelligent electorate than exists in some states where all kinds of rabble are permitted to vote without question." Horace Wilkinson, stockholder of the Art-Craft Publishers, which prints *Alabama* magazine, informed an Anniston civic club, "The poll tax is the greatest protection we have against irresponsible citizens who have no more business voting than a jackass, be they white or black." Instead of abolishing the poll tax, he advocated increasing it to five dollars.

As for the other poll-tax states, something has been said regarding a willingness on the part of the governors to study the effect of the poll tax, but little more.

Of course the states have a right to abolish the poll tax themselves—and if they can all beat Congress to the gun, so much the better. But to argue that the states alone have the right to repeal the poll tax is all wrong. Such an argument is equivalent to asserting that the Germans should have been allowed to dispose of Nazism in their own way if and when they saw fit. . . . For the poll tax is not only a ball and chain upon the South—it has impeded the progress of the entire nation.

The voting record of virtually all poll-tax congressmen demonstrates their subservience to special interests and failure to represent their constituents. Those who perform to the satisfaction of their sponsors are assured of almost a lifetime in office. In the three elections preceding 1944 the turnover among congressmen from free voting states was 70 per cent greater than among those of the poll-tax states. And in the 1944 election, seventy of Polltaxia's seventy-nine congressmen were re-elected. No less than eighteen gentlemen from Polltaxia have been perpetuated in Congress for more than twenty years. By virtue of their seniority the poll-taxers have garnered about three times their proportionate share of dominant positions on House committees and twice their share on Senate committees. With these strategic positions and their intimate knowledge of parliamentary procedure, these veterans actually control Congress. When Polltaxia is "agin" a bill, the United States is often forced to do without it.

Contrary to popular belief, the right to vote is not considered by American jurisprudence to be an inherent, natural, or inalienable right such as the rights to life, liberty, privacy, conscience, pursuit of happiness, et cetera. Rather, it is regarded as a privilege bestowed upon the individual by democratic forms of government. It is interesting to note, however, that Benjamin Franklin not only regarded the right to vote as being inherent in American citizenship, but also considered it to be one of the natural rights of man. It would certainly seem that if liberty is a natural right, then the right to vote must be also; for without a vote no man can be a free member of society.

And yet the Constitution does not grant the right to vote to all American citizens. Except for the Fifteenth and Nineteenth Amendments prohibiting any state from denying anyone the vote because of race or sex, the Constitution leaves the states with complete authority to determine who shall vote in *state* elections, provided they maintain a republican form of government.

With regard to who shall vote for *federal* officials, however, the Constitution does have something to say. Section 2 of Article I provides that "The House of Representatives shall be composed of members chosen every second year by the people of the several states, and the electors in such states shall have the qualifications requisite for electors of the most numerous branch of the state legislature."

The intent of the framers of the Constitution in adopting this provision was expressed in unmistakable terms by Alexander Hamilton: "It will not be alleged that an election law could have been framed and inserted in the Constitution which would have been always applicable to every probable change in the situation of the country; and it will, therefore, not be denied that a discretionary power over election ought to exist somewhere.

It will, I presume, be as readily conceded that there are only three ways in which this power could have been reasonably modified and disposed: that it must either have been lodged wholly in the national legislature, or wholly in the state legislatures, or primarily in the latter and ultimately in the former.

"The last mode has, with reason, been preferred by the Convention. They have permitted the regulation of elections for the Federal Government, in the first instance, to the local administration, which in ordinary cases, and when no improper views prevail, may be both more convenient and more satisfactory; and they have reserved to the national authority a right to interpose, whenever extraordinary circumstances might render that interposition necessary . . . Nothing can be more evident than that exclusive power of regulating elections for the National Government, in the hands of the state legislatures, would leave the existence of the Union entirely at their mercy."

Substantiating Hamilton's statement were the arguments pro and con the provision. The plutocratic opposition was represented by John Dickinson, who warned against "the dangerous influence of those multitudes without property and without principle with which our country, like all others, will in time abound." In like vein, Gouverneur Morris declared, "The time is not distant when this country will abound with mechanics and manufacturers [by which he meant industrial workers] . . . Will such men be the secure and faithful guardians of liberty?" Morris thought not, just as the poll-taxers of today think not; for it is precisely the industrial and agricultural workers whom the poll tax disfranchises.

Fortunately for Americans, the views of Dickinson, Morris, and others of the same sort did not prevail upon the Constitutional Convention. "Who are to be the electors of the Federal representatives?" asked Madison in *The Federalist*. "Not the rich, more than the poor; not the learned, more than the ignorant; not the haughty heirs of distinguished names, more than the humble sons of obscurity and unpropitious fortune. The electors are to be the great body of the people of the United States." Again, with reference to Franklin's views, Madison wrote, "He did not think that the elected had any right, in any case, to narrow the privileges of the electors."

The self-evident fact that the right to vote for federal officials stems from the Constitution, and is therefore subject to congressional control, has been repeatedly pointed out by the Supreme Court: "The right to vote for Members of Congress is not derived from the constitution and laws of the state in which they are chosen, but has its foundation in the Federal Constitution" (*Minor* v. *Happersett*) "and was not intended to be left within the exclusive control of the states" (*Yarbrough*), and "Congress, by appropriate action, may protect such right" (*United States* v. *Moseley*).

Considerable misapprehension was created, however, when in 1937 the Court decided the *Breedlove case*. In this case a citizen of Georgia had been denied the opportunity to vote for both state and federal officials, because he had not paid his poll tax; and the Court upheld the right of the Georgia officials to deny the vote to anyone wishing to participate in a state election without having met all the state's requirements. Poll-taxers—and even some opponents of the tax—generally misinterpreted this decision as giving the states full authority to prescribe qualifications for voters in both state and federal elections.

The Supreme Court itself hastened to correct this misapprehension. Upon deciding the *Classic case* in 1941, the Court said with reference to the Breedlove decision: "When we spoke about the states having power to prescribe qualifications, we meant to the degree that they did it without encroaching upon the Federal prerogative, or to the degree that the Federal Government allowed them to exercise that power."

In addition, the Court proceeded to explicitly enumerate the respective rights of the states and federal government: "While in a loose sense, the right to vote for Representatives in Congress is sometimes spoken of as a right derived from the states, this statement is true only in the sense that the states are authorized by the Constitution to legislate on the subject as provided by Section 2 of Article I, to the extent that Congress has not restricted state action by the exercise of its powers to regulate elections under

Section 4 and its more general power under Section 8 'to make
all laws which shall be necessary and proper for carrying into
execution the foregoing powers.' "

The Section 4 referred to provides that "The times, places, and
manner of holding elections for Senators and Representatives shall
be prescribed in each state by the legislature thereof; but the
Congress may at any time by law make or alter such regulations
. . ." And as was said in *United States* v. *Munford,* "If Congress
can provide for the manner of elections, it can certainly provide
that it shall be an honest manner; that there shall be no repression
of voters and an honest count of the ballot."

Irving Brant, author of *Storm Over the Constitution,* has correctly pointed out, "If the Constitution did not contain a single
word on the subject of Congressional elections, Congress would
have plenary power to regulate them as a part of the implied
power of a supreme government to maintain its supremacy, of
an independent government to maintain its independence, of a
republican government to maintain its republicanism."

The Constitution specifically provides (Section 3, Article IV)
that "The United States shall guarantee to every state in the
Union a republican form of government." Madison very properly
cautioned against calling everything a republic which was not a
monarchy or pure democracy. "We may define a republic to be,
or at least may bestow that name on, a government which derives
all its powers directly or indirectly from the great body of the people, and is administered by persons holding offices during their
pleasure, for a limited period, or during good behavior. It is essential to such a government that it be derived from the great
body of the society, not from an inconsiderable proportion or a
favored class of it."

By that definition—stated more concisely by Lincoln as "government of the people, by the people, and for the people"—republican government has not existed in the Southern poll-tax
states for the past half century. Republican government means
majority rule; poll-tax government means minority rule; therefore
the two are incompatible.

The Fourteenth Amendment provides that when the suffrage
is in any way abridged in a state, that state's congressional repre-

sentation shall be reduced accordingly. But Congress, in reapportioning representation on the basis of the 1940 Census, chose to ignore its duty to carry out this constitutional mandate. Had it done its duty, it would have reduced the congressional representation of the poll-tax states from 79 to 26 (taking the 82 per cent of the potential voters who voted in the non-poll-tax states as a yardstick for measuring disfranchisement in the poll-tax states, where only 22 per cent voted in 1940). There is also a federal statute which provides that when the number of congressional districts in a state exceeds the number of representatives to which that state is entitled, then its representatives must be elected at large rather than by districts. But in the 1944 election this provision was also ignored by Congress as regards disfranchisement in the poll-tax states.

In an effort to bring about adherence to the Constitution and federal law in this matter, the Southern Electoral Reform League in 1944 filed suit in a United States district court in Virginia, claiming $20,000 damages for the state's refusal to admit a candidate named Saunders to the ballot for congressman-at-large, as provided by the afore-mentioned law. In addition, the league instituted proceedings to unseat poll-tax congressmen on the ground that they were not elected in the manner prescribed by the Constitution. As this was written in 1946, neither of these actions had been culminated.

In 1941 the Southern Conference for Human Welfare took the lead in urging that Congress exercise its constitutional power to abolish the poll tax as a prerequisite to voting for federal officials. Eventually this campaign was co-ordinated under a National Committee to Abolish the Poll Tax, which is officially supported by the CIO, AFL, Railroad Brotherhoods, YWCA, National Lawyers Guild, National Farmers Union, National Women's Trade Union League, Townsend Plan, Church League for Industrial Democracy, National Conference on Social Work, National Federation for Constitutional Liberties, the seven leading Negro organizations, and a score of others.

In 1942, when Congress voted to extend voting facilities to servicemen overseas, Florida's liberal Senator Claude Pepper proposed an amendment to free servicemen from poll-tax states of having to pay the tax. This promptly soured poll-taxers on the entire bill. Senator George of Georgia arose to say, "Now the poll-tax question has been raised, and I am going to ask a very pertinent question, one I believe we will have to answer before the war shall be won, whether or not we are more interested in social and political reforms of certain stripe and character and kind than in unity, in the desire and willingness of our people to fight this war. I am going to let that statement stand. It is going to stand right here in the *Record*. The motivating thought behind too many things has been a desire for social and political reform . . ."

It was in 1941 that Senator Pepper introduced his bill to abolish the poll tax, but it was tied up in committee until the following year. Protracted hearings were conducted on the bill, at which the fundamental issue at stake—democracy versus plutocracy—was brought out in sharp relief. Representatives of the various democratic organizations supporting the bills were heard, and then the governors and attorneys general of the poll-tax states were invited to express their views. This they did in classic Defender-of-the-South style. The statement made by Governor R. M. Jefferies of South Carolina was typical. He said, "Bills like that which we are here to discuss today would lead us to believe that a beneficent—and I put a question mark after that—federal government, grown far stronger than the Founding Fathers ever intended, is again trying to reconstruct South Carolina by amending its state constitution on a matter of internal interest only.

"Proof of payment of taxes thirty days before an election is an additional method of collecting the poll tax, which is an integral part of the revenue of South Carolina and is used entirely for school purposes. This poll tax does not keep anybody from voting; that is one thing certain. The criminal statute dealing with nonpayment of the poll tax is enforced against all people and all races fairly and uniformly. It would be ridiculous for anyone to say that the poll-tax requirement in South Carolina prevents people from voting when all who are liable for its payment must pay it or go to jail."

"Do you know of any person now confined in any jail in South

Carolina because of not having paid the poll tax?" inquired Senator Abe Murdock.

"They usually pay it, Senator, without having to go to jail," replied the governor.

After some further remarks by Governor Jefferies, Senator Murdock asked again, "I have inferred from what you stated that the payment of poll taxes in South Carolina is practically unanimous. Everybody pays it; is that right?"

"We do not have much trouble with it," parried the governor. "I will say this: sometimes there is laxity in enforcing it. Senator, I will be absolutely fair. Some counties do not bother with it much. We have tried to collect it, but, like any other law, sometimes enforcement is lax."

In winding up his disquisition the governor reverted to his original contention. "In conclusion," he said, "I respectfully submit that the Congress of the United States has no right to amend the constitution of South Carolina."

The governor was mistaken. The power of Congress to legislate upon matters within the scope of its authority is plenary, as provided by the Constitution itself: "This Constitution, and the Laws of the United States which shall be made in Pursuance thereof . . . shall be the supreme Law of the Land; and the Judges in every State shall be bound thereby, any Thing in the Constitution or Laws of any State to the Contrary notwithstanding."

Next to take the stand was Governor Frank Dixon of Alabama. His impassioned plea for "states' rights" is a classic, though it may not have originated with him. "Once upon a time there was in our land an omnipotent queen—the states," he orated. "The whole empire of sovereignty was hers. But in her wisdom she felt the need of a prince consort who could fight her battles, protect, defend, and guard her from foreign foes, and serve her constituents in those manly ways ill-befitting a queen. So she created such a prince, joined him to herself by sacred vows in holy wedlock, made him king in the sphere she had allotted him, and with him shared her throne. By their vows he was to be supreme in the field of power she delegated him, she in all else. It was to be a perfect partnership.

"He had his scepter—the army and navy. She had hers—the

army of intelligent, virtuous voters selected by her. From time to time, as desirability became apparent, she gave him more and more of her power. He kept all of his and ever exercised more. In spite of the beneficence of his queen, he became jealous of her scepter . . . His yearning grew out of the knowledge that without her scepter she would be but his chattel. But he never once proposed, in the agreed way, that she give it to him. Now, however, this king of her creation, this beneficiary of her generosity, is trying to take her scepter by force . . .

"Throughout the years—I can go back, but it is ancient history —we have been reformed for our own good. Now, nobody has ever helped us in any way where we needed any help. Nobody has ever helped us to overcome the low per capita wealth of our people. Every economic disadvantage has been saddled upon us. It is saddled on us by legislation throughout the years, and then as they bled us white they reformed us. I can tell you how to solve nearly all the problems of the South, but I am not advocating it before the committee here."

"Could you tell us how to solve the problems of New York?" asked Senator Joseph O'Mahoney.

"Well, they say there is a shortage of manpower, but I notice there is a lot of unemployment in New York. I do not understand it. I would hate to have to go up there and reform New York, but I do not want New York to come down and reform me any more."

At this point Senator Pepper arrived at the hearing. "Mr. Chairman," he said, "I understand that Governor Dixon made a very eloquent argument the implication of which was, or part of it was, that this bill was influenced by pressure-group agitation and it was making a false claim to patriotism; it was going to provoke disunity, and all that sort of thing. As the author of the bill I think I am at least entitled to have the record show that I controvert, as strongly as language can, both that statement and its implication.

"My people have been Southerners as long as Governor Dixon's, and since 1600 I have not had a direct ancestor of my people who did not fight for and did not die for the South. So I am sure no one would wish to charge that in the introduction of this bill there has been any scheming or designing by any groups that were trying to provoke disunity in this country. On the contrary, I have offered it as a sincere expression of the belief that if we are going to preach and fight for democracy in the world, the best thing for us to do is to show a good example of it here at home."

From which it may be seen that the South is still capable of producing statesmen as well as demagogues.

Pepper's championship of a tax-free federal ballot was, of course, bitterly attacked by the Southern plutocracy. For instance, the Fort Lauderdale (Fla.) *Daily News* declared:

> This was introduced for the purpose of permitting every irresponsible resident of the South to vote without any qualifications or any definite purposes or interests. The idiots in the insane asylum would be the equal of any thoughtful person on election day. It was designed by the Roosevelt crowd of which Pepper is a leader to break up the Democratic party in the South. . . .

The arguments advanced by the poll-taxers in the House and Senate have been of this same base sort. Representative Sam Hobbs of Alabama, for example, said that every citizen should have "the right to be justly governed, but not the privilege of being one of the governors." However, Pepper's anti-poll-tax bill passed the House in 1942 by a vote of 252 to 84. It was also assured of a substantial majority in the Senate, but a filibuster led by Senator Bilbo of Mississippi and Senator Connally of Texas, lasting nine urgent war days, prevented the bill from coming to a vote. A vote was taken on cloture (debate limitation), but the required two-thirds majority was not forthcoming. And so, by "gentlemen's agreement," the anti-poll-tax bill was shelved.

When correspondents sought to cable the story of the filibuster to British newspapers, U. S. Navy censors refused to let it be sent. But as the New York *Times* rightly observed, "Word will go out —and no censorship can keep it from going out—that this truly democratic country, standing in this war for the right of all peoples to be ruled by governments of their own choosing, permits that right to be denied to a substantial number of its citizens."

There were even some members of the Southern press, in the non-poll-tax states, which spoke out against the filibuster. "Some kind of inter-party chicanery, deeper than anything yet revealed, must have underlain that deal," observed the Asheville (N.C.) *Citizen-Times*. And the St. Louis *Post-Dispatch* declared: "The anti-poll-tax bill died in the last Congress, but the necessity for removing this negation of democracy will not die. Do the obstructionists who stand in the way of this measure not realize how they mock our war aims?"

The anti-poll-tax bill was again brought before the House in 1943 and was passed by a vote of 265 to 110. When in 1944 Vice-President Henry Wallace motioned that the Senate take up the measure, the poll-taxers shouted "no" so loudly they almost drowned out the chorus of "yeas." But, as Wallace said, "the vociferousness of the minority did not overcome its lack of numbers," and so the debate was on. Senator Connally keynoted the proceedings with the stale charge that "pressure groups" were trying to "improve, liberalize, readjust, modernize, and intelligentsia-ize" the South. The vociferousness of the minority found continued expression in a week of filibustering, and when a vote on cloture was finally taken and lost, the bill was shelved by "tacit understanding" (by way of variation from the previous "gentlemen's agreement").

As this was written in 1946, the House had again passed the anti-poll-tax bill by the usual large majority, only to have it again defeated by a minority of Senators who refused to vote for cloture on the hypocritical ground that it would limit "freedom of speech."

But whether Congress frees the federal ballot soon or late, democracy will not be able to come completely into its own in the South until state action has also removed the price tag from the state ballot.

"Votin' Is White Folk's Business"

In addition to the manifold methods by which Negroes are disfranchised under cover of law, there is from time to time a resort to violence as the ultimate form of dissuasion. Generally such action affects only one individual, who serves as an example until such time as the white supremacists deem another example necessary. But at times violent disfranchisement assumes the mass proportions common to the post-Reconstruction period.

For instance, there are the events which transpired in Ocoee, Florida, in the federal election of 1920. As there was considerable fear on the part of the Democratic whites that the Republican candidate would be elected, feeling against Negro voting ran high. When several Negroes objected to being turned away from the polls, a mob of drunken whites, Klan led, set fire to the Negro district and with gunfire drove many Negroes—including children and pregnant women—back into the flames. Approximately thirty-five Negroes were slain, and no Negroes have been permitted to live in Ocoee since.

While there have been no such comparable violent attempts to disfranchise Negroes in recent years, there is as yet nothing to prevent a recurrence of massacre such as took place in Ocoee in 1920.

One indication of this cropped up in 1939. Miami's charter restriction against Negro participation in municipal elections had recently been repealed, and a Citizens' Service League, led by Negro ministers, was urging Negroes to vote, and asked for police protection. One candidate for city commission requested that any Negro votes cast for him be thrown out.

The night before the election, fifty autoloads of hooded Klansmen drove through the Negro section with license plates illegally covered, displayed a hangman's noose, hanged black dummies at the polling places (bearing placards reading *This Nigger Voted*) burned twenty-five fiery crosses at street intersections, and distributed cards reading: *Respectable Negro citizens not voting tomorrow. Niggers stay away from the polls!*

Despite all this, 1,000 Negro votes were cast (in Jim Crow booths); the previous record vote by Negroes had been 150. Negro voters made the same selections as whites, except in the case of this candidate, who was badly defeated.

Of course the main political support of the institution of white supremacy for half a century has been the lily-white Democratic primary. As the 1944 presidential election year approached, the white primary remained inviolate in the eight Deep Southern states already mentioned. And yet in North Carolina, Virginia, Kentucky, West Virginia, Missouri, and parts of Tennessee the bars had been lowered and Negroes were free to vote in the Democratic primary if they would.

Throughout the intervening years a few heroic Negroes had dared to challenge the constitutionality of the white primary. And though the long road to justice has often seemed hopelessly blocked, the end is at last in sight. It began to unwind in 1927, when the U. S. Supreme Court, in *Nixon* v. *Herndon,* declared unconstitutional a Texas statute limiting the Democratic primary to whites. Thereupon the Texas legislature proceeded to delegate the discriminatory power to the executive committee of the state Democratic party; but in 1932 this arrangement was likewise declared unconstitutional in *Nixon* v. *Condon.*

Not to be outdone, the Democratic party of Texas next exercised its racial discrimination by means of a resolution passed at its state convention, rather than by its executive committee. And this time the Supreme Court, in *Grovey* v. *Townsend* in 1935, held that the Democratic convention in Texas had not acted as an organ of the state, and that its denial of a vote in its primary was a mere refusal of party membership with which "the state need have no concern."

Thus the subterfuge of the white primary was given an air of legality it had not enjoyed before, and white supremacists sighed with relief. Their relief was short-lived, however, for in 1941 the revitalized Supreme Court, exercising its established power to re-examine constitutional questions, handed down a decision which caused Justice Reed to declare, *"Grovey* v. *Townsend* is overruled."

This was the historic *Classic case,* which came up from Louisiana and involved the applicability of constitutional guarantees to primaries. The Court ruled that ". . . a primary election which involves a necessary step in the choice of candidates for election as Representatives in Congress, which in the circumstances of this case controls that choice, is subject to congressional regulation as to the manner of holding it . . . the right to participate

through the primary in the choice of Representatives in Congress
. . . is the same . . . as the right to vote at the general election."

The Classic decision was a long step toward democracy, but
it remained for the epochal "Texas case," *Smith* v. *Allwright,* to
sound the death knell of the white primary on April 3, 1944. In
this case a Texas Negro dentist, Dr. Lonnie E. Smith, had sued
an election official who had refused to let him vote in the Democratic primary in 1940. The Court's 8-1 decision, written by Justice Stanley Reed of Kentucky, took cognizance of the fact that
Texas primaries were conducted "under statutory authority" and
that this makes the party "an agency of the state insofar as it de-
termines the participants in a primary election." Said the Court:

> It may now be taken as a postulate that the right to vote in
> such a primary for the nomination of candidates without dis-
> crimination by the state, like the right to vote in a general
> election, is a right secured by the Constitution. By the terms of
> the 15th Amendment that right may not be abridged by the
> state on account of race. Under our Constitution the great
> privilege of the ballot may not be denied a man by the state
> because of his color. The United States is a constitutional de-
> mocracy. Its organic law grants to all citizens a right to partici-
> pate in the choice of elected officials without restriction by any
> state because of race.
>
> This grant to the people of opportunity for choice is not to
> be nullified by a state through casting its electoral process in a
> form which permits a private organization to practice racial
> discrimination in the election. Constitutional rights would be of
> little value if they could thus be indirectly denied.

The reaction of political spokesmen for the white primary
states was only to be expected.

"One of my greatest fears has been realized," confessed Representative John E. Rankin of Mississippi.

"This decision was a shock to me," said Senator Burnet R.
Maybank of South Carolina. "Regardless of the Supreme Court
decision and any laws that may be passed by Congress, we in
South Carolina are going to do whatever we can to protect our
white primaries."

"We've always handled that question . . . and always will,"
declared Governor Sam Jones of Louisiana.

"We'll certainly resist if possible any attempt to have Negroes vote in our primaries," said Tom Conely, chairman of the Florida Democratic Committee.

"We'll find a way out of this," said George A. Butler, Texas state Democratic chairman.

"The Supreme Court nor no one else can control a Democratic primary in Mississippi," said Herbert Holmes, chairman of that state's Democratic committee.

"As for the Negro voting in my primary," said State Representative John D. Long of South Carolina, "we'll fight him at the precinct meeting, we'll fight him at the county convention, we'll fight him at the enrollment books, and, by God, we'll fight him at the polls if I have to bite the dust as did my ancestors!"

In contrast to such verbal fireworks from the politicos (who more or less owe their positions to restricted suffrage) were the editorial comments from Southern states where the white primary no longer obtains.

"Negroes have been participating in Democratic primaries in this state right along," said the Greensboro (N.C.) *News,* "and nothing has occurred, despite this free voting, to upset either the racial or the political applecart hereabouts. Rather we believe that Tarheelia can boast of infinitely better race relations and a much higher quality of placeholders, on the average, than can its discriminating neighbors to the South. Fairness has a way of paying handsome dividends wherever it obtains."

"By a momentous decision upon the suffrage the Supreme Court has cut through various monumental pretenses—including its own—to establish more firmly the American republic," declared the Nashville *Tennessean.*

"Whether held at party or public expense, primaries are an essential part of the machinery for choosing public officials and they should be open to all eligible voters who care to enter," said the Staunton (Va.) *News-Leader.*

"That decision is one more milestone on the way to fairness and justice for the Negro," observed the Richmond *Times-Dispatch.* "If millions of citizens are to be deprived of any voice in choosing their own public officials then we may well ask ourselves

just what the Four Freedoms for which we are fighting amount
to."

For the most part, Deep Southern editorial comment coincided
with that of the politicos. "Political equality is . . . a question it
were well for the Negro race to forget in the South," asserted the
Waterboro (S.C.) *Press and Standard*. ". . . Our Southern duty
is to get around the decision in more ways than one," averred
columnist John Temple Graves.

There were not many editors in the Deep South who dared
oppose the officialdom of white supremacy by endorsing the
court's decision. However, Judge Harry S. Strozier of the Macon
(Ga.) *News* was a notable exception. In a fearless editorial he
declared:

> We cannot honestly fight a war for justice and freedom
> while, on account alone of racial prejudice, we are denying the
> lawful right of citizenship to a large element of our own popu-
> lation. The Supreme Court is right. And we shall be grievously
> wrong if we follow the excited rantings of our politicians and
> disregard or attempt to nullify its decision.

Another effective appeal for a truly democratic primary was
made by Mrs. Glenn W. Rainey, a member of the Georgia Democratic executive committee, who in an open letter to the committee urged that it "take action that will make allies and not
enemies of the responsible people of both races in the South."

Only South Carolina was so rash as to make an official effort
to circumvent the Supreme Court before the 1944 election. Ten
days after the Texas case was decided, Governor Johnston called
a special session of the legislature "to maintain white supremacy in
South Carolina." In a hectic six-day session that body proceeded
to pass 147 bills eliminating from the statute books every discern-
ible reference to primaries. Some legislators gulped when they
realized this involved wiping out even the laws against fraud in
primaries. They also had to abolish their new law requiring the
secretary of state to provide primary ballots for servicemen—thus
making it necessary for servicemen to apply to the secretary of the
party club to which they belonged.

South Carolinians also learned to their regret that a return to
unregulated primaries involves the necessity for *dual registration*

—once for the primary and again for the general election. The parties, moreover, must be left free to set up whatever restrictions they wish as to who may participate in their primaries—and this might easily deprive many whites as well as Negroes of a vote. The poll-tax states, ironically, would also have to cancel their requirement for a poll tax for primary voting should they elect to follow in South Carolina's footsteps.

Furthermore, South Carolina's action left the Negroes of the state with no alternative but to form a party predominantly their own, the Progressive Democrats.

The effect of the Supreme Court decision on the 1944 primaries varied in the several states. In Texas, where there could be no question as to the decision's applicability, Negroes voted in considerable numbers for the first time since Reconstruction. In Arkansas the party chairman saw fit to announce that "Election judges should allow Negroes to vote in the Democratic primary elections this summer, provided they possess a poll-tax receipt and otherwise appear qualified."

Quite a number of Negroes were permitted to vote in Birmingham and Montgomery, and eight Negroes voted in Florida. In Mississippi the secretary of state announced on the eve of the primary that he expected a light vote, with no Negro votes; his expectations were realized. In Georgia an organized effort to get out a large Negro vote led to threats of violence by whites; the Negroes finally agreed to send only a few selected Negroes to the polls for a "token vote," but even these were turned away. There were no reports of Negroes voting in Louisiana, and of course none in South Carolina.

Once the South Carolina primary was over, the Democratic party there set out to impress Negroes with the fact that they were perfectly free to vote for Democratic nominees in the general election. To this proffering of leftovers the Negro *Lighthouse and Informer* declared, "The flatfooted stand must be: all or none." And John H. McCray, chairman of the Progressive Democrats, added, "Where Negroes want to vote is where and when the ticket is being drawn. We don't want to be confined to the amen corner, and prevented by prejudice, schemes, and devices from helping shape the party ticket."

Out of the 1944 primaries the U. S. Department of Justice received only thirteen formal complaints asking for criminal prosecution of election officials who denied Negroes a vote, and five of these were untenable because the complainants were not duly qualified to vote.

Unfortunately there are some indications that something more than prosecution may be needed to render all Democratic primaries democratic. Arkansas provides a case in point. Shortly after the 1944 primary the Arkansas Democratic Convention came forth with an ingenious scheme. First, it recommended that the legislature amend the state's primary law to read as follows:

> Every organized political party shall have the right to prescribe the qualifications for its own membership and shall also have the right to prescribe qualifications for voting in its primaries, provided that no political party shall by rule or otherwise deny to any citizen the right to vote on grounds prohibited by the Fifteenth Amendment to the Federal Constitution.

Then the Arkansas convention proceeded to adopt rules limiting membership in the Democratic party to:

> . . . white electors who have openly declared their allegiance to, and are in good faith in sympathy with, the fundamental principles, purposes, objectives, and practices of the party . . . but party membership shall not be a test for voting in Democratic primary elections.

Next, the party's principles were reformulated to include: preservation of the poll tax, preservation of all existing Jim Crow segregation laws, and preservation of the law prohibiting interracial intermarriage. Applicants for a Democratic primary vote may be required to furnish an affidavit showing that they meet these requirements, and they may be challenged by any election judge, candidate, or candidate's agent.

In other words, while Negroes would not be permitted to join the Democratic party of Arkansas or run for public office on its ticket, they would be enabled by this scheme to vote in the Democratic primary, provided they were willing to swear allegiance to the party's principles, afore-mentioned, and were *otherwise acceptable to party officials.*

What this Arkansas scheme seeks to do is return to the Reconstruction compromise of permitting Negroes to be "just voters," but to deny them an opportunity to become officeholders. The party and its candidates would be kept lily-white, a token primary vote of approved Negroes would be permitted—and white supremacy would still reign. The party evidently feels safe in doing this because it is relying upon the reluctance of many Negroes to endorse Jim Crow, the poll tax, and a party that denies them membership and candidacy; moreover, the party reserves the power to adopt still other principles intolerable to Negroes; and finally, *it* has the discretionary power to decide which Negroes—and thus *how many of them*—meet its voting requirements.

Apart from what the Supreme Court may have to say about this scheme of Arkansas's, there is much that Negroes themselves might do. If they could succeed in voting in the primary in sufficient numbers, it is likely that the competing candidates would soon be bidding for their support by promising to rectify the party's discriminatory practices. Should the Negroes be kept from voting in numbers enough to bring about such changes, they will have no alternative but to go into politics on their own, as they have in South Carolina.

This would shift much of the conflict from the primary to the general election, where Negro voters have the undeniable protection of the federal government. The aim of such a maneuver, however, should not be a permanent political party based on race, but merely to demonstrate to white Southerners that Negro Southerners are determined to shoulder their proportionate share of responsibility in the region's public affairs. By nominating their own candidates and getting out the Negro vote in sufficient strength to pose a threat to a white majority, the Negroes could confidently expect the Democratic party to invite them into the fold. For the sake of an opportunity to demonstrate their solidarity with the rank-and-file white Democrats, Negroes might want to forego for the time being the nomination of Negroes. But that temporary concession should not be made for anything less than equal access, in practice, to the Democratic primary.

One of the white supremacists' whitest hopes is cloaked in their tongue-in-cheek phrases about granting the vote to "qualified Negroes of good character and intelligence." By such widely publicized announcements they hope to lull Negroes into a false sense of certainty that the road to democracy is clear—when all the time what they have in mind are variations of the theme sounded by one Georgia official: "Negroes can still be required to write the Constitution and then be disqualified if they leave out any commas."

A number of the white primary states require the ability to read or write "any" section of the Constitution. In practice, the registrars apply this test almost exclusively to Negroes, although it is increasingly being directed against white union members.

In 1945 the legislatures of Florida, Texas, and Georgia refused to follow South Carolina's lead in abolishing all primary laws. Knowing how strong the opposition would be to that, the white supremacy politicos have hit upon the alternative of going through the motion of "admitting Negroes to the Democratic primary," while tightening their control over registration machinery so that discrimination can be applied there, rather than at the primary. The idea is to keep the Democratic primary dominantly white instead of lily-white, and to do it through discriminatory registrars rather than discriminatory state statutes or party rules.

The most conspicious example of this is taking place in Alabama. A "special" news story apparently released by the state Democratic executive committee has averred that "There is no disposition on the part of Democratic leaders to evade or by-pass the Supreme Court decision. From Chairman Gessner McCorvey of the committee on down, the membership insists that due processes of law must prevail and that the court's decision must be obeyed."

The story went on to say that, "Alabama Democrats have met the Supreme Court's decision in the Texas case by the submission of a constitutional amendment that will, if adopted by the voters in the general election next November, tighten the registration laws and enable registrars to question prospective applicants more closely than in the past. They hope in that way to keep illiterate Negroes out of the election as well as illiterate whites. Many

counties in Alabama have far more Negroes than whites, and if
Negroes vote generally, these counties would be returned to Negro
rule as they had during the Reconstruction era." The story also
carried the reminder, "Every Negro who votes in the primary in
May will have to cast his ballot under an emblem of a crowing
rooster with the words 'White Supremacy' in large letters."

But 'Bama's white supremacists have not always been so subtle.
Chairman McCorvey, in an AP dispatch, has been quoted as follows: "McCorvey said his idea of the way to handle the Negro
voting problem is to see that 'only properly qualified persons are
permitted to register.' This, he added, could be accomplished
through adoption of a constitutional amendment changing registration requirements."

The amendment referred to is the Boswell amendment—named
after its malefactor—which was passed by the 1945 legislature
and is subject to referendum in November of 1946. The Alabama
constitution now requires that, in order to register, a person must
be able to "read or write" any section of the United States Constitution. The amendment would change this to require ability to
"read *and* write, understand and explain" the Constitution. It
would also add the requirement that "no persons shall be entitled
to register as electors except those who are of good character and
who understand the duties and obligations of good citizenship
under a republican form of government." In addition, the amendment would wipe out the present exemption from such literacy
requirements of persons who: own 40 acres of land or $300 worth
of real estate or personal property (taxes must have been paid on
such property for the year preceding the year in which registration is sought).

If the Boswell amendment is passed, the machine-appointed
registrars might conceivably go so far as to deny registration to
Alabama's Supreme Court Justice Hugo Black on the ground
that he did not "understand and explain" the Constitution to
their satisfaction, or was not of "good character," or did not "understand the duties and obligations of good citizenship under a
republican form of government."

In short, under the Boswell amendment the political machine
could not only maintain white supremacy; it could further reduce

Alabama's 14-per-cent democracy by denying the vote to whole masses of whites simply because they belonged to a labor union or would not support the machine candidates.

Still another scheme—which the Southern Conference for Human Welfare says "makes Machiavelli look like a piker"—is that of Roy Harris, Talmadge's political mentor. "If our system is held nonconstitutional," he proposes, "we will change the law at the next session of the legislature—but only by a period or comma. We will hold our primary just as white as a clean sheet. If the Supreme Court invalidates that law too, then we will rewrite it again for the next primary. That will go on ad infinitum!"

That sort of thing borders very closely on the lunatic fringe of Klux-minded folk who would resort to violence in defense of white supremacy. Before open violence became the order of the day, however, economic pressure would be applied to the utmost. Some white overlords would impose sanctions, so to speak, against Negroes with notions of voting. This threat has been operative ever since the Reconstruction Klan drove Negroes from the polls, and is now being intensified.

"The very hands that have given the negro so much are in danger of taking it away," columnist John Temple Graves gravely warns. "The black man in the South must get on with the white man in the South, no matter what Washington orders or New York demands."

This is readily recognizable as a revival of the Reconstruction threat to starve Negroes unless they refrained from voting. Negro tenant farmers and sharecroppers would be denied land, shacks, and rations, and wageworkers would be denied jobs. But just as a continuation of the Freedmen's Bureau and military occupation might have rendered this threat ineffectual during Reconstruction, a combination of such federal agencies as the Department of Justice, Full Employment Commission, Fair Employment Practice Commission, Surplus Commodity Corporation, Farm Security Administration, and Social Security are capable of doing the same today.

As for the more direct forms of violence, their control and punishment are the responsibility of the U. S. Department of

Justice. A few cases of firm enforcement are all that is necessary to banish this method of disfranchisement forever.

One thing which stands in the way of Negro participation in the Democracy of the South is demagogic propaganda to the effect that political rights for Negroes would mean political domination by Negroes throughout the Black Belt. In 1944, when Ralph McGill of the Atlanta *Constitution* reported that a New York Negro congressman-elect had threatened, if the poll tax were ever abolished, to move to Mississippi and run for governor, a white Mississippian assured me, "No need to worry about that, because we'd kill off a certain percentage of the niggers right quick!"

Due to wartime migrations there are no longer any states where Negroes are in the majority, and the number of counties in which they still predominate is steadily decreasing. Mississippi was the last state to acquire a white majority, the 1940 Census giving it a proportion of 50.4 per cent white. The number of Southern counties having Negro majorities has decreased as follows:

$$
\begin{array}{rl}
1900 & \ldots \ldots \ 286 \\
1910 & \ldots \ldots \ 264 \\
1920 & \ldots \ldots \ 221 \\
1930 & \ldots \ldots \ 191 \\
1940 & \ldots \ldots \ 180
\end{array}
$$

The bogey of Black Rule is most horrendous in local circles. The traditional method of dealing with this "problem" has been the system of gerrymandering, whereby political subdivisions are deliberately delineated so as to assure white majorities in each. In other words, Negro districts are never able to elect Negro representatives because their districts comprise the center of pies in which the largest portions of each ward slice are white.

Wherever there are Negro majorities and gerrymandering has not already been practiced, there is a current drive for rezoning, consolidation, et cetera. And whereas such matters are entirely in the hands of the whites, it is difficult to see what Negroes can do about it—until they have organized sufficient political strength to command consideration.

No one should realize better than Southern whites that the

Negro people have no desire to turn the tables and supplant white supremacy with black supremacy. This was conclusively proven during Reconstruction, when a revengeful attitude would have been most understandable and when it had every opportunity to express itself. All the Southern Negro asks is a proportionate opportunity to share the responsibilities and benefits of a working democracy in the South.

The emancipation of Negroes from second-class citizenship is not one of those things which can be postponed any longer. The Deep South is confronted with the absolute necessity of undergoing this democratic revolution now. Somehow violence was avoided in 1944. But in the year 1948 there may be a violent collision at the polls if demagoguery is not sidetracked.

In a real sense the race is between the die-hard white supremacists and the rising demand for democracy. On one hand, for example, columnist Graves declares that "the Southern Negro is not going to be granted the vote now" and that "in part it is the Southern white man's fault that the Southern Negro is less qualified than he might be and should be for the full participation now being demanded." After four centuries of American slavery and four fifths of a century of apprentice citizenship, such accusations of unfitness must seem quite putrid to the Negro. Judged by the standards applied to all other Americans, the Negro is as fully qualified to vote and hold office as anyone else.

Speaking for the new enlightenment (in contrast to Graves), we find Attorney Edward Pritchard telling Charleston Kiwanians: "One thing the South and South Carolina fail to realize is that the day of white elections is gone, never to be revived again . . . As long as we stick to white elections the nation does not want any of our leaders as national leaders . . . There are two courses from which the South must choose: We can adopt a policy of isolationism and buck the Supreme Court and everything else, or we can string along with the Democratic party and stand for something . . . The Negroes can vote and they're going to vote, and there's nothing we can do about it."

There are increasing signs that the officialdom of white supremacy is bowing to the inevitable. Florida's 1945 legislature buried in committee a proposal to go back to unregulated primaries. And though Georgia adopted in 1945 a new constitution which omits all reference to primaries, a special session of the state legislature in 1946 refused to act upon proposals to abolish all primary laws. The people of every Southern state where this is at issue would do well to heed the warning of Georgia's League of Women Voters:

> To most citizens the convention method of nominating candidates is an appalling spectacle . . . Only on rare occasions are the people's voices heard . . . Anything that weakens the direct primary weakens the democratic system. Unregulated primaries may easily become a tool in the hands of the professional politicians and result in the disgrace of our state . . . If we follow the line of freeing our primaries from all regulations, we are jeopardizing our elections, the foundation upon which our government rests.

The choice confronting the Deep South is clear: it can either try to go back half a century to unregulated primaries and rule-or-ruin conventions in which the special interests would have a happy hunting ground, or it can go forward to primaries regulated by the state to assure discrimination against none and democracy for all.

2. All's Hell on the Southern Front

THE $OUTHERN REVOLT

Because of the subversion of democracy in the South by the poll tax, white primary, anti-unionism, and race prejudice, the reactionary forces of the whole nation concentrated their efforts on the region in their all-out 1944 campaign to get rid of "That Man" in the White House and his supporters in Congress. The Southern slavocracy co-operated wholeheartedly in this conspiracy, for the Roosevelt Administration had threatened to uproot their spoils system by giving top priority to solutions for the problem of the South (the Tennessee Valley Authority and Farm Security Administration, to mention but two).

The 1944 campaign was a real showdown between the forces of progress and reaction in the South and nation. The arch-reactionaries revealed as never before their willingness to resort to fascism itself rather than permit peaceful progress in this country. The campaign they waged against Roosevelt was itself 99.44 per cent pure fascist. They tried desperately to turn race against race, religion against religion, farmers and servicemen against labor, region against region, and nation against nation. They sought to provoke pogroms, and they spoke in deadly earnest of stealing the election and assassinating President Roosevelt. And all this while America was locked in a life-and-death struggle against foreign fascism.

In the Southern revolt against Roosevelt, all the rottenness of the slavocracy festered into a boil, came to a head, and broke out in an ugly sore. While it was not a pretty sight, we must examine it rather closely so that we can be prepared to cauterize it properly should it break out again.

The reactionary rash against Roosevelt broke out back in 1936 in the form of so-called "Jeffersonian Democrats." For a proper perspective of the forces behind that early Southern revolt, we are indebted to Senator Hugo Black's Senate Committee Investigating Lobbies. Vance Muse, the Texas head of the "Christian Americans," was called upon to explain the manner in which he had financed the so-called "grass roots" anti-Roosevelt convention called by Eugene Talmadge at Macon, Georgia, in 1936. Ostensibly the sponsor of the meeting was the "Southern Committee to Uphold the Constitution," which claimed to be composed of Southern farmers and businessmen, but which the Black Committee found to be financed very largely by Northern Republican industrial interests.

One of the contributors turned out to be Will Clayton, of the Texas firm of Anderson, Clayton & Company, world's largest cotton brokers. Lamar Fleming and son, of the afore-mentioned firm, also contributed. But the Texas contributions were not enough to satisfy Vance Muse, so he went North and picked up $10,000 more from Pierre du Pont and John Raskob. Thus liberally financed, Muse and Talmadge staged their rabble-rousing shindig in fine style, distributing large quantities of a photograph showing Mrs. Roosevelt being escorted about Howard University by two Negro professors. Gerald L. K. Smith was on hand, and there was anti-Semitism as well as anti-Negroism. None other than Jesse Jones, the wealthy Texan, was "nominated" for the presidency.

That the Northern Republican industrialists who made all this possible were fully aware of what they were doing was clearly brought out in the questioning of Muse by the Black Committee.

"Did you go see Mr. Raskob and talk to him and Mr. du Pont personally?" asked Senator Black.

"Yes sir," replied Muse. "I told them what I wanted the money for."

"After the meeting [at Macon], you received $500 from Henry du Pont, did you not?" he was asked.

"Yes sir."

"And $1,000 on February twenty-fourth from Alfred P. Sloan of General Motors? That was after the meeting?"

"Yes sir."

"So it was apparent that the du Ponts, if they did not know [in advance] of the distribution of that literature [the photograph of Mrs. Roosevelt], did not disapprove of it, because they contributed another $1,500."

In this connection it is relevant to note that Irénée du Pont also gave $116,630 to the Republicans that year. During the same period, 1935–36, the du Pont family and its associates gave a total of $356,667 to such organizations as the Liberty League, Sentinels of the Republic, Minute Men, Crusaders, National Economy League, American Taxpayers League, and the Farmers Independent Council. Joe Pew, Republican boss of Pennsylvania and head of the Sun Oil Company, gave $37,260 to such organizations during the same time; and Will Clayton also chipped in $7,500 for the Liberty League.

Because of the Black Committee exposé of the Northern Republican industrial backing of the Southern revolt in 1936, many of the "Jeffersonian Democrats" paraded under the banner of "Anti-Third Term Democrats" in 1940. After failing twice miserably to split the Solid South away from its savior, Franklin D. Roosevelt, the conspirators got off to an early start for the 1944 campaign. This time they appeared under a wide variety of aliases—"Democrats for Dewey," "American Democrats," "Southern Democrats," "Allied Democrats," "Anti-New Deal Democrats," and "Independent White Democrats."

One of the first of the reactionaries' attempts at political blackmail was the refusal in 1943 of some Southern state Democratic committees to contribute to the campaign fund of the national committee, unless that body would commit itself to "states' rights," "white supremacy," et cetera. Next, certain Southern politicos began to call for an independent "Southern Democratic party," with white supremacy as its principal plank. Sam Jones, then governor of Louisiana, and Frank Dixon, then governor of Alabama, jointly issued such an invitation to the 1943 Conference of Southern Governors. While a few others present thought the idea might have some value as a bluff, they refused to consider it otherwise. Nothing was clearer than that for the South to break with the Democratic party would mean defeat for the party, and a consequent loss of much of the South's congressional power and patronage.

Nevertheless, much of the commercial newspaper and magazine press of the country—catering to anti-Roosevelt advertisers—exploited the "Southern party" propaganda for all it was worth. Most notably, Governor Jones's ultimatum, entitled "Will Dixie Bolt the New Deal?" was published by the *Saturday Evening Post* with the comment: "We believe it typifies the viewpoint of a large and growing segment of Southern voters." Here are some of the more significant passages:

> It is abundantly and increasingly clear that the New Deal high command hopes to use the war as an instrument for forcing the "social equality" of the Negro upon the South. White Southern boys in the armed services, who, perhaps, have an understanding of and affection for the Negro race not shared by their comrades from other sections, do not improve in morale when they are told that one of the things they are fighting for is social equality of the Negro. They would renounce any such war aim, rightly or wrongly.
>
> The New Deal Democrats have their method of solving the race problem, and we have ours. Ergo, let's affiliate with a group which supports our own view. Or create a group, if necessary . . . There is a possibility of an independent Southern Democratic Party . . . consider the result when a bloc of 115 electoral votes takes effect in a college of 531 in all. Subtract those votes from the already-shaky New Deal Democratic column and very little dependable comfort remains for current officeholders. We may support a Democrat, a Southern Democrat, a Republican, or a Mr. No-Party-At-All, but you can be sure that he is going to be a man prepared to speak and act our language. One thing can save the New Deal Democratic Party—that is, a complete reversal of attitude toward the South.

After this thunder all was relatively quiet along the Southern revolt front until late in 1943, when senatorial spokesmen for the South took up the Rebel Yell. The occasion was debate on the soldier vote bill which would have enabled the federal government to extend adequate and uniform voting facilities to servicemen overseas (including Negroes, and without anyone having to pay a poll tax). As Senator Scott Lucas, one of the bill's sponsors, declared, "Servicemen will determine what kind of world we live in. Why not let them help us now in shaping the kind of government they want?"

However, the measure was defeated by a conspiracy of Southern Democrats and Northern Republicans—reactionaries all— which Senator Joseph F. Guffey accurately described as "the most unpatriotic and unholy alliance that has occurred in the U. S. Senate since the League of Nations for peace of the world was defeated in 1919." Far from accepting this eminently deserved rebuke, some Southern senators seized upon it as an opportunity for a broadside against the Administration.

"Mr. President, what is wrong with being a Southern senator?" asked North Carolina's Josiah Bailey. "Let it be said that we are not ashamed, we are proud to be called Southern senators. Now there can be an end to that sort of thing, Mr. President. There is a remedy. . . . They might possibly drive us out, in which event there would never again be a man elected President of the United States on the Democratic ticket. . . . We can form a Southern Democratic party and vote as we please in the electoral college, and we will hold the balance of power in this country . . . By the eternal gods, there are men in the South, and women too, who will not permit men in control of our party to betray or to insult us in the house of our fathers! We will assert ourselves . . . and we will vindicate ourselves . . . !"

After that the blustering subsided for a day or two, until South Carolina's Senator Cotton Ed Smith had collected his wits sufficiently to reopen the affray.

"Mr. President," said he, "I had intended to speak today on the splendid question of Southern senators. . . . If we approve a measure that is introduced, we are all right. But take a measure such as the anti-lynching bill. How many senators who have lived in the midst of an ungovernable, lustful crowd, and had their womenfolk outraged, would sit down and say, 'Let the law take its course'? Let the law take its course? No! We have dealt with these things until we have trained those guilty of these actions so that their crime has almost passed out. There is no lynching in my section of the country. We would lynch some white people if they would go down there—and I think I would join in the lynching—but so far as the Negro is concerned, there are no lynchings. Sometimes I think that all this harping at the South is because of envy of the real character of Southern men and women . . .

"Of course some men call themselves Democrats, but by God, if they are Democrats I never was one, and I want that definitely understood . . . Mr. President, I . . . call on the Southern states to organize a Southern Democratic party, and let us try to get one decent President . . . I have been here with five Presidents and a piece . . . five Presidents and the thing we have got . . .

"God knows I love the Constitution and I love states' rights. I love to have the vote get as near to the people as possible. . . . I have one platform on which I shall live and die—my loyalty to the Constitution, my loyalty to states' rights, and my loyalty to white supremacy. Here, under the driving force of all the power that can be brought to bear on us, attempt is being made to compel us to take the Negro on an equality, to eat with him, to sleep with him. I am not going to do it!

"That reminds me of a colloquy between two men. One man said to another: 'My God, man, has not the Negro been improving?' The other man said, 'Imitatively, yes.' The first man said, 'I do not mean imitatively. How about his instincts?' The other man said, 'I don't know about his *in*stincts, but he *out*stinks hell.'

"There is not a human being on the earth that I love more than I do the old Negroes at home. Old Uncle Bill carried me in his arms. I loved him almost more than I did my mother and my father, but I did not want him to eat at my table or sleep in my bed, and he did not presume to want to do it.

"Mr. President, I want to state here and now that from now on Harry Byrd is my candidate for the presidency . . ."

The press gave such prominence to all this bellywash that more and more Southerners—notably members of the Southern States Industrial Council—were led to take the Southern party proposition seriously. On the other hand, when the newspapers sent reporters to survey the Southern *people,* they found popular sentiment for either a Southern party or the Republican party was virtually nonexistent. A Gallup Poll of July 1944 found Roosevelt to be the choice of 90 per cent of all Democrats, with Senator Byrd being preferred by only 2 per cent.

But the reactionaries—North and South, Republican and Democratic—desperately needed a Southern revolt to bolster their chances of defeating Roosevelt. When they put up big money, and promised to put up still more, there was no shortage of "volunteers" (mostly ex-officio politicos and unemployed promoters) who were willing to try their hand at stirring up a revolt. By and large, the money they took in was spent three ways: (1) on themselves, (2) to collect more money, and (3) to make enough noise to satisfy their sponsors.

Constitutional Democracy Crusaders

This concern, before Roosevelt received the Democratic nomination, was known as the Draft-Byrd-for-President Campaign. It got under way early in 1944, with headquarters in New Orleans under the direction of John U. Barr, proprietor of Federal Fibre Mills and vice-president of the Southern States Industrial Council. I wrote to this Draft-Byrd board, saying I was "interested." By return mail I received a batch of propaganda headed: *"No newspaper or publication publicity, please!"* According to this confidential matter:

> A group of Southerners started the Byrd-for-President movement, in order to arrest or reverse the drift towards bureaucratic collectivism and national bankruptcy. With a view to enlarging this movement, its organizers decided first to contact representative Southerners through personal correspondence, meanwhile on its own strength the movement spread beyond the South. . . . We are urging the peaceful, democratic use of our sharpest and deadliest weapon, THE BALLOT—and only THE BALLOT! No reprisal can be imposed for the use of that weapon, and no "citizen" worthy of that honored title can be scared out of this "Battle of Ballots"! It's a glorious battle

for our Country, for our future! We have established a beach-
head on Capitol Hill and are holding it. It's only a short
distance up Pennsylvania Avenue—march with us!

That Senator Byrd himself was not altogether idle in an organizational way was revealed by an April news report that he and
"a group of farmers and small businessmen have formed an
organization built around 'Four Freedoms on the Home Front.' "
Byrd listed said freedoms as: "Freedom from racketeering labor
leaders; freedom from bureaucracy, red tape, wasteful spending;
freedom of enterprise and individual opportunity; and freedom
of state and local rights from federal domination."

One of the first official tests of sentiment pro and con Roosevelt
in the South came in the Florida primary of May 3, in which
nominees pledged to vote for Byrd at the Democratic National
Convention opposed pro-Roosevelt nominees. On the day of the
primary, Secretary J. J. Kramer of the Byrd-Drafters was in
Chicago conferring with the so-called American Democratic
National Committee. Kramer promised the press that he would
"roll peanuts down State Street tomorrow" if Byrd delegates were
not elected in Florida. Asked by the *Daily Times* what Byrd's
attitude was toward the war, Kramer replied: "Oh, he's a great
internationalist. As the largest applegrower in the world, he is a
man of broad vision in international affairs. He has 4,000 acres
of apple land in the Shenandoah Valley, and his apples are eaten
all over the world."

"Where does Harry Byrd differ from the Republicans?" a reporter asked.

"Oh, gracious me!" exclaimed Kramer. "He's been a Democrat for over thirty years. . . . WE [the Byrd men] are the
Democratic party. THEY [the Democratic party] are a car-
buncle!"

(Be that as it may, when the time came for the Draft-Byrd-for-
President Movement to report its affiliation to the Senate Committee Investigating Campaign Expenditures, the answer given
was "Republican.")

In time Barr partitioned the South into four regions and arranged a secret conclave of big businessmen in each, to set up a
"Southwide Central Committee." It was anything but a grass-

roots movement. Barr himself told the press, "We're not trying to hold any big mass meetings. We don't want them. We're meeting in smaller groups in which we're finding enthusiastic support . . ." At first, he said, much of the financial burden had fallen upon him, but later there were "many contributions ranging from $1 to $100." Altogether the movement took in a reported $10,-527.67.

In this connection the observation of a Washington newspaper is of interest—that Barr "has about him the look of a salesman who has been doing pretty well . . . he calls himself a small businessman, but he fits well against the background of a good suite at the Mayflower."

After every effort to subvert the nomination of Roosevelt had failed, the Byrd-Drafters changed their name to The Constitutional Democracy Crusaders. Thereafter their pledge cards read:

> Enroll me in your crusade for Constitutional government. I am opposed to an election controlled by Hillman, Browder, or Dubinsky.

"The long-suffering Southland will no longer allow alien minorities to remain in control of the party," quoth Barr. He then proceeded to unleash a series of violently worded pronunciamentos, labeled "Message No. 1," "Message No. 2," and so on, which added Red-baiting and Jewish-name-calling to his stock in trade.

Common Citizens Radio Committee

One of the top dogs in the Southern revolt was the ex-flour salesman, Senator W. Lee "Pass-the-Biscuits-Pappy" O'Daniel of Texas. After riding his hillbilly radio band into politics, Pappy, to further his campaign for the governorship of Texas in 1940, launched a paper which he immodestly called the *W. Lee O'Daniel News*. After the campaign, the sheet died a natural death; but as the 1944 election drew nigh, Pappy saw visions of reviving his paper as a national anti-New Deal beat-Roosevelt organ. Consequently, Pappy sent out the following letter:

> This letter is being sent as a test to a group of people who have corresponded with me or the COMMON CITIZENS RADIO COMMITTEE . . . While little of importance was before Congress I took time out and for five weeks I have been going up and down the State of Texas . . . Practically all of the people I interviewed implored me to go on a nationwide radio hookup and broadcast once each day, or at least once each week, and tell the people of America the truth about what is going on in Washington.
>
> They also implored me to again publish THE W. LEE O'DANIEL NEWS . . . they dug down into their pockets and contributed over $100,000 cash . . . I am willing to undertake publication of the NEWS upon one condition . . . that we get at least 100,000 subscribers before we start to print . . . every dollar received in subscriptions will be spent to edit and distribute the newspaper and pay for radio time . . . send your check for $100 to cover 20 subscriptions . . . if you possibly can, send in more than 20 subscriptions . . . With enough people back of this W. LEE O'DANIEL NEWS, and our radio broadcasts, we can whip the NEW DEAL *NATIONALLY,* just the same as we whipped THE NEW DEAL DYNASTY twice here in Texas.

It is an interesting fact that Pappy demanded and got 50,000 gallons of gasoline from the OPA, which he evidently used in stirring up the Southern revolt. No doubt the OPA came across for fear of what O'Daniel might do to OPA appropriations. Ironically, Pappy was a member of the Senate Committee Investigating Gasoline and Fuel Shortages.

Pappy also evidently got the $500,000 he demanded before going to press, for the first issue rolled out on July 4 of 1944. He then issued an appeal saying, "We are trying to locate high-class salesmen in every state who are honest and reliable and have had considerable selling experience; we want these salesmen to call on industries and business establishments and sell the management subscriptions for each of their employees." In other words, Pappy's *News* is strictly an employer's propaganda dish for employees.

When O'Daniel announced publicly that he had obtained enough newsprint to publish 100,000 copies of the *News* for a year, the War Production Board wanted to know "How come?" inasmuch as newsprint was being strictly rationed.

Something of the story of how Pappy's propaganda machine was set in motion was revealed by him in a "Brief History of the Birth and Growth of a Crusade for Democracy." "A few friends set up [May 1943] a committee which they called the Common Citizens Radio Committee. . . . They succeeded in getting out 500,000 copies [of an O'Daniel radio speech]. That was the first phase of this crusade . . . So the Common Citizens Radio Committee expanded and incorporated [April 1944] . . . and put on a short campaign to see whether a foundation fund of $100,000 could be raised for the purpose of buying radio time and publishing a weekly newspaper on a national scale . . . The $100,000 foundation was oversubscribed very quickly . . ."

It remained for the Senate Committee Investigating Campaign Expenditures to dig up some of the more significant facts about Pappy's fund-raising activities. Twice during June of 1944 the Senate Committee invited him to appear and explain himself, but received no reply. Finally, on October 18–19, the committee went ahead with public hearings. One of the first witnesses was the manager of a sound-recording company, who testified that the *O'Daniel News* was paying him about $1,100 per three weeks for making records of O'Daniel's talks, which eventually were broadcast from 124 stations in 44 states.

Next, post-office officials testified that the application of Pappy's *News* for second-class mailing privileges was still pending. They explained that the second-class rate of $1\frac{1}{2}$ cents per pound had been established by Congress to aid bona fide periodicals, and that one of the requirements is that there be a bona fide list of subscribers, with not more than "an insignificant proportion" of the total circulation going to non-subscribers.

Testimony brought out that of the first (July 4) issue of Pappy's *News,* 100,000 copies were printed, although at that time the paper had only 2,500 subscriptions, only 1,229 of which had been paid for by the recipients themselves. Subsequently, 70,000 copies of each issue were printed. A number of requests from the Post Office Department that the *News* supply it with a list of subscribers had not been met.

From that the Senate Investigating Committee moved on to Pappy's so-called Common Citizens Radio Committee. Called as a witness was Garfield Crawford, editor of Pappy's *News* and secretary-treasurer of the Radio Committee, which was incorporated in Texas. Asked to define the relationship between the Radio Committee and Pappy's *News,* Crawford under pressure finally admitted, "Well, we received subscriptions and donations, and I acted as, I guess you would call it, agent-in-trust for moneys received for the *W. Lee O'Daniel News.*"

Crawford was most reluctant about giving out the names of contributors to the Common Citizens Radio Committee. Here's how the Investigating Committee had to probe for it:

". . . your total bank deposit on March 31 is so much greater, more than $80,000, as compared with your $7,705 on March 9, 1944," pointed out one senator. "Now will you give us a breakdown of some of the contributors?"

"Well, I have them all listed here," replied Crawford. "I think the deposits are all listed here."

"Take the deposit slip for March 23, 1944."

"March of which date, sir?"

"March 23."

"You want them all read?"

"Yes sir, please."

"Complete. Let me see. H. R. Cullen, $25,000; Blaine Thompson, $100; I. A. Ogden, $50; M. C. Hagler, $100; Bradford & Elliott, $5; Albert Braune & Co., $5; Peter Daiardi, Inc., $50; W. R. Hughes, $100; M. B. Hughey, $100; F. L. LeBus, $200; Booth Bros., $200; Dewitt Langford, $200; Edwin Lacy, $250; B. A. Skipper, $250; R. T. Morgan, $500; R. Lacy, $1,000. March 25: Kay Kimbell, $2,500; E. H. Moore, $25,000."

"That is [Senator; millionaire oil man] E. H. Moore of Oklahoma?"

"I think it is. . . . He told the newspaper he was glad he sent it in, it was his money, and he had a right to do with it what he wanted to."

"Was that for a lifetime subscription to the paper?"

"I don't know. I never did discuss that with him."

"Where did the money go—into this fund?"

"Yes sir."

"Didn't you say that all of these subscriptions to this fund were for subscriptions to the paper?"

"Well, the way they sent it in, the man sending it in said they would either send a list or for the *News* to supply a list."

Many minutes were consumed by the Investigating Committee in trying to get Crawford to promise to submit the letters which accompanied the two $25,000 contributions. "You are going to get me involved in a lot of stuff," he lamented. In a later communication he told the committee he had been unable to find such letters.

It was found to be impossible to get Crawford to adequately identify the business connections of the contributors. No matter how many large corporations they might be directing, Crawford persisted in describing them as "cow men," or "grocery men," et cetera. At length the senators had to read these connections into the record themselves.

H. R. Cullen, who gave $25,000, is president of the Quintana Petroleum Corporation and a coal corporation. Kay Kimbell, $2,500, is the owner of a large milling plant. Another contributor of $2,500 was Thomas R. Armstrong, whose manifold offices include: director of Huasteca Petroleum Corporation, vice-president and director of Lago Petroleum Corporation, vice-president and director Creole Petroleum Corporation, director of Mexican Petroleum Company, member consulting foreign committee Standard Oil of Bolivia, vice-president and director of European Gas and Electric, vice-president and director of Pan Foreign Corporation, vice-president and director Tamiahua Petroleum Company, vice-president and director Tuxpan Petroleum Company, vice-president and director Compañía Seaboard Dominicana de Petroleo, et cetera.

Maco Stewart of Galveston gave another $2,500. In addition to being an official of Vance Muse's "Christian American" association, Stewart is president of the Stewart Title Mortgage Loan Company, Guaranty Building and Loan Company, president and director Southland Hotel Company, president and director Galveston City Company and Stewart, Burgess & Morris. Two others who contributed $2,500 each were R. W. Briggs and W. O. Yarborough. C. Starace & Bros., Inc., gave $2,000.

In the $1,000 category was Robert M. Harris, a wealthy New York cotton broker who also admitted having contributed to the so-called American Democratic National Committee, Cotton Ed Smith's so-called National Farm Committee, and publisher Frank Gannett's so-called Committee for Constitutional Government. Harris is also said to have helped finance the American Rock party endorsed by Father Coughlin; he has been Coughlin's financial adviser for fifteen years.

Others who chipped in $1,000 each for Pappy O'Daniel's propaganda machine included Lamar Fleming, Jr., of the Anderson-Clayton cotton brokerage firm; J. M. McCauley of the New York Produce Distributors of America; J. S. Bridwell, owner of the Bridwell Oil Company and a big cattle man; Raymond J. Morfa, director of the Brightwater Paper Company of Massachusetts and assistant chairman of the board Chesapeake & Ohio Railroad; John H. Hinsch; J. B. Beach; A. R. Dillards; H. E. Butt Grocery Co.; and R. H. Hawn. From the Mission Provision Company came $1,250; and from the family of Representative Richard M. Kleberg (defeated in the '44 primaries), operators of the King Ranch, a total of $2,500. Kleberg is also a director of the State National Bank of Corpus Christi and chairman of the board of the University of Texas.

Some smaller contributors were C. J. Anderson & Son, proprietors of the United Dairy Company of West Virginia; J. M. Bennett, director of the National Bank of Commerce of San Antonio; A. M. Biedenharn, director of the San Antonio Coca-Cola Bottling Company; William Reynolds Archer, director of the South Texas Feed Company; A. M. Veder, secretary-treasurer of the San Antonio Coca-Cola Bottling Company; William Purlington Bomar, Broad & Bomar flour dealers; and J. H. Frost, president of the Frost Bank Company.

All contributions considered, Pappy's money-raising concern should have been called the Big Businessmen's Radio Committee instead of the Common Citizens Radio Committee.

Some idea of the political complexion of Pappy's *News* may be had from the following story headings: "O'Daniel Puts War on New Dealers First," "Indispensable Man Is Silly Bunk," "Communistic Coronation of Franklin the Fourth," "Democrats Lose Control of Party to Reds," "Democrats of South Rubbed Out at Chicago," "Victory with Hillman Worse than Defeat," "Republic May Perish if New Deal Returned," et cetera. In its report, the Senate Committee concluded "An examination of the issues of the *W. Lee O'Daniel News* disclosed that there were no ordinary news items carried . . . but rather its contents were devoted entirely to cartoons and accounts of a strictly political nature."

However, Garfield Crawford would not admit that either the Common Citizens Radio Committee or its beneficiary, Pappy's *News,* was engaged in political activity.

"Well, here is a $2,500 contribution marked 'Contribution, political,' signed by Marss McLean of San Antonio," said a senator. "What did you do with that?"

"I put it in this fund," Crawford replied. "He came and said, 'This is to go for the newspaper . . .'"

But Crawford would not admit having noticed the notation on the check.

"Would you have sent it back if you had noticed that word 'political' on there?" a senator asked.

"No. I wish I had . . . but not for that reason."

"Why did you wish so many times that you had returned this $2,500 check?"

"I shouldn't have said that," Crawford replied regretfully.

The check was drawn on the Frost National Bank, of which McLean is a director. He is also director of the Trinity Universal Insurance Company, has served as treasurer for the Republican party in Texas, and is a wealthy oil man and rancher. During the 1944 campaign he and the Mrs. gave $9,000 to Republican groups and $1,000 to the "American Democratic National Committee" (affiliated with the Republican party).

Finally it was brought out that such uncommon "common citizens" as these corporation heads had contributed the bulk of the $109,000 which had come in to the committee. Of this, Crawford said he handed over $79,950 to Pappy's *News.*

"Who authorized you to retain $30,000?" asked a senator.

"Well," said Crawford, "the *W. Lee O'Daniel News* will probably be running on for some time to come."

"I am not asking you that."

"That money is left there for the *W. Lee O'Daniel News,*" said Crawford. "You can only go so fast."

"What did you do with that [remaining $30,000]?"

"It is in the bank."

"It is in the bank yet?"

"All excepting what I have drawn out for myself."

Further questioning revealed that only $18,000 of the $30,000 was still on hand. Crawford acknowledged that his contract fee was $10,000 for 1944. It was also found that the "Common Citizens Radio Committee" had another bank account which took in $18,000, all of which had been spent except $1,000.

After the election was over and the Investigating Committee had been disbanded, Pappy boasted in his *News* on February 13, 1945:

> . . . his [Senator Green's Investigating Committee] gumshoe snoopers failed to find a record of even one half of the money the *NEWS* had taken in because most of it was sent to its head office in Washington and deposited in its Washington bank.

In a trial balance of the *News* corporation submitted to the Senate Committee, Mrs. O'Daniel reported a tidy total income of $313,338.24 as of October 31, 1944.

In its Conclusions, the Senate Committee said, "The activities of the W. Lee O'Daniel News, Inc., as a corporation, were directed toward influencing the election of presidential and vice-presidential candidates in 1944 . . . The radio broadcasts were palpably political. All contracts for them ended on election day or shortly prior thereto. Political rates were paid in some instances . . . The committee on February 8, 1945, unanimously voted to refer this matter to the Department of Justice for examination of the facts in relation to section 313 of the Corrupt Practices Act, which prohibits contributions in connection with any election made by a corporation; and in relation to sections 302 and 303 which define the term 'political committee' and require the filing of a complete and accurate account of all receipts and expenditures."

American Democratic National Committee

Thus far we have seen how John U. Barr, the New Orleans industrialist, sought, through secret conclaves attended by certain other members of the Southern States Industrial Council, to "Draft Byrd for President." We have also seen something of how Texas Senator Pappy O'Daniel raised more than $313,000 to attack the Roosevelt Administration through his paper and over the air. But Pappy was by no means the only national figure involved in the Southern revolt. Although the bulk of the nation's reactionary money went into the Republican war chest after Dewey and Bricker were chosen over Wendell Willkie, a very substantial amount—coming from substantially the same sources —was poured into an organized effort to split and thus negate the Democratic vote.

The nationwide "front" organization set up for this purpose was the so-called American Democratic National Committee, formed in Chicago on February 4, 1944. According to testimony given later by Secretary Robert O'Brian (who was once the Christian Front's choice for mayor of Chicago), the ADNC was conceived back in July of 1941, "where a group of five, who were Democrats, two of whom are now dead, were present, and felt something ought to be done. . . . We felt at that time that the only way we could win, or, rather, that the renomination of President Roosevelt could be prevented, would be by a threat which would make it impossible for him to receive the electoral vote of certain states. In the South, that took the direction of independent electors to be placed on the Democratic ballot."

The man first chosen to direct the ADNC was Harry Woodring, the Kansas banker who had resigned as Secretary of War in 1940 in protest against sending even outmoded American arms to besieged Britain. At that time he said, "I have always been, and am now, and expect to remain, a non-interventionist."

The occasion for formation of the ADNC was an address by

Woodring before the Executives Club of Chicago. The audience is said to have been "predominantly Republican" but to have also included "anti-New Deal Democrats from twenty states." In the course of his harangue Woodring suggested as possible presidential candidates on a renegade Democratic ticket: Senator Harry Byrd, James Farley, Pappy O'Daniel, Senator George of Georgia, Governor Jones of Alabama, Senator Burton Wheeler, and Cordell Hull. After the speechmaking, the business of organizing the ADNC went ahead. Robert Harris, the New York cotton broker whose other contributions to the Southern revolt have been noted, was among those present. Woodring revealed that anti-Roosevelt Democrats had been planning such a committee for more than a year, and that they had conferred with "every governor south of the Mason-Dixon Line." Harris, in testimony later before the House Committee Investigating Campaign Expenditures, described the organizational meeting as follows: "I was greatly impressed with his [Woodring's] talk. I was invited to sit in with a smaller group after the meeting [of the Chicago Executives Club], which was held in the late Senator Reed's room. There were twenty-five or thirty people there."

The Senator Reed referred to was eighty-three-year-old James Reed of Missouri, who after World War I led the movement to keep America out of the League of Nations. Among the others known to have been present were J. E. McDonald, Texas commissioner of agriculture and member of Frank Gannett's National Farm Committee, economist Joseph Lee of Boston, ex-Ambassador N. R. Waring, and ex-Congressman Talle of Iowa.

Chosen to serve as vice-chairman of the ADNC were Charles McGlue, a Boston gentleman who turned Jeffersonian Democrat, and Otha D. Wearin, an ex-congressman from Iowa. Edward F. Judge, vice-president of the Scullin Steel Company of St. Louis, became treasurer. Assistant treasurer and national committeeman for Texas was Ralph W. Moore, a professional Washington lobbyist, former master of the Texas Grange, and member of Gannett's National Farm Committee. Ted Ewart, a publicity expert who had been busy putting over the program of Gannett's Committee for Constitutional Government in Texas, was named head of the ADNC's finance committee. Among the national committeemen was Lee Merriwether of St. Louis, president of the "Jeffersonians."

"The ADNC has a fund of $1,500,000 pledged for its campaign to head off a fourth term for President Roosevelt," Woodring boasted on February 25. To push collections for this fund, and to tie in the Byrd men and other Southern revolters with the ADNC, Woodring embarked upon a "grass-roots crusade" of the South. With him went cotton broker Robert Harris. But Woodring and Harris returned from their "grass-roots crusade" virtually empty-handed—neither men nor money had been forthcoming as they had hoped. On April 2, Woodring handed in his resignation as chairman of the ADNC. "These so-called leaders appear too timid, politically and economically, to stand up and be counted," he complained. "In my opinion there is not sufficient time nor are there sufficient funds to organize the rank and file within all the states to such proportions as I had contemplated."

Woodring's statement of his reason for resigning did not coincide with that later given the House Committee by O'Brian. "Mr. Woodring was determined to employ methods of collecting donations which I was confident were in violation of the Corrupt Practices Act," testified O'Brian. "I opposed his ideas strongly and consistently. It is my impression that he resigned in anger over my position in the matter."

Gleason L. Archer, of Suffolk University at Boston, became the new leader of the ADNC. He had been present at the organizational meeting, where he drafted the so-called "Declaration of Chicago," which became the creed, so to speak, of the organization. Archer was also on the advisory board of Gannett's Committee for Constitutional Government and had served as national radio chairman of the Jeffersonian Democrats. His political credo is best summed up in his anti-Roosevelt book, *On the Cuff,* in which he asks: "Can anyone believe that the inevitable inching up of 'social gains' is not a deliberate process of destruction of private property?"

Under Archer's administration of the ADNC, William J. Goodwin of New York served as treasurer. When the House Com-

mittee asked Archer if he would care to list some of Goodwin's
other connections, he replied, "Yes; he was a Democrat; that is
all." But that was by no means all. Goodwin has worked with
the isolationist America First Committee, the Paul Revere Sentinels, and the so-called Christian Front. Upon joining the latter
Goodwin said, "Democracy is nothing but unadulterated slime."

When the House Committee asked Archer to comment on this
statement by Goodwin, he virtually endorsed it by saying:

"There is a difference between democracy as used by the
Constitution and democracy as loosely used here in this country.
Now, democracy, if you go back to the original meaning of it,
means rule by the mob, by Demos. We rejected that in this
country; Jefferson and all the others believed that it would be a
mistake to have democracy here . . ."

Goodwin, asked by the House Committee about the Christian
Front, described it as "an organization formed for the purpose of
combating communism, formed under wonderful auspices, a very
fine organization, of which I have never been ashamed . . . I
am confident that anyone who cares to inquire will find equally
strong objections [to being blamed for supporting the Christian
Front] from the several leading Americans who have been my
fellow victims."

"Such as . . ." suggested a senator.

"Men like Charles Lindbergh, Senator Wheeler, and General
Wood [head of Sears, Roebuck]—men who stand for what America stands for," replied Goodwin.

It is interesting to note that Goodwin managed "Cactus Jack"
Garner's bid for the New York Democratic delegation in 1940.
In 1941 he was busy threatening the Senate Foreign Relations
Committee that "a civil war will break out" if the Lend-Lease
Act were passed. He wrote the committee: "Why should America
destroy Hitler? . . . As between the two nations we are the
violators of international law, not Germany. . . . We are not
champions of freedom of the seas." In 1942, Goodwin and Gerald
L. K. Smith, among others, were campaigning against rationing.
Goodwin is also an admirer of Robert Reynolds, the nationalist
Tarheel fuehrer from North Carolina.

Another of the strong men who worked with Archer was John J. O'Connor, long a congressman from New York, but who was defeated in 1938. That year his picture appeared on the cover of Father Coughlin's *Social Justice* (September 12), and the issue contained an article by him, plus an article in his praise, penned by Father Edward Lodge Curran, clerical fascist. A year later O'Connor was serving as vice-chairman of Representative Fish's isolationist Keep U. S. Out of Foreign Wars Committee.

Cotton broker Robert Harris tightened his financial control over the ADNC, and men like Marshall Wingate, national commander of the United Confederate Veterans, J. M. Futrell, ex-governor of Arkansas, Henry Regnery, Chicago manufacturer, George F. Short, former attorney general of Oklahoma, William Werner of St. Louis, former secretary of the Jeffersonian Democrats, and N. C. Roberts, chairman of the Constitutional Government Club of New Mexico, served as national committeemen.

Archer lost no time in making it clear that he was at least as much of an isolationist as Woodring. "No man," he declared, "whose past record of utterances indicate that he is an internationalist can hope to receive our support . . . we are . . . fed up on repeated participation in the perpetual wars of Europe . . ."

Apparently Archer had almost as much difficulty as had Woodring in getting the boys who had promised $1,500,000 to come across with the cash. In a collection letter sent to ADNC sympathizers of means, Archer said:

> Although several hundred thousand dollars have been faithfully pledged, only a small part of it has been received . . . If the New Deal wins, our liberties are in danger; the education of our youth will be communized; our Christian religion will be in peril; our sovereignty as a nation will be submerged in some dreamy international state, headed by aliens. In the name of our country, we ask your financial help. If you are of moderate means, please contribute $25, $50, $100, $200. If a person of wealth, make it $500 or $1,000.

As the Democratic Convention drew nigh, all the reactionary talk about fusion of all the anti-Roosevelt "Democratic" elements in the country began to aspire after big money. The story of this anschluss, as told by Victor Riesel in the New York *Post* on June 14; was as follows:

> The story behind the creation of a new country-wide isola-tionist machine, built in a series of secret hotel-room confer-ences in New York, Washington, and Chicago, can now be told for the first time. The coalition plans to set up national head-quarters in Chicago's Hotel Sherman Saturday. Then it will campaign against Mr. Roosevelt under the slogan, "Don't be ashamed to be for America First!" This was decided at off-the-record parleys which Byrd's agents—John U. Barr and James Kramer—held recently in Chicago with the Coughlinite Amer-ican Democratic National Committee.
>
> After these conferences Barr, who leads the Byrd-for-President Committee, told friends that he expected "some big development." Barr and Kramer then came to New York and talked with [Gerald L. K.] Smith at the Hotel Pennsylvania. They obtained his pledge of support for the new coalition. Smith also promised to deliver the backing of all America First and Coughlinite cells. Smith, according to reports, was cocky over his ability to deliver because he had been the coalition's walking delegate since last April and had conferred with Na-tionalist leaders in a dozen states.

In New York, Smith was said to have conferred with Goodwin and, the previous April, with Robert Reynolds, head of the Amer-ican Nationalist Committee of Independent Voters. Reynolds' paper, *The American Nationalist,* endorsed the ADNC. More-over, when Gerald Smith staged his America First party conven-tion in Detroit on August 29–30, he distributed a full line of ADNC propaganda.

A two-day political caucus of such anti-Roosevelt forces was held in Chicago June 19–20, prior to the Democratic Convention. "One of the projects to be discussed will be the consolidation of Jeffersonian Democrats, Southern Anti-New Deal Association, and the American Democratic National Committee," it was an-nounced.

Pappy O'Daniel was the keynoter and delivered his usual spiel. Georgia's Gene Talmadge also spoke, but cautiously, keeping his red suspenders under his coat. Many of the Southern revolters on hand were perplexed and disturbed by the injection of nationalism into the caucus by the defeatist-appeasement outfit, "We, the Mothers, Mobilize for America." These ne'er-do-well females broke up the first afternoon session and were again on hand the following day. One of them asked, "Do you realize what kind of a government we have in this country, that uproots people from their homes and takes them to Washington where they are accused of sedition and tried by Jews?" When Serrell Hillman, representing *Time* magazine, tried to question the ladies further as to their anti-Semitism, he was ejected.

Even more terrifying to the Southern Democrats were the many Republicans present (this out of regard for political reputations back home). There was an area of agreement among most of those present in favor of a ticket of Bricker and Byrd, but they could not agree as to which should take top honors. Goodwin announced prematurely that a Bricker-Byrd ticket had been approved, but the caucus itself took action denying this. Finally a resolution was adopted calling upon the Republican party to nominate Bricker and Byrd.

The "Byrd-for-Vice-President on the Republican ticket" boom was short-lived, however. O'Connor talked it up with Republican leaders in Chicago; and Harrison Spangler and Representative Harold Knutson thought it might work. Also, Republican House leader Joe Martin said he thought it would be fine. But the idea was finally rejected, according to Drew Pearson, by Dewey's advisers.

The ADNC-sponsored caucus at Chicago did appoint a five-man "central committee" to watch future developments.

When the delegates began to arrive for the Democratic Convention the Southern revolt held a confab of its own, at the beck and call of the Texas "regulars" led by Garner-man E. B. Germany. Mississippi, Louisiana, South Carolina, and Virginia were also there (plus someone claiming to represent Cuba); but Georgia, Alabama, Arkansas, Florida, and Tennessee were conspicuous by their absence. There was very little agreed upon, and one Texas delegate, Charles Gibson, walked out with the assertion that he would "not be a party to such Republican maneuvers." Properly rebuffed at every turn, the revolters succeeded in getting only eight states to petition for floor consideration of their white-supremacy plank, which read:

> Exercise by the states of their reserved powers to determine the qualifications of their voters and to regulate their public schools and attendance thereon is not subject to control by either the legislative or executive branches of the Federal Government in the absence of Constitutional Amendment ceding such powers to the Federal Government.

When the voting finally came in the Democratic Convention, Roosevelt received twice as many Southern delegation votes as did Byrd.

After the convention the revolters held what amounted to a post-mortem over their plans. It was decided that a "Central Committee of Five," operating through the ADNC, would meet on July 20 to plan for an "American Democratic" convention to be held in New Orleans. But this convention never came off.

It is indicative of the chauvinism of reaction that while the ADNC was fanning anti-Negro prejudice in the South, it was organizing a "Democrats for Dewey" club among Harlem Negroes. It is also interesting to note that the ADNC brought together, in the same movement but at opposite ends of the line, Southern demagogues like O'Daniel and Talmadge and Northern demagogues addicted to the Coughlinite and Christian Front brand of native fascism. The money and goals were the same, but the techniques were designed to appeal to regional prejudices.

Thus, while the Southern revolt was thumping the tub for white supremacy, the ADNC in New York was putting on shows featuring Christian Fronters, et al. One such New York meeting, held in October, was addressed by George U. Harvey, who in the past had been listed to speak with men like Allen Zoll of the American Patriots, Joe McWilliams of the Christian Mobilizers indicted for sedition, John Eoghan Kelly, convicted as a Franco agent, and with Goodwin and Father Edward Lodge Curran for the Paul Revere Sentinels. Moreover, Harvey was one of the sponsors of the "Pro-American Mass Meeting" staged by some fifty "patriots" for the debut of General George Van Horn Moseley as their "man on horseback."

At the World's Fair on June 16, 1940, Harvey had said:

"Hitler lived on the good old-fashioned American theory which is 'If you don't work you don't eat.' " The German-American Bund's *Deutscher Weckruf und Beobachter* praised him for his "activities in behalf of national patriotism."

Among the other speakers at this New York ADNC meet was John J. McNaboe, who had also spoken for the "American Patriots" and had the endorsement of the Nazis' World Service, Coughlin's *Social Justice,* and Mrs. Elizabeth Dilling. John T. Flynn, former state chairman of America First, also spoke. On stage was the Rev. Ed J. Brophy, author of *The Christian Front* and one time character witness for Joe McWilliams. The propaganda booklet *Vote CIO and Get a Soviet America,* published by Kamp's "Constitutional Educational League," was distributed to the audience of 176 persons.

One of the ADNC's last abortive acts was an invitation from Archer to Pappy O'Daniel to become the organization's candidate for President. Pappy advised the press that he was giving the matter thorough consideration and would decide in a day or two. He did not have that long to wait, however, for O'Connor stepped in and informed the press that the "ADNC is not in a position to sponsor anyone."

It was in October that the House Committee Investigating Campaign Expenditures got around to the ADNC. It had the usual difficulty in getting the officials to admit that the organization had been engaged in political activity (despite such statements as that made by O'Brian in Washington on September 22: that the ADNC had spent more money west of the Mississippi for posters and radio time for Dewey than had the Republicans).

Some of the questions and answers at the public hearings had special significance.

"Are you not out trying to uphold the Constitution?" a senator asked Archer.

"Yes," he replied.

"When the Constitution says that the Congress can pass laws relating to elections, and the Congress passes a law known as the Corrupt Practices Act, why does not your organization live up to that act? . . . The legal requirement was that you file [reports] a long time ago. . . . Have you made any attempt to file within the legal requirement?"

"Well, I do not know," said Archer.

The fact was that the ADNC had not complied with the law, but no punishment was meted out.

The list of large contributors to the ADNC, as uncovered by the Investigating Committee, is most interesting. Altogether the ADNC took in $128,465—$90,000 of which is said to have been contributed by about forty Republicans.

H. R. Cullen, the Texas oil man who gave $25,000 to O'Daniel's *News,* gave $5,000 to the ADNC (he and his family also gave $20,000 to Republican groups). Charles E. Merrill of New York City also gave $5,000 (and $13,000 to the Republicans). Another contributor of $5,000 was William L. Volker, Kansas City oil man and manufacturer. Mrs. M. N. Morawetz and Mrs. Victor Morawetz, both of New York City, gave a total of $5,000 (the family also contributed $11,000 to Republican groups).

S. F. Houston, a Philadelphia banker, gave the ADNC $4,000 (and the Republicans $1,750). Robert Harris, the New York cotton broker, gave $3,500 (and $1,000 to O'Daniel's *News,* besides unspecified sums to Gannett's Committee for Constitutional Government and Cotton Ed Smith's National Farm Committee). Another $3,500 came to the ADNC from Harry Weiss of Houston, Texas, president of the Humble Oil Company (he also gave $3,000 to the Republicans).

In the $3,000 class was Edward F. Hutton of Westbury, N.Y., a fund raiser for the Gannett Committee (he and his wife also gave a total of $12,000 to Republican groups). A total of $3,000 was also forthcoming from Irénée and Amy du Pont, and another $500 from a member of the family, W. W. Laird (altogether the du Ponts also gave $106,332.83 to Republican committees). M. C. Fleischmann and Mrs. Van Santvoord Merle-Smith, both of New York City, each gave $2,500 (the latter also giving $1,500 to Republicans). From Dorothy L. Young of Ridgewood, N.J., came $1,500. Robert E. Wood, head of Sears, Roebuck, sent $1,462.73 directly to the ADNC, not to mention $3,500 he sent Suffolk University to pay for Archer's book to be distributed by ADNC (Wood also gave $2,000 to Republican committees).

Topping the contributors of $1,000 was Marss McLean of

San Antonio, who gave the *O'Daniel News* $2,500, while he and his wife contributed $9,000 to the Republicans. The following also gave $1,000 each to the ADNC (amounts also given to the Republicans shown in parentheses):

> Thomas Morrison, Spring Lake, N.J. ($5,500)
> George Monroe Moffet, New York City ($8,500)
> R. D. Wallace, Pleasantville, N.Y. ($1,000)
> Wiley L. Reynolds, Palm Beach, Fla. ($1,000)
> Edward R. Tinker, Syosset, N.Y. ($2,000)
> Henry Regnery, Hinsdale, Ill.
> C. W. Nash (Nash-Kelvinator)
> Charles R. Hook, Middleton, Ohio
> Mrs. W. S. Barstow, Great Neck, N.Y.
> Mrs. P. J. Wigmore, New York City
> Ida Larkin Clements, New York City
> M. X. Fleishmann, New York City

There were two who contributed $600 to the ADNC: J. W. Blodgett, Jr., of Grand Rapids, and Bernard Peyton of Princeton, N.J., the latter also giving $2,500 to the Republicans. William Ziegler, Jr., of New York City (an original member of the Gannett Committee) gave $500—and $7,500 to the Republicans. Others who contributed $500 to the ADNC were:

> John P. Brown, Chicago
> Perry E. Canfield, Seattle
> J. R. Whiting, New York City
> M. Verdi, New York City
> C. Tuck, Roslyn, N.Y.
> R. B. Pierrepont, Palm Beach, Fla.
> Perry Belmont, Newport, R.I.
> W. A. Anderson, Detroit
> Richard Hart, Parkersburg, W.Va.
> Eugene Holman, New York City
> C. L. Kingsbury, Baltimore
> W. W. Laird, Wilmington, Del.
> W. E. Long, Chicago
> Vanderbilt Webb, New York City

It was found that the ADNC had used a contributor's pledge form which carried an assurance that the name of the contributor would be kept secret—a violation of the Corrupt Practices Act.

In its final report the Senate Committee said, ". . . there were certain items entered upon the list of contributors . . . which indicated that corporations had made contributions. . . . These corporations were: The Advance Aluminum Castings Corporation, $100; R. D. Walker Lumber Co., Mobile, Ala., $100; Potash Co. of America, $200."

The breakdown of ADNC expenses should also be of interest, especially to those who contribute to such outfits. As of July 31, 1944, it was as follows: general expenses, $18,100; field expenses, $30,164.67; income procurement expenses, $14,671.98. Just what the leaders got out of it is not known exactly, but O'Connor allowed himself $3,500 for use of part of his New York office by the ADNC, and $3,300 for use of part of his Washington office, and he spent $3,830 on unrecorded personal items such as meals and taxis—the total being $10,630. Goodwin drew $400 per month for use of his office. Ted Ewart, the Texas publicity man who transferred from Gannett's Committee for Constitutional Government to the ADNC, was paid a lump sum of $2,436.84 for his services to the latter, which services lasted less than three weeks. When Woodring resigned, some $4,000 of the money he turned over was unaccounted for as to its contributors; two $1,000 bills had come in the mail in a plain envelope.

Among the significant expenditures of the ADNC was $1,000 to R. C. Rottcamp of Long Island, former Queens chairman of the Coughlinite "American Rock party," and $250 to Nelson Sparks, author of *One Man—Wendell Willkie,* the book which contained the notorious forged letter purporting to show that Harry Hopkins engineered Willkie's 1940 Republican nomination.

"Did you have anything to do with the Committee for Constitutional Government in their essay contest?" a senator asked Ralph Moore.

"None whatever," replied Moore. "I would not be ashamed of it, if I did; but I did not . . . they were spending money on an educational campaign. That, we think, is entirely too slow. . . . We want some direct action. . . . I helped raise some money for O'Daniel radio time, in the O'Daniel outfit . . . this committee [the ADNC] has only spent money for one radio program in the state of Texas; and O'Daniel spoke then . . ."

"Did your committee have any connection with the O'Daniel movement?" it was asked.

"Some people who have been interested in this have been interested in the other," replied Moore. "All I know is I called up a man down in Alabama and arranged for radio and transportation for O'Daniel, and spent the [ADNC] money . . . I have been in all the movements to lick Roosevelt since 1934. . . . I would rather come out of this thing without a dime and get rid of Roosevelt than keep what little I have got and re-elect Roosevelt . . . the re-election of Roosevelt means the end of property rights in the United States."

Dud or Time Bomb?

The master plan back of the Southern revolt was brazenly published in the *Southern Watchman* with the announcement that "This brochure was written by a prominent Southern lawyer early in June—and has been widely circulated in mimeographed form . . ." The plot read in part:

> A plan is here suggested. On November 7 the states will appoint their electors. On December 18 these electors will meet in their electoral college and cast their votes for President and Vice-President. During the interim period let the electors from a state or states (after previous informal consultation) call a convention of the Southern electors and invite those from the border states if deemed practicable. Let them meet, adopt a platform, and pledge themselves to vote for a certain person for President on December 18 . . . There would be no need for such a meeting to be public. The period of public participation will have been over on November 7. The persons at this convention will have in their hands the actual voting power of their states.

While there have been a few cases of individual electors betraying their trust by casting their electoral vote for some candidate other than the one intended, organized plots to disregard the popular vote have taken place only twice before, and each time brought the nation to the brink of civil war. Legally there is nothing to bind electors to their moral obligation to carry out the will of the people. As the historian Edwin Corwin has pointed out, "An elector is an abortive organism. He is not merely functionless, he is dangerous. Electors who bolt are electoral Benedict Arnolds."

According to Drew Pearson in the Washington Merry-Go-Round, it was "Jim Farley's legal counselors" who first proposed the Southern revolt. Be that as it may, there is no question but that Jim Farley, Jesse Jones, and "Cactus Jack" Garner all had a big hand in it.

The chairman of the Texas Democratic executive committee at the time of the revolt was George Butler, Jesse Jones's nephew and attorney for the extensive "Jesse Jones Interests," which include banks, newspapers, radio stations, office buildings, and loan associations.

The Texas phase of the revolt got under way, openly, at the Harris County (Houston) convention, which steam-rollered, without nominations from the floor, the following delegates to the state convention: H. R. Cullen (the oil man who gave money to O'Daniel, the ADNC, and the Republican party), Martin Dies, and those "Christian American" stalwarts, Pappy O'Daniel, Vance Muse, and Val Sherman.

The part played by the "Christian American" in Texas and on other sectors of the Southern revolt was considerable. In this connection it should be recalled that the Caraway Senate Investigating Committee of 1929 found that Vance Muse had served as treasurer of the Republican party in Texas "for quite a considerable period." That Muse took part in the '44 campaign was borne out by a letter he wrote Clarence Miller, chairman of the Harris County Republican Committee in December of 1943, in which he said in part:

> . . . I first intend to organize my own home precinct . . . and encourage both Democrats and Republicans to go into the Republican precinct primaries . . . and see that Willkieites like you are not permitted to attend the county, state, and national Republican conventions . . .
>
> In my limited effort to prevent New Dealers posing as Dem-

ocrats from being elected in the last two state-wide campaigns for U. S. Senator from Texas I formed political contact with some 5,700 patriots who can be depended upon to emulate our Harris County organization . . .

The negro question plus incapable leadership has prevented many citizens from openly affiliating with the Republican party in Texas in the past but since the Democratic party has largely been transformed into the Black New Deal party this question should no longer be an issue. The negroes who want only their just political and economic rights . . . should find a haven of refuge in a reconstructed Republican party in the South, leaving those who believe in social equality bordering on political miscegenation to remain in the New Deal setup.

When the Senate Committee Investigating Campaign Expenditures sent Muse a standard questionnaire, Muse did not reply. A second questionnaire drew from Muse a 380-word telegram violently attacking the Senate Committee and informing it that he had filed the questionnaires in the wastebasket. He claimed that the "Christian American" had contributed "nothing more than a sign" to the campaign between Roosevelt and Dewey.

However, when the Senate Committee looked into the "Christian American" account at the San Jacinto National Bank of Houston (one of the very few banks in the country which does not keep a photostatic record of all checks), some suggestive figures were brought to light. On April 4, 1944, the "Christian American" bank balance was $477.01. The Texas revolt was scheduled for Austin on May 23. From April 4 until May 25 a total of $13,415 was deposited in the "Christian American" kitty, in amounts from $1,000 to $4,550. During the twenty days prior to the Austin convention, $5,250 was taken out of the account, in lumps of $500 and up.

The "Republicratic" complexion of the Harris County Democratic Convention was reflected by the following news items, both of which appeared in the Houston *Chronicle* on May 9:

1.

John H. Crooker, former district attorney and senior member of the law firm of Fulbright, Crooker, Freeman & Bates, was elected temporary chairman of and keynoter of the Harris County Democratic Convention . . .

2.

Carl Stearns, lawyer with the firm of Fulbright, Crooker,
Freeman & Bates, was elected chairman of the Harris County
Republican convention . . .

Crooker, the county Democratic chairman, was also attorney
for Will Clayton and Lamar Fleming of the cotton firm of Anderson, Clayton & Company. George Heyer, president of the
Crude Oil Company, a Sun Oil subsidiary, was another ring-
leader of the revolt, and may have been under orders of Sun-head
Republican-boss Pew of Pennsylvania. Among the other oilers
involved in the revolt were Hiram King, chief lobbyist for Sin-
clair; Clint Small, lobbyist for Humble Oil, a subsidiary of
Standard Oil of New Jersey; E. E. Townes, former chief counsel
for Humble; and Neth Leachman, Lone Star Gas representative.
Another revolter was Charles McCombs of Austin—insurance-
company executive, attorney, and big farmer. A day after the
revolt, McCombs declared at a suite at the Waldorf-Astoria that,
thanks to the revolt, a popular vote for Roosevelt in Texas would
"be but an empty gesture."

Second only to Texas as a hotbed of "revolt" was Alabama.
In Texas it was the oil and cotton interests—largely controlled
outside the South—who financed the fireworks; in Alabama it
was chiefly the steel, coal, and textile interests—also subject to
a large measure of outside control—who took care of the expense
account.

One of the front men for 'Bama's Big Mules was Fred Rucker,
who was associated with Pappy O'Daniel while that unworthy
was campaigning for governor of Texas in 1940. Again, in 1943,
Rucker was instrumental in getting Pappy an invitation to address the Alabama legislature in behalf of the "Christian American" anti-labor bill. Once Rucker proclaimed himself to be a
candidate for the vice-presidency on the "Christian American"
ticket. Asked what his connections were with O'Daniel, Rucker
replied, "I handle all his affairs in this state."

This was borne out by a report in the Washington *Times-
Herald* which said that "Some informed Alabamans here said
that the third party movement in Alabama was an 'offshoot' of

O'Daniel's fight against the New Deal and that Rucker had been promoting the organization under the name 'Facts, Inc.,' since 1941." According to Rucker himself, "more than 100 anti-Roosevelt Democrats" helped him organize the "American Democratic party of Alabama," affiliated with the ADNC.

This Alabama ADNC cabal "nominated" candidates to oppose Senator Lister Hill and Representative Luther Patrick. Fortunately, Alabama's attorney general ruled that the ADNC nominees "had not been selected in such manner as to authorize the placing of their names upon the official ballots."

On August 23 the ADNC shipped Pappy O'Daniel to Alabama to address a "mass meeting." It was attended by about thirty-five persons, mostly Big Mules. His spiel was broadcast, however, also through the sponsorship of the ADNC. When the broadcast was over, the Big Mules urged Pappy to let his hair down and give them the inside dope (the public having been fed the ballyhoo). Pappy was only too glad to oblige, revealing himself to be a rank (reactionary) Republican. This is what he said: "We have no choice except Roosevelt and Dewey, and I am against a fourth term for anybody. The only remedy we have is to vote for Dewey, get these New Dealers out of office, and reorganize the Democratic party." As a token of appreciation, the Big Mules nominated Pappy for President.

Eugene Talmadge tried to get the names of ADNC electors on the ballot in Georgia, but was frustrated by the requirement for a petition bearing 28,000 signatures. And so he worked out a conspiracy with certain Republican elements. As is generally the case in the Deep South, the Republicans in Georgia were split into two factions: the regulars and the lily-whites who refused membership to Negroes. The Republican National Convention had recognized the regulars, but—for the first time in the history of any state—Georgia's secretary of state, John B. Wilson, refused to grant the regular Republican nominees a place on the ballot.

Instead, Wilson certified twelve electors who appeared twice on the ballot, under the headings of both "Republican" and "Independent Democratic." Six of the twelve were lily-white Republicans and six were anti-Roosevelt Democrats. Mayor

R. G. Foster of Wadley, lily-white Republican, explained: "We divided our ticket between Republicans and Democrats because there are a lot of good Democrats who have told us that they would join us if they could, and this will give them a chance. . . . We are prepared to spend considerable money in our campaign . . ." Clint Hager, leader of the lily-white Republicans, added: "This means Negro leadership is out."

Officials of the regular Republicans took court action in which they charged that Talmadge had arranged a meeting with them on August 6. "Talmadge there outlined a scheme to name as electors six Democrats and six Republicans jointly by the Independent Democrats and Republicans," the legal action charged. "The plan was to have each elector individually campaign for votes for himself by appealing to racial and religious prejudices. Talmadge specifically mentioned Negroes and Jews."

The manner in which the Southern revolt fizzled is a matter of record. In Texas a truly Democratic convention was called and its pro-Roosevelt electors were granted a place on the ballot. In Alabama the revolters were denied a place on the ballot. In Louisiana the electors were asked by party officials to declare their loyalty to Roosevelt or resign; two resigned and were replaced. South Carolina, after the Democratic Convention (and Cotton Ed Smith's defeat), lined up for Roosevelt. In Mississippi, when three electors announced that they were going to bolt, the governor called a special session of the legislature which provided for placement of a pro-Roosevelt slate of electors on the ballot. In Florida the revolters were denied a place on the ballot, and a "White Democratic party" (quietly affiliated with the Republican party) advertised against Roosevelt and Pepper, to no avail.

When the votes came in, Roosevelt carried every Southern state by majorities only slightly smaller than in 1940. Even in Texas the revolters received only 11 per cent of the total vote, with 16 per cent garnered by the Republicans, and Roosevelt getting all the rest.

And so the Southern revolt proved to be an attempt to stage a political holdup with a gun loaded with plenty of money but precious few votes. The record of this attempt by reactionary industrialists to bamboozle the South and nation holds many lessons for the future. It revealed that these elements were willing —even while America was engaged in a life-and-death struggle against fascism—to employ the fascist propaganda weapons of racial and religious bigotry to pervert a national election toward fascistic ends. The fact that the South was chosen as the focal point of the attempt shows where the greatest danger lies.

The Southern revolt against democracy fizzled in 1944. But it was not a dud. Unless the fuse is pulled, it may prove to be a time bomb and explode someday in our faces.

THE VISIBLE EMPIRE

While the Southern revolt failed to put the reactionaries in totalitarian control of the nation, its failure weakened but little the slavocracy's strangle hold on the South. The slavocracy's dictatorship over the region's state and local government is both direct and indirect, above ground and under cover. To satisfy its insatiable appetite for excess profits, the slavocracy pays starvation wages and denies democracy to the working people of the South. The result is feudalism for all Southerners, plus white supremacy for Negroes.

Needless to say, in order to maintain such a system, forcible repression is necessary. While the slavocracy has entrusted the burden of day-to-day suppression to officers of the law, in the final analysis the system relies for protection upon the reincarnated Ku Klux Klan. This is no overstatement. The Klan's repressive influence is omnipresent throughout the South, not so much by virtue of its seen handiwork as by the terror engendered by the knowledge that the Klan's unseen lynch law lurks around every corner.

This has ever been the Klan's true function. While some modern Klansmen—like their forefathers during Reconstruction —have conscientiously lynched under the delusion that they were protecting white Southern womanhood or were promoting public morality and the like, they have actually served as storm troopers of the plutocracy which robs them and their neighbors (as well as the Negroes) of the best fruits of their labor.

For more than three quarters of a century, now, the Kloran

of the KKK has superseded the Constitution of the U.S.A. as the governing instrument of the South. The story of the modern Klan is as consistently sordid, from first chapter to last, inclusive, as that of the Reconstruction Klan which with bloody hands wrested democracy from Southern poor whites and Negroes.

While the general theme is notorious enough, a brief review of the modern Klan's criminal record is very much in order.

The gentleman who in 1915 led thirty-four Atlantans to the summit of near-by Stone Mountain, and there beneath a forty-foot fiery cross reincarnated the Klan, was William Joseph Simmons. Addressing himself magniloquently "To All Nations, Peoples, Tribes, and Tongues, and to the Lovers of Law and Order, Peace and Justice, of the Whole Earth," the new Klan's Imperial Wizard declared: "We are dedicated to the exalted privilege of demonstrating the practical utility of the great, yet almost neglected, doctrine of the Fatherhood of God and the Brotherhood of Man; and to maintain forever White Supremacy in all things."

It is reasonably certain that if Simmons had not revived the Klan someone else would have done so. The spirit of Ku-Kluxery was still militantly operative throughout the South and had not relaxed in the least its repressive influence. While Simmons officiated at the Klan's reincarnation, its real spiritual father was Thomas E. Watson, the Georgian who distinguished himself as a leader of Populism, only to disgrace himself in the end by resorting to demagogic racism. The story of how Watson hatched the Klan is still full of significance for the South today.

On April 27, 1913, the body of fourteen-year-old Mary Phagan was found in the basement of an Atlanta pencil factory where she worked. She had been raped and murdered. The superintendent of the factory was Leo Frank—a Jew and a Northerner. Circumstantial evidence pointed to him, and he was charged with the crime. Rival Atlanta newspapers vied with one another in exploiting the lurid details, with the result that a howling mob packed several blocks around the courthouse during Frank's trial. He was declared guilty and sentenced to death, but national organizations interested in justice carried the case to the

U. S. Supreme Court. The "Frank case" competed with the war in Europe as a *cause célèbre*. The sentence was upheld, albeit with many a dissenting opinion.

Tom Watson did not enter the fray until he saw an opportunity to capitalize on it, politically and financially. Then for over a year scarcely an issue of his newspaper, *The Jeffersonian,* failed to inflame the issue. Circulation of his paper increased from 25,000 at the time he took up his anti-Semitic crusade to 87,000 at its peak, at which time it netted an estimated weekly profit of $1,123.

"Frank belonged to the Jewish aristocracy," Watson wrote in a typical diatribe, "and it was determined by the rich Jews that no aristocrat of their race should die for the death of a working-class Gentile." As for Mary Phagan: "Yes, she was only a factory girl: there was no glamor of wealth and fashion about her. She had no millionaire uncle; she had no Athens kinsmen to raise $50,000 for her: no mighty connections . . . While the Sodomite who took her sweet young life basks in the warmth of Today, the poor child's dainty flesh has fed the worms."

Watson waxed even more violent when there arose a nationwide demand that Frank's sentence be commuted to life imprisonment. "How much longer is the innocent blood of little Mary Phagan to cry in vain to Heaven for vengeance?" he asked. Reminding Atlantans how New Orleans mobs had recently lynched a number of Italians, he said, "Now is the time to have a Vigilance Committee APPOINT ITS OWN SENTRIES TO WATCH THAT DESPERATE CRIMINAL . . ." Following up, he wrote, "If Frank's rich connections keep on lying about this case, SOMETHING BAD WILL HAPPEN." And when there was rumor that Governor John M. Slaton might commute Frank's sentence, Watson let go with the headline: "RISE, PEOPLE OF GEORGIA!"

Watson secretly sent Slaton word that if he would proceed with the hanging of Frank, Watson would be his "friend" so that Slaton could become "U. S. Senator and the master of Georgia politics for twenty years to come." Slaton rejected this offer and, on the day before he retired from office, bravely commuted Frank's sentence (he might have left the problem to his successor). On the following day martial law had to be declared in Atlanta, and that night sixteen soldiers were injured in repelling a mob of 5,000 persons who marched on Slaton's home, armed with everything from up-to-date weapons, dynamite sticks, to old-fashioned cap-and-lock firearms, knives, saws, and hatchets.

Watson rose to the occasion with the headline: "Our Grand Old Empire State HAS BEEN RAPED!" In a lengthy defense of the mobs he declared, "When mobs are no longer possible, liberty will be dead."

Having done his worst against Slaton, Watson turned to inciting mob violence against Frank. On August 12, 1915 (all this had been going on over a period of two years), Watson wrote, "The next Leo Frank case in Georgia will never reach the Courthouse. THE NEXT JEW WHO DOES WHAT FRANK DID IS GOING TO GET EXACTLY THE SAME THING THAT WE GIVE TO NEGRO RAPISTS."

Four days later—as was only to be expected—twenty-five armed men, only two of whom were masked, entered the Georgia state prison, removed Leo Frank to Marietta (the home of Mary Phagan), and hanged him. The following day was like a Roman holiday: Georgians came in from miles around—heels were ground into Frank's face, bits of his clothing and of the lynch rope were distributed as souvenirs, and "Fiddlin' John" Carson played the "Ballad of Mary Phagan" (still to be heard) on the courthouse steps.

And thus Tom Watson demonstrated what a demagogue can do with a newspaper. Wrote he: "The North can rail itself hoarse, if it chooses to do so. We've already stood as much vilification and abuse as we intend to put up with; and we will meet the 'Leo Frank League' with a 'Gentile League' if they provoke us much further . . . another Ku Klux Klan may be organized to restore HOME RULE."

And so it was—not to restore "home rule," but to capitalize on the anti-Semitic, anti-Negro, anti-Catholic, and anti-alien prejudices which Watson's rantings aroused. And so the fiery cross which flared atop Stone Mountain in 1915 was ignited not so much by Simmons as by Watson. And it was not only rededicated to the Klan's original creed of white supremacy, but also to the new purposes of anti-Semitism, anti-Catholicism, and anti-alienism.

The reincarnated Klan made little headway until after World War I, when it engaged a publicity expert and went to work cashing in on war-born prejudices. Enticed by liberal commissions, the kleagles launched vigorous membership drives which soon made the Klan a force to be reckoned with throughout America. According to Simmons, "In 1922 our average increase in membership was 3,500 daily and we took in 1,200,000 members. Our daily income was $45,000 from members and sale of paraphernalia." At its peak, in the twenties, the Klan claimed 5,100,000 members.

The Klan's political influence kept pace with its numerical growth. In 1923 it was reported to be in control of Texas, Arkansas, Oklahoma, Indiana, and Oregon, in addition to exercising broad political power in other states. In 1924 it elected the governors of Kansas and Indiana and senators in Oklahoma and Colorado.

Needless to say, acts of violence committed by Klansmen also kept pace with the organization's growth. During the single year ending in October of 1921 the Klan, according to a tabulation by the New York *World,* was guilty of four killings, one mutilation, one branding with acid, forty-one floggings, twenty-seven tar-and-feather parties, five kidnapings, forty-three warnings to leave town, fourteen towns warned by posters, sixteen parades carrying intimidatory placards. The climax came when Louisiana Klansmen laid low some victims with a steam roller.

Naturally, national sentiment for a congressional investigation of the Klan developed. Certain Southern congressmen countered with threats that they would call for investigations of all secret societies—particularly the National Association for the Advancement of Colored People and the Catholic Knights of Columbus.

Nevertheless, a congressional committee to make a preliminary investigation of the Klan was formed in 1921. For the most part it served merely as a sounding board for testimony as to the "high character and public repute" of the Klan's leaders. Significantly, the book *KKK* reports that ". . . a large number of Congressmen were then and now are members of the Invisible Empire."

The congressional investigation did throw light on the Klan's finances. C. Anderson Wright, a former kleagle, testified that the Klan had taken in $1,250,000 since its reincarnation. It was also brought out that "the Klan" had purchased a $25,000 home and "presented it to the Imperial Wizard." Still further testimony exposed the handsome rake-off which the Klan hierarchy made on initiation fees, regalia, and so forth. The book *KKK* frankly admits that "Klan officials ostensibly had regular salaries but it is alleged they took what profits they pleased."

Although the Klan's leaders pretended that the congressional investigation brought them only free publicity and new members, in reality the Invisible Empire lost many millions of its "citizens" as a result of the exposé of the Klan's racketeering.

Although Imperial Wizards are elected for life, a schism developed within the Klan over the issue of "whether or not Simmons should retire." Leader of the rebellious Klansmen was Dr. Hiram Wesley Evans, a Dallas, Texas, dentist. When the insurgents gained sufficient strength to present their demands it was discovered, says *KKK,* "that Simmons personally owned the copyright to everything Klannish that could be copyrighted —name, ritual, constitution, charter, et cetera. So it was necessary to *buy Simmons out.* This was done, Simmons being paid $140,000 cash for his copyrights, after which Simmons 'resigned' and Evans was elected Imperial Wizard in 1932. It was reported that an unknown intermediary manipulated the 'deal,' and that the intermediary received from Simmons $40,000 'commission' for the sale." This must have been approximately correct, as Simmons later admitted receiving $90,000 himself.

The New Deal had no sooner revealed itself to favor a greater measure of economic and racial democracy than the Southern slavocracy instructed the Klan to ride against this new threat to its lecherous existence. And when the CIO announced in 1935 that it was coming South to organize the unorganized— whites and blacks in the same unions—the KKK replied, "We shall fight horror with horror!"

In 1934 there was the case of Frank Norman. He and his wife

were trying to help the citrus workers around Lakeland, Florida, to form a union. One night a car stopped at the Norman home; in it were five men, including a deputy sheriff from an adjoining county. Norman was asked to go with them to that county "to identify the body of a Negro." He entered the car; it drove away —and Frank Norman hasn't been seen or heard from since. Evidence purportedly linking Klan kleagle Fred Bass to the disappearance of Norman was twice presented to a grand jury, but the jury did not return an indictment. Bass has since been claimed by death.

The following year, in 1935, came the mutilation and murder of Joseph Shoemaker at Tampa, Florida. He was the Florida leader of the Workers Alliance, the Depression-born union of WPA workers and unemployed. This was bad enough in the eyes of the Klan, but Shoemaker proceeded to organize Tampa's working folk into an independent political party, the Modern Democrats, whose aim was to rid the city of its notoriously corrupt political machine.

On the eve of the city's election, Shoemaker, Dr. Samuel Rogers, Eugene Poulnot, and several other leaders of the Modern Democrats were arrested without warrants during a meeting in a private home and taken to police headquarters "for questioning about suspected communist activities." No evidence of such activity was found, and the men were released. But as they stepped from the police station, Shoemaker, Rogers, and Poulnot were kidnaped by masked men and driven to an isolated spot where they were stripped, severely beaten, tarred-and-feathered, and ordered to leave town. Shoemaker, who was also castrated and forced to sit in a bucket of hot tar, died in a Tampa hospital after nine days of agony.

Rogers and Poulnot said they recognized certain policemen among their abductors, and in a deathbed statement Shoemaker said the same thing. Eight Tampa policemen were suspended by Mayor R. E. Chancey "for raiding a private home without a warrant." Police Chief R. T. Tittsworth said that "no police officer was involved in the abduction," but soon afterward he resigned "in order to devote all his time to the Shoemaker case."

Eleven men were finally indicted, including six policemen,

several special officers, and a fireman. When it was charged that some of them were members of the Klan, George J. Garcia, Grand Dragon of the Florida realm, said, "The Tampa klavern could not take such an unusual action as a flogging without consulting me." He admitted knowing two of the men, but insisted that he did not know whether they were Klansmen.

Of the last two men arrested, the arresting sheriff said, "These two men are members of the Klan, and Gillam told me he was once a state officer of the Klan." The Tampa *Tribune* reported that they "were among the hundreds of men recruited throughout South Florida, hauled into Tampa, and armed with shotguns, pistols, hoe handles, and other weapons for the city election. Spivey testified that it was known that men were wanted in Tampa on Election Day, and that seven or eight autoloads left Orlando. He said he and Gillam rode all day in a police car, answering radio calls. He was paid ten dollars that night, and his hotel bill was also paid."

After two years of court procedure, all of the indicted men were acquitted.

The next big anti-union job undertaken by the Klan was to unleash terrorism against the CIO's Textile Workers Organizing Committee and Steel Workers Organizing Committee. During 1937 this drive led the Klan to build up its largest membership in fifteen years. In that year the Klan posted hundreds of intimidatory placards around the textile mills of South Carolina. Fiery crosses were planted in front of the homes and meeting halls of the union-minded throughout the South, and there were numerous floggings.

In August of 1938 the East Point (Atlanta suburb) Klan flogged several union employees of the Scottsdale Mills (controlled by the Georgia Savings Bank & Trust Company). "We're going to break up these damn unions!" the Klansmen told one of those flogged, Pierce Toney, organizer for the CIO textile workers.

In its campaign against unions, the New Deal, Negroes, Catholics, Jews, and aliens, the Klan naturally resorted to Red-baiting. In a violently worded pamphlet, *Communism Rampant,*

Imperial Wizard Evans outdid even the Axis signatories of the anti-Comintern pact in going into hysterics over the "menace of communism." He concluded:

> There are millions who have solemnly sworn to defend and protect our Constitution and Government. The time has come for them to fulfill their secret promises. We prepared the Klan for the hour that is now here. We shall seek and find those who have sworn to serve, and shoulder to shoulder we will ride to defend constituted authority against civil strife and rebellion.

Needless to say, publication of this militant declaration attracted the keen interest of other fascist groups in America, whose whitest hopes were based on anti-Negro agitation. The book *KKK* itself admits that "Henry D. Allen, onetime Silver Shirt leader, and a secret agent of the mysterious Mrs. Leslie Fry, alias Paquita Louise de Shishmareff, testified before the Dies Committee that Mrs. Fry sent him to Atlanta to buy the Klan, and Fry offered Dr. Evans $75,000 for the Klan."

KKK might have added that "Mrs. Fry" was the wife of a czarist officer; she came to America about 1936 and devoted herself to furthering a Nazi plot for an American putsch engineered by Baron von Killinger, the Nazi consul general at San Francisco. When the scheme failed she evaded the FBI and slipped back into Germany, but was captured in 1942 while trying to re-enter the United States aboard the S.S. *Drottningholm,* which was bringing home American diplomats and newsmen.

If Klan reports are to be believed, $75,000 was a ridiculously low price for Nazi agents to offer for a money-making concern like the Klan, for which Evans' sponsors had put up a reported $140,000, and which was soon (1939) to be sold again for a reported $220,000. However, it is extremely doubtful that Nazi agents could have purchased the Klan at any price. True, the Klan was actively engaged in furthering the Nazi program of anti-unionism, anti-Rooseveltism, anti-Semitism, anti-Catholicism, anti-Negroism, anti-alienism, anti-communism, and isolationism; but to be most effective in all this the Klan had to do it in the name of Americanism. The incongruity of such a self-

styled "American-American" organization as the Klan selling out
to German Nazis would have killed it instantly. Wizard Evans
did, however, go so far as to discuss with Fritz Kuhn the possibility of a Klan-Bund merger.

"Dr. Evans for some time was active in national politics," the
book *KKK* also reports, "at one time having a Klan headquarters in Washington, D.C. In the 1936 campaign for governor of Georgia he was the right hand of Governor E. D. Rivers,
who was re-elected and who is reputed to be high in Klan favor
and influence." As a matter of fact, Rivers has been a paid lec-
turer for the Klan, and Evans served on his staff while he was
governor.

"Dr. Evans was rewarded for his assistance to Governor Rivers
by being allowed to sell the Georgia State Highway Board a
large amount of paving material, out of which he cleaned up a
large sum, and which was a subject of inquiry before a Fulton
County Grand Jury," *KKK* continues. "Former Imperial Wizard
Evans is scheduled to go on trial in the Northern Georgia U. S.
District Court in 1941, charged with using the mails with intent
to defraud. He has already paid a fine of $15,000 in this Federal
court in one case."

In the case referred to, Evans was fined $15,000, the Emulsi-
fied Asphalt Refining Company of Charleston was fined $4,000,
the Shell Oil Company of St. Louis $5,000, and the American
Bitumuls Company of San Francisco $6,000, for forming a
"competition-restraining association" through which they sold
the state of Georgia asphalt at a price $90,000 in excess of open
competitive quotations (these fines would seem to have left someone an excess profit of $60,000).

When the additional indictments of Evans, Rivers, and others
for using the mails to defraud came up, District Attorney Neil
Andrews said, "After studying these cases it was decided that
the best thing to do was to dismiss them."

This did not, however, put an end to the charges and convictions against Evans. In January of 1942 he was convicted of
"conniving" with a Georgia official (under Rivers's administration) in a conspiracy to make an excess profit of approximately
$11,000 on a state printing job. Indicted with him were Wyly

Tucker, Klansman and head salesman of the (Jesse) Williams Printing Company of Atlanta, and Williams himself. The Williams Printing Company, incidentally, published the Klan's reprint of *The International Jew*, which appeared in Henry Ford's Dearborn *Independent* and was also reprinted in Germany by the Nazi World Service and in Britain by the Imperial Fascist League. It was also in 1942 that a grand jury sitting in Atlanta uncovered one of the most bizarre stories of Ku-Kluxery-in-politics ever brought to light. On Bear Creek, near the Chattahoochee River in the southern part of Fulton County, an artificial lake fourteen feet deep had been created, and in the center of the lake a large fortresslike clubhouse had been built on stilts in 1939. The clubhouse was connected with the shore by a precarious catwalk, and six padlocks barred the way to the front door. Around the entire site an electrified fence had been built (meter readers were admitted by arrangement only; the first bill was $52). Inside the well-equipped retreat were two bedrooms, which could be locked and unlocked from the inside only.

The contracts for all this construction had been let by Imperial Wizard Evans, and he also paid the caretaker. The electricity meter had been installed by D. B. Blalock, a wealthy road-machinery dealer, who also paid the electricity bills. However, there was no deed to the land on file at superior court. All this took place during the administration of Governor Rivers, and it was testified that Rivers, Evans, Blalock, and W. Fred Scott (chairman of the state licensing board for contractors and a colonel on Rivers's staff) met frequently in this Berchtesgaden-like retreat for steak suppers, et cetera.

When Rivers was brought to trial in November of 1942 the judge declared a mistrial, and the following month five indictments against three other persons associated with his administration for using the mails to defraud were nol-prossed by the government without comment.

"Talk in the corridors of the Capitol indicates that an insurgent wing of the Ku Klux Klan plans a revival of that organization with new blood and new purposes," the Washington Merry-Go-Round reported in 1939. This proved to be true. Klan membership and influence had declined rapidly under Evans, particularly after his confab with Bundsfuehrer Fritz Kuhn in 1937, and the notoriety incumbent upon Evans's prosecution for fraud had not helped matters.

As has been mentioned, it is said that this change of Wizards cost someone $220,000. Evans's successor was James A. Colescott, an ex-veterinarian of Terre Haute, Indiana. He has a record of seventeen years as a Klansman, nine of which were spent as Grand Dragon of the realm with headquarters in Ohio. Upon his inauguration, Colescott bellowed: "My administration will be an administration of action!"

By that he evidently meant promotional action, for he promptly launched an intensive and extensive membership drive. Numerous parades were held, and full-page advertisements were inserted in newspapers across the country, calling upon old and new Klansmen to rally around the fiery cross.

Colescott's Wizardry brought to Ku-Kluxery certain changes in techniques and emphases, but nothing more fundamental. Under Evans's program of violent opposition to "Communism and the CIO," the Kluxers effected something of a rapprochement with their old enemies, the Catholics. But Colescott had no sooner sounded off than Bishop O'Hara of the Atlanta Catholic Diocese took the new Wizard to task for his announcement that the Klan would "promote the interest of the native-born, white, Protestant, Gentile population of America." Bishop O'Hara pointed out that the Klan was distributing propaganda literature to this effect, and that "the KKK has practically proclaimed through its newly elected head that there is no room in Georgia or America for Catholics."

However, Colescott was soon to prove himself anxious to soft-pedal, or at least disguise, some of the Klan's traditional methods of intimidating minority groups. For example, the following story appeared in the Miami *Herald* not many weeks after Bishop O'Hara's rebuttal:

Klan's Methods of Intimidation Are Abandoned
New Imperial Wizard Says He Will Not Tolerate Such
Practices
J. A. Colescott, new imperial wizard of the KKK, said to-

day he did not "intend to tolerate" such methods of intimidation as the burning of fiery crosses and parades of white-robed figures through negro sections that occurred before a city election here last fall.

"There are more intelligent American ways to handle such problems," Colescott said. "I would rather see the Klan disbanded than see it continue its old policy of anti-Semitism, anti-Catholicism, or anti-alienism. We have not compromised the basic creed of the Klan, however. We have not added to or taken away any of our aims."

In pursuance of his purpose of convincing the public that the Klan is an educational rather than a terroristic society, Colescott in 1940 issued an edict banning the use of a mask or visor by any Klansman either in public or private, limiting the use of the fiery cross to ritual ceremonies, and forbidding public parades or demonstrations by Klansmen without the prior consent of the Klan's high command, the public authorities, and the owner of the property where the affair is to be staged.

However, the record does not speak at all well of Colescott's promise that the Klan would stop intimidating Negroes, Catholics, Jews, and aliens. It is significant that back in 1936, when Colescott was merely a Grand Dragon, he had informed the press, "Right now we're concentrating on obtaining passage of legislation to drive 3,500,000 unnaturalized foreigners from the United States to better our employment conditions."

Without attempting to be exhaustive, here are but a few of the innumerable instances of Klan intimidation which have occurred *since* Colescott became Imperial Wizard:

June 1939, California—Grand Dragon Snelson issued an instructive, "A poll is to be taken of all members belonging to rifle and trap-shooting teams, National Guard units, ROTC, and those willing to form shooting clubs. Please forward to State headquarters, using numbers instead of names." The instructive also said that the Exalted Cyclops had collected "maps of all territories in your klanton," and taken polls of available automobiles.

August 7, 1939, Mattituck, N. Y.—Klansmen displayed a ten-foot fiery cross with signs reading: "The Jews Are Invading Mattituck. No Jews Wanted Here. K.K.K."

Jersey City, 1939—The Klan burned five crosses in the vicinity of Catholic churches, distributed leaflets attacking "Papism and Romanism."

October 3, 1939, Greenville, S. C.—Fred. V. Johnson, Grand Klokard, announced in the Greenville *News:*

> Our fathers and grandfathers, Klansmen of old, saved this State from negro rule and Northern political domination during Reconstruction days. . . . Almost the same influences which caused the trouble 70 years ago are again at work in our country. These influences have set in motion forces which threaten South Carolina. Only the Knights of the Ku Klux Klan can and will curb these forces. Preserve white supremacy in South Carolina! Ride on, Klansmen, ride on! The order prohibiting you from appearing in public in your robes is hereby rescinded.

Thereafter began a reign of Klan terror during which a number of Negroes who had registered to vote were run out of town. A Negro veteran of World War I, named Neely, was seized by the Klan, questioned, disrobed, and forced to walk naked to the home of a white attorney whose wife was alone; she gave him a pair of trousers and called a taxi to take him home. The home of William Brier, local president of the National Association for the Advancement of Colored People, was ransacked by the Klan, and the NAACP secretary, William Anderson, was questioned by the Klan, arrested thrice, and jailed for thirty days and fined $100 for allegedly telephoning a white girl and asking her for a date (this "atrocity" story was also prevalent in the South during the War for the Four Freedoms). An NYA camp for Negro youth was invaded by the Klan, which left a sign saying, "Niggers, your place is in the cotton patch!"

February 1940, Rosedale, N. J.—Twenty hooded Klansmen burned a thirty-foot cross outside a Jewish synagogue and distributed leaflets saying, "All Jews are communists or are communistic." One Klansman explained that the Jews "had been too damned fresh and too darned powerful in New Jersey politics." Another added, "If this doesn't shut the Jews up, we'll cut a few throats and see what happens." Two of the Klansmen were arrested for "disorderly conduct." The Rev. A. M. Young,

Grand Dragon, said there would be a "riot" if the Klansmen were convicted.

May 1941, Atlanta—The Klan's Imperial Kloncilium decided to raise a $1,000,000 "Americanization" fund and attacked the USO as being dominated by Catholics and Jews. Said *The Fiery Cross:* "In view of the effort by official sources to cram the Catholic doctrine down the throats of Americans in camp, it is time for the Ku Klux Klan to distribute real American literature into every Army and Navy camp in the land."

August 1941, Southern California—James Harvey, state Klan leader, said, "Someone, some organization must be ready to take over the country when it finds itself in chaos, and we are best equipped to do it. . . . Here in Southern California is a fertile field for the Klan to grow. We must concentrate on the motion-picture industry which is controlled by the Jews and the Catholics. . . . On the surface the USO is good, but who is running it? The Jews and the Catholics. . . . The Catholics are backing the Axis and the Jews are backing England, Soviet Russia, and the United States. We don't want any part of it."

August 19, 1941, Miami—The John B. Gordon Klan, 200 strong, planted four fiery crosses on the site of a projected housing project for Negroes, while a Kluxer with an amplifier said, "Yes sir, ladies and gentlemen, it's the KKK. We are here to keep niggers out of your town. . . . You don't have to put up with things the way they have over at Miami Beach where they sleep with niggers. . . . When the law fails you, call on us!"

October 8, 1941, Pittsburgh—Colescott said that two of the Klan's leaders—one in New York and one in the West—wanted to support Hitler. He added: "Now is not the time to say anything about religious groups . . . but after the war we will have plenty to say about them!"

October 10, 1941, Pittsburgh—Colescott addressed the Klan, alias the Keystone Patriotic Society, alias the Mantle Club. "The Klan's chief enemies," he said, "are Jews, Negroes, and newspapermen. . . . Italian-Americans, German-Americans, Russian-Americans, and Jewish-Americans will either become full-fledged Americans or they will be driven out of the country!"

After this meeting, Colescott, Grand Dragon Samuel G.

Stauch, Walter H. Klinzing, Frank S. Fite, and John V. Waite were indicted for soliciting funds without registering with the department of welfare, and for conspiracy "to foment hate and strife." State Police Sergeant Willard Schauer testified that he had attended the meeting and heard Colescott "urge reorganization of the Klan as a militant, fighting, Protestant, white, native-born group of Americans" and mention "fighting the Jews, the Negroes, and Catholics."

"He [Colescott] went into the subject of the movie industry," continued Sergeant Schauer, "and said that the names of the Senate Committee investigating the industry would be found to be similar to if not the same as former Klansmen." The Senate Committee referred to "investigated" the motion-picture industry in 1941 for producing anti-Nazi films; it was headed by Senator Gerald P. Nye, Senator Burton K. Wheeler, and Senator D. Worth Clark. In this connection it should be recalled that Count Anastase Andreivitch Vonsiatskoy-Vonsiatsky, fuehrer of the All-Russian National-Socialist (fascist) Labor party in America (later jailed for espionage in connection with Nazi agent Gerhard Wilhelm Kunze), said to John Roy Carlson (author of the book *Under Cover*) just a few months before Colescott's talk: "That America First Committee does good work. . . . It is all very, very good education for nationalism. In America you will have it. It is must when Hitler wins. Your Wheeler, Nye, and your D. Worth Clark will save your America for you Americans."

KKK, published in 1941: "At present it may be stated with authority that Klansmen everywhere are in a vast majority opposed to the Roosevelt Administration. This is caused by the fact that many, very many, of the Washington administrative offices, some of great importance, are filled by Jews."

1941, Atlanta—The Klan reprinted *The International Jew.*

1942—Colescott wrote Georgia's Grand Dragon Samuel Green enclosing Waldo Frank's article in the *Saturday Evening Post* criticizing Jews, with the comment, "I call your attention to the similarity in this article with the statement made by me in the foreword of *The International Jew.*"

August 1942—The Klan reprinted an editorial from the

Gadsden (Ala.) *Times,* based on the book *Washington Is Like That* by W. M. Kiplinger (publisher of a reactionary news letter for businessmen), which observed that the Roosevelts were promoting a sympathetic attitude toward Negroes. The editorial concluded that the effect of such an attitude would be to "mongrelize" the South, and that "the Klan had saved the social order in 1866" and was prepared to do so again.

August 1943, Beaufort, S. C.—The *Gazette* carried a full-page advertisement of a Klansman astride a horse, reading: "Ku Klux Klan Rides Again—There Is Work To Do!" It called upon white men to "Wake up and stop something brewing here . . . Don't be cold-footed all the time! Have a little guts and fighting blood in your veins! We are still the old red-blooded Southerners ready to protect our women and children . . . God give us men to protect the innocent women of this country!"

December 1943, Porterdale, Ga.—A Klan klonklave in this textile-mill town featured a turkey dinner served by the Parent-Teachers Association. The mayor acted as master of ceremonies, and ex-Governor Eugene Talmadge, his bodyguard, burly Johnny Goodwin (fuehrer of Vigilantes, Inc.), ex-Fish and Game Commissioner Zack Cravey, and State Treasurer George Hamilton were guests of honor. Talmadge's speech was the big event; he inveighed against the FEPC, scored reciprocal trade, and ranted against the admission of Jewish and Catholic refugees from Nazi Europe. His conclusion: "Christian Democracy and White Supremacy are the greatest things which should emerge from this terrible catastrophe!"

January 1945, Atlanta—Dr. Samuel Green told Stanley High of the *Reader's Digest* that as medical examiner for Selective Service in the second ward he had found a disproportionate number of Jews seeking deferment.

May 1945, Atlanta—Dr. Green charged that Attorney General Francis Biddle, being a Catholic, had appointed a Catholic priest, two Jews, and two Communists to rule upon what literature could be circulated during the war.

Despite all the foregoing and much more besides, and despite his reference in 1939 to the Klan's "old policy" anti-minorities, Colescott wrote me on September 23, 1943: ". . . the Ku Klux

Klan has not been anti-Semitic, anti-Negro, anti-Catholic, nor anti-alien. . . . The Klan itself is strictly pro-American. You may view some of the literature sent you as anti material. We do protest the shortcoming of some minorities and point out their inability to completely assimilate Americanism. This we don't view as being anti."

The book *KKK*, written with Colescott's co-operation, does its bit to portray the Imperial Wizard as being non-anti. "Colescott doesn't hate negroes," the volume solemnly avers. "He even has a negro maid take care of his daughter when he is away organizing the Klan."

Perhaps the best way to sum up the evidence is to cite the reaction of an Atlanta Klansman to whom I showed the Wizard's letter saying the Klan is not anti anything: "It don't make one damn bit of difference what he nor nobody else says about it. Every man who joins the Ku Klux does it 'cause he considers it sumpum another to kill niggers!" And this same sort of inspired hatred—directed against Catholics, Jews, and aliens—is what motivates the Klan in other parts of the country.

"The Klan has no fight with any labor union," the Imperial Wizard informed me on January 21, 1944. But an examination of the record reveals that this assertion has no more validity than his denial that the Klan is opposed to racial and religious minorities. Under Colescott there has been, however, a change in the Klan's anti-union technique. To some extent the flogging, kidnaping, and murder of union men which was rampant during Evans' regime has been discouraged by Colescott in favor of more subtle forms of intimidation, plus a new Klan policy of "boring from within" the unions.

In an editorial in *The Fiery Cross* shortly after he became Wizard, Colescott said, "I call upon those affiliated with labor organizations to organize themselves in groups and take over active leadership . . ." In addition, the following letter was sent out:

MY FAITHFUL KLANSPEOPLE:
    . . . each exalted cyclops shall contact immediately all members of our organization holding membership in units of the

Workers Alliance, CIO, and the AFL. Each group so represented with membership in the local unit shall be instructed to . . . present themselves as a solid block within their labor organization unit for the purpose of sponsoring . . . the name of a member of their labor organization whose Americanism is beyond question as president and to every other office within the labor unit . . .

Faithfully yours,
In the sacred, unfailing bond,
(signed)
J. A. COLESCOTT

The effect of this new Klan policy of subverting the unions became manifest in the race-hate strike at the Packard plant which helped precipitate the disastrous Detroit race riot, the Philadelphia Transit strike, and many other wartime work stoppages brought on by Klansmen through the injection of race prejudice.

There has also been under Colescott a continuation of anti-union violence, to wit:

1939, Anderson, S. C.—"They said they were beating me because I didn't give my wife enough money and because I beat my five-year-old boy; but I have never been married and have no children," said one of several union men flogged by Klansmen.

December 6, 1939, Aberdeen, Wash.—Klansmen and members of the so-called "Better Business Builders" sped in autos through the streets, stoning and breaking windows at the AFL Central Labor Council and CIO headquarters.

May 1941, Detroit—"I am contacting the employers, through the Chamber of Commerce and Employers Association, and influencing them to see that it is to their advantage to give unemployed Klan members the preference during the layoff in the auto industry," said A. H., reporting to the Detroit Klan. He and a Pontiac company agent attended the 1941 Imperial Kloncilium held in Atlanta.

March 31, 1942, Holt, Ala.—In a whirlwind climax to weeks of flogging and terror, the Klan planted fiery crosses in front of the CIO Steelworkers Organizing Committee hall and in front of the union leader's home, on the eve of an NLRB election at the Tennessee Coal, Iron & Railroad Company (a U. S. Steel subsidiary).

July–August 1942—Colescott said in *The Fiery Cross* that the Klan was promoting "100 per cent Americanism . . . in CIO unions throughout the country, as well as in unions of the AFL."

1942, Decatur, Ga.—Klansmen drove menacingly around a CIO meeting hall and said, "We've given you your last warning; we mean for you to get out and stay out!"

September 15, 1943, Apopka, Fla.—"Hey, you nigger, we've got your union button and know you're a CIO member!" yelled one of the Klansmen in the parade of masked men who drove through the Negro section on the eve of an NLRB election at the Phillips Citrus Packing House. A number of soldiers (from the North) stopped several carloads of Klansmen and commanded them to "Take those damned hoods off! You ought to be saving that gasoline for war use!" When I queried Colescott about this parade, he replied, "If such a parade were held, it was no doubt for the purpose of getting new members and creating interest in the Klan."

December 20, 1942, Orlando, Fla.—Fred Bass, Florida kleagle, called at the newly opened office of the CIO Citrus Workers Union, introduced himself as "a boilermaker from New York," and inspected the premises thoroughly. He left with the observation that maybe they would succeed—and maybe they wouldn't.

January 30, 1943, Orlando, Fla.—The Klan broadcast a mobilization "call for all Klansmen" over the local radio.

January 31, 1943, Orlando, Fla.—The Klan inserted in the Orlando *Sentinel-Star* a "help-wanted" ad for "4,000 of the 8,000 Klansmen from Orange, Seminole, and Osceola counties— there is work to do." (Similar notices appeared in newspapers in various parts of the country.)

Shortly after the Klan broadcast and advertisement, an NLRB election was scheduled at the Fosgate Citrus Packing Plant. The day before the election, Klansmen, watched over by kleagle Fred Bass, distributed leaflets to workers at the company gates, quoting Eddie Rickenbacker, smearing unionism, and winding up "The Ku Klux Klan Is Watching You!" I asked Colescott if such intimidatory advertisements and leaflets were not at variance with his professed opposition to intimidation, and he replied: "I not only approve of the ad appearing in the Orlando *Sentinel* and the quotations from Rickenbacker, but I personally assisted in its preparation."

January 15, 1944, Orlando, Fla.—With a CIO Citrus Workers Union contract due to expire fifteen days later, the Klan sent one hundred of its robes to the American Laundry, where CIO workers were also employed.

February 17, 1944—Colescott told the Colorado *Citizen* that he planned to conduct a "unity meeting" with Tom Watson, Florida attorney general who sponsored the "Christian American" amendment banning union security in that state, and who is also given to anti-Semitism and the championing of white supremacy.

So much for the Klan's continuing anti-unionism, direct and indirect, subtle and not-so-subtle. As Ralph McGill, editor of the Atlanta *Constitution,* recently said: "The KKK may protest that it now is a reformed organization, but if you could see one of their rituals or sit in on a klavern meeting you would find the same old Klan . . ."

The fascistic inclinations of the Klan—which were clearly manifest during Evans's regime—became even more apparent after Colescott took over. Most damning was the "monster anti-war, pro-American mass meeting" jointly sponsored by the Klan and the Bund at Camp Nordland, N. J., on August 18, 1940. The Kluxers had a field day, burning a forty-foot fiery cross and denouncing (among other things) "Romanism" and "dumb ring-kissers."

August Klapprott, acting as Bundsfuehrer due to the arrest of Fritz Kuhn, informed the assemblage that, "When Arthur Bell, your Grand Giant, and Mr. [James Edward] Smythe asked us about using Camp Nordland for this patriotic meeting, we decided to let them have it because of the common bond between us. The principles of the Bund and the principles of the Klan are the same." Klapprott is prominent among the thirty-odd persons indicted for sedition on October 26, 1943, and again on January 3, 1944, by federal grand juries.

James Edward Smythe also addressed the Klan-Bund rally,

saying, "Fritz Kuhn and I have tried for three long years to bring about a meeting like this. Fritz is not in our midst today, God bless him! His only crime was in trying to bring friendship between the United States and German dominion." Smythe—who was leader of the so-called Protestant War Veterans of America, a supporter of Father Coughlin's *Social Justice,* a collaborator with Joe McWilliams's Christian Mobilizers and John Cassidy's Christian Front, and a contributor to the Bund's *Weckruf und Beobachter*—was also doubly indicted for sedition and conspiracy to establish a fascist government in America.

The book *KKK* represents another link between the Klan and other native fascist groups. In his foreword the author, Colonel C. Winfield Jones (no relation to Attorney Winfield Jones, also of Atlanta), says, "Once I had gained the confidence of the Imperial Wizard [Colescott] and the high officials they frankly and sincerely laid everything before me concerning the Order." *KKK* was published by The Tocsin Publishers of New York City, formed by Colonel E. N. Sanctuary, twice brought under indictment for sedition. The author thanks him "for kind and efficient assistance in publishing this book, in preparing the Mss. for publication, and in assisting in reading proofs and other matters connected with the work."

The mercenary motives which inspire the dime-a-dozen fuehrers were revealed in this case by the following letter from Jones to Sanctuary:

> I delayed answering until today so I could see Mr. Colescott again. He has agreed to take 500 of the first-edition books and send them to as many heads of the different Klans, with strong and urgent letters asking them to order and pay for as many books as possible. He intends to tell the members that this book is the only book on their organization ever written that is worth buying and having—in other words, he is back of it full strength. In New York, New Jersey and continuous territory there are more than 10,000 Klansmen. We ought to sell from 50,000 to 100,000 of these books alone through the Klan campaign.
>
> I have made him a price of $1.40 net per copy, giving the Klan a profit of 60 cents with which he expressed himself as satisfied. As we can probably get these books for not more than 40 cents per copy, as soon as we get going there is $1.00 net

per copy for us—a pretty handsome sum from this source alone.

On August 2, 1943 (one month before Sanctuary was indicted), Colescott wrote me, "I am sending under separate cover certain information which will give you an excellent picture of our background and activity." One of the things he sent was the book *KKK,* published by Sanctuary.

Carlson, in his book *Under Cover,* tells of visiting Sanctuary in 1941 shortly after *KKK* was published: "I expressed surprise at Sanctuary's friendship with the Klan. 'They are 100 per cent American,' he explained. And when I asked how he had met Colonel Jones, Sanctuary replied: 'General Moseley put me in touch with him.' "

This was the retired Major General George Van Horn Moseley of Atlanta, who was invited to speak at a "Pro-American Mass Meeting" held at the New York Hotel Commodore under the sponsorship of some fifty "superpatriots." The plot was the brain child of Baron von Killinger, German consul general and Nazi agent at San Francisco. The baron's blueprint for an American putsch called for a general staff of thirteen men: "three Germans (Nazi sympathy), three white Russians (anti-Soviet sympathy), three Italians (fascist sympathy), four Americans (Republican sympathy). All native-born or naturalized." And, he went on, "In each area we must study the composition of the population about us and agitate accordingly."

No doubt Moseley was chosen because of his public proposals that Jewish refugees fleeing to this country from the Nazi terror should be sterilized, and because of such statements as this, which he made in an interview by the Atlanta *Journal* in 1940:

> Democracy, hell! It's nothing but Communism. My motto is "Restore the Republic." A democracy pulls everything and everyone down to the level of an average and that makes it Communistic. . . . We don't want the mob rule of democracy.

One of those who co-operated with Nazi agent Killinger was George E. Deatherage of St. Albans, West Virginia. A member of the Klan, Deatherage also formed the Knights of the White Camellia and the American Nationalist Confederation which eventually embraced seventy-two such outfits. He distributed vast quantities of propaganda, including Hitler's speeches and material from the Nazi World Service. Tarheel Fuehrer Robert Reynolds also presented him with a sack of his speeches for distribution. Adapting his Ku-Kluxery to Nazism, Deatherage sent out detailed instructions to "Christian Leaders" on how to prepare and display fiery swastikas. He, too, was doubly indicted for sedition.

When the Klan joined with certain Atlanta organizations to sponsor an address by Martin Dies (then chairman of the House Committee to Investigate Un-American Activities), Colescott and other Klan leaders occupied prominent seats on the stage. "How faithfully he followed the doctrine which the Klan has been laying down for the past twenty years," Colescott observed after Dies had spoken. "One needs but to look back through the files of the Klan's publications to find repeated ten thousand times the same warnings which Mr. Dies sounded. His program, which unquestionably is the program of all real Americans today, so closely parallels the program of the Klan that there is no distinguishable difference between them."

In this connection it is interesting to note that Parker Sage, leader of the notorious National Workers League which reprinted vast quantities of Klan and Bund propaganda and played a large part in bringing on the Detroit race riot, wrote the author of *Under Cover:* "Hell, we found out Dies was or is a Klansman. *We* have nothing to fear from him. The FBI have never bothered us and we never concern ourselves about them." Eventually, however, Sage was twice brought under indictment for sedition, and also for inciting to riot at the Detroit Sojourner Truth Defense Housing Project for Negroes in 1942.

Still another Klan-Bund link uncovered by the author of *Under Cover* was James Banahan, alias Mike Strahinsky, alias Hermann Schmidt, leader of the Iron Guard, alias the American Phalanx, whose watchword was "Faith, Hope, and Terror!" Banahan told his Nazi-saluting outfit: "The Iron Guard was financed with German money. . . . The Phalanx is now affiliated with the Ku Klux Klan. We are also officially connected with the Bund. . . . In time of war we are all saboteurs. We'll blow the hell out of this country!" Inexplicably, Banahan was not indicted along with the rest.

William H. Sahli, California kleagle, appeared as a character witness for Baron Frederick Van Meter, charged by the American Legion with being a Bundsman, before the State Committee Investigating Un-American Activities, October 18, 1941. Sahli said both he and Van Meter had been members of America First. Asked whether the Klan approved of violence, he replied, "Positively not! Manpower where manpower is necessary, but not violence." Declaring he was "sick and tired" of "all the pussy-footing around" by other "Americanism" groups, Sahli smacked the table with his fist and told the legislative committee, "I could take on your whole bunch one at a time! When I see things not going according to Hoyle, I smack 'em down!" Then he handed out cards reading:

America—Love It or Leave It!
Act American; Be American; Think American;
Talk American; the Ku Klux Klan Is American!

Among the other arch-reactionaries who have been in one way or another associated with the Klan are William Gregg Blanchard, Jr., of Miami, leader of the white-supremacy, anti-Semitic "White Front," who spent most of the war in an army detention camp (Blanchard's *Nation & Race* praised the Klan to the skies); Court Asher, who claims to have been a member of the Klan (he publishes *X-Ray*, consorted with William Dudley Pelley, Parker Sage, et al., was indicted for sedition); David Baxter, author of *The Corporate State—A Practical Plan for American Nationalists,* and *Tactics,* a study course for fascist revolution, doubly indicted, placed the Klan high on his list of approved organizations; Harry Augustus Jung (no indictments, but included on the Nazi World Service approved list) directed the American Vigilant Intelligence Federation, shared offices with Gale S. Carter, Klan leader for Illinois, who was number 37 on Jung's list of "reliables"; and Donald Shea, director of the National Gentile League, who regarded Hitler as "one of the world's greatest and most merciful leaders," spoke for the Italian fascists, the Christian Mobilizers—and the Klan.

KINGFISH AND SMALL FRY

Many people have said that to a large extent the South is already under the heel of fascism. As Franklin D. Roosevelt said at Gainesville, Georgia, "When you come down to it, there is little difference between the feudal system and the fascist system. If you believe in the one, you lean to the other. With the overwhelming majority of the people of this State, I oppose feudalism."

But modern feudalism is not the only manifestation of fascism. Unfortunately, many Americans have been taught—often deliberately—to think of fascism as a disease confined to the Axis nations—and completely cured by the Allied victory. This misconception, if not speedily righted, might prove even more costly than America's original sin of failing to recognize and help stamp out Axis fascism the moment it appeared. We would do well, therefore, to clarify our conception of fascism as it has manifested itself both nationally and universally.

As O. John Rogge, special assistant to the U. S. Attorney General and prosecutor in the 1945 sedition trial, has said, "International fascism, though defeated in battle, is not dead. Fascism is not dead in England, nor is it dead in the United States . . . It is simply reconverting. But even in reconversion, American fascism has been unable to avoid falling into a readily recognizable pattern . . . Mere word substitution—such as 'Nationalist' for 'Fascist'—is a poor disguise."

It was Benito Mussolini who imposed the first modern system of fascism, and for that reason, if for no other, his definition of it should come first. *After* he had been installed in power by re-actionary monied interests (when he was no longer obliged to appeal for popular support with progressive-sounding slogans), Mussolini said:

> Fascism, which did not fear to call itself reactionary when many liberals of today were prone before the triumphant beast (democracy), has not today any impediment against declaring itself illiberal and anti-liberal. Fascism knows no idol, worships no faith; it has once passed, and, if needful, will turn to pass again over the more or less decomposed body of the Goddess of Liberty.

Hitler's German Nazism was based upon the same philosophy as Mussolini's Italian Fascism, but was given such Teutonic trim-mings as the Theory of the Master Race. *After* Hitler had been installed in power by reactionary monied interests, his Propa-ganda Minister, P. J. Goebbels, had this to say:

> We National Socialists have never maintained that we were representatives of a democratic viewpoint, but we have openly declared that we only made use of democratic means in order to gain power, and that after the seizure of power we would ruthlessly deny to our opponents all those means which they had granted to us during the time of our opposition.

This willingness on the part of Axis fascism to confess its anti-democratic nature was one of its most remarkable attributes.

But to get at the whole truth about fascism we must see it through anti-fascist eyes. Here first honors must go to the an-tithesis of fascism, which is communism—the Soviet-German non-aggression pact of 1940 notwithstanding (both Soviet and German sources later confirmed that each nation entered into that pact as a mutually distasteful but necessary expedient to gain time needed to prepare for the inevitable conflict between them). The 13th Plenum of the Executive Committee of the Communist International declared: "Fascism is the open terrorist dictatorship of the most reactionary, most chauvinist, and most imperialist elements of finance capital."

It is important to note what fascism is not, as well as what it is. Totalitarianism does not necessarily mean fascism. Distinctions between totalitarianisms must be made on the all-important basis of the ends to which they are employed. Italian-German-Japanese-Franco totalitarianism has been devoted to the fascistic purpose of enhancing the vested interests of a minority-exploiting class within the nation by all means, including imperialist military aggression.

In contradistinction, the totalitarianism of Soviet Russia is described as a "dictatorship of the proletariat" deemed essential to the socialization and ultimate communization of the country, but which is expected to wither away as internal and external opposition disappears; its function has been anti-fascist, anti-aggression, anti-imperialist, and anti-exploitation. Similarly, the wartime totalitarian techniques employed by the United States and Great Britain are not to be regarded as fascistic, but, on the contrary, as democratic weapons adopted to win the war against fascism as economically as possible. Thus it may be said that totalitarianism is of two kinds: majority and minority; democratic and fascistic; good and evil.

For a "Made in the U.S.A." description of fascism we can do no better than to cite the great anti-fascist, Henry Wallace: " 'Old-fashioned Americanism' is the last refuge of the fascists, but by 'old-fashioned Americanism' they do not mean what is implied by the term, but mean the situation that existed when great corporations rose to power economically and politically. The reason Mr. Roosevelt is so hated by many big businessmen is the fact that he stopped making Washington a way station on the road to Wall Street." Speaking of the future of the Democratic party, Wallace said he would fight to the last ditch to keep control of it out of the hands of "men and corporations who put money rights above human rights."

The late Heywood Broun, the noted American columnist, also knew fascism for what it is. "Fascism is a dictatorship from the extreme Right," he said, "or, to put it a little more closely into our local idiom, a government which is run by a small group of large industrialists and financial lords. . . . I think it is not unfair to say that any businessman in America, or public leader, who goes out to break unions is laying foundations for fascism."

Because the War Against Fascism taught most Americans to think of fascism in terms of such trappings as black shirts, swastikas, Sam Browne belts, goose steps, and Nazi salutes, the day of cheap imitations of those things in this country is probably over. For American fascists to use such badges of identification now would be to invite frustration. Fascism's only hope in America is to fill the prescription of its precursor, Kingfish Huey Long of Louisiana: that fascism appear in the guise of anti-fascism. Americans must therefore learn to distinguish between anti-fascism and fascism disguised as anti-fascism. The cloak is actually quite thin. It is safe to say that anyone who is given to racism, religious bigotry, anti-unionism, or plutocracy is potentially if not actually a fascist.

The peculiar characteristics and techniques thus far adopted by American fascists and their witting and unwitting fellow travelers are worthy of close scrutiny. Among the hypocrisies commonly practiced by American fascism are:

Instead of standing for statism, its cry is for "states' rights, home rule, the grass roots."

Instead of proclaiming its imperialism, it tries to hide behind slogans like "America First, Last, and Always."

Instead of confessing its unchristianity, it brandishes the cross of Christ in one hand while furiously waving the Stars and Stripes in the other.

Instead of endorsing totalitarianism, it calls for "Constitutional Government and Free Enterprise"—by which it means free exploitation.

Instead of being frankly reactionary, it pretends to be "truly liberal."

Instead of admitting its undemocratic nature, it professes to be "republican."

Instead of being admittedly anti-labor, it poses as a champion of the laboring man against "radical, alien union racketeers."

Instead of acknowledging its discriminations against minorities, it speaks facetiously of "majority rule" and "the best interests of all concerned."

Instead of openly professing its divide-and-rule policy, it proclaims "we are not anti-anything; we are simply pro-American."

Instead of ruling directly through a dictator, it seeks to rule indirectly through corruption of democratic processes.

Instead of an armed putsch, it hopes to ride into power on a wave of votes misled by the afore-mentioned propaganda techniques employed by its subsidized press and radio.

This is not to say that everyone who speaks for some of those things is necessarily a fascist at heart; this is to say that those are some of the hypocrisies which American fascists must perforce practice *until* they come to power.

Southern-style fascism has all those earmarks and then some. There are, of course, all degrees of fascism. It is often difficult to say where reaction ends and fascism begins. But if we accept Nazi Germany as a measuring stick, as a 100-per-cent fascist country, how does the South measure up?

In the matters of peonage, feudalism, exploitation, and denial of suffrage to her own citizens, the South is 100 per cent as fascistic as was Nazi Germany. The overlords of the South are at least as adept as the Nazis in the techniques of divide-and-rule. Southern sectionalism, often bordering upon nationalism, serves essentially the same reactionary purposes as Nazi nationalism. In many respects the South's racial discriminations are more gross than the peacetime discriminations of the Nazis. The segregation and confinement in black ghettos of the South's ten million Negro citizens is at least as rigorous as the Nazis' peacetime segregation of the Jews. In the South the Kloran of the KKK has been substituted for the Constitution of the U.S.A. in much the same manner as the Nazis subverted the German Constitution. There are in the South an uncounted number of would-be fuehrers, and an untold number of organizations every bit as fascistic as the Nazi party. And, finally, the storm troopers of Southern fascism—the Klan, police, state guardsmen—are preparing for *Der Tag* when they can demonstrate that they can be just as terroristic as the Nazis.

This is not meant to suggest that Southerners (not counting Negroes, peons, and union organizers) do not fare appreciably better than did the Germans in peacetime. The point is simply this: That native-born fascism has established a Southern redoubt, and it may sally forth to infect the entire nation if the forces of democracy do not combine to cauterize it.

Because of its very nature, fascism can never get anywhere without high financing. Hence the financiers of fascism must be

regarded as the number-one culprits, in America no less than in
the Axis countries. One of the most telling indictments against
native American fascism was that issued by the War Department
for use in Army orientation courses. In inserting it into the *Congressional Record,* Representative Adolf Sabbath said, "I only
regret that the rules and regulations of the War Department pre-
cluded the naming of outstanding American fascists, such as
the du Ponts, the Pews, the Girdlers, the Weirs, Van Horn
Moseley, H. W. Prentis, Jr., Merwin K. Hart, and others, including the thirty fascists charged with conspiracy and seditious
activities. . . ."

A great deal of money has been spent on the promotion of
fascism in the United States, and the great bulk of it has come
from the ultra-reactionary segments of capital and industry. The
financing of the more overt fascist organisms has generally come
from individual corporate interests, while the task of producing a
"climate" conducive to reaction has been assumed by the various
industrial and financial associations. It goes without saying that
no blanket indictment can be made of all the firms comprising
such organizations, though all must share the responsibility of
tolerating reactionary leadership.

Altogether the nine thousand members of the NAM control an
aggregate corporate wealth of $60,000,000,000 (billions, that is).
According to the report of the LaFollette Senate Committee investigating *Violations of Free Speech and Rights of Labor,* "The
National Association of Manufacturers is largely financed by a
small group of powerful corporations, representing . . . less than
10 per cent of its membership. . . . A much smaller clique of
large corporations, not more than sixty in number, have supplied
it with active leadership. Through the National Association of
Manufacturers and its affiliated national network of employers'
associations in the National Industrial Council, this small group
of powerful interests have organized the strategy for a national
program of employer opposition to labor unions and to government action to improve conditions of labor."

The NAM, launched in 1903, has several times been the subject of congressional investigation. The first occasion was in 1913,
when "Colonel" Martin M. Mulhall, who had been employed by

the NAM as a secret lobbyist for more than a decade, exposed the organization's methods. An investigating committee, headed by Finis J. Garrett of Tennessee, thereupon proceeded to take sixty volumes of testimony regarding the NAM's activities, which were summed up thus by Representative William McDonald, a committee member:

"They did, by the expenditure of exorbitant sums of money, aid and attempt to aid in the election of those whom they believed would readily serve their interests, and by the same means sought to and did accomplish the defeat of others whom they opposed. In carrying out these multifarious activities, they did not hesitate as to means, but made use of any method of corruption found to be effectual . . . they instituted a new and complete system of commercialized treachery. . . .

"Their plain shown attitude was that the American Congress was considered by them as their legislative department and was viewed with the same arrogant manner in which they viewed their other employees, and that those legislators who dared to oppose them would be disciplined in the same manner in which they were accustomed to discipline recalcitrant employees."

In summing up the findings of that earlier investigation, the LaFollette Committee in 1938 reported, "The activities of the National Association of Manufacturers became so bold and sometimes indiscreet that a scandal occurred in 1913, when public charges were made that agents of the Association had given 'financial rewards' to congressmen to promote its legislative program. Both Houses of Congress passed resolutions to investigate the lobbying activities of the Association. These investigations disclosed that 'the Association had placed an employee of the House of Representatives on its pay rolls in order to obtain information not available to the public; the Association's agents had contributed large sums of money to congressional candidates in their campaigns for re-election and had opposed representatives friendly to labor; the Association had carried on a disguised propaganda campaign through newspaper syndicates and through the chautauqua circuits by placing publicists on its pay roll and by distributing large quantities of propaganda material to schools, colleges, and civic organizations throughout the country; the

Association's agents had promoted employees' alliances as an aid in opposing candidates friendly to labor.' "

Summarizing its own full report, the LaFollette Committee's digest says, "The 315-page report identifies the large interstate corporations which finance the operations of the National Association of Manufacturers and guide its policies; describes the traditional opposition of the National Association of Manufacturers, dating back to 1903, toward the principles of collective bargaining and toward liberal legislation; discusses the promotion of company unions; and analyzes the extensive publicity and propaganda campaign conducted by the Association." With further reference to this latter, the report added, "The National Association of Manufacturers has blanketed the country with a propaganda which in technique has relied upon indirection of meaning, and in presentation upon secrecy and deception."

The LaFollette Committee also found that "The National Association of Manufacturers deliberately organized and coordinated the efforts of employers and employers' associations in a planned nationwide campaign to nullify the administration of the National Labor Relations Act, impairing the successful operation of the law." It was further revealed that the 207 firms which largely supported the NAM purchased 60 per cent of the tear gas purchased by American industrialists for use against labor; that they were the greatest employers of labor spies and strikebreakers; and that NAM directors were the chief sponsors of such outfits as the "Christian Crusaders," "Liberty League," "Sentinels of the Republic," "Farmers' Independence League," and the "Johnstown Citizens' Committee."

After the liberation of France, Frederick C. Crawford, board member and ex-president of the NAM, returned from that country with praise for Nazi occupation as compared to Allied liberation. "A fine conservative Frenchman I had known for years told me that if it [the Nazi occupation] had gone on a year and a half more, he believed the French working people would have settled for things as they were," Crawford told the New York Chamber of Commerce.

Another congressional exposé of the NAM came from the O'Mahoney Monopoly Investigating Committee, whose Monograph 26 reports on the NAM's political and propaganda activities, while Monograph 29 deals with America's two hundred ruling families (available at twenty-five cents and two dollars respectively from the Government Printing Office, Washington, D.C.). Some idea of the extent of the influence of NAM men in politics may be had from the fact that they contributed $9,500,000 to the Hoover campaign fund in 1928.

In recent years the NAM has conducted most of its propaganda through its "National Industrial Information Committee" (NIIC) and special "Committees on Co-operation," with Agriculture, Church, Labor, Teachers, and Women. Of the NIIC's eleven regional offices, three are in the South—at Atlanta, St. Louis, and Dallas. While it is difficult to obtain exact figures as to the amount of money spent each year by the NAM on propaganda, a congressional committee was told that the NAM's budget for "non-political education" in 1944 was $1,385,000.

"People in the mass are unconcerned about details," NIIC spokesmen have assured the NAM in convention assembled. "They tend to think in blurs. They are moved primarily by simple, emotional ideas. The NIIC will capitalize upon this fact with an aggressive program designed to inspire a crusade that will sweep free enterprise into public favor."

Although the NAM succeeded in seducing the leaders of the National Education Association, it did not fare so well with the Federal Council of Churches, for that organization insisted that representatives of organized labor be included in the Industry-Church "conferences" which the NAM proposed. While the NAM made this concession with what grace it could muster, it proceeded on the side to organize, wherever possible, Industry-Church confabs without Labor.

"The National Association of Manufacturers, with plenty of what it takes to do the job, has turned to the task of converting the clergy to its point of view," reports *The Witness,* news magazine of the Episcopal Church. "The stunt is to get some highly respectable parson, innocent to the ways of the NAM, to invite the brethren to a nice dinner or luncheon, feed them well, pass out fat cigars, and then turn on the line through a paid employee who generally is a clergyman delighted to be on such a generous pay roll."

When such an affair was arranged in Memphis in 1942, the Rev. S. E. Howie, president of the Memphis Ministerial Alliance, berated businessmen for opposing the inclusion of labor representatives. "The church emphasizes human values, and capitalism emphasizes profits," said the Rev. Howie, "and between these two emphases there is a fundamental antagonism."

All over the country, conscientious representatives of many faiths have spoken out in similar vein.

"This is an attempt to line up the churches, not merely in support of the present program of the NAM to destroy labor and social legislation, but also behind its plan to control the postwar economic situation," says the Rev. Harry Ward of Union Theological Seminary.

"On the basis of its past record, I don't put much faith in any 'progressive' social movement initiated by the NAM," says the Rev. John Paul Jones, Presbyterian.

"The important point is that the ideas expressed in the latest speeches of NAM spokesmen still are poles apart from the Christian social tradition as it is applied to modern economic conditions by papal encyclicals of the last fifty years," writes Edward Skillen, editor of the *Catholic Commonweal*.

"The NAM is endeavoring to deceive clergymen, especially in the smaller communities, into support of an economic system that is largely responsible for the collapse that has overwhelmed society," observes Rabbi Sidney E. Goldstein.

"Until businessmen learn that both Judaism and Christianity correctly and traditionally insist that human values come before profits," concludes the Rev. Guy Emery Shipler, editor of the Protestant Episcopal *Churchman,* "they will find themselves basically at war with religion."

Despite equally strong criticism from the real leaders of Farm, Labor, Women, and Teachers groups, the NAM is still finding it possible to obtain unsuspecting local sponsorship for its "conferences."

But more and more the NAM is operating through peripheral organizations, while the product bearing its own label is being heavily coated with sugar.

One of the most effective transmission belts is the "Associated

Industries" setup in each state. Indicative of the intimate relationship which exists between the NAM and Associated Industries is the following account from *Alabama* magazine in 1945:

> Like a general touring his battle front, President Ira Mosher of the National Association of Manufacturers swung through Alabama last week, stirred anew his captains' spirits. . . . In speeches at Birmingham and Montgomery, before members of his Association and the Associated Industries of Alabama, Ira Mosher made no bones about the purpose of his mission. He was out to keep industrialists alert to the peril that hangs over free enterprise and to help management "plan its strategy of survival." Frankly, he said, management should quit muttering into its beard, instead should do a thorough job of convincing the public and the lawmakers that free enterprise must not be sacrificed.
>
> "But," he said, "it isn't an armchair job, or one for timid souls . . . we are reluctant dragons. We flinch from the steel of open combat. We're such delightful, rugged individualists that we can hardly agree on a plan of battle. We're an army of generals. We've got to learn the art of modern propaganda warfare. . . . That job begins at home—right here in your town. . . . It's a rare chance. . . ."

Very often of late the NAM, Associated Industries, and Farm Bureau Federation have teamed up. For example, in April of 1946 a joint conference of the Georgia Farm Bureau Federation and Associated Industries of Georgia convened at Macon, with "agriculture and business delegations" from Alabama, Florida, and South Carolina also attending. Significantly, this meeting was important enough to have as speakers Robert R. Wason, president of the NAM, and Edward A. O'Neal, president of the American Farm Bureau Federation. A pre-session circular issued by Associated Industries reported the CIO's plans to organize 1,500,000 Southern workers and asked, "Is the CIO's $1,000,000 drive Georgia industry's $64 question?" According to the INS, "A follow-up regional convention of the National Association of Manufacturers will be held in Atlanta Friday, with many of the delegates expected to attend that conference also."

Next to the NAM, the U. S. Chamber of Commerce has been prepotent, although its record in some respects has not been quite so bad. During the war the Chamber did sign a concordat with the CIO and AFL, which mutually recognized Labor's right to organize and Management's prerogative to manage; but the NAM abstained. It is also significant that in 1942 the resolutions committee of the NAM voted against "Win the War" as its slogan, adopting "Free Enterprise" instead. And, though it may have been purely coincidental, representatives of the NAM appeared in Texas in 1943 when the notorious Manford anti-union bill was pending, and again in 1945 when the "Christian-American" anti-union-security amendment was being debated.

For the most part, however, reactionary corporate interests have subsidized various "front" organizations to wage their overt fight against the unions and progress. Prominent among such fronts are the so-called "Committee for Constitutional Government" and "Constitutional Educational League."

There are also some organizations of "small" businessmen which have fallen under reactionary domination. Primarily, there is the "National Small Business Men's Association," which has been carrying on since 1937. Embracing any firm with one thousand or less employees, the NSBMA agitates for "Christian-American" legislation to abolish all forms of union security; it champions the O'Daniel-Rankin proposal to enable and encourage veterans to violate union security contracts; it favors regulation of unions on the ground that they are "monopolies"; it would ban political activity by unions; emasculate the Wagner Act; defeat the Wagner-Murray-Dingell public health bill; reduce corporate taxes; defeat FEPC; et cetera.

In 1943 the NSBMA launched a campaign to raise a quarter of a million dollars "for the purpose of organizing public opinion." In its fund-raising drive it led with the question, "Would you, Mr. Manufacturer, pay out one cent to save a dollar?" Then its circular went on to claim that the NSBMA, through pressure on Congress, had helped kill a proposed 1-per-cent increase in the Social Security tax in 1943:

> Similar action on Social Security taxes will have to be taken later this year for 1944 pay rolls, and in the meantime there

are a great many other things which need attention, particularly the union labor situation. This Association has already
projected itself into the organized labor problem in a big way—
see enclosed folders. . . .We need your $10 in dues. . . .
Also at the proper time we will need your assistance in bringing pressure on Congress.

The reason advanced by the NSBMA's president, DeWitt
Emery, for his opposition to Social Security is peculiar to say the
least. "Our creator intended that life should be a struggle from
the cradle to the grave," Emery avers, "and I for one am perfectly
willing to bow to his judgment."

Since 1942 the NSBMA has been aided and abetted by a self-
styled "Conference of American Small Business Organizations."
This is operated out of Chicago by Frederick A. Virkus, publisher
of family trees and likewise head of the Illinois division of the
NSBMA. In addition to its violent campaigning against FEPC,
this conference is the sponsor of a "Declaration of Independence
from Post War Regimentation and Socialization of Business,"
which it would have Congress adopt as "simply and exclusively
ALL AMERICAN."

In addition to the machinations of the national associations
which follow the reactionary big business and big farm line, the
South must contend with the "Southern States Industrial Council," a self-styled "voluntary, non-profit organization of industrial,
commercial, and agricultural interests." Claiming to represent
"6,000 of the leading concerns of the Southland," the Council,
in addition to its mercenary concerns, goes on to say, "The South
has certain traditions, certain principles of living, and certain
philosophies of life which must be preserved for its people." It is
not surprising, therefore, that the Council took a "leading part"
in the fight against FEPC and solicited ten-dollar contributions
"to help in creating sentiment in other sections," adding, "of
course we would appreciate a larger amount."

The Council did not hesitate to distribute a piece entitled
"Shall We Be Ruled by Whites or Blacks?" which was based on
one of Rankin's diatribes against the FEPC. The Council also
stooped to make erroneous statements about FEPC, to wit: "The
employers of labor—of all kinds and in any number—would have

to take in their office, factory, store, workshop, or any other place of business, employees selected by the Agency . . . without regard to race, color, experience, or ability."

Significantly, this Council was organized the year after Roosevelt took office. Robert Rast Cole, former president and present executive committeeman of the Council, is president of Monsanto Chemicals, a frequent advertiser in the anti-Rooseveltian, anti-union, white supremacy *Alabama* magazine; he has also been a director of Associated Industries of Alabama. John U. Barr, vice-president of the Council, was, as has been noted, the leader of the "Draft-Byrd-for-President" movement in 1944, which was closely tied to the so-called "American Democratic National Committee." Barr is also a director of the NAM and Louisiana Manufacturers Association. Thomas A. McGough, a director of the Council, is president of the McGough Bakeries chain, which advertises regularly in the *Southern Outlook,* a weekly paper which employs arch-reactionary tactics in its attack on unions.

As might have been expected, the Council's board of directors met at Jacksonville, Fla., late in 1945 and resolved to henceforth "devote every energy" to combating the union shop. It had long been suspected that Council members were among the sponsors of the "Christian-American" front's anti-union-security lobbying. Now that the "Christian-American" has been publicly discredited, it would seem that the industrialists have decided to come out in the open with their drive to abolish union security.

The Council's president for 1946, Remmie L. Arnold, has issued an appeal for a Council budget of $150,000. In making this appeal the Council says it has been "very active" against the Pepper bill to raise the minimum wage to sixty-five cents and was also "very active for" the Case anti-union bill.

Sometimes the presumptiveness of the industrialists surpasses all understanding. For example, when the Southern Governors' Conference convened in 1945, Governor Millard Caldwell of Florida announced that the Southern Association of Science and Industry "proposes to act for the Southern governors at its own expense, to establish an office and to provide a secretariat for the Southern governors." To this Governor Chauncey Sparks of Alabama replied that he saw "no more reason for the Association of

Industry and Science furnishing us with a secretary than for the CIO. . . . These people are high type, but there is no more politically minded group. . . . You don't see them on the stump; but you find them behind closed doors."

The unhappy truth about the whole matter is that the big business and big farm blocs have made a deal: the big farmers are helping big business fight labor, and in return big business is helping the big farmers to defeat government programs to aid small farmers.

The postwar putsch whereby reactionary industrialists sought to break the back of unionism on the strike front seems to have failed miserably. But the reactionaries have not given up. From here on out, more and more of their money will be poured into the political war chest, with barrels of it earmarked for the subsidy of divisive organizations.

The political kingfish are the incumbent officeholders whose demagoguery is surpassed only by their reactionary voting records. Nationally, we find such men as Senator Pappy O'Daniel of Texas, Senator Theodore Bilbo, Senator James O. Eastland, and Representative John Rankin of Mississippi, Senator Allen J. Ellender of Louisiana, and Representative Eugene Cox of Georgia exercising inordinate control over the Congress of the United States and filling the halls and *Record* of that body with all manner of demagoguery. These are by no means the only Southern offenders, but they are perhaps the most flagrant.

The record of such "representatives" is too notorious to require rehashing here.

But, simply as a reminder, let us recall a few words of Rankin. When in 1942 Carl Sandburg—the great American poet, biographer, and champion of democracy—declared that America has "yet another front to conquer—the color line," Rankin retorted with the asinine charge that Sandburg is a "communist-front propagandist" who was "trying to mongrelize America." Again, on December 15, 1943, Rankin said in the House, "Mr. Speaker, we never reduced the Negro to slavery. We elevated him from the position of savage to that of servant."

One such man in Congress would be one too many. The task of the Southern people—in which the rest of the American people have a tremendous stake—is to eliminate such men from the offices to which they have risen through restricted suffrage, demagoguery, and corporate backing. There is also the parallel task of preventing other such men from coming to power—for the South's reservoir of ex-officio demagogues is virtually bottomless.

On the state level, the 1946 bid of Eugene Talmadge for a comeback as Georgia governor is particularly fraught with possibilities. He has the backing not only of such corporate interests as the Georgia Power Company, but also the Ku Klux Klan. It is openly stated in Georgia klaverns that if Talmadge is elected he will give the Klan a free rein in the event of interracial violence before calling out the militia. Klan support is also promised Tom Linder, Georgia's isolationist white-supremacy commissioner of agriculture, no matter what office he seeks. And Georgia is but typical of other Deep Southern states where men and machines, representing big money, stand ready to resort to racism in bids for power.

The multitudinous disruptive organizations and publications which plague the South are all designed to further the cause of reaction. Some are operated by outright agents of reactionary industrial and financial organizations. Others are one-man creations which the creator hopes will carry him to power. And finally there are the aberrations of the conscientious crackpots—the well-known "lunatic fringe" who are, for the most part, too irresponsible and incompetent to ever enlist enough followers or financial supporters to do much harm.

The *Ku Klux Klan* is potentially the most dangerous of the anti-democratic forces in the South. This is true because of the prevalence of unorganized Ku Klux sentiment and the fact that, although the press has succeeded in convincing "respectable" people that the Klan is no longer essential to the maintenance of the interracial status quo, its prestige among the illiterate and semi-literate who now compose its rank and file has declined not at all.

The entry of America into the war against the Axis found the Klan in the uncomfortable position of playing the Axis game of disunity and disruption. The indictment of thirty-odd Americans for sedition and conspiracy to foment fascist revolution did not improve the Klan's outlook—for it had been dealing with a good many of those arrested. Imperial Wizard Colescott admitted that two Klan leaders—one in New York and one in the West— wanted to support Hitler.

But, of course, the Klan had to do an abrupt about-face. There ensued the incongruous spectacle of the Klan denouncing the Axis, canceling its klonvokations to conserve gasoline, boosting war bonds, and calling upon B'nai B'rith and the Knights of Columbus to join it in national broadcasts appealing for "unity of all factions to win the war." Moreover, the Klan suspended publication of its official organ, *The Fiery Cross,* and withdrew from circulation its reprints of *The International Jew.* As has been noted, however, the Klan continued its activities against unions and minorities, even provoking race-hate strikes in vital war plants.

It was not until April of 1944 that Walter Winchell—ever on the alert to expose disruptionists—revealed that the Klan was going deeper underground, hiding behind the name "American Keystone Foundation" and other aliases. I asked Colescott about this, and on May 4 he replied:

> As usual when speaking about the Klan, Mr. Winchell is wrong. The Klan has not disbanded and has no intention of doing so. This may be verified by writing to the clerk of the Fulton County Circuit Court. A meeting was held here on April 23, at which routine matters were discussed.

However, on May 5, the day after Colescott dictated the above letter, a group of thirty-eight men met in Atlanta, accused the Klan of "disbanding at a time when most needed," berated local ministers for wanting to "give a fair break to the Negro and Jew," and proceeded to call for members (fee, $6.00) of the "Fact Finders" to carry on where the Klan left off. (Fortunately, a blast of editorial censure stopped the "Fact Finders" in their tracks.)

A month later, on June 4, Winchell was proven to have been right (as usual) about the Klan. In a copyrighted story by Fred Moon in the Atlanta *Journal* it was revealed that the Klan's imperial offices were empty and that Colescott had sold his At-lanta home and "retired" to Miami. Colescott explained that the ("routine") klonvokation of April 23 had voted unanimously "to suspend the constitutional laws of the Knights of the Ku Klux Klan, Inc., to revoke all chartered klans, and to order the disbandment of all provisional klans."

He went on to make it clear, however, that "This does not mean that the Klan is dead. We simply have released local chapters from all obligations, financial and otherwise, to the imperial headquarters. I still am Imperial Wizard. The other officials still retain their titles, though, of course, the functions of all of us are suspended. We have authority to meet and reincarnate at any time." When asked what the chances were that the Klan would be reincarnated, Colescott replied, "About that, you can't tell. The Klan has always come out, and come out on top, when it was needed. Lots of people tell us that it is more needed now than at any time in history. . . ."

When Colescott was asked the reason for the Klan's "suspension," he replied, "I do not regard it as a matter for discussion outside the Klan." Asked specifically whether a reported tax assessment levied by the Treasury Department were a factor, Colescott referred the press to the Treasury Department.

Press service reports caused a national sigh of relief by mistakenly conveying the impression that the Klan had "dissolved." In an article in the *Southern Patriot* of the Southern Conference for Human Welfare I pointed out that actually the Klan was merely going through the motion of suspending its activity as a corporation, leaving the local klaverns to do as they pleased, while divorcing the imperial hierarchy from all responsibility. I also recalled that when Grand Wizard Forrest issued his edict in 1868 that the Klan was "dissolved forever," autonomous local Klan activity actually increased in scope and violence.

That many klaverns continued to operate on their own is certain. A bit of prowling led me on November 8, 1944, to a Marietta Street address in Atlanta (made available to the authorities). Upstairs there was a large meeting hall, the padlocked door to which was equipped with a peephole. By pretending to be interested in renting the hall for a meeting, I learned from the caretaker that it was being used for regular meetings by the "Masons, Railway Trainmen, and Ku Klux."

Moreover, I found that the Atlanta telephone directory, printed after the Klan's reported disbandment, still contained a number listed under "Knights of the Ku Klux Klan." Upon calling the number, I was asked by the operator whether I wished to call the Imperial Wizard or the Imperial Palace. When I said either, there was a long pause, after which I was informed that the Klan had a new private number and that they had requested that it not be given out.

In Florida, Klansmen incorporated on September 7, 1944, as the "Knights of the Ku Klux Klan of Florida, Inc." A. B. Taylor of Orlando, H. F. McCormack of Apopka, and A. F. Gilliam of Clarcona were listed as directors.

For the most part, however, Klan activity was carried on under a variety of aliases. The "American Keystone Society" label exposed by Winchell is still in use and serves as a front for a complete line of patented Klan insignia, pins, and lapel buttons which bear the Klan recognition word, "Akai." In New York the Klan operates as the "Circle Club," in Detroit as the "Dreamland Club," in Pittsburgh as the "Mantle Club," in Knoxville, Tennessee, and Des Moines, Iowa, as the "American Fellowship Club," in Texas as the "Order of American Patriots" and "Independent Order of Minute Men," et cetera.

In March of 1944 one J. B. Stoner of Chattanooga achieved notoriety by petitioning Congress to "pass a resolution recognizing the fact that the Jews are the children of the Devil," and urging Congress to take "immediate action against the Jew-devils."

It soon developed that Stoner was Klan kleagle for Tennessee and that he had been liberally distributing business cards listing himself as "Ku Klux Klan Organizer" (see photostatic layout) and mailing out thousands of applications for membership in the form of return postcards (also in photostatic layout). These were ordered in batches of five thousand and mailed to males in the city directory whose names did not sound Jewish or did not have "(c)" after them. These cards are headed "White Supremacy" and bear the return post-office-box address of "R. W. Byerley." Although the cards do not bear the name of the Klan, the princi-

WHITE SUPREMACY

If you are a Native Born, White, Protestant, Gentile, American Citizen of good character and believe in our principles..an opportunity to join a secret organization that stands primarily for WHITE SUPREMACY awaits you.

Our Organization stands for:

Christianity.

America First.

White Supremacy.

Upholding Constitution of U.S.A.

Racial Segregation.

Racial Purity.

Pure White Womanhood.

Opposition to Communism.

America for Americans.

State Rights.

Separation of Church and State.

Freedom of Speech and Press.

No Foreign Immigration, except pure White.

Law and Order.

American Leadership of American Labor Unions.

Closer Relationship between American Capital and American Labor.

If you truly desire to do your part for Christianity, your Country, and your Race by joining our organization, sign and return this card at once. Every real American should be able to honestly say: "I do my part." Tomorrow may be too late. ACT NOW!

Name_____ Res. Address_____

Occupation_____ City and State_____

Bus. Address_____ Phone_____
  *Reasonable initiation fee.

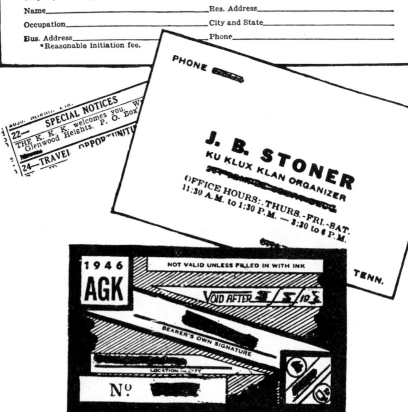

PHONE

SPECIAL NOTICES

THE K. K. K. welcomes you. W.
Glenwood Heights. P. O. Box

22—

24—TRAVEL OPPORTUNIT

J. B. STONER

KU KLUX KLAN ORGANIZER

OFFICE HOURS:. THURS.-FRI.-SAT.
11:30 A. M. to 1:30 P. M. — 3:30 to 6 P.M.

TENN.

1946 AGK

NOT VALID UNLESS FILLED IN WITH INK

VOID AFTER

BEARER'S OWN SIGNATURE

LOCATION — CITY

N°

ples printed thereon coincide with those in the printed *Kreed* of
the Klan, and they were sent out in envelopes bearing "KKK"
under the flap. R. W. Byerley, I later discovered, is apparently a
Miss Ruby Byerley, to whom Stoner sends applicants for inter-
viewing. The cards themselves come to his desk in a Chattanooga
office building.

To interviewers Stoner recommended such "literature" as the
Patriotic Bulletin of Elizabeth Dilling (who was indicted for sedition), as well as her *Red Network* and *The Octopus; The Tal-
mud Unmasked* and *A Foundation of Sand,* by Eugene Nelson
Sanctuary (who was also indicted for sedition); *With Lotions of
Love,* by Joseph P. Kamp of the so-called "Constitutional Edu-
cational League"; Gerald L. K. Smith's *Cross and Flag;* Eugene
Talmadge's *Statesman;* Hubert Baughn's *Alabama* magazine;
and "The International Jew," from Henry Ford's Dearborn
Independent. In addition to these, Stoner had in his own library
such volumes as *Concise German Grammar,* the *Philosophy of
Nietzsche,* and the *Discourses of Machiavelli.*

Of those indicted for sedition, Stoner said that most of them
were "good patriotic Christian Americans who oppose Jews and
Communists." Practically all professors are communists, he thinks,
who spread communism under the guise of liberalism. "Liberalism, or democracy, as it is sometimes called, means something
too much like communism," said Stoner. He went on to say that
America was "fighting to preserve and spread communism." He
opposed American aid to Russia, or even to "liberal" nations. And
if the United States participated in the United Nations, he said,
it would soon lose its sovereignty in the same way that Virginia
was absorbed in the United States. He favored the United States
taking over the North American continent and deporting all
Negroes to Brazil. The Latin races he described as more black
than white.

Stoner voiced the opinion that Hitler was "too easy" on the
Jews—let too many of them get away. "Anti-Semitism and white
supremacy go hand in hand," he said. "A politician who doesn't
believe in white supremacy and anti-Semitism can't get far now."
Stoner thought Pappy O'Daniel and Charles A. Lindbergh would
make good Presidents, and he also had high praise for Henry

Ford. In Congress, Stoner's favorites were Bilbo, Rankin, Dies, Nye, and Hoffman.

After the war, Stoner anticipated depression and revolution—and hoped that the Klan would "put it down." Viewing the struggle in terms of Right and Left, he said, "I favor the Right."

Explaining that the Klan had suspended its interstate machinery "until a deal could be made on the tax assessment," Stoner said that the local and state machinery was still operating under the Klan name. Two klaverns were then meeting in Chattanooga, he said, one during the day and one at night. The initiation fee was ten dollars and the dues fifty cents per month. Receipts were inscribed "Realm of Tennessee" and gave the Klan's address as "P. O. Box ——, Atlanta, Georgia." Stoner said he looked for support from the Chattanooga *News-Free Press* and did not look for prosecution from the FBI.

Attendance at the Chattanooga klaverns ranged from about thirty to fifty at that time, with a half dozen or so new and reinstated members being inducted each week. The membership was predominantly middle-aged, with only a few white-collar persons among them. He delivered many a spiel against Negroes, Jews, the FEPC, et cetera, and urged all Klansmen to "buy Gentile." There would be an anti-Jewish candidate against Representative Estes Kefauver in 1946, Stoner declared. When one Klansman suggested that the Klan pay all fines of members who might get into trouble with Negroes on busses, Stoner agreed to call a special meeting in such an eventuality.

In acquainting new members with the *Kloran,* Stoner emphasized the sections on the military organization of the Klan and the fact that all Klansmen, including the exalted cyclops and kleagles, are directly responsible to the Imperial Wizard.

Charles H. Still, who until recently was manager of a Chattanooga service station, told customers that he "had been a member of the Klan until it got mixed up in the black market."

During 1945 Klan activity increased considerably. In May, Georgia Grand Dragon Green said, "The Knights of the Ku Klux Klan, Inc., is dead now, but the Knights of the Ku Klux Klan are not dead. They're as strong as they ever were. They're meeting all over the country right now."

It was also in May that the Klan touched off a fiery cross at Trenton, N. J., on the site of a Negro housing project. At Roanoke, Virginia, Dr. H. T. Penn, Negro dentist, received a letter on Klan stationery, warning him to cease urging Negroes to vote. In Atlanta I acquired a summons (see photostatic layout) to a "special klonklave" of Klan No. 297, dated February 10 and signed by Exalted Cyclops G. T. Brown. At Houston, Texas, cards were distributed reading:

> THE KU KLUX KLAN IS RIDING
> GOD GIVE US MEN
> SAM HOUSTON KLAN NO. 1

The card also bore a post-office-box number.

In Miami the John B. Gordon Klan No. 5 erected two billboards along the highways leading into the city, saying, "The K.K.K. Welcomes You," and giving a post-office-box number. Similar advertisements were inserted in the want-ad sections of Miami newspapers (see photostatic layout).

It was in August of 1945 that I visited Imperial Wizard Colescott at his comfortable home in Miami.

He spent most of the evening inveighing against the Jews, accusing them of controlling the press, radio, motion pictures, et cetera.

I asked him what he expected from returning Negro servicemen who had experienced social equality overseas.

"That's the thing that took me into Klan," he replied. "I don't believe in interracial intermarriage or social equality. I've got a nigger maid, treat her good, pay her better than most, but I don't want to eat with her or marry her."

I asked whether he specifically endorsed the booklet *Negro Suffrage—Its False Theory,* written by his predecessor Hiram Evans, which he (Colescott) had previously mailed me under a blanket endorsement.

"Personally, I'm in favor of repeal of the Fifteenth Amendment," he replied. "I believe we should have restrictions on Negro voting so that only qualified ones are admitted to the polls."

Feb. 10. 1945
Box ■ Sta A
Atlanta Ga,

Esteemed Klansman.

There is Work to be done - are you doing your Part? Do you Know what happened Sunday Night Feb 2nd. on Ormone Street and on Grant St.? Would you have been ready if Called?

There will be a Special Klonklave of your Klan, Thursday Night Feb 15th 7³⁰ P.M. in your Klavern. ■■■ St. Sw. Be There, Duty Calls

yours Itsub

G.V. Brown
Exalted Cyclops.
Klan # 297

The Records of the Kligrapp Shows your Dues Are Paid Thru _ _ _ _ _ _ _ _ _

Rules and Regulations Recomend Supension if Dues Are in Arrears Three Months.

I asked if by this he meant literacy requirements.

"Literacy, educational, moral standards, and all the rest," he said.

I then asked about a recent press report to the effect that he planned a "unity meeting" with Tom Watson, Florida's attorney general. "I don't know what they mean by a 'unity meeting,' said Colescott, "but I've known Tom Watson well and favorably for many years." He went on to reveal that Watson had been in on his scheme to present a "united front" with Catholics and Jews for the duration.

When I asked him to define what he meant by "radical unions" —which he had said the Klan opposed—he replied, "The Klan believes that unions should be officered and led by Americans." He cited the CIO-PAC as what he regarded as an example of "radical-alien" union activity.

I mentioned that the Scripps-Howard papers had reported that the United Sons of America were spreading into the South. "That's Charlie Speer's outfit which he started in Detroit," said Colescott. "I wouldn't be surprised if he were trying to expand. It might be that some Klansmen are joining him. Speer ran out on the Klan when I went to the Dies Committee with all my papers and records. He wouldn't stand fast. Apparently he was afraid that there was something in the records which would get him in trouble. He started the United Sons purely as a racket to make money and to influence Michigan politics."

I next raised the question of Reynolds's Nationalist party (the Klan's *Fiery Cross* frequently printed Reynolds's propaganda and, in its August 1941 issue, said "Senator Reynolds has made and is making a noble fight for America"). Colescott admitted that he knew Reynolds and said, "He is an old member of the Klan." He went on to say, "Of course I'm strictly a Nationalist. The Klan stands for strict restrictions on immigration. I believe in a job for every American before we hand out jobs to any aliens. I once suggested an editorial and cartoon on that subject to Bernarr Macfadden, and he carried them both in *Liberty Magazine.*"

Earlier, in January, Colescott had said to an interviewer, "There is no doubt in my mind that patriotic organizations will carry on after the war. . . . It might be a reorganized KKK or made up of former America First Committee, but I am sure there will be a revival of Nationalist feeling."

The most significant thing I got out of the Wizard was his reply to my question about the reported tax assessment against the Klan.

"When I took over the Klan from Evans in 1939, he told me that we had a tax-free corporation certificate as a fraternal organization," said Colescott. "The Klan was incorporated in 1915, but it wasn't until 1941 that the Government said we were liable for taxes for the entire period and assessed us $700,000. What could we do but suspend our activities? We liquidated all our assets and our attorney turned it over to the Government. Maybe it can make something out of the Klan—I never could."

When I asked Colescott about the possibility of recalcitrant Klansmen reincarnating without his permission, he replied: "No one has any authority to reincarnate the Klan but me. I have the corporate charter and intend to hang onto it. All Klansmen are sworn to obey me."

My next intimate association with the Klan came on the night of October 10, when Kluxers touched off a gigantic fiery cross atop Stone Mountain near Atlanta. Due to an advance tip-off, I was on hand for the event. Grand Dragon Green did not exaggerate when he said the cross could be seen for sixty miles. Instead of the usual contraption of wooden frame and gasoline-soaked burlap, this cross consisted of hundreds of barrels of fuel oil and sand, so strung out across the face of the mountain as to constitute a cross one hundred yards long.

I circumvented the carloads of Klansmen who guarded the roads leading up the mountain and climbed to the summit through the underbrush with my camera; but there were no Klansmen in evidence there. The next day, however, a card-carrying Klansman assured me that some four thousand Kluxers had been assembled on the far side of the mountain in Gwinnett County.

At the foot of the mountain I talked with the proprietress of a drink stand who has witnessed all cross-burnings on the mountain, including the cross of the reincarnation of 1915. She said that one Klansman had told her that the big new cross was "just to let the niggers know the war is over and that the Klan is back on the market." And he added, "We'll be back soon and often!"

When the Associated Press interviewed Dr. Green about the cross, he said it was the work of one of the Atlanta klaverns, of which he said there were nine. "Probably there are 25,000 Klansmen in good standing in Georgia right now," he added, claiming a 20-per-cent increase in the number of klaverns in the state during 1945. Green said that Georgia Klansmen were "assessed an initiation fee of ten dollars, annual membership fee of six dollars, and all chipped in two dollars for an insurance fund for the benefit of families of deceased members."

Shortly after the Stone Mountain cross-burning, Green told Allan Swim, author of the Scripps-Howard "Dixie Disruptionists" series, that J. B. Stoner "can give you the dope about the Klan in Tennessee, although he is not the head of the organization."

Early in 1946 I got around to visiting Stoner at his Klan office in Chattanooga. I was escorted into his presence by a rugged young character and was surprised to find that Stoner himself is but twenty-one years old. He walks with a decided limp, his hair is close-cropped, and he rolls his eyes ceilingward at intervals of about thirty seconds.

"Stetson Kennedy," he said. "I've heard that name somewhere before."

I hastened to assure him that I was "just a Florida boy," and that it was most unlikely that he had heard of me, and changed the subject. I could see, though, that he was still trying to remember.

A native of Georgia, Stoner explained that he had been busy organizing the Klan for three years. When I asked how he happened to take up the work, he replied, "Because I want my children to be white Gentiles. I am against racial equality in any form—whether with niggers, Japs, Chinese, Filipinos, or what have you. I believe in white supremacy—social, political, and economic. I haven't anything against niggers personally, but only as a race."

He went on to say that "There is bound to be violence if niggers seek to vote in the Democratic primary in the Deep South." He indicated that the Klan would take a hand, "not violently," but "through Klansmen in the Democratic party—we have them in the party especially in Georgia, Tennessee, and South Carolina, including some of the top officials."

Stoner's "solution" for the "Negro problem" is "the expatriation of all Negroes to Africa, with the Federal Government providing them better conditions than they have here."

But Stoner is far more concerned about Jews. He proudly displayed a rubber stamp reading "Down with the Jews!" with which he decorates his correspondence. He urged me to read Eugene Sanctuary's *The Talmud Unmasked* and gave me Sanctuary's address from memory. Stoner said this item would soon be available again.

Stoner's solution for the "Jewish problem" was anticipated by Adolf Hitler. "I would get them out of the country," says Stoner, "and I don't mean send them to other countries. I'll never be satisfied as long as there are any Jews here or anywhere. I think we ought to kill all Jews just to save their unborn generations from having to go to hell."

Stoner went on to say he was nearing completion of a book which would prove with Biblical quotations that "all Jews are Jew-Devils." Then he says he plans to help organize a "National Anti-Jewish party." When I asked who else was interested in forming such a party, he replied, "So far it's mostly just a lot of individuals all over the country who do know each other and have enough influence to get it started." He has hopes for such a party winning out in the 1948 election. The Democratic and Republican parties are lost, he says, because of their subservience to Jewish and Negro minorities.

I asked Stoner what he thought of Reynolds's Nationalist party, and he said, "I like his party all right. . . . But I believe in coming right out and saying a party is anti-Jewish."

I also asked him what he thought of the Masons.

"Oh, we're all for the Masons," he said. "We've got lots of

Masons in the Klan. Colescott himself is a Mason. In Atlanta the Klan has one meeting place jointly with the Masons and another with several other organizations."

On all questions relating to Klan activities outside Tennessee, Stoner referred me to Dr. Green.

And then suddenly Stoner's face lit up and he exclaimed, "Southern Conference for Human Welfare!"

At this I tried to keep one eye on Stoner and another on the reaction of the Kluxer across the room.

"What about it?" I asked innocently.

"That's where I saw your name!" said Stoner.

Grasping at the remaining straw that he hadn't yet recalled my having authored an anti-Klan piece in the Conference paper, I said, "I wouldn't be surprised—I've been interested in every sort of organization operating in the South."

It worked long enough for me to make my departure.

In Atlanta in 1946, Klan No. 1—headed by Dr. Green—was meeting on Monday night, and Klans Nos. 066 and 297 were meeting on Thursday night. Three other klaverns were also reported to be holding forth in other neighborhoods—East Point, Buckhead, and Stone Mountain. The regular application and reinstatement forms of the Ku Klux Klan, Inc. (Forms K-115 and K-131; see photostatic layout), are being used, although in some instances a pencil line is drawn through the "Inc." Klan membership cards bear Klan seals, and members are identified by number rather than by name. The old recognition rigmarole is still in effect, with the seeker asking, "Ayak?" ("Are you a Klansman?") and the other replying, "Akai." ("A Klansman am I.")

The Georgia Klan is still offering for sale the booklet *Klannishness* and other items from the Klan's old line of prejudice propaganda. The Atlanta meetings are violently anti-Negro, anti-Semitic, and anti-Catholic in nature, with numerous "horror stories" being told to arouse the prejudices of the ghouls. For instance, it is declared that because Justice Murphy is a Catholic and a member of the Knights of Columbus, Klansmen cannot look for justice from the Supreme Court. It is boasted that Klan money

Form K-115

APPLICATION FOR CITIZENSHIP

IN THE

INVISIBLE EMPIRE

Knights of the Ku Klux Klan

(INCORPORATED)

To His Majesty the Imperial Wizard, Emperor of the Invisible Empire, Knights of the Ku Klux Klan:

I, the undersigned, a native born, true and loyal citizen of the United States of America, being a white male Gentile person of temperate habits, sound in mind and a believer in the tenets of the Christian religion, the maintenance of White Supremacy and the principles of a "pure Americanism," do most respectfully apply for membership in the Knights of the Ku Klux Klan through

Klan No. _____, Realm of _____

I guarantee on my honor to conform strictly to all rules and requirements regulating my "naturalization" and the continuance of my membership, and at all times a strict and loyal obedience to your constitutional authority and the constitution and laws of the fraternity, not in conflict with the constitution and constitutional laws of the United States of America and the states thereof. If I prove untrue as a Klansman I will willingly accept as my portion whatever penalty your authority may impose.

The required "klectokon" accompanies this application.

Signed _____ Applicant

Residence Address _____

Business Address _____

Endorsed by _____

Kl. _____

Kl. _____ Date _____, 19 ____

The person securing this application must sign on top line above. NOTICE—Check the address to which mail may be sent.

APPLICATION FOR RE-INSTATEMENT

and

APPLICATION FOR PERMANENT ENROLLMENT

I, the undersigned, herewith attach Three Dollars ($3.00), to this form and make application to the Knights of the Ku Klux Klan, Inc., of Atlanta, Georgia, for a LIFE ASSOCIATION KARD, as provided in the Constitution and Laws in Section 4, Article 3, Page 7; Section 6, Article 4, Page 9; Section 18, Article 18, Page 83; and Section 26, Article 18, Page 35.

I joined as a member of Klan No.............., located in .... Realm of................
I hereby agree to abide by the Constitution and Laws and all edicts and mandates, rules and regulations of the Knights of the Ku Klux Klan, Inc., and/or this Klan.

Name.. Age..................

Business Address.. Bus. Phone..................

Residence Address.. Res. Phone..................

Remarks..

Have you ever received a Life Association Kard?...

What is the number of your Life Association Kard?...

Has your mail address changed since you received Kard?...

Dated ....
Applicant's Signature.

Detach this Coupon at perforation and give to applicant as his temporary receipt.

No. ....
Solicitor's Signature.

helped eliminate Secretary of the Treasury Henry Morgenthau and Attorney General Biddle, and that senators and congressmen are now being enlisted in a campaign to get rid of Justice Murphy.

When Atlanta Negroes petitioned that Negro policemen be employed in Negro sections, the Klan sent committees to protest to city officials. No Negro policemen have yet been hired.

All Georgia Klansmen were urged to write letters to Senators George, Russell, Bilbo, and Representative Rankin, urging them to carry on the 1946 filibuster against FEPC and enclosing dollar bills to help carry on the fight.

The Klan was especially upset by the defeat of "Brother" Ben T. Huiet in the special election in February to replace Representative Robert Ramspeck, resigned. Huiet polled only 2,704 votes as compared to the 11,067 votes received by Helen Douglas Mankin, the winner. The Klan has collected affidavits that Negro ministers in the district read from their pulpits a letter from Mrs. Mankin, and these affidavits are to be used "against" her when she comes up for re-election in the fall of 1946.

Initiation teams have been sent from Atlanta to Elberton, Dalton, Gainesville, and other points. At Elberton, on February 18, Klansmen appeared with hoods over their faces; and soon afterward Georgia Klansmen were instructed to prepare summer robes consisting of white trousers, white shirt, and a cap which would serve both as hood and mask. Grand Dragon Green subsequently issued an order that masks *must* be sewn back on the hoods and that they were to be worn at a special meeting on February 25. Later an order was issued for all members to acquire robes. A contract was signed with a Griffin, Georgia, textile mill for the cloth. The robes are to be made by the Klan's ladies' auxiliaries and sold through the Grand Dragon's office.

Klansmen have been informed that as soon as the President's wartime powers have been abolished, the Klan will "ride forth" in a manner "the country has never seen before." Immediately upon the abolition of the President's war powers, all Ku Klux Klansmen will be summoned to a gigantic demonstration on Stone Mountain. The call will be, "You must go!" The only excuse tolerated will be confinement to bed or death in the family.

Night riding, cross-burning, flogging, and all the rest will be resumed. A feature of the meetings are the displays of weapons which the Klansmen bring with them—pistols, blackjacks, brass knuckles, et cetera.

But enough of Ku-Kluxery. The only question is what can be done to put a stop to it.

The prime—and probably final—solution is for the Treasury Department, aided by the FBI, to again call upon the Klan for payment of the $700,000 it owes the United States. It is difficult to understand why the Klan has been allowed to continue its activities since 1941. Of course since 1944 the Klan has been making a feeble pretense of having suspended its activities as a corporation, but the documentary evidence of its continued operation as such (see photostatic layout) is more than sufficient to warrant prosecution. Prima-facie evidence of the continuation of the Klan's corporate activities is the certificate of registration which the Klan's attorney, Morgan S. Belser, filed for the "Knights of the Ku Klux Klan, Inc.," with the Georgia secretary of state on March 22, 1946, together with the required fee covering the years from 1940 to 1946 inclusive (see photostatic layout).

Even without such evidence, it is not the custom of the Treasury Department to permit corporations to escape payment of taxes by pretending to suspend operations and yet carry on in disguise or out. Under the law, the current Klan can be prosecuted as either the de jure or de facto Klan, Inc.

Should the Klan somehow satisfy its tax debt and continue its machinations, other remedies may be required. Unfortunately, a good deal of hysteria has mitigated against some of the past attempts to curb the Klan. The federal "Ku Klux Act" of Reconstruction days was declared unconstitutional because it went beyond enforcement of the Constitutional Amendments. There remains, however, Section 51, Title 18, Chapter 3 of the United States Code, titled "Offenses Against Elective Franchise and Civil Rights of Citizens," which provides:

"If two or more persons conspire to injure, oppress, threaten, or intimidate any citizen in the free exercise or enjoyment of any

Form F-38

STATE OF GEORGIA
CERTIFIED STATEMENT FOR ANNUAL REGISTRATION OF A CORPORATION

NAME OF CORPORATION: KNIGHTS OF THE KU KLUX KLAN, INC.

PRESIDENT: J. A. COLESCOTT _____ GENERAL MANAGER: _____

PRINCIPAL OFFICE: (Street and No.) _____ (City) Atlanta _____ (State) Georgia

PRINCIPAL OFFICE IN GA.: (Street and No.) Atlanta, Georgia _____ (City) _____

AUTHORIZED AGENT IN GA.: IF FOREIGN _____

AGENT'S ADDRESS: IF FOREIGN (Street and No.) _____ (City) _____

NATURE OF BUSINESS: Fraternal Association _____

WHEN INCORPORATED: (Date) July 1, 1916 BEGAN DOING BUSINESS IN GEORGIA: (Date) July 1, 1916

WHERE INCORPORATED: (City) Atlanta _____ (County) Fulton _____ (State) Georgia

BY WHAT AUTHORITY INCORPORATED: Superior Court _____ CAPITAL STOCK Non-stock
(Secretary of State, Legislature, Superior Court, or other authority)

TO THE HONORABLE SECRETARY OF STATE, Atlanta, Ga.:

I HEREBY CERTIFY that the above statement, furnished the Secretary of State of Georgia for record, as required by an act of the General Assembly of Georgia, approved August 16th, 1906, is correct. Date March 21, 19 46.

Signed by: Morgan Belser /s/ _____ Title Secretary _____
(Law requires that President or General Manager must sign)   (OVER)

Charter amended Feb. 1, 1935, extending 20 years from date of amendment.

right or privilege secured to him by the Constitution or laws of
the United States or because of his having exercised the same, or
if two or more persons go in disguise on the highway, or on the
premises of another, with intent to prevent or hinder his free
exercise or enjoyment of any right or privilege so secured, they
shall be fined not more than $5,000 and imprisoned not more
than ten years. . . ."

Though responsibility for the enforcement of this statute rests
with the Civil Liberties Division of the Department of Justice and
with the district attorneys, both of which rely upon the FBI for
investigation, all these have in the past neglected their sworn duty
by frequently refusing to investigate and prosecute such cases.
Very often this reluctance may be traced to the influence of local
politics in the appointment of district attorneys.

Were it so inclined, the Department of Justice might well
prosecute Klansmen for treason. The courts have ruled that to be
guilty of treason by "levying war" there must be (1) an assembly
of armed force, or of *a force sufficient to intimidate by its
numbers,* and (2) there must be an intent to overthrow the government or to *defeat the enforcement of one of its laws.* During
the early days of our country, in the Shays, Fries, and Whisky
rebellions, men were convicted of treason and sentenced to death
for such deeds as tar-and-feathering federal marshals, preventing
tax collections and intimidating tax collectors, and effecting jail
deliveries—all deeds which Klansmen have duplicated and surpassed.

As for treason by giving aid and comfort to the enemy, the
courts have ruled that, among other things, this may consist of
"acts against the Government" and "acts which tend to defeat,
obstruct, or weaken the country's arms." If the Klan's divisive
propaganda both in and out of army camps didn't weaken our
arms, nothing did. The *Yale Law Journal,* in an article "What
Is Giving Aid and Comfort to the Enemy?" has pointed out that
treason may consist of words as well as deeds. "All those who
perform any part, however minute, or however remote from the
scene of action, and who are actually leagued in the general conspiracy, are to be considered as traitors," Chief Justice Marshall
ruled.

Should the executive branch of the government continue to default in its obligation to defend the civil liberties of the people, there would yet be recourse to the legislative branch. New York State, for example, has a law enacted in 1923 which provides that any corporation or association (other than labor unions, fraternities, benevolent societies, et cetera) having more than twenty members and requiring an oath as a condition of membership must file with the state a sworn copy of its constitution, by-laws, rules, regulations, and oath, together with a roster of all members and incumbent officers. All persons who become members of, retain membership in, or attend meetings of such an organization with knowledge that it has not complied with the law are liable to prosecution.

A Klansman named Bryant was convicted of the latter charge, but he contended that the law was discriminatory class legislation which denied him equal protection of the laws. When brought before the Court of Appeals the conviction was upheld with the observation that "The danger of certain organizations has been judicially demonstrated . . . it seems reasonable to separate the known from the unknown . . . the sheep from the goats."

Upon being appealed to the U. S. Supreme Court in 1928 (*Bryant v. Zimmerman*, 278 U.S. 63), the court held that many secret organizations do not violate the peace or interfere with the rights of others, but on the other hand *the state may take notice that certain societies are evil and dangerous and may legislate against them,* provided the classification in such regulations is reasonable. Other states might therefore do well to adopt similar statutes. Moreover, the Congress might do likewise. Because the Klan is a national organization, constituting a national menace to the public safety and welfare, Congress has a perfect right to legislate on it, the same as in enacting the prohibition, narcotics, kidnaping, and alien registration laws.

The motto of the Reconstruction Klan was *"Resurgamus"*— We shall resurge.

The motto of the modern Klan is, "Here Yesterday! Here Today! Here Forever!"

America must answer firmly, "No—not even tomorrow."

The "United Sons of Dixie" was incorporated in Chattanooga on December 28, 1943, by Charles G. Simmons, Roy F. Simmons, Earl D. Simmons, Sanford J. Harwood, William B. Powell, E. E. McDaniel, and Everette F. Poe (some of these may have been unaware of what they were getting into; at least McDaniel assured me that such was the case with him).

The United Sons consists of two degrees—the Sunshine City and the White Legion. The first order was set up as a mere front for the rank and file and bore a heavy coat of—of all things—unionism.

But in the second degree—the White Legion—the United Sons reveal their true aims. Candidates must answer satisfactorily the following questions:

1. Do you believe that the negroes should have better treatment in the U.S.A.?
2. Do you think that negroes should hold public offices in the U.S.A.?
3. Do you think that negroes should have social equality in the U.S.A.?
4. Do you believe in allowing white and negro children to attend school together?
5. Do you think that the white and negro races should intermarry in the U.S.A.?
6. Should these United States of America be a white man's or negro's country?
7. Do we want another Pearl Harbor from the negro in this country?
8. Will you fight to make the U.S.A. a white man's country?

Following the oath-taking (on the Bible and Confederate flag), the president pretends to turn the meeting over to regular business. A "letter" is read from a near-by unit of the Sons of Dixie, calling for 150 men to come at once to help put down rioting by Negroes.

"I was aware of the fact that the negroes intended to try to take control in the South but did not realize it was this close," comments the president. The ritual then calls for up to thirty minutes of discussion from the floor, after which the president calls for volunteers to help put down the "riot." If all candidates for the degree volunteer, they are commended. If any do not,

the president says, "I am surprised that you forgot your obligation
so soon. Are you afraid that you will get killed or wounded? Or
are you just plain coward? What have you to say for yourself?"

After the candidate makes his explanation, someone from the
floor suggests that he be thrown out the window, but the president intervenes and, if the candidate is willing, the ritual proceeds. Among the oaths taken is the following:

"I promise and swear to do all in my power to increase the
white birth rate."

The lecture connected with the White Legion degree is highly
inflammatory. It opens like this: ". . . The negroes are demanding more privileges every day. They want social equality with the
white race in schools, cafés, theaters, trains, and busses. In fact,
in everything—even in your own home. They want to be able to
step out with your mother, wife, daughter, or sweetheart. Men,
we will not stand for this here in the South—here in Dixie!"

(The Sons of Dixie do stand for partitions between whites and
Negroes on public conveyances, barring of Negroes from Pullman
cars, dining cars, and from walking through white coaches; they
want two doors and two conductors on city cars and busses, with
Negroes using the rear door only.)

Summing up, the president declares: "These United States of
America must, and shall be, a white man's country for white people, the master race! We must keep it that way! The white people
of the world must compose the Master Race not only here but in
other countries—just so they are white people. . . . Men, do
you ever get mad? Do you ever feel like getting out and blasting
the negroes until there are none left in this country?

"We must nominate and elect members of our Order and put
them in state, county, and city public offices. These men will be
able to put laws on our statute books which will help us. They
can also help us to get arms and ammunition in order to defend
ourselves and the white people of the United States.

"Most of the white people take the negro for granted and do
not think about what is taking place here at home, while the
negro is quietly arming himself. We want 15,000,000 members in
the United States, and every one of them with a good gun and
plenty of ammunition—ready to fight when it starts. This is plain

talk, Brothers, but we must face the facts. Let us prepare now, before it is too late, and be ready to protect our loved ones from the negro, whatever the price. Eventually we must eliminate the negroes in this country.

"So, my Brothers, live up to your oath. . . . Be ready to fight for your Honor, your Home, and the Master White Race of white people and white supremacy here in the United States of America—our country. Forever—right or wrong—may she endure forever."

The Sons of Dixie represent nothing more nor less than a reversion of Ku-Kluxery to the treason and open terrorism of the Reconstruction Klan. Fortunately, the FBI lost little time in going after the Sons of ——, and there have been no signs of their continued activity. But their lasting significance lies in the foretaste they provided of what the Klan might yet become unless it too is curbed.

Should the Klan be effectively frustrated, there will still be danger that the *state guards* will carry on where it leaves off. At the entry of the United States into the war, the state militia—otherwise known as the National Guard—was inducted into the Regular Army. But during the war the states organized what they called "home guards," which in most instances in the South were officered and in large part manned by so-called "blue bloods." These home guards were equipped and trained specifically to put down "civil insurrection"—which in practice will doubtless prove to be strikes or interracial violence.

Little or no attempt was made to conceal the function of the state guards. Governor Olin Johnston of South Carolina, in addressing his state guard shortly after the Detroit race riot, said, "Segregation is the only way to handle the race question. . . . If any outsiders come into our state and agitate social equality among races, I shall deem it my duty to call upon you to expel them."

In Miami in 1943, Major T. E. English told the junior chamber of commerce, "We have certain elements among us who, through lack of enlightenment or understanding or false leadership, may create situations before the war is over or after it ends, which will require policing with a larger and more forceful organization than our present law-enforcement agencies." Governor Millard Caldwell has added, "We will so equip ourselves in the form of a state guard that we will not have to depend on others."

In similar vein, Brigadier General George L. Cleere of the Alabama guard told the Montgomery chamber of commerce in 1945, "The state guard needs hundreds of additional members, for we must be prepared for the day when Negro soldiers will come back with new ideas and get into trouble."

Although the home-guard units are now being absorbed into the reconstituted state militia (National Guard), they will still be commanded by the governors, and no federal troops can intervene without gubernatorial or legislative invitation.

Also in the potential storm-trooper category are the "Vigilantes, Inc." This outfit was formed in Atlanta on October 10, 1942, by John E. Goodwin, John J. Cummings, and Fred Derrick; attorneys for the incorporators were T. F. Bowden and Hewlett & Dennis. Goodwin was head of the state highway patrol under Talmadge and appeared with Talmadge at the Klan rally in Porterdale, Georgia, in 1943. Talmadge's link with the "Vigilantes" has been exposed by the book *Under Cover*.

The "Art-Craft Network" would perhaps be the best label to apply to the most influential sector of the South's disruptive press. Such papers provide the written word, while the demagogues provide the spoken word, to poison the mind of the South against democracy. The papers spade the ground for the demagogues' campaigns and in some instances are personal organs of the demagogues themselves. But the papers, like the politicians, must be regarded as mere instruments of the employers they serve—for without financing, the papers would not be printed and the demagogues would not choose to run.

The Art-Craft Publishing Company was formed in Birmingham in March of 1945, buying out the DuBose Publishing Company. According to *Alabama* magazine, which is printed by the establishment, "Financial spark plug of the deal was portly Attorney Horace C. Wilkinson, whose interest was partly in keeping a place to print the *Woodlawn News* and probably turn out more scatter sheets in future political campaigns."

Horace Wilkinson was the principal stockholder at the time of incorporation, with Fred Rucker (secretary) taking the next largest amount. C. G. Thomason, another stockholder, is also the publisher of the *Industrial Press, Northside Press,* and *Shades Valley Press.*

In the past the Art-Craft presses (then the DuBose Publishing Company) ground out Jim Simpson's 1944 race-hate campaign sheet, the Alabama *Sun.* Currently the same presses are turning out a weekly tabloid newspaper, the *Southern Outlook,* and the monthly slick-paper *Alabama* magazine—to mention the two most outspoken. The *Southern Outlook* is nominally published by T. E. Blackmon, while *Alabama* is published by Alabama News Magazine, Inc. However, a Birmingham credit bureau reports that Art-Craft and the *Outlook* are "one and the same company . . . there are a bunch of smart people in Birmingham who are behind this paper . . . they publish and Mr. Blackmon plays the part as manager." W. D. Samuel, president and third largest stockholder of Art-Craft, is listed as the publisher of Wilkinson's *Woodlawn-East Lake News,* but a local credit bureau says it is "actually published" by Art-Craft, and they have the same telephone.

The *Southern Outlook,* "Feature Newspaper of the American Way of Life," is by all odds the most complete of the Southern hate sheets. Its anti-union, anti-OPA, anti-Negro, anti-Semitic, isolationist, reactionary propaganda is thoroughly mixed with photographs, comics, mystery stories, illustrated Sunday-school lessons, cartoons, and crossword puzzles. This is the paper described by the Montgomery *Advertiser* as "one of the most viciously unfair and contemptible distortions of truth . . . ever to come from the typewriter of any man save the late Adolf Hitler. . . ."

The *Outlook* arose out of an organization called Facts, Inc., which was formed in Birmingham in January of 1943. Among the incorporators of Facts, Inc., were R. DuPont Thompson, an attorney who has advertised in the *Outlook* and who played a prominent part in the so-called "American Democratic Party of Alabama"; Sherwood A. Moore of the Moore Ornamental Iron Works, who advertises in both the *Outlook* and *Alabama;* and W. C. Strickland of the Strickland Paper Company, whose name is used by the *Outlook* as a reference; and J. J. Scarborough, also named by the *Outlook* as a reference.

The paper's claim to be "First, an American; second, a Southerner; and third, a Democrat" is hardly substantiated by its contents. Its use of material from Colonel McCormick's Chicago *Tribune* is not good and sufficient evidence of Americanism; the use of this same material is sufficient to disqualify the *Outlook* as Southern (despite the Chicago *Tribune's* apologies for the Klan); and the *Outlook's* advertisements, editorials, photographs, and "news stories" favoring Republican candidates can hardly be called Democratic.

It may have been through contagion from the Chicago *Tribune* that the *Outlook* contracted a bad case of isolationism and nationalism. Straight from the *Tribune* came an editorial praising Reynolds's "Nationalist Party" as the "only hope" unless the Republican party improved (became more effectively reactionary). Other symptoms were such headings as these:

"Britain's Nigger in Our Woodpile," "John Bull's Same Lion," "U. S. Versus John Bull's Trained Diplomats," "Britain, Russia Play Cat and Mouse; U. S. in Santa Role," "Will We Give Aid to China's Communists?" "UNRRA the Most Expensive Setup Ever Put Together," "Who Gets What Benefits from Reciprocal Trade Treaties?"

With such as this sprinkled through its pages, it was little wonder that the *Southern Outlook* came to the defense of those who were charged by a federal grand jury with sedition. The paper also branded Carlson's book *Under Cover,* which exposed them, as "New Deal propaganda."

Indicative of the *Outlook's* anti-unionism was a full-page advertisement headed: "Small Industries Will Find a Welcome in Clanton, Alabama." The advertisement read:

> Abundant Native Labor, Efficient, Reliable, Congenial. Friendly co-operation by a People 99% Native Born who Believe in Free Enterprise, Who Welcome New Enterprise, Who Are Intelligent, Co-operative, and Friendly. No Hostile Union Here and None Desired.

Furthermore, the *Outlook* has reported "Caution Urged by NAM for Plan to Increase Pay," it has followed the NAM line

for emasculation of the Wagner National Labor Relations Act,
and hailed the adoption by Arkansas and Florida of the "Christian-American" constitutional amendment abolishing union security.

In its disruptive propaganda the *Outlook* has been orthodox
rather than original: "FEPC Perils South; Robs White, Negro
of Postwar Jobs; Strikes Up Racial Antagonism," "Southerners
Furious Over Equality Issues," "What the New Deal Has Now
Done to Alabama's Well-Known Ku-Kluxer; Just What Kind of
Hi-Life the New Deal Used on This, Our Great Southern States-
man and Former Ku Klux Orator, Is Still a Military Political
Secret."

In its continuous attacks upon Jews, the *Outlook* has gone so
far as to print the so-called "Franklin prophecy," long since
proven to be a forgery.

For some time the *Outlook* has advertised that "full-time agents
can earn up to $500 per month" selling subscriptions, which are
$2.00 per year. Also for some time one Raymond Parks, a former
Huey Long newsman, was busy soliciting bloc subscriptions by
telephone in Birmingham. Although his sales talk varied from
time to time, his favorite seemed to be to describe the purchase
of the *Southern Farmer* by Marshall Field as an attempt to
socialize the South. To forestall this, Parks would suggest that the
industrialist take as many bloc subscriptions as possible, which
would be sent "to a list of 10,000 key farmers." To some of his
big prospects Parks added that the *Outlook* could help save the
South's electoral votes "for free enterprise."

Claiming a circulation of 20,000 in the Southern states, Parks
solicited industrialists for anywhere from $10 to $200 "to push
circulation to 50,000." Promising that bloc subscribers would be
sent individual receipts showing to whom the subscriptions went,
Parks said, "As for using your name in any way, that is entirely
up to you. Some of the men whose names I have mentioned have
been good enough to let us use them as reference, giving us moral
as well as financial support, while others who would like to do so
have been unable, for business reasons."

Among the names given as references were "the DeBardelebens
—both C. F. and Prince." C. F. DeBardeleben, Jr., is head of the

Red Diamond Mining Company, and Prince DeBardeleben is head of the Alabama Fuel & Iron Company. Among the other references given were Ike Roser of the Alabama Mining Institute, Thomas McGough of the McGough Bakeries chain, and Carl Hotalen of the Alabama Temperance Alliance. It may be, of course, that these "references" are not aware of the use of their names.

Alabama, the "News Magazine of the Deep South," comes out in imitation *Time* format, with the imprimatur (advertising) of many of Alabama's industrial Big Mules. Among its regulars are Coca-Cola, Alabama Power Company, DeBardeleben Coke & Coal, Alabama Mills, Monsanto Chemicals, Southern Bell & Telephone, Birmingham Trust and Savings Company, Bama Mills, Sherwood Moore Ornamental Iron Works, National Life Insurance, Stockham Valves, McGough Bakeries, et al.

The important fact is that these corporations are not advertising in an ordinary magazine, wherein reaction is dispensed in the more disguised forms. During the '44 campaign *Alabama* published on its cover several of the photographs of Mrs. Roosevelt accompanied by Negroes, and it has never failed to exploit the white-supremacy line.

Alabama not only carries ads of the National Association of Manufacturers, but gives complete coverage to the NAM's comings and goings in the state. In addition, it might be said that the magazine is the ex-officio organ of Associated Industries, Chamber of Commerce, and Farm Bureau Federation. Whereas the *Southern Outlook* is designed for mass propaganda, *Alabama* is the esoteric voice of the Big Mules, braying at all things democratic.

In other forays *Alabama* has fought against state legislation to raise unemployment compensation to the national level, charging that the bill was "An Act to Compensate Intentional Idleness." It took a leading part in defeating repeal of the poll tax by the 1945 legislature, upholding the tax as the last bulwark of white supremacy against Social Equality and Black Rule. It was pleased to note passage of the "Christian-American" amendment banning union security in Florida and Arkansas. Periodically it attacks the CIO and the Southern Conference for Human Welfare.

Upon Roosevelt's death, *Alabama,* with indecent haste, began to express its hopes for the "New Setup" which it said had replaced the New Deal. The magazine's anonymous (as well he might be) "Major Squirm" said: "I have high hopes of Harry. . . . His pappy put on a Confederate uniform back in the sixties and tuk out after them Yankees hot and heavy." Said *Alabama* itself: "This does not mean that the critics of Mr. Roosevelt will now have their way about everything, but rather that true progress is made with a scalpel instead of the broadax."

Another Art-Craft-printed paper which has recently resorted to racism is Hugh DuBose's weekly tabloid, *Radio News,* which is said to have a circulation of about ten thousand among Birmingham's white-collar folk. DuBose, of course, was the former proprietor of the printing establishment. His *Radio News* still uses the Art-Craft address, and so does the *War II Vet,* another weekly tabloid, issued by the "War Two Veterans International," an organization launched in Birmingham with DuBose's help. DuBose ran against Luther Patrick for Congress in 1944 and is trying again in 1946. After bidding unsuccessfully for union support, DuBose has turned to vitriolic attacks on PAC. And when Birmingham Negro vets marched to the courthouse to register to vote, DuBose published a call for a new Klan to ward off "social equality." The Klan thereupon emerged and touched off five fiery crosses.

Still another rather influential member of the Southern "white supremacy" press—not related to Art-Craft—is the *Southern Weekly,* "Militant Journal of the Awakening South," edited by Peter Molyneaux at Dallas, Texas. Prior to 1944 the magazine was known as *Texas Banking and Industry.* Two of its most faithful advertisers have been the Chase National Bank of New York and the Dallas Union Trust Company.

"In these times, when the people of the South are facing the most serious menace to their local institutions since the days of Reconstruction, such a periodical is necessary to every loyal Southerner," says the *Southern Weekly* in advertising itself. The magazine is not, however, a rabble-rouser. On the contrary, it provides a sober analysis of events and trends for the guidance of rabble-rousers. No Southern demagogue should be without it.

Because it does serve as something of a mentor for reactionary financial, industrial, and editorial circles, the *Southern Weekly's* political perspective is significant. Upon the final re-election of Roosevelt it predicted: "The rejoicing of Southern officeholders and office seekers over the 'great victory' is likely to be short-lived, for measures included in the anti-Southern pro-negro program will come up in Congress as soon as it reassembles. . . . The South will receive no consideration."

Denying that the collapse of the 1944 Southern revolt made things hopeless for the Southern Democratic tories, the magazine said: "Our own view is that it only demonstrates that nothing can be accomplished through the organized party machinery. . . . Instead of a collapse of the Southern revolt, the happenings of the past five months may turn out to be the beginnings of such a revolt. . . . In 1948, after four years of the kind of experience which seems certainly ahead of the South, the storm may break with southwide fury."

Apparently, however, the death of Roosevelt gave the Southern tories new hope of regaining control of the Democratic party, for in 1946 the *Southern Weekly* had resumed its old line: "New Deal Repudiated Democratic Platform."

In going about the South, recording the struggles of working folk to organize, I have often heard complaints about a small monthly paper calling itself *Militant Truth*. Usually this paper appears mysteriously in workers' mailboxes on the eve of National Labor Relations Board elections. Sometimes it crops up only for the election; sometimes it keeps on coming every month for a year or more. It says inside that the subscription price is thirty-five cents a year, but these workers do not pay anything for it. According to an inside notice, it comes to them free, "With the Compliments of a Friend."

Some employees have detected that *Militant Truth* is addressed to them in *exactly* the same way as things sent them by the company. Of course no employer will admit he is the one who put up the money and the mailing list—that would get him into hot water with the NLRB for violating the National Labor Relations Act, which prohibits employers from trying to stop their workers from forming a union. And when the NLRB sent a field examiner to see Editor Sherman A. Patterson of *Militant Truth,* Patterson said he kept no record of his contributors!

However, the NLRB has pinned down one employer on the *Militant Truth* deal, and it has other cases pending. Just last year the Blue Ridge Shirt Manufacturing Company of Lafayette, Tennessee, was found by a NLRB trial examiner to be "chargeable" for the act of one of its foreladies who handed out *Militant Truth* to an employee on company time and company property.

Patterson lowered his guard sufficiently to write me in part on December 3, 1945:

> Quite a number of mill and factory workers throughout the south are receiving MILITANT TRUTH, and results indicate that it is well read. The group rate of 35¢ each, per year, includes mailing direct to the homes, of the employees, as is now being done by a large number of industrial people.

Again, on January 5, 1946, he wrote me:

> Regarding your friend whom you think would be interested in taking subscriptions for his employees, I would be very glad to come down to Jacksonville and call on him, if you feel that this procedure would meet with his approval. This would not obligate him in any way, but would give me an opportunity to outline to him the procedure we have followed in similar situations in other communities.

Militant Truth was first published in 1940 at Dayton, Tennessee. The advertisements of R. E. Winsett, a religious-songbook publisher located there, appear regularly in the paper.

The South's long-suffering textile workers are having to suffer *Militant Truth* to a greater extent than any other group of workers. In Georgia alone, *Militant Truth* was sent during 1945 and/or 1946 to workers at the following mills: Exposition Cotton Mills, Piedmont Cotton Mill, Gate City Cotton Mills, Rushton Cotton Mill, Thomaston Cotton Mill, Lowell Bleachery, Inc., Crompton-Highland Mill, Dundee Mills (Nos. 1, 2, 3, and 5), Athens Manufacturing Company, A. D. Julliard (Floyd Mill Division), Anchor Duck Mill, Mandeville Mills, Caroline Mills, Dallas Mill, and Douglas Mill.

During December of 1945 I called at Editor Sherman Patterson's office in Chattanooga. He wasn't in, but there were two young ladies busily cutting address stencils from mailing lists. They assured me that Patterson was seldom in the office, as he spent most of his time traveling, occasionally stopping by the office at night to catch up with his work there. However, since it was presumed that I was there to talk "business" with Patterson, I was given an appointment to see him upon his arrival several days later.

I found Patterson to be a slight, smooth-talking man in his early thirties. His first words were, "Sorry I wasn't in the other day—I'm very hard to catch."

Patterson said that the circulation of *Militant Truth* is 45,000, almost entirely in the South. He added that he "can't make any money" until he reaches 50,000 circulation, but that "in the meantime I am receiving a few contributions from businessmen which take care of the deficit."

When I intimated that a friend of mine was having "union troubles," Patterson said, "All he has to do is send in the mailing list and I'll take care of the rest."

At the outset Patterson assured me that "Of course *Militant Truth* is not put out to fight unions; its purpose is to promote fundamental Christianity and constitutional Americanism."

However, when I tried to feel Patterson out as to which particular unions he regards as undesirable, he did not hesitate to condemn the entire CIO "lock, stock, and barrel." An examination of the contents of *Militant Truth* reveals that he has also opposed AFL unions. In other words, if it's anything but a company union, he's against it.

Militant Truth's anti-union line is peculiar. First it takes as its text the Biblical admonition, "Be ye not unequally yoked together." Then the non-Rev. Patterson interprets this as meaning that Christians should not join any organization which includes people of other creeds. And the final step is a vicious attempt to demonstrate that unions are not Christian.

So virulent is *Militant Truth's* attack upon labor leaders that in some instances even the most confirmed anti-union employers have declined to make use of it. For example, A. B. Salant, of the mill chain of Salant & Salant, wrote G. C. Gambill of his Lawrenceburg (Tenn.) plant, on March 10, 1944: "Thank you ever so much for the January and February copies of *Militant Truth,* which I read with a great deal of interest. . . . On the first page of the January number there is a reference to Hillman as 'an alien-born communist.' . . . We are fighting the Amalgamated [Clothing Workers of America-CIO] and fighting Hillman as strenuously as we can, but we don't care to use poisoned weapons in this or any fight. . . ."

Besides its unfailing month-to-month attack on unions, *Militant Truth* put out in 1945 an undated "Special Labor Edition" which is the one usually distributed on the eve of NLRB elections. Patterson confided to me that he was planning another such edition for publication early in 1946, of which he hoped to sell an extra 100,000 copies.

Among other things, Patterson confided that "the NLRB has been after me, especially through the Post Office." He went on to say that at one time the Post Office subpoenaed him to produce the records of his subscribers and contributors. Rather than do this, he decided to give up his second-class mailing privilege.

In addition to the purchase of *Militant Truth* by employers for their employees, Patterson informed me that "through the courtesy of some businessmen" he is sending subscriptions to "several thousand working people selected from the Knoxville, Tennessee, city directory."

As I was about to leave I mentioned the Southern States Industrial Council. Patterson beamed. "They support *Militant Truth,*" he said. "You can write either to C. C. Gilbert [the executive secretary] or Thurman Sensing [director of research]. Sensing writes the unsigned 'As I See It' column which appears on the front page of *Militant Truth* every month."

Because *Militant Truth* carries regular ads of Joseph P. Kamp's "Constitutional Educational League" propaganda, I was not surprised when Patterson reached into a steel cabinet and began handing me such Kamp booklets as *Vote CIO—And Get a Soviet America* (five times the Nazis' "World Service" propaganda bureau recommended *Join the CIO—And Get a Soviet America*), *With Lotions of Love* (an attempt to smear Walter Winchell, who has often exposed Kamp), and other propaganda of the same stripe.

Patterson told me he had distributed "thousands" of Kamp booklets. According to the Friends of Democracy, Kamp's salesmen keep 25 per cent of the take, and "one representative made upwards of $16,000 in one year." Kamp used to have a Southern office of his "Constitutional Educational League" in Birmingham. I asked Patterson about it, and he said the office is now closed but that he has "some friends there who are carrying on."

"The material for these Kamp booklets came from the files of the Dies Committee," Patterson went on. Speaking of the Wood Committee, which has taken the place of the Dies Committee, he added, "Winchell attacked it recently, which is enough to recommend it to me."

This man Kamp whom Patterson serves deserves further mention. For some time Kamp was executive editor of a paper called *The Awakener,* which was twice recommended by the Nazis' "World Service." Associate editor of *The Awakener* was Lawrence Dennis, author of *The Coming American Fascism.* The editor was Harold Lord Varney, who was also managing director of the "Italian Historical Society" and was decorated by Mussolini.

Kamp also served on the "Committee of Honor" of some fifty "super patriots" who sponsored the debut of Atlanta's Major General George Van Horn Moseley (retired), whom both native and German fascists evidently chose to be their "man on horseback" in this country.

Needless to say, Kamp had many supporters among the thirty-odd persons indicted for sedition by the federal government. Among them were William Dudley Pelley, Joe McWilliams, George Deatherage, James True, Robert Edward Edmondson, Gerald B. Winrod, Elizabeth Dilling, Charles B. Hudson, Eugene Nelson Sanctuary, William Kullgren, Court Asher, C. Leon de Aryan, and Elmer J. Garner.

In view of all this, it is not surprising that when two successive federal grand juries returned indictments against such persons for sedition and conspiracy to foment fascist revolution, Joe Kamp's "Constitutional Educational League" was named in both indictments as one of the channels through which their propaganda flowed. Kamp himself was indicted in 1944 for refusing to furnish a list of the officers and contributors of his League, which had been requested by the House Committee Investigating Campaign Expenditures.

Kamp is by no means the only *Under Cover* character with whom Patterson does business. In fact, *Militant Truth* has gone out of its way to make excuses for all those indicted for sedition.

Militant Truth has carried advertisements of indicted Eugene Nelson Sanctuary's propaganda (after Pearl Harbor). Also, *Militant Truth* has printed the propaganda of the "Anglo-Saxon Federation," an outfit organized by William J. Cameron while he was editing the anti-Semitic Dearborn *Independent* for Henry Ford. The "Anglo-Saxon Federation" still publishes a slick magazine called *Destiny*. The Federation has also distributed large quantities of the forged "Protocols of the Elders of Zion," strongly recommended by Hitler.

Still another *Under Cover* character whose poison has been spread through the pages of *Militant Truth* is George Washington Robnett, whose "School for Revolution" appeared in the July 1945 issue. A lot more of Robnett's stuff appears in *Militant Truth,* but, instead of being "credited" to him by name, gives his front-organization names, such as the so-called "Church League of America," "National Laymen's Council," and *News and Views.*

According to John Roy Carlson, author of *Under Cover, "News and Views* seemed to be merely another outpost of reactionary 'big business' interests, mixed with a brand of hysterical Red-baiting and flag-waving paralleling those of Mrs. Dilling. Robnett was backed by important industrialists. General Robert E. Wood [head of Sears, Roebuck] once sent him a personal check, followed by another substantial check by R. Douglas Stuart, Jr., youthful founder and a director of the America First Committee . . ." Carlson called on Robnett and reports that he began at once a tirade of bitter invective against minority groups. Among Robnett's friends, says Carlson, were Kamp, Sanctuary, Dilling, Harry A. Jung, Merwin K. Hart, Walter S. Steele, John B. Snow, Charles B. Hudson, Charles W. Phillips, and E. A. Rumely of the so-called "Committee for Constitutional Government."

And so *Militant Truth,* while claiming to stand for Constitutional Americanism, actually works hand in hand with many of those who have been indicted for sedition and conspiring to overthrow the American Constitution and government.

Although *Militant Truth* makes a great pretense of being a Christian publication, month after month it prints an ad of a book called *20th Century Reformation,* written by one Carl McIntire. This book seeks to "scandalize" the good name of the Federal Council of the Churches of Christ in America, which represents twenty-four denominations, including Baptists, Methodists, Presbyterians, Episcopalians, and Congregationalists, embracing nearly 28,000,000 church people all told. As if attacking this great confederation of Christians were not enough, *Militant Truth* also attacks the YWCA and YMCA.

One must wonder if *Militant Truth* would not be more truthful if, instead of calling itself "Fundamentally Christian," it frankly admitted that it is fundamentally anti-Christian.

Besides attacking unions and the churches, *Militant Truth* has gone out of its way to attack co-operatives and has also printed a recommendation of "more, better, and bigger poll taxes, and restrictions on the right to vote."

The "Union of Christian Crusaders," led by the priest-without-a-parish Arthur W. Terminiello, is currently one of the most ominous cabalistic factors operating in the South. Often referred to in the press as the "Father Coughlin of Dixie," Terminiello was born in Boston on April 11, 1906. He received B.A. and M.A. degrees at St. Mary's Seminary in Baltimore and also a degree from the James Law School at Montgomery, Alabama. He was ordained for the diocese of Mobile in 1933.

In 1939 Terminiello launched a monthly paper, *Rural Justice,* at Troy, Alabama. Like Coughlin's *Social Justice,* Terminiello's paper attacked the Roosevelt Administration, Britain, et cetera. Hate sheets such as the anti-Protestant, anti-Masonic, anti-Semitic *Malist* (published by F. H. Sattler of Meriden, Connecticut) advertised *Rural Justice,* which soon waxed anti-Semitic itself. It was not until May of 1943, when the paper had acquired a claimed circulation of 20,000, that its publication was suspended upon the order of Bishop T. J. Toolen of Mobile. The final issue carried an article by Carl H. Mote, president of the Nationalist segment of the National Farmers Guild and publisher of the hate sheet *America Preferred* which attacks Negroes, Jews, our Allies, the Federal Council of Churches, et al. (Mote is a part owner of the Commonwealth Telephone Company and the Northern Indiana Telephone Corporation; he also chaired the 1944 convention of Gerald L. K. Smith's "America First Party.") Another contributor was Earl Southard of Chicago, secretary of the "Citizens U.S.A. Committee" and a top dog in the "America First Party."

Terminiello was not silenced for long. In June of 1944, at his new parish in Huntsville, Alabama, he broadcast over station WBHP a series of nine addresses in honor of Our Lady of Victory at the Church of the Visitation. Utterly defeatist, these speeches came to the defense of the "Peace Now" movement which even the Dies Committee had exposed. Under such titles as "Victory through Peace" and "Victory through Charity," Terminiello spoke of the "so-called atrocities" of our enemies. Subsequently these speeches were published in booklet form, bearing the imprimatur of Bishop John Francis Noll of Fort Wayne, Indiana.

Again, on October 22, 1944, Terminiello broadcast over the North Alabama Network a speech entitled "The Cross of War— Is It Due to Stupidity or Cupidity?" Among numerous other statements hardly calculated to improve American morale, Terminiello said, "We must stop joining the refrain 'We must win the war.' . . . More important even than victory is to stop that slaughter as soon as possible." He went on to defend "the 26 old men and women who are now being persecuted for their convictions in the so-called 'sedition trial' . . ."

Needless to say, this speech was widely disseminated by the self-styled "patriots." Among those who aided in its circulation were Mary Leach, secretary to Elizabeth Dilling; Court Asher, publisher of *X-Ray;* Charles B. Hudson of Omaha; William Kullgren of California, publisher of *America Speaks* (the preceding four were all charged with sedition); the "Citizens U.S.A. Committee"; the "Independent Music Publishers Service" of

Aberdeen, Washington; George T. Foster speaking before the "Constitutional Americans" in Chicago; H. L. Beach of Portland, Oregon; and favorable mention also came from C. Leon de Aryan, publisher of *The Broom.*

Evidently encouraged by such manifestations of "solidarity," Terminiello decided to launch an organization of his own. In a broadcast sermon entitled "Santa Claus or Christ?" delivered at Midnight Mass on Christmas Eve, 1944, at his church in Huntsville, Terminiello issued a "Call for a Christian Crusade" to fight against "a cause which is becoming more UNJUST every day. . . . Our soldiers," said he, "must not be the victims of the crooked cross of Nazism or of the DOUBLE CROSS of the Allies." A claimed million copies of this speech were sent to "persons who requested it," resulting in a *claimed* enrollment of 40,000 in the Union of Christian Crusaders by the end of 1945.

Terminiello also got out a multigraphed sheet, *The Crusader,* and a diagram entitled "The Double Deal Cross of War" which sought to blame President Roosevelt for America's participation in the war. When the war was over, Terminiello issued a hysterical appeal for funds, making the ridiculous charge that B'nai B'rith (a staunchly democratic Jewish fraternal group) "is now conducting a campaign to raise four million dollars to carry on their anti-Christian plot to exterminate those who opposed their plans for world domination and the rape of the Holy Land." Calling Zionism "treason," Terminiello called for a constitutional amendment "to outlaw Zionism and British-Israel."

Then Terminiello went from bad to worse. In a mimeographed release entitled "The World Plot Unfolds," he called upon his "Christian Crusaders" to stage a "March of Death" on Washington and suggested hanging for John Roy Carlson, author of *Under Cover,* Eugene Segal, author of a Scripps-Howard exposé of the Nationalists (including Terminiello), and Harry Monsky, president of B'nai B'rith. Charging that all civilization is going to be destroyed by Fascism and "Red Fascism," Terminiello said, "All this is to be accomplished in the name of 'brotherhood' and 'democracy.' Then the work of the Judeo-Masonic British-Israel will be complete." Elaborating still further, Terminiello explained that the "world plot" includes "the financing and building of the capital of the World Empire in the Jewish Homeland," and "the fomenting of revolution in the remaining Christian countries of the world—Spain, South America, and Ireland."

Terminiello spewed up this sort of thing despite a statement from Bishop Toolen in May of 1945 that he would "not allow Father Terminiello to go along the lines of Father Coughlin." Finally, on November 27, it was revealed by the AP that Bishop Toolen had issued a formal statement as follows:

> Reverend Arthur W. Terminiello, having refused to obey the order of his bishop to cease sending out literature which we feel is detrimental to the church and the unity of our country . . . is no longer considered a priest in good standing in the diocese of Mobile, nor has he the right to use his facilities as a priest in the diocese.

While divesting Terminiello of some of his prestige, this suspension order evidently had the effect of limbering his tongue and giving him more time for disruption, for early in 1946 he decided upon a speaking tour of the North. In Philadelphia—the city chosen for his first stand—he was refused permission to use a Catholic hall, and so spoke at the hall of the "Current Events Club." He appeared in full frock, however, and used the title "Reverend" on the announcements. Among other things, Terminiello said that American servicemen had not fought for democracy, but for "a capitalistic Zionist group which is now trying to control America." The meeting was concluded by Paul Meinhart, assistant national secretary of the "Christian Veterans of America," who charged that the American Legion, Veterans of Foreign Wars, and other veterans' organizations are "pro-Jewish." Still another speaker was C. Daniel Kurtz, of the Queens "Christian Front."

Accompanied by Gerald L. K. Smith, Terminiello also spoke at such cities as Cleveland, Pittsburgh, Detroit, and Chicago. In Cleveland, speaking under the auspices of the America First party, Terminiello declared that in opposing the Jews he was acting "on the Pope's order to the faithful." In Pittsburgh his sponsors were the "Defenders of George Washington's Principles." There he said, "Let's never use that word 'democracy' about our country again. . . . I don't want unity; I'm not organizing a party but a crusade."

In Detroit Terminiello spoke to about seven hundred women, mostly members of the "United Mothers." "Every member of the America First Party is marked to be the first killed when the Jews take over," said Terminiello, "unless the Christians stick together to fight back and to organize for a bloody revolution." In Chicago he spoke under the auspices of the "Christian Veterans." On stage was an all-star cast, including Elizabeth Dilling and Ellis O. Jones of the sedition trials; Eugene Flitcraft and James Dies of the Gentile Co-operative Association; Frederick Kister, chairman of the "Christian Veterans"; George Vose, Smith henchman; and anti-Semitic candidate for Congress, Charles Anderson, Jr. Terminiello, Smith, and Kister were arrested and charged with creating a diversion tending to produce a breach of peace.

In February of 1946, Terminiello produced the first issue of an eight-page tabloid version of *The Crusader* ("Successor to *Rural Justice*"). Printed in Birmingham, it announced the opening of Terminiello's "Unique Publishing Service" in that city, offering the propaganda of such people as Elizabeth Dilling, Sivert Erdahl, Samuel Pettingill, Jeanette Rankin, George Armstrong, Garet Garrett, William Hard, John T. Flynn, et al.

The idea of a *Nationalist party* was among those of the arch-isolationist Representative Ham Fish, but it remained for ex-Senator Robert R. Reynolds of North Carolina to launch the party early in 1945.

Reynolds was elected to the Senate in 1932 after touring his state in a jalopy and displaying a menu in French and a jar of caviar ("Red Russian fish eggs at that"), which he alleged was the fare of the incumbent, asserting the while that "good ole North Carolina hen eggs are good enough for me."

After being elevated to the Senate, Reynolds showed his isolationism by voting against repeal of the arms embargo; he was the only Southern senator to vote against both lend-lease acts; he voted against revision of the Neutrality Act, against the transfer of Axis ships, against extension of the draft, and against arming merchant ships. He voted thus despite his elevation through seniority, on May 15, 1941, to the position of chairman of the Senate Military Affairs Committee.

In addition to his isolationism, Reynolds introduced a series of deportation and immigration bills. In April of 1939 he inserted in the *Congressional Record* an inflammatory article, "The Refugee Invasion," from *Il Grido della Stirpa* ("Organ of Italian Fascist Propaganda in America"), whose editor, Domenico Trombetta, was sent to an internment camp in 1942 as a "dangerous enemy alien."

Reynolds decided to further air his views in a newspaper which he founded, the *American Vindicator,* which soon received the endorsement of men like William Dudley Pelley and George Deatherage, both of whom have been charged with sedition. Reynolds apparently found such company congenial. In 1942 he wrote Gerald L. K. Smith, "Let me congratulate you with my full heart upon your first edition. . . . We have arrived at the hour when we must have more 'two-fisted' talking and real action." Similarly, on October 9, 1943, Reynolds dispatched the following letter:

Personal

Rev. Gerald B. Winrod
Wichita, Kansas
My dear Rev. Winrod:

Your friend, Rev. William T. Watson, president of the Florida Bible Institute at St. Petersburg, Florida, was good enough to send me a full-page advertisement from the *Independent* which carried your answer to the smear charges of sniper Nelson Poynter.

I read every word of your reply with deep interest. These character assassins are still at large, but the day of reckoning will arrive and is on its way.

With assurances of my highest esteem, I am,

Very sincerely yours,
(signed)
Robert R. Reynolds, U.S.S.

In September of 1942 thousands of anti-Semitic leaflets were enclosed with a Senate speech by Reynolds and distributed in his franked envelopes in New York subways. Rubber-stamped on the envelopes was the slogan "Buy from Christians."

While in the Senate, Reynolds also corresponded with Elizabeth Dilling, later indicted for sedition; and when, on November
12, 1943, he was mentioned by Gerald L. K. Smith for the
presidency on an "America First" ticket, Reynolds said he was
"highly flattered and honored." To cap all this, it is not surprising that after a visit to Nazi Germany, Reynolds returned
to say that "in all fairness" he thought "the dictators are doing
what is best for their people."

Perhaps deciding that discretion was the better part of valor,
Reynolds decided not to seek re-election in 1944. Instead, he
organized an "American Nationalists' Committee of Independent Voters" for the purpose of "bringing about the election of
congressmen, senators, a vice-president, and president who are
for AMERICA FIRST." Shortly afterward he sought the aid
of Republican Senator Taft "for a plan which he claimed would
bring under the Republican banner a coalition of strict nationalists of all political affiliations."

After those abortions, Reynolds announced in January of
1945 that he was launching a Nationalist party under the sponsorship of the American Nationalists' Committee and the Nationalists' Confederation. Claiming that the party was already
organized in New York, Michigan, Illinois, and California, Reynolds said that its greatest support would come from Republicans, anti-New Deal Democrats, America Firsters, and veterans.
Charging that Communists had sabotaged the America First
Committee, Reynolds said his plan called for tightly knit units
of ten persons each.

"By 1946," he said, "we will have reached such a state of
organization that we will be able to make our weight felt in each
congressional district. If we don't approve of the candidates in
the field, we'll be able to enter a candidate of our own. By 1948
we will either support a presidential candidate who is in accord
with our views—or we will be strong enough to place our own
candidate in the field."

On February 21, 1945, it was reported that Reynolds had
approached a member of a firm of newspaper promotion experts,
asking whether the individual would be interested in syndicating
a weekly newsletter to be published shortly by Reynolds together

with Gerald L. K. Smith and Joseph P. Kamp. Reynolds added
that he had just opened an office with these two gentlemen in
Washington.

About this same time Major General George Van Horn Moseley of Atlanta stated that Reynolds had offered him a job in
uniting the various nationalist groups. It was also reported that
Reynolds had commissioned the "Christian Mobilizer" Joe Mc-
Williams to tour the South in search of nationalist money from
businessmen.

The letter of introduction which Joe McWilliams, traveling
as "Mr. Jack Williams," carried from Reynolds said in part:

> I am sure that you will be interested in hearing what the
> plans are regarding this new party in fifteen Southern states.
> We know that you will be greatly interested for the very par-
> ticular reason that part of our program directly affects your
> business, which subject is fully set forth in the enclosed state-
> ment entitled "Freedom for Management."

But apparently Reynolds's plans for a Nationalist party are not
faring very well. His paper—whose name he had changed in
May of 1943 from the *American Vindicator* to the *National
Record*—was suspended late in 1945. And though he tried to
gloss over the suspension with plans for a weekly Nationalist
paper, no such organ has yet appeared. The future of nationalism
in America depends not so much upon little men like Reynolds
as upon the intolerable possibility that really powerful imperialist
elements might succeed in forging for a time an Anglo-American
anti-Soviet Axis.

The "Commoner Party of America" was organized at Conyers, Georgia, in 1944, as a "Gentile block to combat the Jewish
and Negro political blocks." Charles H. Emmons, its secretary-
treasurer, had previously proposed the formation of a "Dixie
Party." Emmons has evidently fancied himself as an exponent of
racism for some time, for in 1945 he mailed me a leaflet labeled
"Racial Problems Considered," bearing the printed notice,
"Copyright, 1939, by Chas. H. Emmons," but also bearing his
penned notation, "Not copyrighted." Emmons is now seventy-
nine years old. A native of Kansas, he came to Atlanta about

ten years ago. In the 1944 campaign he worked for John W. Goolsby, who polled 11,500 votes against Senator Walter George's 81,000 votes. In a letter pro-Talmadge Goolsby has said that Emmons "is an able man and a man of good intentions, and I feel he has some excellent ideas; they only need to be put into effect."

When Emmons first began to show his Commoner party program he was assured, "You'll never get anywhere with it."

"You'd be surprised," he replied. "We may make quite a bit of money out of this thing."

Taking leave of his relatives in Atlanta, Emmons took up residence on the Conyers farm of James L. Shipp, who became chairman of the Commoner party. Shipp is sixty-four years old and has been in the coal business in Atlanta for some time. Together these two got out a thirty-two page program unique in its commingling of racism, religious bigotry, prohibitionism, old-age pensions, "cures" for juvenile delinquency, et cetera. "A National Gentile Political Block should go into control of the American Government in 1948 and proceed at once to break the strangle hold of the Jew Dynasty . . ." the program asserts.

On the "Negro question" the Commoners employ classic Ku Klux jargon: "Primarily and fundamentally the United States is a 'White Man's Country.' Unquestionably, it shall so remain." Under the heading "A Double Standard Voting Franchise" the program says: "The Commoner Party demands repeal of the Fifteenth Amendment to the Federal Constitution and the reduction of the Negro race to citizenship without the right of franchise. It proposes the establishment of Franchise Courts in all states for granting the franchise privilege to Negroes upon proof of voting qualifications." As a substitute for the Fifteenth Amendment the Commoners propose:

> The right to vote and to hold office shall be limited to white people who are citizens of the United States of America, and to other racial individual citizens who can qualify under the franchise standard fixed by the Constitution and Acts of Congress.

Internationally, the Commoners would have spheres of influence rather than the United Nations Organization. The program goes on to say, "The Commoner Party welcomes the support of Gentile organizations of every kind: the Churches, the Teachers, the Prohibitionists, Old Age Pension Clubs, the Ku Klux Klan, if there is such an organization, and all other societies that feel to travel down this 'Great White Way' with it."

In a letter Secretary Emmons has said, "While Mr. Shipp and I fronted for this movement, it has behind it some of the best men in Georgia. We drove many miles over Georgia to consult with men who felt the need of such an effort." The names of Georgia bankers, industrialists, attorneys, railroad men, and politicians who have contributed to the Commoner party in one way or another are known, but are being withheld from publication pending further developments.

Emmons wrote me that a Mississippi merchant who ordered a quantity of the program "said a vice-president of a farm organization took a copy of the book to a state convention and made a speech for the movement." To me he concluded, "Trusting that you will be able to 'crack the pot' our enemies talk about. . . ."

When I went to see Talmadge about the thing, he first said, "I don't know anything about it." But shortly afterward he commented that "It was not the usual way to start a political party. . . . If it was me, I'd call it something else—something like the 'American party.' "

That the Commoners got together with Talmadge is borne out by a letter from Shipp to Talmadge on February 17, 1945, in which he said, "In further reference to our talk while in your office with regard to the matter of changing name of the Commoner Party to the American Party, it is our decision at this time, after due consideration, and with the association of True Americanism carried throughout our platform, to permit the present name to stand."

Nevertheless, it was not long before the Commoners acquired a rubber stamp with which they subtitled their program booklet "Pro-White Gentile American Party."

Shipp has said that the Commoner party is backed by two wealthy men—one in New York and one in California.

Among others, the Commoners have been corresponding with Terminiello; Joseph P. Kamp; Carl Mote; Winfield Jones (author of *KKK*); James A. Colescott; the Christian American; John R. Irwin; Charles B. Hudson; Gerald L. K. Smith; Robert Reynolds; Phil W. Davis, Jr., a Tulsa attorney who tried to form a Nationalist party in 1945; and Ainsley E. Horney, publisher of the *Hoosier Patriot*, Indiana. When asked specifically by Allan Swim of the Scripps-Howard papers whether the Commoners were working in co-operation with such groups as America First and Christian American, Shipp replied, "Where their programs are in line with my program we naturally are in the same road. Therefore, in that case, we are traveling together."

On May 7, 1945, Shipp spoke before a meeting of Vesper Ownby's "We the People" in Atlanta. Shipp also says that Emmons says he has spoken to William J. Cameron of the Ford Motor Company, who he says promised to supply some back copies of the Dearborn *Independent*. Shipp has said further that he expects William Dudley Pelley to take over when he gets out of prison.

On June 4, 1945, Emmons wrote Ainsley Horney, "I am mailing the enclosed suggestions for consolidating the scattered third-party forces to five leading men with a request for their reaction to its proposals. . . . I am sending this suggested plan to Carl H. Mote of Indianapolis, Gerald L. K. Smith of Detroit, Phil W. Davis, Jr., of Tulsa, Oklahoma, Robert R. Reynolds of Washington, D.C., and yourself." The enclosure was titled "A Suggested Plan for United Political Action by the Various Patriotic Units Now Organized in the United States." Calling for consolidation into "one gigantic powerhouse," the Plan suggested a meeting on October 12, 1945—the anniversary of the discovery of America—to "Recover National America from a dangerous International Leadership." The meeting was to adopt a name, principles, establish a national committee and a publication, and name candidates for president and vice-president. On June 11, Smith replied:

> I am very much interested in the suggestion you make, and at a time that is mutually agreeable I would be happy to meet with you and others in Washington, D.C.

By 1946, however, the Commoners' plans had bogged down to such an extent that, in desperation, they concocted another outfit, to be known as the "American Gentile Army." This was not too surprising, in view of the fact that the Commoners had previously enclosed with their propaganda a "Call to Action—No Softies Need Apply" from Frederick Kister's "Christian Veterans of America." Membership cards for the "American Gentile Army" have been printed, and it is planned to enlist veterans to sell them at three dollars each around bus stations, train terminals, et cetera, the veterans keeping two dollars for each membership sold. This "Army" is described as "an Organization for Independent Political Action," and the membership cards bear the legend, "National Independence Will Save the American Way of Life." Companies are to be formed, under cover, of ten men each. The co-operation of some "twenty other organizations" in the enterprise is hoped for.

It is unlikely that either the Commoner party or the American Gentile Army will get anywhere, in view of the caliber of their present leaders, unless new leadership and more money are forthcoming. The Commoner party's chief significance is as a symptom of the extremes to which Southern-style fascism may go in the event of widespread unemployment with its consequent frictions.

The "Christian-American" association—better known in labor circles as "Heathen American"—has been by far the most effective promoter of labor regimentation laws on the American scene. While the products peddled by the "Christian Americans" vary from time to time, they have of late specialized in the following concoctions:

1. "God-Given Right-to-Work" constitutional amendments. (These amendments would abolish all forms of union security: the union shop, closed shop, maintenance of membership, et cetera.)

2. "Anti-Violence-in-Strikes" laws. (Under such laws, unions and strikes can be broken by jail sentences and/or fines meted out on the testimony of a single person that a unionist or striker

has threatened—not necessarily committed—violence to deprive him of his "right to work.")

3. Union registration laws. (These would establish burdensome residence and licensing requirements for union organizers and make union finances a matter of public record, thus facilitating strikebreaking, and so forth.)

The record of the "Christian Americans" has become so notorious as to require but little recounting here. In 1944 I prepared a full-length documented exposé of the outfit, which was published by the Southern Conference for Human Welfare and 150,000 copies distributed by unions and other progressive groups. Subsequently, other exposés have appeared in *Collier's*, *Reader's Scope*, and the Scripps-Howard papers.

While the "Christian American's" principal product is anti-union legislation, it has not hesitated to resort to racism and bigotry to that and other ends. According to Vance Muse, secretary-treasurer, the "anti-violence bill would implement the power of our peace officers to quell disturbances and keep the color line drawn in our social affairs." According to the Houston *Post*, he has described the miragelike "Eleanor Clubs" as a "RED RADICAL scheme to organize negro maids, cooks, and nurses in order to have a Communist informer in every Southern home."

Mrs. Muse, chief clerk, confided to Victor Bernstein (as he reported in the *Antioch Review*) that she was worried about the "Eleanor Clubs" because they stood for "$15 a week salary for all nigger house help, Sundays off, no washing, and no cleaning upstairs." As an afterthought she added, "My nigger maid wouldn't dare sit down in the same room with me unless she sat on the floor at my feet!"

Letting herself go still further, the little lady went on to say, "Christian Americans can't afford to be anti-Semitic, but we know where we stand on the Jews, all right. It doesn't pay us to work with Winrod, Smith, Coughlin, and those others up North; they're too outspoken and would get us into trouble. . . . You'd be surprised how many important corporations support our work."

The lair of the "Christian Americans" is Houston, Texas, from which Muse and Val Sherman, his hired hand, sally forth in search of sponsors. The man Muse is quite a character. He is six four, wears a ten-gallon hat, but generally reserves his cowboy boots for trips Nawth. Now over fifty, Muse has been professionally engaged in reactionary enterprises for more than a quarter of a century.

From time to time he has fought against women's suffrage, against the child-labor amendment, helped collect $250,000 from the railroads for the cause of nullifying the eight-hour-day bill, fought for high tariffs, for sales taxes, for a 25-per-cent limitation on federal inheritance, gift, and income taxes (a pet project of the "Committee for Constitutional Government"), and for "Americanization of the Supreme Court" (Austrian-born Frankfurter's decisions in labor cases have been distasteful to employers).

It is interesting to note that Muse cuts little ice in his own bailiwick. When he ran for Congress in 1942 against Representative Albert Thomas, he received 500 of the 90,000 votes polled.

Back in the twenties Muse worked as agent and collector with the "National Council of State Legislatures," "Southern Tariff Association," and "American Taxpayers Association," for which Muse and his fellow workers collected over a million dollars. When in 1930 Senator Thaddeus Caraway's "Committee Investigating Lobbying Activities" looked into these things, they described them as "highly reprehensible." The Committee found that of $860,574 collected by Muse and his associates during a four-year period, Muse received $20,434, his sister, Mrs. Ida M. Darden ("her stage name for collecting money," said the Committee), received $24,898, and her husband, W. F. Myrick, got $14,958. There was an agreement whereby Muse and his sister were to get 40 per cent of all checks they took in and 10 per cent of everything over $100,000 collected in their domain of eighteen states.

After that investigation and exposé, Muse went to work with a "Texas Tax Relief Committee" and "Southern Committee to Uphold the Constitution." This time, in 1936, Senator Hugo Black's Lobby Investigating Committee called Muse in to testify. The Committee discovered that he had succeeded in collecting some $41,000 from some of the country's biggest industrialists, including $10,000 from the du Ponts, $5,000 from John J. Raskob, $1,000 from Alfred P. Sloan of General Motors, et cetera. Other sums came from H. P. Hopson of Associated Gas & Electric, Ogden Mills, former Secretary of the Treasury, E. W. Mudge of Weirton Steel, Stone & Webster, Pittsburgh Plate Glass Company, the Armours, Wideners, Sam Insull, Crawford Johnson of Coca-Cola, Robert Ingalls of Ingalls Iron & Steel, and Charles DeBardeleben of DeBardeleben Coke & Coal. Ed O'Neal, president of the American Farm Bureau Federation, also co-operated with Muse and the "Southern Tariff Association."

One of Muse's long-time financial godfathers was the late John Henry Kirby of Texas (said to have been worth $30,000,-000), who informed Senator Black's Committee that he was chairman of the Kirby Petroleum Company, president of the Kirby Lumber Company, and president of the Kirby Investment Company. He also said he had been chairman of the "Southern Committee to Uphold the Constitution," an executive committeeman of the "Sentinels of the Republic," and a member of the "Order of American Patriots." Another heavy contributor was the late Maco Stewart, Sr.

It is not certain just where and when Muse crossed trails with Lewis Valentine Ulrey, the present chairman of "Christian American." According to CA literature, Ulrey is a "university-trained man of wide learning and experience," who came from Indiana to Texas for his health, and became geologist for Maco Stewart & Son, also taking charge of their "anti-radical activities."

The genesis of the "Christian American" is likewise clouded. In 1936 the Rev. Ralph E. Nollner formed the "America Forward Movement for Religion and Americanism," otherwise known as the "Christian American Movement." Nollner's magazine, the *Christian American,* announced a conference in Asheville, North Carolina. Among the sponsors were Sanctuary, Dilling, Robert Edward Edmondson, William Kullgren, Ernest F. Elmhurst, and Ulrey. When the conference came off there was a schism, with an anti-Semitic faction being led away by Deatherage, Gerald Winrod, Ulrey, et al.

Muse incorporated the "Christian American" in Texas in

1936, and until 1940 the magazine was edited by the Rev. Harry Hodge of Beaumont (minister to Martin Dies). Then Ulrey took over as chairman and managing editor. He had already achieved notoriety by writing for Winrod's *Defender,* where he charged that Colonel House had "conspired with foreign Jews for the establishment of the League of Nations," and complained that "Our President has sent two insulting messages to Hitler . . ." Ulrey has jumped almost everybody: the Federal Council of Churches, Methodist Federation for Social Service, American Civil Liberties Union, Union Theological Seminary, NAACP, CIO-PAC, World Trade Union Congress, et cetera.

It was in 1941, when Governor Pappy O'Daniel was trying to push the first "anti-violence" bill through the Texas legislature, that the "Christian American" stuck its nose into the anti-union feed bag. Ever since then Pappy has been at their beck and call, coming in to speak to other state legislatures after the "Christian American" has done its softening-up job.

While their batting average has not been perfect and has dropped precipitately of late, the "Christian Americans" have had considerable success. On April 24, 1944, Muse wrote me:

> We have successfully sponsored anti-violence laws in Texas, Arkansas, Mississippi, Florida, and Alabama. We are directing a campaign in Arkansas for a RIGHT TO WORK amendment to the state constitution and are co-operating with Attorney General Tom Watson, who is sponsoring a somewhat similar movement in Florida.

According to *Collier's,* "Christian American has ballyhooed for anti-labor union legislation in forty-four states and claims credit for success in eight." The additional states mentioned were Kansas, Idaho, South Dakota, and Colorado. In referring to the mailing lists which he said he used "just as long as it's productive," Muse said blandly to a Scripps-Howard interviewer, "Call them sucker lists, if you like."

One of the CA's first setbacks came in Louisiana, where the legislature not only rejected their "anti-violence" bill, but charged that the CAs had "harassed, annoyed, and threatened" them, and asked the FBI to investigate. . . . In 1942, Pappy introduced the thing in the Senate, where it received one vote. In 1944,

Florida and Arkansas adopted the so-called "Right-to-Work" amendment, with the CAs spending an admitted $67,873.49 in the latter state.

That same year California voters rejected the amendment, perhaps because the CAs were not called in. There the Merchants and Manufacturers Association carried the ball, but chambers of commerce, the Democratic party, church groups, city and county commissions, union groups, newspapers, American Legion posts, and the Veterans of Foreign Wars all got together to nail it. Said the VFW: "The proposed 'Right of Employment' initiative will not create one additional job. . . . It will, however, if adopted, create a condition under which reactionary employers can ruthlessly exploit working men and women. . . . This amendment proposes to restrict the very liberty and freedom our brothers and sons are fighting for overseas."

When the amendment was brought before the Texas house in 1945, it voted 111 to 14 to investigate the "Christian American's" lobbying activities. It was charged that "the Christian American, acting by and through its agent, one Buck Taylor, had continually had the privilege of the floor of the house. . . ." The investigating committee reported that Taylor "denied ever having been associated with the Christian American or with Vance Muse." However, the report went on, "Vance Muse, upon being questioned concerning his relationship with Buck Taylor, stated that in 1943 he asked Buck Taylor if he would make a tax survey through Louisiana and other Southern states for the Christian American. Buck Taylor made such a trip, according to Muse, and was paid his traveling expenses. . . ."

The committee resolved "We do condemn the methods of high-pressure propaganda sponsored by Muse in an effort to pass any type of legislation." And so the amendment was killed in Texas. It was also killed in Tennessee and Georgia the same year.

It is significant that employers have been among the most militant contestants of the legality of the "Right-to-Work" amendments in Florida and Arkansas. The thing is clearly a violation of the constitutional right to enter into contracts— which in their case is the right to contract for a stable labor supply. Certain Southern spokesmen of the AFL have even had the nerve to warn employers that adoption of the amendment would "open the doors" to the CIO by nullifying AFL closed-shop contracts. Moreover, both the National Labor Relations Board and War Labor Board have ruled that the amendment is superseded by all management-labor union-security contracts under their jurisdiction. It only remains for the Supreme Court to kill the project altogether.

The "Christian Americans" are undaunted, however. They still have hopes of getting thirty-two state legislatures to force Congress into considering a "Right-to-Work" amendment to the Federal Constitution. Now that the National Association of Manufacturers, National Small Business Men's Association, Southern States Industrial Council, et al, have openly taken up the fight against union security, the peril is even greater than before.

With the "Christian Americans" seriously crippled by exposés, a new group known as "Fight for Free Enterprise, Inc." was chartered in Texas in January 1944, as an "educational" society. Its incorporators were William Walker, chairman, M. D. Spindler, and William Crockett O'Hara. FFE proceeded to open an office in a San Antonio building. In the same building State Representative Marshall O. Bell maintained his law office (Bell authored the Texas "Christian American" anti-union-security amendment and also sponsored a bill—endorsed by the "Committee for Constitutional Government"—to prohibit the state from levying an income tax).

In a preliminary report dated March 31, 1945, a Texas house committee investigating lobbying activities in connection with the anti-union-security amendment said it "did receive a letter from one of [FFE's] executive officers advising that they had not and were not taking any part, either for or against, any legislation" before the legislature. Nevertheless, on May 20 and 30, 1945, when the amendment was still pending, FFE sent telegrams to all Texas senators, urging its passage. Also, according to the Houston *Press* on November 29, 1945, Phil Hopkins, FFE's vice-president, stated that the FFE had spent $700 on telephone calls that spring, drumming up support for the amendment.

But the "Fight for Free Enterprise" boys have not only fought for "Christian American" laws. Among the organization's objectives are: no repeal of the "Christian American" so-called "anti-violence in strikes law"; no repeal of the Manford Act regimenting unions; no reinstatement of Homer P. Rainey as president of the University of Texas; maintenance of a white Democratic primary by repealing all state laws governing primaries; retention of the poll tax; adoption of a constitutional amendment disfranchising all federal employees in Texas elections.

In addition, according to the AP on January 28, 1945, Vice-President Hopkins said that the FFE advocates: (1) A six years' residence requirement for all union organizers in the state. (2) A law requiring union leaders to wear identifying headgear while on duty: red or orange caps for the CIO, fawn or light brown for the AFL, and gray or black for the brotherhoods and independents. To cap the self-portrait of the FFE, Chairman Walker said in a letter dated February 1, 1945: "You are entirely correct in your statement that our aim is Nationalism— with a large capital 'N.'"

In May of 1945 a "Confidential Memorandum," unsigned, went out in envelopes bearing the return address of the FFE, together with a letter signed by FFE Chairman Walker asking the recipient to "Please read the enclosed memorandum at once." In its foreword this memorandum said, " 'The Organization' is . . . NOW FIGHTING to protect BOTH Labor and Capital from exploitation (indeed enslavement and destruction) by the Communistic Revolutionists, Extortionists, Racketeers, Thugs, Goons, and Common Thieves of the C.I.O." It also pointed out that "the Source which prepared this program, and which now has it in actual preliminary operation, is for obvious reasons referred to in this memorandum only as 'The Organization.'"

Continuing with an "Outline of Basic Measures," the memo described plans to get out special editions of the "Organization's" newspaper attacking the CIO, and a plan to apply for a Writ of Mandamus against the attorney general of Texas, "citing him to show cause why he has not or should not proceed against various CIO unions . . ." The memo further explained:

> It should be noted that, quite regardless of the chances for success of this suit, it affords an opportunity to make allegations of a sensational nature without regard to libel, and allows the newspapers of the state TO PRINT these allegations with complete immunity from any action by the CIO or its leadership . . . If lost, these suits would be kept alive for harassment of the CIO by continued appeals—meantime bombarding the public with details of the story set forth in pleas for injunction, which will carry great weight through being dignified by forming part of court records.

Also on the program was a weekly radio broadcast against the CIO, over stations KRGV, Weslaco, KTSA, San Antonio, KXYZ, Houston, and KGKO, Dallas. Item 4 stated: "It is intended that periodical sensations will be created by the publication and distribution of documents, letters, publications, leaflets, et cetera, *clearly* of C.I.O. origin, and which 'The Organization' is in a position to produce, when and as most appropriate and timely."

Item 5 of the program declared:

> Discharged veterans of this war . . . will be carefully selected for toughness and peculiar abilities and set to work organizing "Americanism Protective Committees" . . . These Committees to be organized on the basis of observing, reporting, and opposing CIO activities, and to become political campaign organizations in the spring of 1946. They will also become direct action committees, when, as, and if this should be necessary or desirable . . .

Item 6 called for "stern corrective and punitive action against those newspapers of the area which are running with the CIO wolf pack," with "intense pressure" to be "exerted on all advertisers to withdraw their patronage from them . . ." Item 7 called for the erection of anti-CIO billboards, while the final Item 8 concluded "The whole of the foregoing (AND such additional measures as determined by events) to form the background for an intensive campaign in the 1946 primaries to nominate Democratic candidates bitterly opposed to the CIO and completely committed to assisting in its eradication from Texas."

On July 17, 1945, two months following the appearance of the foregoing memorandum, FFE petitioned the attorney general to investigate the CIO. In its answer and counterpetition the CIO said it would welcome investigation and called for investigation of the FFE as an illegal conspiracy.

Then, on October 21, 1945, FFE sought an injunction against the Oil Workers International Union-CIO on the ground that the Union was not duly chartered to engage in activities in Texas. It developed that non-profit organizations such as unions do not require charters from each state in which they operate. Thereafter, on November 3, the AP reported that a "board of trade" had been issued a Texas charter under the name "Congress of Industrial Organizations, Inc." FFE Vice Chairman Hopkins and other FFE members were among the incorporators of this new "CIO." A week later the corporation sued for an injunction against the CIO Oil Workers, demanding that the union be denied use of the designation "CIO." At the same time other CIO unions in Texas were warned to stop using the name, and newspaper and radio stations were likewise warned not to use "CIO" with reference to what the new corporation called "self-styled" CIO unions.

FFE Chairman Walker has refused to name his financial backers. The Austin *American Statesman,* on January 15, 1945, reported him as saying that he had previously worked in the East with Joe Kamp's "Constitutional Educational League" which he said "sponsored the Dies Committee." Walker claimed that the FFE represented 9,000 members and was not only anti-CIO but "most definitely anti-New Deal."

In addition to those already named, FFE has listed the following officers, directors, and members:

> Austin F. Hancock, vice-chairman, Dorothy Adams Hay, treasurer, B. P. Matoocha, legislative counsel. *Directors:* Dr. L. R. Brown, Victor C. Rodgers (contractor), A. P. Rheiner (contractor), Fred Lehr (contractor), Howard Bumbaugh (contractor), F. H. Eckert (investments), Hilton T. Howell (insurance), Peter B. Reed (Candle Company), Geo. L. Taft

(produce shipper), J. L. Lytle (real estate), A. K. Polis, O. W. Killam (oil refiner), Anna M. Kelsey (investments), H. J. Moreland (Dr. Pepper), Dr. Oliver A. Keith, Clyde H. Alexander (Crosslyn Oil Company), A. B. Syptak, Dr. F. B. Kelly, Judge F. B. Crawford (attorney), G. E. Burford (Burford Oil), D. M. Jones (investments), Judge E. A. Arnim, Jr. (attorney), A. L. Ligon (machine works), W. J. Ellinghausen (merchant), Hugo Kallenberg (merchant), Walter R. Smith (oil operator), John S. Atkins (county judge), Judge Lee Wallace (retired attorney), Gus Schreiner (cattleman), Lem L. Allen (oil operator), Fred Turner, Jr. (oil operator), Mrs. E. R. H. Taggart (Macon, Ga.), Mrs. W. S. W. Farnum (Philadelphia). *On FFE letterhead:* Henry Knolle (board of *Dirt Farmer Stockman*), Mrs. Ed Auge (Auge Packing Company), Frank Marek (accountant), I. K. Howeth (oil), Clinton Lunberg (San Antonio livestock commission), W. C. Evans (contractor), J. W. Perry (contractor), Dr. J. W. Goode, Dr. W. B. Russ.

It is, of course, possible that some of those people had no idea what "Fight for Free Enterprise" stood for. . . .

I happened to be in Chattanooga when the "Veterans and Patriots Federation of Labor" made its debut on January 11, 1946. In an announcement to the press, it was reported that the corporate charter had been applied for by a group of fifteen veterans "whose names were not available."

"The most important thing we are interested in right now is to get jobs for veterans without holding them up on initiation fees," said Ulis Keith, president. A long-time resident of Chattanooga, Keith is about fifty years old and a paper hanger. Attorney for the incorporators was Harry Berke, who announced that the group would be "more conciliatory" than the established labor unions. Berke went on to say that "for all practical purposes" it would "be a competitive labor organization with the AFL and CIO."

The day after the press story I dropped around to the "Veterans and Patriots" office and learned from the janitor that not a single caller had been in, despite the publicity. The office was barely furnished with a table desk, a few chairs, a pencil, and a pack of file cards—unopened.

That same day B. T. Judd, CIO representative in Chattanooga, pointed out in the press that the CIO does not charge veterans any initiation fee at all and that the maximum charged by CIO unions is five dollars, the average being two dollars. "I doubt very seriously that this projected outfit called the 'Veterans and Patriots Federation of Labor' will turn out to be either for veterans, patriots, or labor," said Carl Stafford of the Chattanooga Industrial Union Council. "The announcement made by their attorney strongly indicates that what its backers have in mind is a subservient company union and a union-busting propaganda and lobbying concern."

This evaluation was soon proven to be correct. When the CIO Steelworkers strike reached Chattanooga in February, anonymous newspaper ads appeared offering steel jobs and training to veterans. Many veterans who answered the ads refused to work when they discovered that they were expected to scab. A few crossed the picket lines and took jobs at the Mascot Stove Works, however, precipitating violence.

Evidently the self-styled "Veterans and Patriots" are doing business, for they have advertised for a secretary and a file clerk. When I went by the office again, just a few weeks after its opening, I found it well equipped, including venetian blinds.

"We the People"—whose relations with the Commoner party have been noted—is the misnomer assumed by a group incorporated in Atlanta on January 31, 1944. Significantly, the attorney and mentor of the group, Vesper M. Ownby, also ran for a seat in the Georgia legislature in 1944. The incorporators are Marvin W. Thompson, Henry C. Parker, and Mack H. Stowe, all of Atlanta. Official notice of the incorporation was inserted in Talmadge's *Statesman*.

"We the People's" application for membership asks, "Do you believe that the white and negro races should continue to pursue their separate social paths, without hindrance from moronic agitators and intermeddlers who set themselves up as would-be leaders?" The meetings, reportedly held at a hall on Marietta Street, are said to be anti-Negro, anti-New Deal, and anti-Russian. In May of 1945, Ownby claimed a membership of

2,000, said that he had acquired a public-address system and had ambitious plans for getting out printed propaganda. There was some talk that the organization might change its name to "The Falcons" when the war was over.

Now that the war is over, "The Falcons" have not yet emerged into the light of day; nor is it likely that "We the People" will prove to be more than one man's attempt to forge a political implement.

Woodford's Slant is the name of a monthly newsletter published by Jack Woodford in conjunction with the "International Writers Club" in Houston, Texas. Slant's price is six dollars per year, or, if you prefer it autographed and air-mailed, fifteen dollars. The theme is simply that a Jewish monopoly over the publishing, radio, and motion-picture industries prevents Gentile geniuses from making good, while mediocre Jewish writers are pushed to the top. Woodford suggests that if struggling Gentile authors will write about cowboys with Jewish names, success will be theirs. He is especially peeved at the Anti-Defamation League, an adjunct of the Jewish B'nai B'rith fraternity, which does an effective job combating anti-Semitism and other fascistic factors. Woodford's personal category is indicated by his suggestion that the Jews may have to be wiped out in droves.

The *White Horse* is the name of a small monthly paper launched in Atlanta early in 1946 by J. A. Dennis, a minister of the Church of Christ. The *White Horse* rides the Catholics unmercifully, gives the Pope hell for having "blessed Franco" and entered into a concordat with the Nazis. According to Dennis, the Church of Christ is Christ's church, whereas the Catholic Church is a presumptor founded in 606, from which the various Protestant branches have since sprung. On the other hand, Dennis points out, "Christ was a Jew and so were all the Apostles. No Christian can hate, persecute, or kill even one Jew and please Christ."

Progressive Labor is the name of an anti-labor paper published at Knoxville, Tennessee, by Sam H. Scandlyn, Jr. Besides opposing the union shop and strikes, it has also attacked price control. It suspended publication for a time during the war, after the NLRB found a Tennessee manufacturer guilty of unfair labor practice in sending the anti-CIO *Progressive Labor* to his employees. Another *Progressive Labor* has also cropped up in Shreveport, Louisiana, where it is published, facetiously, by the "Free Enterprise League, Inc."

The Individualist, published by Guy C. Stephens at Danville, Virginia, sells for twenty-five cents for twenty-four issues—and is worth every cent of it.

"The Constitutional Christian Party" apparently consists of one Frank Lowson of Huber, Georgia. To the Senate Committee Investigating Campaign Expenditures, Lowson reported spending several dollars during the 1944 campaign. However, during the war Lowson authored the following lengthy booklets, which were printed on slick paper and distributed by the J. W. Burke Company of Macon, Georgia:

Trail of the Serpent of Gold of Babylon; The Army of Christ; Come Out of Babylon, My People; Listen Deluded Democrats and Republicans; Match (?), Master (?), or Slave (?); The Cross of Gold.

In these almost pathetic volumes Lowson attacks the "World Government Machine of the Judeo-Mongolian Money Changers," and charges that both the gold standard and free enterprise are part of a Jewish bankers' conspiracy to control the wealth of the world. He calls upon the American people to "throw out that Money Changer System, and adopt a system based upon Thomas Jefferson's Government Owned and Operated Banking System and a Superstructure of the Christian Commonwealth Co-operative System of Enterprise." Lowson signs himself, "A Scribe in the Army of Christ." A native of Scotland, he is sixty-six years old.

The "Free White Americans, Inc." broke into print in August of 1945, when President C. E. Mills, an insurance man of Jellico, Tennessee, announced that a charter had been obtained and that groups were being formed in other states. Asked what the organization's "Fifth Freedom" slogan stood for, Mills replied, "Freedom from forced mixing of the white race with other races." The group also advocates a federal Jim Crow segregation statute. Moreover, the "Free White Americans" objected to such pictures as *The Fighting 69th* and *Going My Way* because of the emphasis on Catholics. They sent a letter of protest to thirty movie producers against pictures which "advertise favorably one religious faith to the exclusion of others." Furthermore, they objected to movies which "play up Communistic Russia in a heroic role." According to the secretary of the "Free White Americans," a letter he sent to Senator Bilbo outlining the group's principles was inserted in the *Congressional Record* by "The Man."

The "Mason-Dixon Society, Inc." was incorporated in Kentucky in the fall of 1945 and established offices in Covington and at Washington, D.C. The corporation's subtitle is, "The National Association for the Advancement of White People." Its prime purpose is to defeat passage of a permanent FEPC bill. The Society was founded by its vice-president, J. Lawrence Dooley of Covington, long-time industrial representative in that area. Its president and Washington lobbyist-collector is Beecher Hess of Norwood, Ohio.

More in the rumor category of small fry are the "White Waves," which a man named Pitman of Stone Mountain, Georgia, was promoting via petition in April of 1943. The purpose of the "White Waves," Pitman is said to have said, "is to get rid of all the Jews in America."

But we have come from the vicious to the ridiculous Southern organisms of reaction. These are not even small fry. Many fascist eggs are spawned, but few mature into fuehrers. In order to mature, they must be fed and they must have a congenial environment. Therefore, if we do not want a fascist South or fascist America, we must cut off their food supply and build a democratic environment in which fascism cannot survive.

3. The Road Ahead

MANY THINGS MONEY CAN BUY

Having thus far probed some of the economic, social, racial, and political aspects of the problem of the South, let us now consider approaches to solution of the problem.

There is little or nothing wrong with the South that money can't cure.

Southerners do not eat corn pone and fat back out of preference, nor live in tumble-down shacks out of sheer attachment, nor shy away from doctors out of fear, nor till other men's land to avoid responsibility, nor work for low wages willingly, nor quit school simply because the curriculum doesn't fit their needs. . . .

On the contrary, Southerners do those things largely because they can't afford to do otherwise.

It does not require professional prescience—particularly for Southerners—to see that the South is poverty-stricken, prejudice-ridden, half starved, sick, ill-housed, and badly educated. These shortcomings must be provided for if the squalid South is ever to become a solid South.

In the important matter of health, North Carolina has demonstrated what the Southern states themselves can do, within the financial limitations peculiar to each. As a result of organized public demand, the governor of North Carolina has appointed a commission on Hospital and Medical Care, which, after a careful survey, has recommended:

1. The appropriation of $5,000,000 to aid communities and counties to build new hospitals and health centers, and to expand present facilities.

2. Expansion of the state's public health service, including an adequate program of disease prevention, provisions for a general examination of all school children and treatment of the remedial defects found.

3. Hospital aid for low income groups, and encouragement of health insurance and group medical care plans.

4. Expansion of the University of North Carolina's medical school from a two-year to a four-year institution with scholarships for promising youths, and the establishment in co-operation with neighboring states of a regional medical school for Negroes.

But North Carolina is one of the most prosperous of the Southern states; what she can afford, others cannot. To meet the South's most urgent health needs, the Southeastern Regional Planning Commission has urged that health and diagnostic centers be established in those 312 Southeastern counties which lack general hospitals. It has also urged that the number of public health personnel be increased in all instances where it falls below at least 4 per 10,000 population; that all agencies interested in dietary problems become acquainted with the crop-adjustment program of the U. S. Department of Agriculture, and that programs of nutritional education be inaugurated, employing mobile clinics among other things.

In urging the construction of a considerable number of both government-supported and non-profit hospitals, and in regard to the entire program recommended, the commission concluded, "Federal aid will be needed to provide the original capital for instituting and temporarily maintaining this program. Alongside the institutional development will be needed a plan of hospital care insurance to insure utilization of the services provided."

The specific need for increased hospital facilities for the general public has been carefully studied by the Senate's Sub-Committee on Wartime Health and Education, headed by Senator Claude Pepper of Florida. This committee has proposed networks of medical facilities on a regional or state basis, to make high-quality medical care available to every citizen regardless of where he may live. The health centers recommended by the Pepper committee would combine all three aspects of modern medical care: the preventive, the diagnosis, and the cure. It proposes the development of a co-ordinated network of small neighborhood and community health centers, rural and district hospitals, around a large base hospital.

The recommendations of the Pepper committee are embodied in the Hospital Construction Bill, introduced jointly by Senator Lister Hill of Alabama and Senator Burton of Ohio. The bill would provide $5,000,000 for planning and $100,000,000 for building new facilities, with additional yearly appropriations to be made as needed.

New hospitals will not be enough, however; there must be some provision for getting people into those hospitals and getting them whatever medical care they need. To accomplish this is one of the purposes of the Wagner-Murray-Dingell bill for the expansion of social security. Besides enlarging upon the benefits of unemployment and old-age insurance, this particular bill would also establish a system of health insurance which would provide complete medical and hospital services, including maternity benefits. The insurance fund would be financed by a small pay-roll tax on salaries up to $3,000, paid equally by the employer and employee.

For reasons beyond all understanding, the incumbent leaders of the American Medical Association have viciously opposed public health insurance as "socialistic" and charge that it would result in political domination of the medical profession. But despite their intensive propaganda campaign to that effect, a good 68 per cent of the American people are still in favor of public health insurance.

The medicos may be satisfied with their present private fee system whereunder they assuage their consciences with an occasional reduction or outright charity case, but the millions of Americans who suffer untold misery for lack of treatment are not at all satisfied. Nor need they be satisfied with anything less than full access to all that medical science affords. An adequate public health program can provide that now. Democracy in action can cure the sick, reduce disease to a minimum, raise health to a maximum. Any doctors whose desire to make money takes precedence over those goals will remain perfectly free to do business as usual.

The job of adequately housing the South is also plenty big enough for both private and public enterprise to work side by side without getting in each other's way. But, sad to say, certain real-estate interests, for reasons best known to themselves, have bitterly fought public housing programs. The "reasons" they advance (for public consumption) consist of ridiculous complaints that "public housing projects are tax-exempt, collectivist, communistic, conducive to social equality," et cetera. But the real reason—which they keep to themselves—is a mistaken belief that somehow public housing will deprive them of some of their profits. It is too bad that they have not yet realized that public housing has invariably stimulated private construction.

The basic philosophy which *must* govern our housing program has been clearly stated by the National Association of Housing Officials:

1. The health of any community and its social and economic stability require the maintenance of a certain minimum standard of housing accommodation for all its families. The community cannot afford the continuing degeneration of the living standards, the discontent, and the expense thrown upon public services by the blighted areas and slum conditions which follow any failure to maintain such a standard in housing.

2. Experience shows that private enterprise, working on ordinary commercial lines, cannot afford to provide this minimum of house room and amenity for the lower-income groups in a community. Consequently the duty of securing the *standard* must be regarded as a public responsibility, and, as in the case of education and water supply, must be undertaken as a public service.

While those truths should be self-evident—to realtors above all—there is as yet little indication that they are willing to recognize just how obsolete their position is. The extremities to which they have gone in combating public housing are almost beyond belief. As a single example—typical rather than extraordinary—when the Farm Security Administration announced in 1939 that it was going to erect housing facilities to accommodate 2,250 of the 20,000 migratory farm workers in the Everglades who were sleeping, sometimes forty in a room, in foul shanties (500 of which had been condemned), and even on the ground behind shelters made of soft-drink signs, the landlords took the following action, as reported in the press:

> *Property Owners Fighting Project*
> Belle Glade, Fla.—A copy of a letter and petition recently sent to Senators Pepper and Andrews by L. J. Rader and other owners of tourist camps and negro quarters in the vicinity was read, setting forth their objections to the $500,000 federal housing project which is scheduled to be started here. . . . It was pointed out that such camps would not be taxable for revenue to the city and that they would draw considerable business away from the present merchants and landowners.

Very much the same arguments have been advanced by realtors against various forms of public housing throughout the country. Needless to say, politicians have frequently joined the attack. For example, R. W. Farnell, "a good sport and a good friend to everybody," speaking in behalf of his candidacy for congressman from Florida over a Jacksonville radio station in 1938, declared, "Just look at the modern little cottages, landscaped grounds, playgrounds for the kinky-headed children, and recreation halls for the grownup niggers, while many a good tax-payin' white citizen wanders by without a job or a place to rest his head!" This, despite the fact that the government has provided housing projects equally for whites and Negroes, despite the relatively greater need of Negroes.

It should not be assumed that the South has an exclusive monopoly on this sort of thing. Cyrus C. Willmore, as president of the National Association of Real Estate Boards, has charged that "some of these governmental slum-clearance projects are just a fraud on the American people." And he went on to try to agitate Miami realtors by telling them of a Cleveland project for Negroes which he said was erected in a white residential neighborhood.

Much of the howling against "bureaucratic dictatorship" originates in this same quarter in protest against OPA ceilings. One Southern realtor actually told me during the war that the only freedom he was interested in fighting for was "freedom from the OPA."

The organized and unorganized attempts of real-estate interests to sabotage the public-housing programs adopted and considered by Congress are too notorious to require citation. Having failed to completely subvert the workings of democracy for better housing on the national level, the realtors have now opened a supplementary flanking attack on the state and local levels. The first citadel to fall has been Birmingham, Alabama; believe it or not, the 1945 Alabama legislature passed a local bill prohibiting the expenditure of federal funds for public housing in Jefferson County! The purveyor of this bill, interestingly enough, was legislator Jim Simpson, unsuccessful "white-supremacy" opponent of Senator Lister Hill in 1944.

If the South's people—as well as Americans generally—are not both vigilant and militant, they may find themselves denied decent housing by this Jefferson County formula.

The delayed industrialization of the South has served at least one good purpose, in that it has enabled the region to largely escape the housing horrors which have everywhere characterized the steam age. The replacement of steam by easily transmittable electricity as industrial motive power (not to mention the potentialities of atomic power) has made it possible to decentralize industry as never before. "The development of vast electric power in the Tennessee Valley has put the Southeast in a particularly favorable position," says the Southeastern Planning Commission. "Its situation is analogous to that of the Scandinavian countries a short time ago, especially Norway, which, having been late in starting industrialization, was able very nearly to begin at the electric power stage and avoid an enormous amount of smoke, grime, and slums."

Still other advantages which the South possesses over some other regions include the lack of highly inflated land values. Consequently, even though the South may have its share of slums to eliminate, it will cost less for the land with which to do the job. This means too that instead of apartment houses—which experience has proven are not so good for child-raising—much of the South's rehousing can afford to take the form of single family units with plenty of yard space and porches.

Half a century ago, Ebenezer Howard wrote a volume entitled *Garden Cities of Tomorrow,* in which he painted a fascinating picture of ideal communities combining the advantages of urban and rural housing. Constructed according to a meticulous master plan, each dwelling was to have ample light, air, and garden space. In Great Britain two such garden cities, Letchworth and Welwyn, have made their appearance and have proven to be as practical as they are desirable. As a single indication of their superior capacity to promote life and the pursuit of happiness: while the infant mortality rate of England and Wales has been 62 per 1,000, those of Letchworth and Welwyn have been only 33 and 25.

"On a smaller scale," says the Southeastern Planning Commission, "some of the farmstead communities of the Farm Security Administration, which have brought industry within reach of their members, are a laboratory experiment in decentralized industry and combined town and country life, not too far from the Ebenezer Howard model. If something such as the garden city is to be the industrial and living pattern of the future, and if overgrown cities will sooner or later pass, it will be easier for such a region as the Southeast to swing into step than for regions where the metropolis is now dominant."

A sound start in the rehousing of the region has already been made. During the eight years prior to 1942 the Southeast—in relation to population and not including war housing—built twice as much urban public housing as did the nation at large. By the end of 1941, sixty-five U. S. Housing Authority projects had been completed in the region, providing a total of 15,537 dwelling units and creating over 19,000,000 man-hours of on-the-site employment. Yet this has merely laid the foundations for rehousing that half of the South's people who must have it; to fill that need in the Southeastern states alone will cost something like four billion dollars.

Besides good health and good homes, the South needs good schools. Poor as the South's provision for education is, the region does spend a much larger proportion of its income for education than any other section. The South collects in taxes only about half as much per capita as the nation as a whole, and must educate one third of the nation's children with only one sixth of the nation's school revenue. Some sections of the country have sixty times the ability to support education as some others. For Mississippi to achieve the national average in educational expenditures would require the use of 99.3 per cent of her entire tax income. Likewise, for the Southern states as a whole to spend the national average per pupil would require an additional quarter of a billion dollars of revenue.

It would require $240,000,000 to bring the per pupil investment in Negro schools up to that of the whites, and an additional investment of one billion dollars to bring the combined white-Negro expenditures in the South up to the national average.

Much of what the South spends on education is lost to the region through the migration of many of its young people to other areas. It has been estimated that the South's rural areas—which suffer the greatest disparity between the number of children and the means of educating them—lose something like $250,000,000 per year in the cost of rearing and educating their youth who move to cities. Whether or not these Southerners constitute assets or liabilities to their new communities depends in large measure upon the quality of education imparted to them in the South. It is therefore both sensible and just that the richer sections share the educational burden of the poorer.

Of course federal aid to education is nothing new, but its history and scope are generally unknown to its beneficiaries, the American people.

In 1862 Congress granted 30,000 acres of land from the public domain to each of the states for each senator and representative to which the state was entitled, with the provision that the moneys derived from the sale of such land should constitute a perpetual and irreducible fund, the income from which was to be devoted to the establishment and maintenance of colleges for the "benefit of agriculture and mechanic arts."

While this land grant enabled the states to establish colleges, they soon experienced great difficulty in maintaining them. Consequently in 1890 a law was passed appropriating $15,000 to each state for the current year, with an increase of $1,000 each year for a period of ten years, after which the amount for each state was set at $25,000 per year. Again in 1908 the federal govern-

ment came to the assistance of the land-grant colleges, providing
an additional appropriation of $5,000 to each, with an increase
of $5,000 per year for the next four years, after which each state
would receive $25,000 per year.

Thus the total annual amount provided each state under both
these acts became $50,000; and it continued at this figure until
1935, when the Bankhead-Jones Act was passed. This act provides for an additional $20,000 per year to each state, plus an
additional $1,500,000 which is divided among the states on the
basis of population. And so each state receives—from the three
funds afore-mentioned—a total of $70,000 a year, plus its popu-
lation basis allotment, which for each Southern state ranges from
about $20,000 to $30,000 per year. Despite all this, as of 1930 the
federal contribution amounted to less than 1 per cent of the total
spent on education in the South; and the proportion is still very
low.

A major cause of the inadequacy of federal aid to education
has been the refusal of the South's white supremacists in Congress
to approve such appropriations for fear they would be earmarked
in such manner as to put Negro education more on a par with
that afforded whites. Inasmuch as a racial educational differential is essential to the socio-politico-economic system of white supremacy, the system's opposition to federal aid to education has
dated from Reconstruction. Here's how the Gainesville (Fla.)
Weekly Bee viewed the matter with alarm in 1881:

> Dr. Curry, agent of the Peabody Fund Association, recently
> deplored the present illiteracy of the colored population of the
> South, and seemed to imply in his remarks that he was in favor
> of aid from the United States Government. He can hardly
> have reflected, however, that the effect of such action in the
> present state of our civil service would be to supplant the state
> schools or reduce the influence of local sentiment upon the
> conduct and teachings of the schools to a minimum, unless, as
> is suggested in some quarters, the money appropriated by Con-
> gress for education in the South be handed over to the state
> authorities, to be used according to the judgment of the state
> authorities. In a word, "national" schools in the South, it is
> feared, would be but a reproduction of the Freedmen's Bureau,
> a political propaganda.

That warped trend of thought still sets the pattern for white supremacy's opposition to federal aid to education. White supremacy has ever made it clear to Congress that any federal money appropriated for education in the South must not be so earmarked as to reduce the racial differential. Until now the effect of this position has been to deprive both Southern whites and Negroes (as all Americans) of further benefit of federal funds.

In recent years, however, the South's precious few statesmen in Congress have introduced bills which would appropriate something like $300,000,000 for federal aid to education—not for the land-grant colleges, but for primary and secondary schools. The portion allotted to each state would be based upon two things: (1) the number of children in each state between the ages of five and seventeen, and (2) the total net per capita income of the people in each state. Needless to say, the Southern states, having the most children and the smallest income, would benefit most. While the bill would not of itself decrease any racial differential, it does provide that there be "equitable apportionment of funds for the benefit of public schools maintained for the minority races, without reduction of the proportion of state and local money." Thus the federal money would be used to raise the standards of both white and Negro education, and the states would be given a greater opportunity to use their own money to reduce the racial differential, if they would.

Supreme Court Justice Hugo Black of Alabama, while a senator, was one of the first to introduce such a bill, and subsequently bills have been introduced by Senator Lister Hill of Alabama and Senator Claude Pepper of Florida. In 1943 its passage seemed almost assured, but a group of Republicans, led by Senator Taft of Ohio and Senator Langer of North Dakota, saw fit to put across an amendment to the bill providing that no state be granted any money until it had first completely eliminated all racial differentials in its educational system. Needless to say, this amendment proved fatal to the bill. Senator George of Georgia promptly interpreted the amendment as a move to force co-racial education upon the South, and so the unholy coalition of fiscally conservative Republicans and racially conservative Southern

Democrats deprived the children of the South and nation of better education.

The old bugaboo of "federal control" does not enter the picture at all, actually. As the Asheville (N.C.) *Citizen-Times* has pointed out, the bill "does not in any way extend federal control, for the money to be distributed would be expended directly by the state agencies themselves . . ." This fact, however, has not deterred such as poll-tax Senator Harry Byrd of Virginia from making such charges as "The federal government would dictate our schools and tell us how to run them. That was the story of federal aid for building highways, and it would be the same story in the schools. There isn't a state in the Union which isn't able to educate its own children."

And so the long struggle to give America's children equal status with its Indians, hogs, forests, and wild life, as being entitled to the aid of the federal government, continues. While there is life in democracy there is hope for all things democratic. The National Opinion Research Center has found that eight out of every ten persons are in favor of more federal aid to education. Even in the South the opposition constitutes only 11 per cent. Politicos please note.

WHOSE GOOD EARTH?

Because the South continues to be a predominantly agricultural region, solution of its farm problems is essential to its economic progress.

It has been noted that Southern farming is still dominated by the antiquated tenant-cropper plantation system, suffers from a disastrous overconcentration on such cash crops as cotton and tobacco, and is sadly lacking in farm machinery; while at the same time the new system of highly mechanized big business farm enterprises, ofttimes operated by absentee corporations, threatens with its resources and efficiency to tractor off the land the South's small farmers, tenants, and croppers, leaving them the grim prospect of becoming hired hands.

In short, the technological revolution in agriculture has at last come South, posing the question of whether the new system of mechanized farming is to be monopolized for the profit of a few or democratically controlled for the benefit of the many. Reduced to its simplest terms, the question boils down to: Who is going to own the farm machinery? By extension the question also asks: Who is going to own the good earth?

Unless social controls are established (if freebooting is allowed to continue on its way), both the machines and the land will very soon be monopolized as a big business, and the South's farm folk will become exploited hired hands. This is not meant to imply that the Southern farmer should not welcome the appearance of farm machinery, nor even that the Southern cotton picker should look with terror upon the mechanical cotton picker. It simply means that Southern farm folk had better put democracy to work to put farm machinery to work *for* them instead of *against* them.

There is nothing whatever to indicate that private financial interests are either equipped or inclined to conduct farm financing and advisory programs to make this possible. On the contrary, many financial groups have conspired to deny long-term credit to the small farmer and at the same time have gone all-out financing big business farms and processing plants. By coupling this with a political campaign against adequate government programs for small farmers, these financial interests hope to establish a monopoly over farming whereby the surviving small farmers will be denied loans by the banker unless they agree in advance to sell their crops at the combine's processing plant at whatever prices are offered.

Obviously, only the federal government can cope with such a plot. By making available long-term cheap credit for the purchase of economic, family-size farms, the construction of farmhouses, and establishment of co-operatives for the purchase of farm machinery, livestock, seed, fertilizer, markets, and processing plants, the federal government can make it possible for Southern farmers to compete successfully with the big-business outfits—and thus find security and prosperity instead of insecurity and poverty.

The late President Roosevelt fully appreciated the seriousness of the Southern farmers' position, and he appointed a Committee on Farm Tenancy to study the problem. In 1937 this committee issued a report of its findings, which became the basis of the program subsequently conducted by the Farm Security Administration, to the enormous benefit of American farmers generally and Southern farmers particularly. The primary purpose of the FSA has been to help the ambitious tenant or cropper to purchase his own farm and to launch it on a sound basis. To this end the FSA has provided both long-term cheap credit and "show how." Loans have been made for the purchase of land, houses, seed, fertilizer, livestock, machinery, and other farm requirements. During the first seven years after its establishment in 1936 the FSA loaned a total of $809,000,000 for such purposes, of which 87 per cent of all matured loans had been repaid by that time, with many clients paying off in advance of maturity.

The FSA has also helped small farmers to establish 10,000 co-operatives, 3,500 of them in the South. The crying need for such co-operatives was fully revealed by the Department of Agriculture, just before America entered the war. In a survey of the South Atlantic states the department found that the average tractor was in use but 372 *hours* a year (there are about 5,000 daylight hours per year). Peanut pickers were in use only 170 hours, horse-drawn mowers 66 hours, and planting machines 56 hours. This means that the well-to-do planters who own such machinery store it away when they finish with it, while their less fortunate neighbors have to let much of their land lie idle for lack of equipment.

Not even the nation's great wartime need for increased food production was sufficient to force this idle farm machinery into greater use. "In 1943," declared the Department of Agriculture, "examples of all-out co-operation were the exception. . . ." When the FSA surveyed the situation, it found that 160,000 Southern farm families were in need of co-operatives for the purchase and use of machinery.

Despite such evidence of the need for expansion of the FSA's services, and despite the fact that FSA clients increased their production of critical war crops far more, proportionately, than did other farmers, the Big Farm Lobby redoubled its efforts to scuttle the FSA.

Indicative of the nature of this plot was a letter sent out in 1943 by the National Cotton Council, informing its members and fellow travelers of its plan to "charge the FSA with mismanagement, waste of funds, decreased production, and Communistic activities, with a view to curtailing the scope of this agency." It urged that any "general rumors" of that nature be forwarded to the council.

After such "charges" against the FSA had been aired in the public press and halls of Congress, a Select Committee of the House Committee on Agriculture was delegated to "investigate" the FSA. In its report made in 1944 this committee sought to smear the agency by calling it "an experiment station of un-American ideas." The committee also charged that the FSA co-operative farmstead communities "followed the Russian pattern of collective farming." Instead of confessing its opposition to co-operatives as such, the committee based its objections on such charges as "The heads of the families have been given gratuitous advice as to the number of children they should have."

The committee proposed legislation which would "prohibit loans to any co-operative association," called for the breakup of all existing FSA co-operatives or their sale to "individuals or corporations capable of engaging in farming on a large scale," urged that all FSA housing projects for migratory farm workers be liquidated after the war, and that the FSA's loan service be transferred to a "Farmer's Home Corporation" which would offer "practical guidance in farming and farm home plans and operations of the same type and character now being rendered by the Extension Service."

Fortunately for farmers, Congress did not swallow all of this Big-Farm-bloc-endorsed legislation. However, the smear campaign against FSA did cause such a drastic cut in the agency's appropriation that it was able to grant only one out of every twenty loan applications received during the ensuing year. While the Agricultural Appropriations Bill was still before Congress, Chairman Tarver of the House subcommittee said, "I am frank to say that the Farm Bureau Federation, with regard to some of the more controversial [FSA] items, has been all-powerful in the consideration of the pending bill."

"The Farm Bureau is against price control, against unions, against closed shops, and for the extension of the work week," the book *Roots in the Earth* (Harper) has pointed out. "This is a program to aid manufacturers, not farmers. It is part of a deal whereby the Farm Bureau does not attack wartime profits and the National Association of Manufacturers does not attack food prices. But both attack labor."

When reduced to its simplest terms, as per *Roots in the Earth,* the FSA controversy resolves thus: "Shall the government aid 3,000,000 farm families to keep going and expand production on their farms, or shall it allow them to be driven off their farms in order to supply cheap labor for 200,000 big farmers?" Still more specifically, the question is whether the government should aid in the establishment of family-size farms, co-operatives, or both.

The answer given by the President's Committee on Farm Tenancy (which included representatives of the Big Farm groups) was "both," with emphasis on the family-size farm, as follows:

"In general the aim should be the establishment of family-size farms. . . . Certain economic disadvantages of the family-size farm can be, and should be, overcome through the co-operative ownership of the more expensive types of farm machinery and breeding stock, and through co-operative buying, processing, and marketing. In some cases it may be found desirable for small holders to be co-operatively associated for the employment of technical supervision. The FSA should be authorized to aid the formation of local co-operatives, either by technical assistance or by loans."

While subscribing to the committee's report in general, the Southern Tenant Farmers' Union appended a minority opinion discounting the feasibility of the small farmstead and strongly endorsing co-operatives, as follows:

"We believe the report's references to co-operative activity are wholly inadequate. They seem only incidental, almost accidental. We believe that in the cotton South the small homestead visioned in many of the present proposals is an economic anachronism, foredoomed to failure. We strongly dissent, therefore, from the 'small homestead' philosophy as the solution for the majority of the Southern agricultural workers. It is the more readily accepted by the present landlords because they know it to be relatively ineffective and consequently harmless from their point of view. It runs contrary to generations of experience of croppers and farm workers in the South—experience which, we believe, could be capitalized in co-operative effort under enlightened federal supervision."

There is much evidence, economic and social, to support this view. In addition to having long worked together on large plantations, Southern farm folk have a virile tradition of neighborly co-operation in accomplishing those tasks requiring group action, such as "fence raisings" and the like.

It is all too evident that family-size farms cannot compete with mechanized big-business farms except through co-operatives. Congress has the responsibility of seeing to it that the family-size farm is protected; that co-operatives are aided and encouraged; that the "factories in the field" are made socially responsible and their workers extended the benefits of wage-hour laws, social security, employment service, housing and health façilities.

It is unlikely, however, that Congress will fully accept its responsibility in these respects until small farmers unite in democratic unions of their own. Just as the hope of the Southern industrial worker lies in the industrial labor unions, so the hope of Southern farm folk lies in such organizations as the National Farmers Union and Southern Tenant Farmers' Union. While the Farmers Union has acquired formidable strength in the Midwest, it is still baby-weak in the South.

And yet it should be recalled that the depression of 1884—aggravating as it did the unmitigated thralldom of the lien and cropper-tenant systems—sent more than three million Southern farmers (more than a third of them Negroes) headlong into the Farmers Alliance during the several years preceding 1890; and soon Alliance-sponsored co-operatives were thriving throughout the region. Now history bids fair to repeat itself. The evils of the lien and cropper-tenant systems are still upon the South, and the "factories in the field" threaten even worse in the form of wage slavery. Southern farmers can wait for the worst before doing anything about it—or they can organize to prevent the worst from happening.

The program of the Farmers Union is designed to meet the most urgent basic needs of the small farmer. It emphasizes the potentialities of farmers' co-operatives, and how much can be done through collective effort to improve local conditions. But equally important is the influence such an organization can have in the promotion of legislation to aid the small farmer. Already the National Farmers Union has earned an enviable name for itself as the champion of the small farmer in legislative matters. Like David against Goliath, it has frequently stood and smitten the Big Farm bloc in the temple, killing bills which would have spelled ruin for the Southern farmer. A broad Southern membership, needless to say, would greatly strengthen the Farmers Union's political arm.

The organizational drive is now under way and in many sections is being led by returned farmer-veterans. Labor unions and all other democratic organizations would do well to lend a hand; for the labor movement in the South, democracy in the South, and democracy in America can never be entirely secure until Southern farm folk are democratically united.

The technological revolution in agriculture is on the march. The farm machines, spearheaded by the mechanical cotton picker, have crossed the Mason-Dixon Line and are bearing down upon the South at top speed. Through organized co-operative action the South's farm folk can acquire title to those machines and drive them to prosperity such as they have never known; otherwise the machines will bulldoze them into poverty such as they have never known.

TVA LEADS THE WAY

"It is clear that the Muscle Shoals development is but a small part of the potential usefulness of the entire Tennessee River," said President Roosevelt in proposing in 1933 that Congress establish a Tennessee Valley Authority. "Such use, if envisioned in its entirety, transcends mere power development: it enters the wide fields of flood control, soil erosion, afforestation, elimination from agricultural use of submarginal lands, and distribution and diversification of industry. In short, this power development of war days leads logically to national planning for a complete river watershed, involving many states and the future lives and welfare of millions."

And so the Tennessee Valley Authority was created, not as an ordinary government agency, but more as a public corporation "clothed with the power of government, but possessed of the flexibility and initiative of private enterprise." Made responsible directly to the President, TVA was charged with the regional but sizable task of promoting closer integration and better balance between industry and agriculture, broadening economic opportunity, and generally to insure a rising standard of living.

Perhaps the best exposition of the basic role of TVA is that of its capable director, David Lilienthal, in his book *TVA: Democracy on the March* (Harper). "There is a grand cycle in nature," he writes. "The lines of those majestic swinging arcs are nowhere more clearly seen than by following the course of electric power in the Tennessee Valley's way of life. Water falls upon a mountain slope six thousand feet above the river's mouth . . .

it comes together in one stream, then in another, and at last reaches a TVA lake where it is stored behind a dam. Down a huge steel tube it falls, turning a water wheel. Here the water's energy is transformed into electricity, and then, moving onward toward the sea, it continues through ten lakes, over ten such wheels.

"The electricity, carried 200 miles in a flash of time, heats to incredible temperatures a furnace that transforms inert phosphate ore into a chemical of great possibilities. That phosphatic chemical, put upon his land by a farmer, stirs new life in the land, induces the growth of pastures that capture the inexhaustible power of the sun. Those pastures, born of the energy of phosphate and electricity, feed the energies of animals and man, hold the soil, free the streams of silt, store up water in the soil. Slowly the water returns into the great man-made reservoirs, from which more electricity is generated . . .

"Such a cycle is restorative, not exhausting. It gives life as it sustains life. The principle of unity has been obeyed, the circle has been closed. The yield is not the old sad tale of spoilation and poverty, but that of nature and science and man in the bounty of harmony."

What this "closing of the circle" has meant in transforming the lives of the people of the valley has been graphically described by Benton J. Strong in the *National Union Farmer*. "I saw the enormous success of the Tennessee Valley Authority in an alfalfa patch," he wrote. "Once the field had probably been a 'shotgun' cornfield. (So steep that, according to local legend, the owner has to plant it by shooting seed into the field from the opposite hillside.) Then it had become one of those deeply gullied wastelands which covered the Valley, thick with underbrush and tiny streams that carried away the little remaining soil.

"But when I saw the field this month it was covered with a green blanket of alfalfa and blue grass; its deep scars wiped away and replaced with terraces. It was part of the 55-acre hillside farm of Henry Clark which had been restored by TVA phosphate, lime, and the work of a family to whom TVA has brought an entirely new life.

"Ten years ago Henry Clark scratched his hillside with a little black mare and a sled and got little more than $200 cash income. Last year he cultivated it with a tractor, a mowing machine, grain drill, and the most modern equipment and took in $4,600 from hay, dairy products, tomatoes, tobacco, and poultry. Ten years ago Henry Clark's home was a cabin. Today it is a fine farmhouse with electric lights, electric range, electric washing machine, and electric refrigerator."

What TVA has already done for Henry Clark is typical of what it has done for thousands of others. Throughout the valley it has brought about an increase of 75 per cent in per capita income, as compared to a national increase of 56 per cent for the same period.

Since its establishment, TVA has erected 16 large dams, created 650 miles of 9-foot navigable channel for river commerce (which has increased fivefold), provided more than 13,000,000 acre-feet of flood-control storage, produced 47,000,000,000 kilowatt hours of electricity, provided 153,000,000 seedlings for reforestation, manufactured 600,000 tons of phosphatic fertilizer, developed numerous new machines and processes, and opened up for use many latent resources of water, soil, forests, and minerals. Perhaps most significantly, by 1943 the average TVA customer was using 53 per cent more electricity than the average American consumer—and was paying 18 per cent less for it.

The year after TVA's low mass-consumption rates were inaugurated, the Tennessee Electric Power Company's sales of electrical appliances—ranges, refrigerators, and water heaters—increased threefold, and other companies in the region experienced similar increases. Together the customers of three private power companies supplied by TVA spent $60,000,000 for electrical appliances during TVA's first four years alone.

Industrial growth in the valley—which roughly consists of some 40,000 square miles in the states of Tennessee, Kentucky, North Carolina, Virginia, Georgia, Alabama, and Mississippi—has been appreciably greater than elsewhere in the South or nation. In the prewar year of 1939 the valley had 721 more manufacturing establishments and nearly 41,000 more industrial workers than in 1933—an increase of 53.4 per cent in plants and 33.9 per cent in industrial wage earners. The corresponding increases for the

Southeast had been 41 and 34 per cent, and for the United States, 30 and 30.2 per cent.

It did not take business long to recognize that its original opposition to TVA had been unjustified. Indicative of this recognition was an article entitled "TVA Aids Private Business," which appeared in *Business Week*. "Industry is beginning to cash in on TVA's research," the article stated. "For example: A simple machine developed by TVA engineers plows furrows in the hard sod and drops grain and fertilizer, all in one operation. A private manufacturer, B. F. Avery & Sons of Louisville, began production of such a seeder. The low price ($22.50) has encouraged sales to farmers in eight states.

"Other research has developed walk-in types of community refrigerators, electric hotbeds, electric heating systems to maintain steady, uniform conditions for curing and storage of sweet potatoes. At Norris and other TVA communities there have been extensive trials in electrical heating of homes and stores. TVA's work in developing a new quick-freezing process promises similar benefits both to local growers and to equipment manufacturers.

"In North Carolina were primary China-clay deposits, which had been worked in a limited way for fifty years. . . . TVA carried on research in a laboratory at Norris, in co-operation with representatives of the ceramic industry. Last year 10,000 tons of kaolins refined by a new process were produced.

"Farmers in the TVA program are found to be buying more from the hardware store, the lumber yard, and the department store than they did before they agreed to follow new farming practices, and markedly more than their neighbors who are following the earlier methods.

"What TVA has done to further navigation, electric power, flood control, and soil conservation is aiding not only the region, but private business."

Came the war, and TVA proved to be as powerful a weapon in the global conflict as it had been in the peacetime fight for freedom from want. TVA power became the principal source for aluminum production, without which the nation's phenomenal output of planes would have been impossible. Eventually 75 per cent of TVA's total electrical output, which was increased more than a third, was going to huge aluminum, chemical, electro-metallurgical, and munition plants. Huge quantities of elemental phosphorus, a vital munition, were produced, and 10,000,000 feet of timber were harvested from TVA lands during 1943 alone. Because of TVA's work, the Tennessee River provided an invaluable means of transporting grain, coal, petroleum, pig iron, and military vehicles. TVA-invented prefabricated houses were copied by war-housing agencies. With approximately one third of the commodities listed as strategic by the Munitions Board to be found in the region, TVA's ready surveys greatly facilitated their extraction.

In its twelfth annual report TVA revealed that during 1945 it produced nearly 12,000,000,000 kilowatt-hours of electric power—more than any other integrated system in the country. With the dropping of atomic bombs on Japan, the War Department also revealed that TVA's abundance of electric power was the major factor in locating the atomic-energy plant at Oak Ridge, Tennessee, making possible the bomb's timely appearance. In a very real sense, then, TVA can be credited with saving an untold number of American lives which would have had to be sacrificed to conquer Japan without the atomic bomb. In war, as in peace, TVA has proven to be a blessing to mankind.

And yet, as the Southern Conference for Human Welfare has pointed out, "Much of what TVA has accomplished, both for war and peace, and what it has come to represent in contemporary American life, cannot easily be interpreted by statistical tables and summary paragraphs. Precise columns of figures cannot evaluate the practical idea of an integrated regional development in which all the varied facets of Valley economy are weighed and treated as related parts of the whole. Nor can they measure the impact of the regional development program outside the Valley, both in America and abroad, as perhaps suggesting the approach to the solution of problems in other regions."

A good many of the specifications for postwar regional development programs like the TVA have already been set forth by the National Planning Association. "The TVA—an experiment designed to test the efficacy of unified and autonomous management located physically in a region—has furnished us with the most acceptable and workable answer thus far developed," the association states. "The impetus may come from the top, but the actual integration of resource development and social progress must come from the areas where the problems of the people occur and where adjustments can be realistically achieved."

It is the suggestion of the Planning Association that twelve or fifteen regional development agencies be established throughout the United States, each centered around a major river system and its watershed, but with flexible boundaries to permit inter-regional planning and collaboration. Various "guesstimates" place the cost of such national development on a regional basis at from $20,000,000,000 to $50,000,000,000 for the first twenty years. But, as TVA has proven, there is no reason why the entire program should not pay for itself through direct charges for its services and through increased tax revenues derived from a rising level of productivity.

THE SOUTH JOINS THE UNIONS

Just as the organization of farm folk into democratic unions is essential to the success of all other programs for Southern agricultural progress, so must unionization of the South's industrial workers go hand in hand with the region's industrial progress.

The equalization of freight rates and the expansion of river-valley development à la TVA will give rise to an industrialized South. But the South has already learned through sad experience that prosperity does not automatically accompany industrialization. At the turn of the century the South was taken in by the glamorous word pictures of the "New South" which Georgia's Henry W. Grady assured them would be ushered in by railroads and industry. But the railroads came, and, instead of bringing prosperity, hauled off the South's natural wealth for the enrichment of other areas. Industries came South too, but often they were secondhand, and instead of fat pay rolls they paid starvation wages for long hours of work performed under sweatshop conditions; and instead of proving to be a blessing to the community they became a blight; and when the workers sought to organize unions for protection they were ruthlessly broken up by violence and terrorism. In short, the "New South," as it has thus far materialized, has in large measure supplanted the planter slavocracy with a corporate slavocracy, as often as not subject to outside control, and dedicated to the purpose of keeping the South in semicolonial status.

In other words, industrialization is not to be regarded as a cure-all, nor even as good medicine, unless it is accompanied by adequate social controls. Industry in the South must be made to live up to its full responsibility to its employees and to the public. The only way to accomplish this is through economic and political action, and the only type of organization in a position to do this is the democratic labor union.

Southern workers, handicapped as they are by poverty, ill-health, poor education, inculcated racial prejudice, and an overdose of anti-union employers and secondhand industries, have been having an especially difficult time organizing. A *Fortune* magazine poll in 1943 found that only about 30 per cent of Southern industrial workers and 12 per cent of Southern Negroes were organized, as compared to respective figures of 53.5 and 43.8 per cent in the rest of the country.

We have already seen how anti-union employers, individually and in concert, are spending large fortunes through "Kingfish and Small Fry," trying to lynch the unions with both ropes and laws. We ought now to look at the other side of this picture and see how Southern labor is organizing despite all the obstacles which are thrust in its path.

Even where anti-union activity has been most violent and successful the workers are still able to laugh—and while there is laughter there is always hope. As the textile worker at Danville, Virginia, said shortly after Pearl Harbor, when invasion jitters were at their peak: "I'm not worried a-tall about the Japs movin' in on us; the chamber of commerce has kept the unions out, and I reckon as how they can keep the Japs out too." However, anti-union activity in the South "ain't what she used to be." As one organizer recently pointed out to me, "They used to kill you for tryin' to organize a union; now they just knock all your teeth out."

Among the first labor unions in the South were importations from Cuba. Cigar manufacturers moved from Havana to Key West, Florida, in an effort to escape the unions; but the Cuban cigar makers came along and brought their unions with them. These unions were firmly established in Key West before 1870. There were bitter strikes, and Spanish strikebreakers were imported from Cuba. Again the manufacturers moved, this time to

The Growing Menace of Closed Shop

CIO IS COMMUNISTIC

COMMUNISM

The Right NOT To Organize

WE ARE 100% Non Union AND PROUD OF

WILL NOT BE TOLERATED

KU KLUX KLAN RIDES AGAIN!

HERE

esterday—Today—Fore

WHAT THE WHITE MILL WORKER MAY EXPECT FROM LABOR ORGANIZATIONS

ARE YOU ON THE JOB?
KU KLUX KLAN Is Watching

The following is an editorial from the Textile Bulletin October 1, 1944

TO MERGE WITH NEGROES

SINCE EIGHTEEN HUNDRED SIXTY-SIX

THE KU KLUX KLAN

Has been riding and will continue to do so as long as the WHITE MAN liveth.

WANTED. 4,000 OR MORE of the 8,000 KLANSMEN from Orange, Seminole and Osceola Counties.

work to do

orid

Do We Want Labor Unions Or Industrial Expansion?

Citizens of Bay Minette are being insulted. It seems as though the American Federation of Labor is launching a drive to

tial election. They have too much such power as it is.

It is reported by one who knows that e of the paid organizers working here a prison record. It is not un unions to use thi

se th

NOTICE

WE ARE AMERICANS AND BELIEVE IN AMERICAN PRINCIP IF YOU ARE HERE TO INTERFER WITH OUR RIGHTS, THIS IS THE PLACE TO TURN AROUND

EMPLOYEES OF ACNAR MILL

Watch Your Ste

I am appealing to you in the name of all that is good right that in this crisis of making a choice for the future devel ment of your community not to support the C. I. O. in We VOTE AGAINST IT and stamp it out.

sons is sufficient to make the

Tampa. The unions were just as militant there, however, and there was a series of strikes, two of them lasting ten months each. Community soup kitchens set up in the streets by the unions were overturned by law officers. Finally the union was broken when the manufacturers arranged for the kidnaping of twenty of its leaders, chartered a schooner, and had them deposited on the coast of Honduras.

The Knights of Labor, pioneer of the American labor movement, made some headway in the South. It met with such violent opposition from anti-labor industrialists that it was forced to operate in secrecy until 1878.

Unions of the craft variety, affiliated with the American Federation of Labor, have made considerable progress in the South since the turn of the century. However, the exclusivist and monopolistic policies of some such unions have tended to circumscribe their beneficial influence. Craft unionism, addicted as it frequently is to practices of Negro exclusion and segregation, has proven particularly inappropriate to the needs of Southern labor. The progressive industrialization of the South, with its logical requirement of industry-wide unionization, has further detracted from the effectiveness of craft unions.

It was the United Mineworkers of America who spearheaded the advent of the new industrial unions to the South. The Mineworkers' organizational drive began in 1933 and, despite the most violent opposition, fought its way to success.

Typical of the opposition to the Mineworkers was that of the Alabama Fuel & Iron Company, whose president, Charles De-Bardeleben, was accustomed to deliver monthly staff dinner speeches, flanked by posters reading:

> WE ARE 100% NON-UNION
> AND PROUD OF IT

There were also monthly meetings for the Employees' Welfare Society, at which free popsicles and apples were distributed. The company's property was surrounded by a barbed-wire entanglement, there was a lookout tower atop the water tank, and armored blockhouses were erected at strategic points. Investigations made by the Coal Labor Board also revealed that in 1934 the company made plans to dynamite the road leading to the mine. Until 1937 a sign at the entrance of the company's property read:

NOTICE
We are Americans and believe in American principles. If you are here to interfere with our rights, this is the place to turn around.

Subsequently the sign was changed to read:

This is a happy and satisfied community. We need no paid advice. We have our own union. We tolerate no agitators. Our interest is in our homes and our work. Meddlers and agitators will not be tolerated.

Farther down the road a sign warned:

ENTER AT YOUR OWN RISK

In 1934 and 1935 an abortive attempt to organize the Southern textile industry was made by the AFL. A general strike ensued, and employer-sponsored opposition to the union grew into open terrorism. A typical situation developed in a town in Georgia. Eugene Talmadge was governor then, and he called out the militia, which proceeded to evict the strikers from their company-owned homes. One of the striking workers was bayoneted and killed during the eviction proceedings. The evicted families were then transported to Atlanta and confined in a barbed-wire concentration camp.

An overseer's car drove up behind another of the strikers, and someone in it began shooting at him. He was permanently crippled.

An affidavit signed by still another of the striking union members said, ". . . I recognized —— and —— ——, who stepped out from behind the car, then others raised up from the inside of it and I again was able to recognize one of the others who was in the car as —— ——. They then drew guns on me and told me to throw up my hands, but before I had a chance, they began to beat me over the head and face with the pistols they held and I was knocked down." A sack was put over his head and he was driven out of town and given a terrific beating. "They were sure they had me more than knocked out this time. They would bend my fingers back as well as beat me on the leg again to see if there was any life left. After they pulled me out of the car, they placed me in a ditch on my face—then started beating on me again . . . I played off that I was knocked out. Then they started up the car and left."

He worked his head out of the sack and started back to town. When he saw the car returning to look for him he hid in the bushes, and later said he recognized the driver of the car as an overseer at the mill. A few days later a note was thrown in his yard reading:

> ROBERT HENRY:
> After what happened the other night we would suggest that you leave ——, and this is to notify you that you have thirty days from now to move yourself and family out of this town. It will be the best interests of ——, yourself, and family to heed this friendly warning, else we will have to do something that we do not want to do.
> CITIZENS OF ——

The grand jury failed to indict in the case, and a union leader reported that the jury "resembled more a stockholders' meeting of the textile manufacturers than it did a grand jury."

By such methods the textile manufacturers broke the strike, and with it almost every vestige of the union. So disastrous was the strike for the workers that the cause of unionism was actually retarded.

But then in 1937 the CIO established regional offices of its Textile Workers Organizing Committee in Atlanta, and the drive to organize the textile industry was again under way. Again characteristic violence arose around the mills at ——.

The first to be beaten arrived in —— on May 19, 1937, were arrested "on suspicion," then jailed and fingerprinted. Union cards were found on them, and they were tried *that night* before a special court session attended by twelve businessmen. The charge was "hoboing and bumming"; the fine was fifteen dollars and costs or thirty days—with a suspended sentence if they would leave town in thirty minutes.

The judge asked which way they were going. When they told, a fingerprint man came forward and volunteered to give them a lift in that direction. After being let out on the highway, they came upon a parked car and three men who pretended to be out of gas. One of them struck ——— over the head with a flashlight, exclaiming, "You union son-of-a-bitch!" One of them ran, but the other two were beaten with a hickory stick and blackjack. When they also ran, shots were fired after them.

The following month a worker in the mills wrote the CIO in Atlanta:

> A number of my friends here in the mill want to be signed up. We have to be awful careful because three or four have been beat bad. If you have cause to write me, please mail it in a plain envelope without return address.

The same month a tear-gas bomb was thrown into the home of T. H. Burson, the union organizer. George Mathews, driver of a dry-cleaning truck (his parents were members of the union), saw the bomb thrown; a few days later he was ambushed and shot—dead.

Among those beaten were Paul Swanson and his wife. According to a report made at the time, "He was struck across the forehead with a blackjack. The other man ran around to the other side of the car and beat his wife nearly to death. She is in the hospital now. He was knocked unconscious but he's up now. Swanson gave the law the two men's names that did it, but they made no arrests." Later the union organizer wrote the Atlanta office:

> As to the ——— thugs: They called the case of the two that beat up Swanson and his wife for the third time and it was put off again. You just can't get court action if it doesn't suit ———. All the cotton mills around ——— are watching him because he's the main cog in the wheel and the way he turns over they will turn. The workers in ——— are scared to talk to anybody on the streets for fear of a beating. I suppose I have been accused of being scared because of the bombing of my house. I am not scared, just uneasy in the dark, for that bunch will do anything for a dollar. But as long as I work on this job I am going to put my time and self into it. Then I will have nothing to regret.

An affidavit of another union member, dated October 29, 1937, says: "Last Saturday dynamite was thrown in my yard and there was a couple that saw this . . . they gave me the number of the car from which it was thrown. . . . I called the police and two came out and they said there was nothing they could do about it but that the city detective would have to investigate it. It was the car of the city detective from which the dynamite was thrown."

The tie-up between so-called public officials and law officers with anti-union employers was everywhere apparent. Often there was little or no camouflage of this infamous link. For instance, Horace White, while handing out CIO literature in Georgia in 1937, was attacked by thirteen men, including the chief of police, who struck him four times with a blackjack while he was down. White was then given a drink of whisky—and jailed for being drunk!

Frequently the mayors of Southern cities have joined in the anti-CIO terrorism. For instance, the mayor of Macon, Georgia, proclaimed that he would "put under the jail" any CIO organizer who dared enter the town, and the mayors of Memphis and other Southern cities have said much the same thing. Nor has this fascistic sort of edict yet disappeared. In 1945 the mayor of a small Alabama town threatened the lives of union organizers if the Southern Tenant Farmers' Union was not disbanded immediately.

One might suppose that this sort of thing would not occur where the National Labor Relations Board had arranged for a federally supervised election, but such is not the case. As a single example of terrorism being used to frustrate the functioning of federal law and federal officials, there is the case of the NLRB election scheduled at Brownsville, Tennessee, in 1944. Two days before the election, Joe Hellinger, CIO representative at Memphis, was informed by one of the Brownsville members that "the Negro workers in the compress are being terrorized and threatened with violence because of their affiliations with the CIO."

Hellinger promptly went to Brownsville, where he was met by the banker, the undertaker, and several other leading citizens, who advised him to get out of town. However, Hellinger got in touch with the compress workers and reassured them that the NLRB election would be conducted under government auspices and they need not fear violence.

"You just don't know Brownsville," one of the Negro workers told him. "Uncle Sam may be able to handle things like that in other places, but we don't think he can do it here. We know what the white folks have told us."

The afternoon before the election Hellinger met with the leaders of the community who told him that "the town doesn't want the CIO or any other union messin' with our niggers."

On election eve a mob of vigilantes so terrorized the Negro members of the CIO that the president of the local fled from town. The vigilantes also searched for Hellinger, and the next morning the chief of police informed him, "A group of farmers, maybe two hundred of them, called at the hotel for you. They wanted the CIO man to make them a speech. They were particularly anxious to hear what your last words would be."

The police chief went on to explain how "Brownsville folks handle people they don't like—sometime during the night they just disappear from their homes and sometime later a body is found in the river." He recalled how, four years previously, the bodies of a dozen Negroes had been found in the river, after local Negroes had ignored a warning not to participate in the Democratic primary.

Needless to say, when the NLRB examiner opened the polls to give the employees of the company an opportunity to express their free choice for a union, not a single employee dared appear.

The difficulties encountered by the United Steelworkers of America (USA-CIO) in organizing the Reynolds Corporation Naval Ordnance Fuse Plant at Milledgeville, Georgia, were more or less typical, and therefore worthy of note. In April of 1944, at the request of workers in the plant, the USA assigned its international representative R. E. Starnes (a Georgia boy) to assist in organizing a local.

The Milledgeville city council promptly adopted an ordinance requiring all union organizers to establish a local residence of one year, and pay a $5,000 license fee, before operating. To test this ordinance, Starnes violated it, was arrested and convicted. Bond was posted and appeal made. However, it became necessary to hold the union meetings outside the city limits—an enormous handicap under gas rationing. No one would rent Starnes a meeting place in Milledgeville, anyway.

A Workers Welfare Association, Inc., was established at the plant. It proceeded to publish literature describing the CIO as "an international group of bloodsuckers" which "was communistic and fomented unpatriotic strikes." By joining the Workers Welfare Association instead of the CIO, local money would be kept out of the hands of Northern radicals, the literature asserted. By word of mouth, leaders of the association charged that the CIO would force white employees to work beside Negroes, et cetera. A number of workers who displayed CIO buttons were discharged for "absenteeism," et cetera. The Reynolds Corporation gave expensive barbecues for the employees, thus forcing the union to do likewise.

The workers at the plant were assembled during working hours and addressed by Lieutenant Commander Banks and Harry G. Smith, general manager. Said Commander Banks: "I speak of dissension among workers, taking of so-called sides, personal arguments, or anything that will cause you to take your minds off your business. . . . We, the Navy, would be guilty of neglect of duty to the country and to you if we failed to make every effort to prevent this. . . . Anyone—male, female, manager or worker —who willfully commits an act that will retard production . . . is as guilty of treason as the deserter who assists the enemy. . . ."

To this manager Smith added: "You will not be required to belong to a union in order to hold your job here. . . . Finally, ask yourself, do you need a union to enable you to enjoy your work, earn good pay, or to have a clean and pleasant place in which to work? Personally, I can see no reason for a union in this plant."

Whenever CIO organizer Starnes announced a meeting, rumor was rife that it would be broken up, that a horsewhip was being plaited to drive him out of town, and so on. On one occasion Starnes was struck in the eye with an apple filled with axle grease, and finally he was beaten as he distributed CIO literature along the highway leading to the plant. But despite all the threats against his life, he stayed in Milledgeville and organized.

The first ray of justice broke through the clouds in August of

1944: five months after its passage, the Milledgeville ordinance against organizers was declared unconstitutional by Judge George S. Carpenter, on the ground that the $5,000 license fee was excessive and the requirement of a year's residence was a violation of free speech. Costs were assessed against the City of Milledgeville (this discouraged moves to adopt similar ordinances elsewhere in the South).

Then in December—nine months after the organizing drive began—the National Labor Relations Board rendered a decision that the Reynolds Corporation had "interfered with, restrained and coerced employees in the exercise of the rights guaranteed in Section 7 of the [National Labor Relations] Act."

The NLRB found that James Sibley—a Milledgeville businessman—arranged to have the anti-CIO literature of the Workers Welfare Association printed, "took an active part in promotion of the Association and financed some of its activities. His sister, Martha Sibley, was personnel manager at the plant and editor of the plant's paper. Sibley advertised in the paper. Smith, the plant manager, lived with Sibley. Meetings were held in the courthouse with Sibley presiding, and the mayor spoke in opposition to the CIO."

The board ordered the Reynolds Corporation to withhold all recognition from the Workers Welfare Association, to reinstate and reimburse those discharged for CIO activities, and to post a notice for sixty days throughout the plant assuring employees that they were free to become or remain members of the CIO or any other union.

Sometimes anti-union employers come up with something novel in the way of violent anti-union techniques. For instance, on the night of February 6, 1940, some 250 employees of the Republic Steel Corporation plant in Gadsden, Alabama, were invited to attend a meeting at the YMCA building on the company grounds "to discuss the company's representation plan." D. S. Campbell, an office employee of Republic Steel, presided, and introduced the show which followed.

"During the meeting there were many references made to condemn the CIO to the lowest-down meaning that could be," reported a CIO member who attended, "but when the show came on I was very much surprised to see that it was a show of five naked women. The leading girl of the show announced that the more the audience would applaud the more show they would get, or the better the show would be. The photograph hereto attached and initialed by me is a photograph of one of the girls who was in the show."

In due time the strip-teasers stripped to nothing but slippers and costume jewelry and then donned cellophane garments.

Subsequently the Alabama *News Digest* published the following interview with one of the teasers:

> Q: "You were engaged directly by the Republic Steel Corporation in Gadsden to stage this show, weren't you?"
> A: "Yes. We were paid by Republic, but we received more than the six-fifty apiece for a night's performance we usually charge. In addition, they paid for gasoline for our car up there and back."

The daily press has had so much to say about strikes by workers that someone—for the benefit of the record at least—should prepare a set of volumes reporting all the unjustifiable strikes by management. Sometimes reactionary industry employs the shutdown, lockout, and sit-down for politico-economic purposes, as during the notorious sit-down of capital during Roosevelt's second administration. That was a deliberate plot whereby capital, by refusing to expand and invest, sought to prevent Roosevelt from leading the country out of the Depression and around the corner to prosperity. To a large extent their sabotage succeeded—and the entire country suffered proportionately. Even more infamous was the blackmail employed by certain sections of industry at the outbreak of the war, when patriotism as well as community responsibility should have entered in. By refusing to convert to war production until assured by the government of "cost-plus" or other excess-profit guarantees, many industries held up our production of arms with costly consequences at the front.

For the most part, however, strikes by industry have been an ultimate method of intimidating employees out of joining a labor union. As a single wartime Southern example, consider the case of a textile-mill chain in Alabama. Workers at the chain's mills were joining the CIO Textile Workers Union. So, notwithstanding the armed forces' critical shortage of textiles, it was announced in 1944 that three mills had been sold to another corporation which in turn said it was offering the mills for sale—to South America if necessary.

When the president of one of the CIO locals called upon one of the general managers of one of the plants, he reported that the manager declared: "The mill would be reopened this week but we won't recognize your damn union! We'll rehire whom we please, on whatever basis we please, without regard to seniority, and your people can go to work or not, just as they damn please!"

It is often difficult to distinguish between violent and nonviolent forms of union busting. What could be more violent than depriving a man with a family of his job? While in 1935 the Wagner Act established the right of workers freely to organize unions of their own choice without interference from their employers—thus estopping employers from firing or blacklisting workers for union activity—it is taking many Southern employers a long time to live up to the law.

One reason why some employers still do not hesitate to fire workers in an attempt to discourage union organizing is that they have relatively little to lose. Although the employer may be reasonably certain that the NLRB will eventually order him to reinstate and reimburse workers discharged for union activity, the cost is generally small in comparison to the amount saved by the resultant intimidation of the other workers, and the consequent setback or breakup of union organization. A major reason for recent strikes has been the length of time required to obtain a decision from the shorthanded NLRB; in many instances the unions have simply found striking to be cheaper than appeals to the NLRB.

It is interesting to note to what extent some Southern employers are still defying the Wagner Act. The following typical case was related to me by a Negro worker in Atlanta:

"I had no sooner joined the union and put on my union button than the foreman told me the bossman wanted to see me in his office. I went in and sat down and he asked me:

" 'George, what do you mean by joinin' a union?'

" 'Well, sir, I just figured it was the right thing to do.'

" 'Who told you to get in it?'

" 'Didn't nobody have to tell me, sir; I joined it for my own benefit.'

" 'What's the matter? Haven't I been treatin' you right?'

" 'Well, sir, to tell the truth: not exactly.'

" 'Then go get your pay—you can't work for me and boost the union.' "

And so the Southern worker is rapidly awakening to the potentialities of unionism. Hasn't a Negro local down in Texas secured a contract providing for a paid holiday on Emancipation Day? And hasn't a white local in the Georgia foothills secured similar provision for Confederate Memorial Day?

More seriously, the Southern worker is aware that union workers over the country have a median monthly wage of about $150, as compared to a median of only $95 for unorganized workers. On top of that, the good word is getting around that those Southern workers who have achieved a high degree of unionization have all but wiped out the regional wage differential, and the "Black Dispatch" grapevine also has it that real unions can wipe out the racial wage differential.

All in all, it is little wonder that during the decade since Roosevelt took office in 1932 Southern unionization increased 1,000 per cent, as compared to a 200-per-cent increase in the remainder of the country.

Recently a Southern worker said to me, "I have only been in the union a few years, but from the benefits I have already derived from it, I wish I had been born in it!"

Yes, it is much later than the would-be union busters think.

BROTHERHOOD—UNION MADE

It is within the power of the unions not only to propel the South toward economic solidity, but also along the path that leads to interracial justice and harmony.

That indispensable prerequisite to Southern progress, the unity of Southern working folk, black and white, has twice been set back for generations: first by the abolition of Reconstruction, and subsequently by the perversion of Populism. Now the mantle of responsibility and opportunity has fallen upon the unions, many of which are striving, with far-reaching success, to reawaken Southern workers to the potentialities of strength-through-unity.

But, sad to say, some unions have not accepted this opportunity and responsibility. Of the two hundred major unions in the United States, nineteen of the big craft unions have constitutional bars against Negroes and about thirty others have other excuses for not admitting Negroes. Many other unions, while not practicing outright Negro exclusion, do insist upon separate Jim Crow locals for Negroes. Such Negro locals usually are affiliated with the nearest white local and are generally dominated by it. Ten of the nineteen unions which have constitutional bars against Negroes are affiliated with the American Federation of Labor. And so it is that nearly a third of the craft and semicraft membership of the AFL, as well as the entire membership of the operating railroad brotherhoods, is limited to those who are "white, sober, and of good moral character."

In the railroad industry Negroes have been methodically squeezed out for the past several decades. This is being done through unconscionable union-company agreements—sometimes formal and sometimes tacit—to keep Negroes off the higher paid jobs without regard to seniority, and to bar Negro youths as apprentices. As a result, by 1940 only 9 per cent of the employees of the Class I railroads were Negroes, and 97 per cent of these Negroes were in the following jobs: janitors and cleaners, extra gang, section and maintenance-of-way men, laborers and helpers, baggage-room and station attendants, cooks, waiters, and train attendants. In the higher classifications, embracing 1,297,563 employees, only three tenths of 1 per cent were Negroes.

During the war there were a number of tests of the closed shop when maintained by unions which refuse to admit Negroes to membership. One such case developed at San Mateo, California, when Charles Sullivan, Negro, was denied work at the Bethlehem Shipbuilding Company because the International Association of Machinists, AFL, had a constitutional ban against Negro members. Ultimately the FEPC referred the case to President Roosevelt, who in turn called upon William Green, head of the AFL, to take appropriate action. Finally the International Association of Machinists wrote its local: "It is now our duty to advise you that there is no other course to follow than to instruct the membership of Lodge 68 to make the necessary arrangements to comply with the Executive Order of the President of the United States." However, the Negro machinist was not admitted to the union, but was merely "cleared" for work.

There can be no legitimate excuse for such behavior on the part of a union. As the Louisville (Ky.) *Courier-Journal* has observed, "Brotherhood is a term that will not be without its qualifications and contradictions as long as human beings are what they are; however, when Brotherhood denies even a minimum economic chance to a man on account of the color of his skin, it makes us think of Free Enterprise."

The International Mineworkers were the first to spade Southern soil for non-discriminatory unionism. As one Negro miner puts it, "With the union it's all the same; white or black, you're a coal digger still."

Nevertheless, in 1935, when the CIO appeared under its

standard "to bring about the effective organization of the working men and women of America regardless of race, creed, color, or nationality . . ." the South of white supremacy was deeply shocked, as well it might be. The simple truth is that, to be effective in the South, unions must be non-discriminatory. Employers know this and have issued many an invitation to CIO representatives to organize their Southern plants—on a lily-white basis—but all such offers have been impolitely declined.

Southern Negroes are also well aware of the potentialities of non-discriminatory unions. As a bishop of the African Methodist Episcopal Church puts it, "When I first heard of the CIO, I asked, 'What does it stand for?' The answer I got was, 'White and colored in the same union.' When I heard that, I put on my war boots and my preachin' coat, and I been preachin' the principles of CIOism ever since!"

So high is the prestige of the CIO among Southern Negroes that CIO organizers often have difficulty convincing them that the various international unions—each of which has its own alphabetical designation—are really the CIO. Negroes want their membership buttons to read "CIO" in big letters, not "UCAPAWA" or something of the sort with a mere footnote reading "Affiliated with the Congress of Industrial Organizations."

White Southerners, on the other hand, are learning the necessity for non-discrimination the hard way. By all odds the most effective appeal to them is that of self-interest: the prospect of wiping out the regional wage differential by first wiping out the racial wage differential. Put another way, the Southern white worker can see how bringing Negroes into the union will keep them from undercutting wages or strikebreaking. (Significantly, I can find no instance of Negroes lending themselves to strikebreaking since the CIO came South a decade ago.)

Despite the CIO's huge success in building better race relations where they are most needed, it has not discovered any magic touchstone which will instantaneously convert prejudice into brotherhood. Sometimes it has found it necessary to advance toward non-discrimination a step at a time. As one organizer pointed out to me, "You can't promote equal job rights for

Negroes until you've got a union and a collective-bargaining contract."

In other words, neither Southern Negroes nor Southern whites would be helped by a union which went so far and so fast in the field of race relations that a reaction was provoked which would either prevent the formation of a local union or break up one already established. Southern Negroes are keenly aware of this fact and voluntarily conduct their activities in the unions accordingly. The CIO is not trying to impose union democracy from the top so much as it is trying to build it from the ground up. Generally speaking, this upbuilding is proceeding at the maximum speed possible without endangering the existence of the union. True, much of the initiative comes from the (duly elected) top; but for the most part it is being administered by Southerners who have risen above prejudice. As one of them said to me, "You just don't find men on the CIO pay roll who have it in their hearts to discriminate."

In the fusion of whites and Negroes into one union, the organizer functions as a catalytic agent. Often the difficulties involved in the process depend upon the relative proportions of the two ingredients. "If there are only 15 to 30 per cent Negro employees, you have a mean situation," an organizer explained to me. "But if there are from 35 to 60 per cent Negroes, everything is jake. But again, if there are more than 60 per cent Negroes, the white employees are likely to say: 'I went down to the union hall and there wasn't nothin' but blackbirds there; I ain't joinin' no black man's union.' "

Of course anti-union employers seldom fail to turn the anti-Negro prejudices of their white employees against the union. The first charge in the anti-CIO arsenal is: "The CIO is a nigger union!" This propaganda line is to be found in employer-sponsored scatter sheets, anti-union newspaper ads, and even in the mouths of prostitute preachers. Some employers have indirectly purchased quantities of the CIO pamphlets *The CIO and the Negro Worker* and *Working and Fighting Together Regardless of Race, Creed, Color, or National Origin,* and distributed them among their white employees in the hope of thus turning them against the CIO.

Again, in 1945, the Miami local of the International Association of Machinists, AFL, being confronted with stiff CIO opposition at an impending election, published a pamphlet entitled *Debate on the Fair Employment Practices Committee, Excerpts from the Congressional Record.* The contents consisted, not of the words of congressional champions of labor, but selections from the anti-CIO, anti-Negro, anti-Semitic rantings of Bilbo and Eastland. To cap the sacrilege, this racist propaganda bore the union label!

Whether inspired by the employer, a rival union, or other factors, prejudice is sometimes so rife that the CIO organizer must perforce—if he wishes to see a democratic union established —circumvent the race issue temporarily. One organizer recently described such a situation to me, as it developed in a Georgia plant where about 15 per cent of the employees were Negroes.

Quietly he took some of the Negro leaders aside. "Y'all know what the policy of the CIO is regarding racial discrimination," he told them, "but y'all also know how the whites in this plant feel. If I start right in organizing you fellows, I won't have a chance with them, and then nobody will have a union. So I'm asking you people to stand fast, and, when the time comes, vote for the union."

Then he went to work with the whites. When the election was finally held, the majority voted for the union, despite violent opposition from the employer. Now the organizer was in a position to say to the white members, "The colored have helped us by voting for the union. Without their votes we would have been licked. Now, as you know, the CIO is opposed to racial discrimination. Furthermore, the NLRB says the union has got to represent *all* employees in the plant. On top of that, the plant's contracts with the government specify that there be no discrimination. We're in for some hard sledding in the postwar period, and we can't expect the Negroes to stick by us if we don't give them a square deal. And so no matter how you look at it, it's up to us to take the colored in."

By that time the whites were sufficiently converted to unionism to put aside their prejudices—and thus another non-discriminatory Southern union was born. Short of a democratic revolution, this would seem to be one of the devious paths which democracy-in-evolution must take in the South.

The CIO has sometimes found it necessary, moreover, to tolerate for a time separate meetings of white and colored members in some of its Southern locals where prejudice is deep-rooted. Quite often the employer is more responsible for segregation sentiment than anyone else. In a recent Alabama case, the employer offered to stop fighting the union if it would agree to hold separate meetings for whites and Negroes. "All right," the organizer countered, "if you'll agree to build separate plants and commissaries for white and colored." And that settled that.

For the most part, what separate arrangements as have existed within the CIO have been mitigated somewhat by a measure of democracy for the Negro members in conducting the affairs of the union; although the problem of adequate Negro representation among the elected officials of mixed unions is another matter that is usually solved gradually. At present there remain but a handful of CIO locals which still cling to separate meetings, and these occur mainly among Southern textile workers. Indicative of the trend was the recent unanimous decision, without even a dissenting comment, of an Atlanta steelworkers local to consolidate, after having met separately for four years.

Among independent and AFL craft unions, however, the Jim Crow auxiliary continues quite common. This undemocratic and unhealthy situation cannot long endure. While much has been said about the equal rights afforded white and Negro members segregated in "Local 101A and 101B," in reality the result is second-class union membership for Negroes. In a typical situation, the FEPC found that Negro auxiliaries of the International Boilermakers had "no voice in the conduct of the union's affairs and must accept as their business agent the business agent of the supervising lodge in whose election the auxiliaries have no part," and that there was further discrimination in insurance benefits, et cetera.

On at least two occasions—at Mobile and New Orleans—AFL central labor councils have actually refused to seat duly elected Negro delegates. In both instances, however, the AFL revoked the central bodies' charters and saw to their reorganization with

Negro participation. The AFL also has within its ranks international unions which have courageously fought discrimination.

Inevitably the non-discriminatory policies and practices of the
CIO have had a salutary effect upon the AFL, even in the South.
For example, some three thousand Southern delegates in a regional AFL conclave in Atlanta in 1943 resolved: "This conference declares that it is in hearty accord with the fundamental
principle of the AFL, that the labor movement should serve the
workers without regard to race, creed, or color, and further declares that there should be a condition of absolute equal rights on
jobs and job opportunities without any discrimination whatsoever
between the workers on account of race, creed, or color."

On the other hand, when it has come down to actual cases the
AFL leadership has not always practiced the non-discrimination
it preaches. When AFL Negro unionists cited chapter and verse
of AFL discriminations at its 1943 convention, William Green
countered with the charge that Negro leaders have an "anti-AFL"
bias. To this the Chicago *Defender* properly replied:

"The hope of Negro America is in the trade-union movement,
because the preponderant majority of us labor with our hands for
a living. Precisely because we see in labor the chance of genuine
freedom and economic emancipation do we fight so hard to open
wide the doors of the AFL without regard to race or color. And
until the AFL learns that the darker brother is part of the American labor movement without reservation, we cannot but continue
to favor the CIO over the AFL in every instance."

(Some may think that the author is also prejudiced against the
AFL. As a matter of fact, he is prejudiced against prejudice; and
if the evidence showed the CIO to be most prejudiced, he would
be prejudiced against the CIO in that respect.)

The 1943 AFL convention finally contented itself with resolutions urging educational programs within its unions to combat
racial prejudice and urging continuance of the FEPC. In its 1944
convention at New Orleans, after a bitter floor fight by Negro
members, the AFL adopted a resolution endorsing a permanent
FEPC; but at the same time it also approved its executive committee's report describing the pending FEPC bill as "most objec-
tionable and dangerous."

In sharp contrast, pronouncements of the CIO have been uncompromising in their adherence to non-discrimination, as exemplified by the following resolution adopted at the 1944 convention:

Resolved, that (1) the CIO again reaffirms its unwavering opposition to discrimination against the Negro people or the people of any other minority.

(2) The gains that have been achieved must not be lost in the postwar. The CIO urges all affiliated unions to renewed vigilance against any form of racial discrimination, against all conditions that make fertile grounds for such discrimination, and to prevent anti-union employers from taking steps which are designed to return to previous conditions of discrimination and thereby reduce the gains that all workers have won.

We recommend that the CIO unions seek the incorporation into collective bargaining agreements of a provision that no person seeking employment shall be discriminated against because of race, creed, color, or place of origin.

(3) The CIO commends the President's Committee on Fair Employment Practices for its splendid work and important achievements procured in spite of the opposition of its enemies. We call upon Congress to enact legislation that will make the Fair Employment Practices Committee a permanent agency and confer upon the agency authority to enforce its decisions.

(4) Out of this war must emerge a complete understanding and determination on the part of the American people that full political and economic equality must be accorded to all Americans. Jim Crowism, the abominable poll tax, and any other form of discrimination and bigotry must be excised from our national life. The struggle against these vicious practices would be the strongest weapon in forging an effective national unity among all decent-minded Americans.

It is interesting to note that, in furtherance of its policy of non-discrimination, and under the stimulus of its National Committee to Abolish Discrimination, various CIO unions have established nearly one hundred similar committees on a local and state basis, and some of the CIO internationals have likewise set up anti-discrimination committees of their own.

In addition, the United Auto Workers (CIO) became the first union to enter into a contract with the FEPC for the purpose of co-operation in the elimination of discrimination. Moreover, when Ku-Kluxers infiltrated the UAW and inspired wartime race-hate strikes at the Packard and Hudson plants, the union's officials uncompromisingly warned "all members who feel disposed to violate the principle of 'no racial discrimination' that they cannot expect to get the support of the union in any discipline they may suffer from the company."

The influence of the CIO's policy of non-discrimination is by no means confined to the union, but carries over into community life. As a result of their working relationship on the job and in the union, white and Negro members are in a position to approach their common community problems on a basis of friendship instead of prejudice, and understanding instead of misunderstanding. . . . Too, the CIO exerts its influence for non-discrimination directly upon community agencies; whenever any of the welfare bodies solicit contributions from the CIO, the union's prime condition is: "The fund must be expended without discrimination."

Anti-union forces have striven mightily to create a public impression that the CIO is dedicated to a revolutionary program for bringing about "social equality." In clarifying the practical application of the CIO's resolution against discrimination, director George L. P. Weaver, of the union's Committee to Abolish Discrimination, reported in 1945: ". . . the phrase 'social equality' has always been used to create confusion. To illustrate, the following public services are often included within its scope: Equal access to all residential areas, to all public transportation, public recreation, hotels, restaurants, public schools and other facilities used by the public and supported wholly or in part by public funds. These services must be removed from the realm of private social activities and considered as public facilities to be equally enjoyed by all citizens.

"Private social activities may be defined as the right of individuals or groups to make purely arbitrary selections, such as marriage, friendships, home entertainment, and participation in organizations concerned with social uplift. To attempt to regulate or dictate to an individual in this sphere would be a violation of his constitutional rights and outside the scope of our jurisdiction."

While the CIO has thus condemned compulsory segregation, it has not sought any overnight revolution against the laws and practices of segregation which exist in the South. Within its own ranks, however, the CIO is doing what it can to discourage segregation in the South. What it can do varies within geographical (and psychological) boundaries. For example, in Alabama and Georgia, I have seen Negro delegates segregate themselves on one *side* of the hall at state CIO conventions. On the other hand, at a Tennessee convention there was no segregation, although one individual white delegate did take the trouble to inform me that "This section has been reserved for the colored." However, I have not encountered any instance of a CIO staff member insisting upon segregation, while many have actively discouraged it. The position of the majority is, "We don't have anything to say about it; the Negroes segregate themselves."

A related question has to do with the recreational activities of mixed unions in the South. I have attended such affairs in Georgia. White members served the Negro members refreshments and then served themselves. There was a tendency on the part of both groups to sit apart while eating. Whatever talent there was in the union, white and Negro, took turns performing. Whenever there was music for dancing, either the white couples danced at one end of the hall and the Negroes at the other or the two races took turns dancing alternately. Throughout the entire proceedings there was an evident spirit of comradeship, and there were no incidents or friction. I describe these events here, not because either the CIO or I regard them as ideal, but because they are significant mileposts marking the South's transition from white supremacy to democracy.

Another such milepost, whose significance lies largely in its symbolism, is the manner in which the abhorrent "etiquette" of white supremacy is gradually being discarded by the CIO's white Southern members. As a single example of this, I recall what took place after a Negro delegate to a recent Alabama CIO convention had delivered a stirring speech. Several white staff members shook the Negro's hand in congratulation. Slowly a few white delegates moved forward to do likewise.

"You goin' to shake his hand?" I heard a white delegate apprehensively ask his companion behind me.

"I don't know," came the answer cautiously.

"Come on," said the other, "everybody else is. I don't care if he is colored; he made the best union speech of the convention."

And so the white brothers shook hands with their darker brother; and the walls didn't come tumbling down; and the union and the South were stronger.

In a very real sense, the conflict between progress and reaction on the Southern front is the struggle of the CIO versus the KKK, for these two organizations spearhead the opposing forces: democracy vs. white supremacy. It is a fact that some of the South's best unionists, from every viewpoint, are former Klansmen. The emphasis here is upon the *former*. On the other hand, some of the most disruptive forces in the Southern labor movement are those active Klansmen who hold union cards. While there are some such in the CIO, they largely infest the craft unions.

As evidence of the CIO's technical knockout over the KKK there is the fact that several of the union's recent Southern state conventions have barred members of the Klan. As one union member related to me, "We give the Ku Klux hell at almost every meeting now, and nobody gets up to protest like they used to."

The metamorphosis from KKK to CIO is no mean accomplishment. It involves a process of de-education and re-education comparable with that of making democrats out of Nazis and Nipponese. But it can be done. An organizer described the job succinctly when he said, "All we got to do is make the white and colored folks see that the boss has tied their tails together and hung 'em over a line to keep 'em from clawin' at him."

Some may wonder just how this realization is being brought home. Does the CIO conduct an intensive educational campaign in the South against racial prejudice? The answer is: no. The absence of such a program is due to a deliberate policy of the CIO's Southern officials and editors. Their belief is that the best education is for their members to work together in the union, and the less said about the "race question," the better. Consequently, members are regarded as members, and race distinctions are kept at a minimum. Only when the situation demands it are interracial problems discussed as such on the floor, and then diplomacy governs both groups.

Surprisingly often, completely non-discriminatory locals come into being spontaneously without any apparent indication that different races are involved. Just recently, in south Alabama, white and Negro lumber-mill workers, having worked side by side for generations, proceeded to organize a completely democratic CIO local without it occurring to anyone to set up a separate or segregated organization. It was a "natural"—as every union would be if it were not for the agitation of certain employer groups bent upon maintaining the disunity cheapness of labor.

One Southern labor institution which deserves special mention for its contribution to effective unionism and racial democracy is the Highlander Folk School at Monteagle, Tennessee. "The purpose of Highlander Folk School is to assist in the defense and expansion of political and economic democracy," the school's program states. "Since unions are basic to the achievement of democracy, the strengthening of unions through education is the school's primary task."

Since its founding in 1932, Highlander has provided instruction in labor history, economics, parliamentary law, public speaking, labor-management contracts, grievance machinery, and labor journalism—all subjects direly needed by Southern unions. Union locals are invited to select the most promising from their membership to attend the residence sessions, where the charge covering both tuition and board is only fifty dollars per month. Highlander is now raising a new-building fund in order that it may offer instruction to many more Southern unionists the year round; the library will be dedicated to members of Southern unions who lost their lives in the War Against Fascism.

In addition to its residence program, the Highlander staff conducts a field-training program, carrying instruction to unions throughout the South.

Follow-up surveys of Highlander students have revealed the truly miraculous extent to which they have provided top-notch native leadership for the Southern union movement. But one of the most significant Highlander contributions is in the field of race relations. The school has always actively fought with facts the prejudice it encountered and, since 1945, has been able to conduct its sessions on an interracial basis. Recently Myles Horton, director of Highlander, described the sessions to a Negro scoutmaster at Chattanooga.

"I'd like to bring my Boy Scout troop up to Highlander just to show them that such a thing does exist, and that there are white Southerners without prejudice," said the scoutmaster. "We wouldn't bother you any. We could camp out in the woods and just look in the windows once in a while. It would mean so much to my boys while they're growing up."

Various other organizations, such as the Southern Conference for Human Welfare, Southern Regional Council, National Association for the Advancement of Colored People, and Anti-Defamation League of B'nai B'rith, are in various ways clearing the right-of-way to brotherhood in the South. But the actual job of road building is in the hands of the unions. And the road is progressing; and the end is in sight. *Everybody* cheered when a Negro delegate to a recent Southern union convention concluded: "If we ever goin' to get anywhere, we got to get there together."

FAIR EMPLOYMENT FOREVER!

While the unions have an unequaled opportunity to abolish discrimination and build brotherhood on the job, the over-all task of assuring equality of economic opportunity is primarily a public one.

Heretofore, equality of opportunity has been in the anomalous position of cornerstone of the American ideal—but without any legal status. While countless individual members of minority groups have sought and found opportunity in America, minority groups as a whole have been subjected to all manner of discriminations in employment. And they have had no recourse at law. As Westbrook Pegler has pointed out, it has been the privilege of employers to "look a man in the face" and refuse to hire him solely because of his race, creed, or national origin.

There is a great deal that the unions can do to abolish such discrimination. As has been pointed out, the CIO has already taken the lead in urging its unions to use their collective-bargaining power to secure contractual guarantees that employers will not discriminate in hiring or upgrading. But in the final analysis, the assurance of equal job opportunity is a public responsibility, which can and should be met by all levels of government. So far, New York City, New York State, and New Jersey have enacted anti-discrimination laws, and have found them altogether salutary. But such laws are most needed where they are least likely to be enacted—in the South.

The duty of the federal government in this matter is clear. Although there is nothing in the Constitution that makes real the

American ideal of equal opportunity, there is much in it that imposes upon Congress the right and responsibility to do so. It is simple justice that laws be enacted requiring that there be no discrimination in the expenditure of public funds which are acquired through indiscriminate taxation, and this proscription against discrimination should apply not only to public agencies but to all concerns doing work under contract or subcontract for public agencies. From a different—but none the less positive—view, Congress, under its power to regulate commerce and promote the general welfare, has the right and responsibility of prohibiting discrimination by concerns engaged in both interstate and foreign commerce. And of course this right extends to prohibition of discrimination by unions.

In peace, racial and religious prejudice as manifested in job discrimination costs America dearly, both morally and materially. In war, the same sort of discrimination was indulged in at the cost of many American lives. But even before America became directly involved in the War Against Fascism, her role as the "Arsenal of Democracy" made intolerable the failure to fully utilize the nation's manpower because of prejudice. The very nature of the global conflict, in which America allied herself with the democracies in opposition to the forces of racism, required that positive steps be taken to combat racism as a bottleneck to production.

And so on June 25, 1941, President Roosevelt issued his epochal Executive Order 8802 establishing a Fair Employment Practice Committee (FEPC) "to provide for the full and equitable participation of all workers in defense industries without discrimination because of race, creed, color, or national origin." One of the order's most significant provisions was a requirement that all contracts let by the government include a clause obligating the contractors not to discriminate in employment.

So much has been said concerning the FEPC's alleged "dictatorial and highhanded" methods that the facts of the matter ought to be stated without further delay. Upon receiving a complaint of discrimination coming under its jurisdiction, the FEPC investigates. If the complaint appears to have been warranted, the offending employer or union is consulted, and if satisfactory adjustments are made, the case is closed. If such adjustments are not made, public hearings are sometimes held, at which both parties may appear in person or be represented by legal counsel. The full committee reviews the transcript of the hearings, and on that basis issues recommendations or directives to the offending parties.

The committee has commonly required offending employers and unions to notify one another, and employment agencies, of their intention not to discriminate because of race, creed, or color. When an offender refuses to comply with an FEPC directive the committee may recommend to other government agencies that punitive steps be taken, and ultimately such cases may be referred to the President for enforcement. The FEPC has never urged an employer to hire a quota of minority group workers; each individual complaint is considered on its own merit.

No federal agency since the Freedmen's Bureau has been confronted with so colossal a task—nor given such a minute staff to tackle it. For the first two years of its existence the FEPC's entire personnel consisted of only thirteen officials and twenty-one clerical workers. By 1945 its staff still consisted of less than one hundred and twenty persons. Considering the immensity of its task and the diminutiveness of its staff, the FEPC has done a superlative job. It has made some mistakes, of course; but its road has been rough and uncharted. On the whole its effect has been definitely positive, making itself felt not only in those cases handled but, by indirection, throughout the industrial and governmental life of the nation.

The FEPC has established a record of satisfactory adjustment of cases at the rate of 95.7 per cent per month. During the eighteen-month period from July 1943 through December 1944 the FEPC docketed 5,803 complaints as having face value but dismissed 64 per cent of them for lack of merit. In 69.4 per cent of the complaints, private industry was charged with discrimination, federal agencies were charged in 24.5 per cent, and labor unions in 6.1 per cent. Complaints against unions were most prevalent in the South. The percentage of satisfactory adjustments was considerably lower in the South and Far West than in the East and Midwest. About 81 per cent of the complaints docketed were allegations of discrimination because of race, and 97 per cent of these involved Negroes. Of the complaints based upon religious creed, 73 per cent came from Jews and the remainder from Seventh-Day Adventists, Jehovah's witnesses, Catholics, et cetera.

Due in no small measure to the influence of the FEPC, the utilization of non-white workers in war industries was increased appreciably. Whereas less than 3 per cent of all war workers were non-white in 1942, the percentage had risen to 8.3 per cent by November of 1944. In addition, the FEPC aided in settling some forty strikes caused by racial friction during the eighteen months preceding December of 1944 and warded off many more.

Another significant effort on the part of the federal government to abolish job discrimination was a 1943 decision by the War Labor Board on a Texas case, abolishing the wage classifications "colored laborer" and "white laborer," and granting all laborers the same rate of pay regardless of race. The WLB's decision, penned by President Frank P. Graham of the University of North Carolina (a public member of the board), said, "This equalization of economic opportunity is not a violation of the sound American provision of differentials in pay for differentials in skills. It is rather a bit of realization of the no less sound American principle of equal pay for equal work as one of those equal rights in the promise of American democracy, regardless of color, race, sex, religion, or national origin."

Although the War Labor Board expired with the war, the influence of that particular decision, at least, lives after it.

Lincoln's Emancipation Proclamation sounded the knell of chattel slavery for the American Negro; the Supreme Court's white primary decision implemented—after three quarters of a century—his political rights as asserted by the Fifteenth Amendment; and Roosevelt's Executive Order 8802 paved the way toward equal job opportunities.

Naturally, all three of these auspicious events were given exceedingly warm receptions by the lords of the Southern manor. Atlanta had no sooner been chosen as the site of the FEPC's Southeastern regional office than the city council charged that the

The nationwide campaign of false and misleading propaganda against F.E.P.C. has derived much of its inspiration from the Southern States Industrial Council. The cartoon below is from Talmadge's Statesman.

agency "planned mixed employment of the races in one of the office buildings," and called upon Southern congressmen "to insist upon the removal of said office from the city of Atlanta."

Likewise, when the FEPC opened a Southwestern regional office at Dallas, Governor Coke Stevenson of Texas put to it the following questions:

> 1. By what authority do you conduct your activities in Texas?
> 2. What is the scope of your operations and what is the objective you seek?
> 3. Do the purposes of your activities include the violation of any of the segregation laws of this state?
> 4. Is it the purpose to establish policies which are in violation of state laws?

In reply, Chairman Malcolm Ross of the FEPC said, "The committee has never taken the position that segregation per se is contrary to the provisions of Executive Orders 8802 and 9346 . . . Where the issue of segregation is involved, as in all cases, the committee's action will depend upon the existence or absence of prohibited discrimination.

"We regret to inform Your Excellency that we have reports that industries located in Texas have recently barred Negroes from work which traditionally they have done for years," Ross went on to say. "We have reports that in Texas employers have placed white and Negro workers on the same job, requiring the same skill and experience, yet paid them different wage scales. We have reports that in one city in Texas, Negro welders trained at the expense of the government have been denied an opportunity to use their skill in Texas so that it has been necessary to refer them to other states for employment. We have reports that in Texas there are in effect union contracts which forbid the use of Negroes or Latin Americans above a certain skill level, regardless of their qualifications."

In addition to asking the FEPC to state its business and to get out, the Southern slavocracy has resorted to violence. A foreboding instance of this took place in 1944 in a town in Louisiana, where eight of the town's leading Negro citizens were beaten and driven away for having joined in a protest to the FEPC against plans to establish a government welding school for whites only.

The protest was registered by the local chapter of the National Association for the Advancement of Colored People, and as a result, Negro instructors were assigned to the school. Among the enrollees was the Negro father of two sons in service in the South Pacific. The first afternoon two white men called for him at the school, saying, "We're officers; come with us!" They took him to the office of the sheriff, where he was confronted by the sheriff and the superintendent of the parish schools.

The sheriff accused him of writing letters to the superintendent, which he said were insulting. The sheriff then went into a tirade against the NAACP (which is regarded as a revolutionary organization in the rural white South). Then the superintendent warned the father not to write any more letters to the FEPC or War Manpower Commission or any other outsiders. He wound up by telling the sheriff that the father was organizing the Negroes to overthrow the whites and that he had a good notion to run him out of town.

"It's up to you," said the sheriff.

"Then run him out!" the superintendent ordered after a pause.

The sheriff thereupon gave the father until ten o'clock the next morning to make his departure. But he was unable to leave on schedule, and that evening he was picked up by four deputies and again taken to the sheriff's office. There, according to an affidavit later sworn to by him, "The sheriff became enraged and began to use a deal of abusive language; he began slapping me on both sides of the face, then using his fist very forcefully, kicking me two or three times."

After being jailed for a time, the Negro was driven about a mile out of town, slapped in the face with his own necktie, and told to "Walk, and walk fast!" As he walked, a pistol was fired after him. For several miles the car followed him, and he was warned never to return to . . . The treatment accorded the seven other Negroes followed much the same pattern.

While it is true that there are few if any employers in the South who do not discriminate against Negroes, the race is also discriminated against in other sections, albeit somewhat less grossly. In the Southwest and on the Pacific coast, discrimination against Mexican-Americans is almost as rampant. And everywhere there are other racial and religious minorities which are discriminated against daily. In other words, discrimination is reactionary rather than Southern, its efficacy as a means of thwarting democratic unity having been universally recognized.

It is not at all surprising, therefore, to find certain employer groups actively engaged in attacking the FEPC. Among these is the Southern States Industrial Council, which in a letter to me said it was doing everything that it could in order to defeat this measure, and that it had "contacted every trade association in the United States, some 2,800 in number, in an effort to enlist their assistance."

But by no means all of the opposition to the FEPC has come from the South. Ever since industry arose in America there has been a deliberate effort on the part of some industrialists to foster prejudice among Americans in order to assure a divided and cheap labor supply. Thus we find not only the Southern slavocracy opposing the FEPC as a threat to its cheap labor, but also such nationwide reactionary-led employer groups as the so-called "National Small Businessmen's Association."

There is no question but that Roosevelt's Order creating the FEPC, like Lincoln's Emancipation Proclamation, came primarily as a war measure to strengthen the fighting power of the United States, physically and morally. The FEPC expressed the determination of the American people that prejudice was not to be tolerated as a bottleneck to war production. As American soldiers of all races fighting side by side at the front said, they didn't care what color hands turned out their weapons, just so they kept coming at top speed.

Lincoln's Emancipation Proclamation was given sanction and permanency through adoption of the Thirteenth Amendment abolishing slavery. But Roosevelt's Economic Emancipation Proclamation establishing the FEPC must yet be made permanent by congressional action. In 1944 Senator Chavez in the Senate, and Representatives Morton, Scanlon, Dawson, and LaFollette in the House, introduced bills which would not only make the FEPC permanent, but would extend its jurisdiction over employment in interstate and foreign commerce. In its

Findings and Declaration of Policy, the Fair Employment Act states:

> The Congress finds that the practice of denying employment to, and discriminating in employment against, properly qualified persons by reason of their race, creed, color, national origin, or ancestry, foments domestic strife and unrest, deprives the United States of the fullest utilization of its capacities for production and defense, and burdens, hinders, and obstructs commerce.
>
> It is hereby declared to be the policy of the United States to eliminate such discrimination in all employment relations which fall within the jurisdiction or control of the Federal Government as hereinafter set forth.
>
> The right to work and to seek work without discrimination because of race, creed, color, national origin, or ancestry is declared to be an immunity of all citizens of the United States, which shall not be abridged by any state or by an instrumentality or creature of any state.

The act applies to "Any employer having in his employ more than five persons, who is (1) engaged in interstate or foreign commerce; (2) under contract with the United States or any agency thereof; (3) performing work, under subcontract or otherwise, called for by a contract to which the United States or any agency thereof is a party . . . This Act shall apply to any labor union which has five or more members in the employ of one or more employers covered by the preceding paragraph."

Just as the slavocrats have subverted the Thirteenth Amendment through more or less subtle forms of peonage, the wage slavers have gone all-out to sabotage the Fair Employment Act even before it is adopted. As drawn, the act properly provides that "Any person aggrieved by a final order of the Commission . . . may obtain a review of such order in any circuit court of appeals . . ." Whereas circuit-court cases are decided by federal judges, district courts provide trial by jury. Hence the would-be saboteurs are trying to amend the act, substituting the district courts for the circuit courts, in the hope of frustrating the agency through a refusal of prejudiced local juries to convict.

Of course the white supremacists in Congress have wailed that equality of opportunity must certainly lead to social equality, while the reactionaries among the Republicans echo the Pegler

line that Americans have a constitutional right to discriminate.
Both groups argue that legislation is powerless over prejudice.
While it is true that the holding of prejudice cannot be prohibited by law, the *expression* of prejudice certainly can. The
fact is that the Fair Employment Act will bring about the most
effective education against prejudice—the experience of working
together without discrimination and co-operating for progress
through democratic unions.

Besides the various Negro, Jewish, and Catholic organizations
which support the Fair Employment Act, there is the Federal
Council of Churches of Christ in America, the Young Women's
Christian Association, Southern Conference for Human Welfare,
Southern Regional Council, and a great many labor unions,
municipal interracial committees, and other such democratic
organizations.

"To abandon at this time the fundamental principle upon
which the Fair Employment Practice Committee was established
is unthinkable," President Truman wrote the House Rules Committee in June of 1945. "Discrimination in the matter of employment against properly qualified persons because of their race,
creed, or color is not only un-American in nature, but will lead
eventually to industrial strife and unrest."

The President's plea that the House be given an opportunity
to vote on a bill providing for a permanent FEPC came after the
House Appropriations Committee deleted funds for the temporary FEPC from the war agencies appropriations bill, thus
threatening the life of the agency after June 30. Truman's message also came in fulfillment of the Democratic party's 1944
campaign pledge: "We believe that racial and religious minorities have the right to live, develop and vote equally with all
citizens and share the rights that are guaranteed by our Constitution. Congress should exert its full constitutional power to
protect those rights." On the other hand, some Republican congressmen have failed to act upon their party's specific pledge to
support a permanent FEPC.

The filibustering against appropriations to continue the FEPC
during the fiscal year beginning July 1, 1945, reached an all-
time low for such lowly performances. Senator Bilbo, "The

Man" from Mississippi—veteran leader of filibusters against the anti-poll-tax and anti-lynching bills—led the anti-FEPC gab fest in the Senate. "There are a few Catholic priests in this country, who, along with some Jewish rabbis, are trying to line up with the Negroes in teaching social equality . . . some of them are rotten," The Man said. Senator Eastland, also of Mississippi, took a notorious part in the proceedings, going so far afield as to seek to impugn the good record of America's Negro servicemen. In the House the anti-Semitic rantings of Rankin of Mississippi touched off a Southwide wave of Jew-baiting.

The FEPC request was for the pitiably small sum of $446,200 as a part of the $771,538,765 appropriation for a score of other war agencies. But for thirteen days the funds of all these agencies were held up by the opponents of the FEPC—Southern Democrats and reactionary Republicans—who finally compromised on the measly sum of $250,000 for the FEPC, which was ordered to liquidate itself. Significantly, neither the House nor the Senate would permit a record vote on the issue.

Again, when the FEPC bill was finally brought before the Senate in February of 1946, the Southerners once more thwarted democracy by a filibuster which lasted nineteen days. Again the Senate evaded a controversial issue by refusing to limit debate.

And so the FEPC passed away on June 30, 1946 A.D.

But it shall be resurrected, and fair employment will reign forever. . . .

THE RACE RACKET

Prejudice Is Made, Not Born

Since race prejudice is by all odds the greatest obstacle to democratic unification of the South—and hence is the greatest barrier to Southern progress—an understanding of how prejudice is made, not born, is essential to an understanding of "how come" the South is so sorely afflicted in this respect.

Needless to say, such prejudice is not indigenous to the South alone, nor does it arise from any innate propensity of Southerners.

Before man, prejudice was. Prejudice came into being when the first animal developed sufficient memory to enable it to sustain anger, and human prejudice is simply animal prejudice in its most intricate form. Instinctive xenophobia—fear of the unknown—is common to man and many other animals. A gift of natural selection, its efficacy as a lifesaver in a predatory world has brought it down to us through eons of time. Thus the child's first thought upon being confronted by a strange animal, human or otherwise, is "Will it bite?" If it does bite, then the child's worst fears are confirmed and a complicated sequence of emotional and psychological reactions sets in which may culminate in prejudice and hate.

Primitive men no sooner became aware of their racial and cultural divergencies than they began to band together in tribes of their own kind—and individual xenophobias merged into group xenophobias. As such, they acquired the characteristics of mass psychology. The individual's fear of strange tribesmen was re-enforced by the identical fears of all his fellow tribesmen; and the trepidation which had begun as a protective instinct now took on the infallibility of a verity imputed by socially consistent sensation.

Man thereupon proceeded to erect an institutional, legalistic, traditional, religious superstructure to proclaim the normalcy of his xenophobia. In all of this the high visibility of difference was what set in motion the suspicion-distrust-fear sequence, so that the intensity of intertribal prejudice was usually proportionate to the degree of difference in physical appearance, language, and custom.

Although it is entirely natural for people to first make issues of their differences, it is equally natural for them to resolve those differences and to work out ways of co-operation. This means that race hatred can be kept alive only by forces foreign to the folk themselves. The whole monstrous mass of racial and religious animosities, despite their instinctive and traditional background, are not bona fide folkways, but a deadly virus that has been artificially cultivated by the few who profit from the disunity of the many. Exploitation, imperialism, fascism, and war would all be impossible without forced feeding of these asocial instincts.

All exploiters, oppressors, and aggressors have fostered diversionary and divisive hatred in order that they might divide and rule and divide and conquer. Fascism represents the ultimate expression of this policy. Here in the twentieth century the forces making for democratic unification of the peoples of the world are so irresistible that the exploiters have resorted to the extremity of fascism in a desperate effort to prolong the inevitable. By means of fascist dictatorship, the exploiters first suppress all forms of democratic expression and then proceed to divert popular discontent against both foreign and domestic scapegoats.

For example, Hitler once said, "My Jews are a valuable hostage given to me by the democracies. Anti-Semitic propaganda in all countries is an almost indispensable medium for the extension of our political campaign." And Goebbels added, "Nothing will be easier than to produce a bloody revolution in America. No other country has so many social and racial tensions. We shall be able to play upon many strings there. North America is a medley of races." Goebbels also said, in *Das Reich* in 1942: "The world has fallen into two parts. There is a world of love and a world of hate. A hard century has begun. Only those who know when to love and when to hate are standing on strong ground."

Of course the Nazis are not the only ones who have deliberately promulgated race hatred; their counterparts in the South and elsewhere have proven equally adept.

Professionally made hate comes in two packages: one bears the label of nationalism, contains an inordinate spirit of animosity toward other nationals, and is designed to prevent international democratic unity; the other bears the label of racism or bigotry, and contains hatred against racial and religious minorities within the nation, and is designed to prevent democratic national unity.

The relative status of majority and minority groups within competitive societies is a peculiar phenomenon which has both economic and psychological substance. In order to be such a minority, a group of people must be *recognizable,* and the more easily recognizable they are, the more sharply defined their status is likely to be. This is true because the conduct of any member of such a group is unconsciously attributed to the entire group, whereas similar behavior by someone whose race is not *noticeably* different from the majority is only associated with the individual.

At bottom, however, racial and national minorities have been kept in a disadvantaged position not because of prejudice, but because industry has fostered prejudice as a means of assuring the disunity cheapness of labor. When American industry gained economic and political ascendancy over the nation following the Civil War, it began a feverish search at home and abroad for cheap labor. Successive immigrations of Irish, Italian, and Polish labor were encouraged.

These groups had no sooner arrived than industry began to fan the prejudice of native American labor to such an extent that it culminated in the Know-Nothing movement and Ku Klux Klan. The function of such inspired prejudice has been to keep minorities isolated so that they may be more readily discriminated against. This policy reached its logical conclusion in the legalized segregation of the South's Negroes, which could not have been accomplished or maintained without the connivance of Northern industry through its influence on Congress. By isolating minorities and discriminating against some more than others, industry is able to dictate its own wages, whereas if the minorities were allowed to integrate, labor unions would ensue and force wages up.

In the past, man's physical inability to produce the basic necessities of life in sufficient quantities for all has been a prime cause of international hatred and war. Have-Nots have always been a threat to Haves, and understandably so. Now, however, technology and atomic energy promise plenty for all, and the mere prospect of freedom from want has done a great deal to allay selfish rivalry and bring mankind closer together. Moreover, man's cumulative knowledge is at last bringing him to the realization that, from a purely selfish viewpoint if for no other reason, he must help others to live if he himself wishes to live and enjoy freedom from fear of depression and atomic disintegration. He not only must not hate others, but he must also see to it that there is no cause for others to hate him.

We have seen how social prejudice comes into being naturally and can be overcome naturally through co-operation and education, while institutionalized prejudice, on the other hand, is deliberately fostered and nurtured to serve the ends of economic and political reaction. Social prejudice is a growing pain incident to the process of becoming civilized, but institutionalized prejudice is the cause of untold suffering, war, and depression. The task of eliminating the latter type is therefore most urgent.

Myth of the Master Race

In order to cope effectively with institutionalized prejudice in its reactionary politico-economic role, its basic dogma, the

Theory of the Master Race, must be exposed as the infamous rationalization that it is. The thing was virtually unheard of a century ago. The first comprehensive exposition was Count Arthur de Gobineau's *Essay on the Inequality of Human Races,* which appeared between 1853 and 1857. Variations on the same theme were forthcoming in 1899 in Houston Chamberlain's *Foundations of the Nineteenth Century.* To a considerable extent such racial "interpretations" of history—and the climatic and geographic "interpretations" which appeared contemporaneously —were intended to counteract the economic interpretation by Karl Marx.

Far from being based upon scientific evidence (intelligence tests were then in a prenatal stage), the Myth of the Master Race was mere idle or sponsored speculation (Gobineau was a writer of fiction, and Chamberlain a Britisher who worked for the Kaiser during World War I). But this has not deterred latter-day disciples of racism from citing the founding fathers of the dogma as though they knew more about the comparative intelligence of races than do modern anthropologists—who are frank to admit their ignorance on the matter.

By the outbreak of World War I, racism had been firmly established as an adjunct of nationalism for purposes of aggression. The war itself inspired a host of popular and pseudo-scientific variants of the Myth—most notoriously, Madison Grant's *Conquest of a Continent,* Lothrop Stoddard's *Rising Tide of Color,* and Adolf Hitler's *Mein Kampf.* Grant and Stoddard were journalists; Hitler a paper hanger. Hitler's bally-hoo about an Aryan-Nordic-Teutonic "Superman"—made ridic-ulous by the "honorary Aryan" appellation bestowed on the Nipponese, and the mad hunt for fair-haired Nordic ancestors for the Italians in general and Mussolini in particular—was *not* borrowed from Friedrich Nietzsche, the German philosopher of the past century, who was actually one of the Germans' severest critics.

Nietzsche's Superman was by no means a racial or national concept. His thesis was that warfare and the law of the jungle were desirable to render the Law of Natural Selection—with its struggle for existence and survival of the fittest—again operative among humans, so that the "inferior" would be exterminated and a "Superman" evolved. Never would Nietzsche have bestowed the title en masse on Nazis or Germans or Nordics or Aryans or Southern "whites." In passing it should also be noted that the atomic bomb has completely invalidated war (if ever it had such validity) as a means of promoting the survival of the fittest. Atomic war means mass destruction of both civilians and combatants without any regard for their intrinsic worth.

Although the South took a fancy to white supremacy long before the Nazis, the latter went raving mad on the subject, while the South continues to hover around the lunacy fringe. The standard exposition of Nazi racism, Hermann Gauch's *New Elements of Racial Instruction,* carried the Theory of the Master Race to its illogical conclusion:

> We can advance the assertion that at the base of all Racial Science there is no concept of "human being" in contradistinction to animals separated by any physical or mental trait; the only existing differentiation is between Nordic man, on the one hand, and animals as a whole, including all non-Nordic human beings, or sub-men, who are transitional forms of development. It has not been proven, moreover, that the non-Nordic man cannot be mated with apes.

Some idea of what the Southern Negro had to preserve in fighting the Axis may be had from Hitler's own concept of white supremacy: "From time to time it is demonstrated . . . that for the first time here or there a Negro has become a lawyer, teacher, even clergyman, or even a leading opera tenor or something of that kind . . . it is a criminal absurdity to train a born half-ape until one believes a lawyer has been made of him, while millions of members of the highest culture race have to remain in entirely unworthy positions . . . it is a sin against the will of the Eternal Creator to let hundreds of thousands of His most talented beings degenerate in the proletarian swamp of today, while Hottentots and Zulu Kafirs are trained for intellectual vocations."

The Nazis applied the theory of the master Aryan race in a program of selective eugenics on the phony basis of Aryanism. Loans up to one thousand marks were made to newlyweds who were "free from hereditary mental or physical defects" (Semitic or other non-Aryan ancestry) and who were also "politically right-minded" (Nazis). A portion of these loans was canceled upon the birth of each child to the couple, and large families were granted tax exemptions and housing priorities.

So anxious were the Nazis to increase their brood that—as reported in Erika Mann's *School for Barbarians*—the periodical *Rasse* (Race) declared in 1937: "Every healthy child of every German mother means one more battle won in the fight for existence of the German people. And so, in an ethical sense, it is impossible to deny to the unmarried German woman the right to become a mother." To this Alfred Rosenberg, the high priest of Nazism, added, "And so the German Reich of the future will have to regard the childless woman—regardless of whether or not she is married—as an incomplete member of the National Commonwealth."

Carrying the tribal tripe still further, Professor Ernst Bergmann, in an essay on *Knowledge and the Spirit of Motherhood,* said, "Lifelong monogamy is perverse and would prove harmful to our race. Were this institution ever really enforced—and fortunately this is almost never the case in reality—the race must decay. Every reasonably constructed state will have to regard a woman who has not given birth as dishonored. There are plenty of willing and qualified youths ready to unite with the girls and women on hand. Fortunately, one boy of good race suffices for twenty girls. And the girls, for their part, would gladly fulfill the demand for children, were it not for the nonsensical so-called civilized idea of the monogamous permanent marriage, an idea in complete contradiction to all natural facts."

Nazi racism reached its ultimate expression in the deliberate efforts to exterminate the "inferior" races of Europe, which reached its maximum intensity when the defeat of Germany became certain. This policy was bluntly enunciated earlier by Dr. Karl Rudolf Werner Best, Nazi minister of Denmark. Said he: "The extermination or elimination of foreign races is not contrary to the rule of history, provided this process is brought to completion." He went on to say that Nazi racism relegated the rest of humanity to four categories according to their relative quality, and that politically under the New Order this would find expression in alliances (as with Italy and Finland), supervision (as of France and Norway), direct administration (Moravia, Bohemia), or colonies (such as Poland).

The quackery of racism has been fully exposed in such authoritative volumes as *Heredity and Politics* by J. B. S. Haldane, professor of genetics at the University of London; *Man's Most Dangerous Myth: the Fallacy of Race* by M. F. Ashley Montagu; *Race, Language, and Culture* by Franz Boas; *Race* by Jacques Barzan; *Race: Science and Politics* by Ruth Benedict, professor of anthropology at Columbia; and *The Genetic Basis for Democracy* by Henry Wallace. In addition to these, such reliable scientists as Hrdlička, Herskovits, Davenport, Steggerda, Krauss, and many others have discounted the Master Race Myth.

Dr. Haldane, in addressing the Congress of Anthropological and Ethnological Sciences, debunked the Race Myth in a single sentence when he said ". . . on a knowledge of their ancestry alone we cannot yet say one man will and another will not be capable of reaching a given cultural standard." As Robert Redfield, professor of anthropology at the University of Chicago, has said, "There is no evidence that the races differ inherently in any ways which would justify a differential treatment among them. One might put it succinctly this way: There are no inferior races; there are only inferior opportunities."

While not even Nazi "science" was able to demonstrate any innate intellectual inequalities among the races, on the other hand, it is true that science has also failed to prove that all races are intellectually equal. The intelligence tests thus far devised are too imperfect to eliminate environmental and cultural factors, and so are unreliable as a basis for interracial comparisons. This indeterminate situation has left the field clear for the race racketeers.

I, for one, suspect the motives of persons and races who pronounce themselves superior. Is it not strange that no two races have ever agreed as to which race is superior? Real superiority would not have to identify or favor or protect itself with such artificial devices as compulsory segregation. It would not matter a great deal if science were to someday find that the races do differ somewhat, intellectually as well as in other respects. What does matter is that we know now that there are no differences of any sort which can possibly justify compulsory segregation or any other form of racial discrimination.

And yet the rabble-rousing yell of the South's white supremacists—like that of their Nazi prototypes—continues to be "mongrelization!" Both groups blithely ignore the diversity of their own backgrounds. And particularly do they ignore the contemporary scientific evidence that the white-Negro combination results in a sound ethnic type with physical and mental characteristics equal and often superior to their parents. The same has been scientifically found true of other racial combinations. As Dr. Montagu has pointed out, "Hybridization is one of the most fundamental processes of evolution. In man it is an age-old process which was unquestionably operative among his proto-human ancestors. The genes combine to produce new types which are always novel and often recognizably superior in some traits to their parental stocks."

James Crow, Ph.D.

We might let the matter drop, were it not for a somewhat novel note recently injected into the Myth of the Master Race. The discordant key was struck by Dr. W. T. Couch in his Publisher's Preface to the admirable book *What the Negro Wants,* which he reluctantly published in 1944 as director of the University of North Carolina Press.

To state the Couch case briefly, it is that history demonstrates the inferiority of the Negro, and that therefore the white majority in the South has a *democratic* right to impose segregation in order to protect its posterity from degeneration.

Dr. Couch looks at the matter this way:

> Since all people are equal, so the assumptions go, the explanation of apparent inequalities must lie in environment.

All of us, in this view, are products of the conditions under which we have lived. No informed person would ever think of blaming the Ashanti, Dahomeans, or Yoruba for anything they do or do not do. If they had the proper environment, so we are led to believe, they could have produced everything in which western man prides himself.

We have long been accustomed to hearing such remarks from Imperial Wizards of the Klan, and from the likes of Bilbo, Rankin, and Ellender in Congress. But Dr. Couch can scarcely plead ignorance. He is certainly aware that there were great Negro states in Africa when Europe was yet a wilderness. The rich civilizations of Egypt and Babylon flourished while our forebears in Europe were stone-age cave men. African Negroes were fashioning iron tools and weaving fine fabrics when the fair Europeans were still wearing hides.

The best available evidence points to the accident of the priority of the industrial revolution in Europe as being largely responsible for the current ascendancy of Western culture. The industrial revolution was itself the result of fortuitous circumstances—Marco Polo's discovery of highly civilized China, the consequent opening of trade between Europe and Asia, and the importation, among an infinity of other things, of printing and gunpowder—with which the Chinese had already operated power engines.

As Paul S. Martin, curator of the Field Museum's department of anthropology, has said, "There is more confusion and more smug and false thinking on the subjects of race, culture, and language than on almost any other subject. In order to prove that our culture is superior to all others, we are wont to compare other civilizations with our own. And the more they differ from ours, the lower they are thought to be. This is illogical, immature, provincial. We, like so-called 'primitive people' and 'savages,' think of our own way of life as the best possible in the world. All civilizations are the end results of contributions and borrowings from other peoples and civilizations. There is one human race, and everybody belongs to it." To this he added (Supermen please note) that Caucasian whites have more resemblance to apes than do some other races.

But Dr. Couch is not content with impugning the record of the Negro in Africa. He has the nerve to ask:

> What is the Negro doing of importance in agriculture, in industry, in the professions? What is he inventing, discovering, writing? What is he contributing that is new and valuable? Can it be that Negroes in this region now have all the educational opportunities they can use?

Judged by any standards, the Negro has made outstanding contributions in all these fields. And judging from the amount of Negro ability, talent, and genius that has fought its way to expression despite all the imposed handicaps, there is every reason to believe that, given equality of opportunity, Negroes can contribute at least as much as any other group.

Dr. Couch seeks to advance some more legitimate excuse than prejudice for the business at hand: forced segregation and prohibitions against interracial intermarriage. He seeks to do this more by asking questions than by making direct statements.

"Can [Negroes and whites] remain racially separate and distinct and at the same time avoid inflicting disabilities on each other?" he begins. The question is lopsided, inasmuch as the Negroes as a race have never imposed disabilities on the whites —not even during Reconstruction, when they could have. Moreover, the question is academic. *Theoretically* the whites might be able to remain racially separate and not impose disabilities; but *practically* the economic and political role of Jim Crow (maintenance of the disunity cheapness of Southern labor through white supremacy) does not lend itself to the evolution of separate-but-equal opportunities.

"Does the white man have no right to attempt to separate cultural from biological integration, and help the Negro achieve the first and deny him the second?" Dr. Couch goes on to ask. "Can biological integration be regarded as a right?"

To answer one question is to answer the other. When a man and a woman of different races marry and have children they are simply enjoying the basic individual human right to do so without any arbitrary restrictions imposed by society on the grounds of race. They are not motivated by anything so inhumanly abstract as a desire for "biological integration." Races, being comprised of individuals, are likewise innocent of such intent. The answer to the question is: Yes, there is a right of two individuals to marry regardless of race, come what "biological integration" there may. If the master racists had the courage of their professed convictions, they would be calling, not for prohibitions against miscegenation, but for legalized eugenics which would deny the right to have children to all mentally incompetent persons, regardless of their race.

Dr. Couch's misapprehensions are further exposed by his question: "What happens to the case for the Negro if it is tied up with things to which he not only has no right, but which, if granted, would destroy all rights?" He will have to answer that one himself.

But at least we are getting somewhere. "If any two people have a right to lead their own lives," Dr. Couch leads on, "certainly any two others or ten or twenty million have a right to opinions on what ought to be allowed and what forbidden. To say that the twenty million have no right to make and enforce decisions that they think necessary to the well-being of all is to say that society has no right to govern itself."

This is reminiscent of a letter I received from Imperial Wizard Colescott in 1944, in which he facetiously declared, "The Klan, after all, believes in majority government." The Klan literature he enclosed made perfectly clear what he meant: white supremacy—government by the white majority "without any political influence by inferior groups."

Dr. Couch carried this Ku-Klux concept of majority-rule-minus-individual-and-minority-rights still further in a letter to me in 1945:

> I take it you believe in democracy. Perhaps you would agree with me that a belief in democracy necessarily involves belief in the good will and sound judgment of people generally. However, the argument you make in your chapter involves the assumption that the majority of the people in the South have bad will and unsound judgment.

I do believe in democracy, above all. But belief in democracy does not require belief in the good will and sound judgment of people generally at all times and places. I do not, for example, believe in the good will and sound judgment of the German people generally at this time, not because they are Germans, but because they have been Nazified for a generation. Moreover, in the matter of racial attitudes I do not believe in the good will and sound judgment of the majority of the Southern people at present, not because they are white Southerners, but because they have been inoculated with race prejudice for many generations. All such attitudes, fortunately, are subject to change within a single generation if not sooner.

The right to hold an opinion is something no earthly power can deny; but the right to express or act upon certain opinions is subject to certain limitations. Such limitations are most likely to be for the good of the majority when they are determined by democratic processes, which means majority rule. Inherent in the concept of democracy, however, are the concepts of individual and minority rights which may not be transgressed by a majority. Prominent among such rights is the right of a man and woman to marry regardless of their race.

But Dr. Couch seems to feel otherwise. Returning to his Preface, we find him saying:

> The assumption of a better, a more valid authority, one that can be understood and that ought to be accepted by all rational beings, one that speaks with the voice of reason and justice, is the only foundation for appeals against majority decisions . . . But the spokesmen for minorities have followed the fashion of the times and denied the existence of any such authority.

Once Dr. Couch's erudite exposition of Negro "inferiority" and his "justification" of segregation have penetrated the semi-literate circles of reaction, he can scarcely avoid much veneration from the demagogues of Dixie.

In his correspondence with me (which I have permission to publish), Dr. Couch continues:

> Of course many other problems are involved. I suppose the most important is the question whether there is anything right or wrong. If you argue that segregation is wrong and that no people ought to choose deliberately to do anything wrong, then you have taken on yourself a real task.

Of course there is right and wrong. Of course segregation is wrong, because it restricts the personal freedom of whole races for no demonstrably legitimate reason. Of course no people ought deliberately to choose to do anything wrong. Of course to insist upon this is a real task, but it is one we cannot dodge much longer.

But to let Dr. Couch continue:

> A lot of people object to what they call compulsory segregation. Under democratic theory the people have a right to follow any laws and customs they please. Can it be said that any people except the Southern people is responsible for the segregation that exists in the South? Was segregation in the South enforced by the United States government or any other power partly or wholly external to the South? If the answer is no, what then is the meaning of "compulsory segregation"?
>
> The meaning would seem to be limited to the fact that the South uses compulsion to get compliance with its laws and customs. But every society does this. Now if this kind of compulsion is present in every society, whether democratic or of another kind, is it not possible that it is indispensable? Can any society reasonably be expected to dispense with something that can't be dispensed with? You need to decide whether you intend to join those who are attacking democracy. If you do not intend to attack democracy, you ought to show wherein the view you represent is not an attack.

This is Southern sectionalism carried to its logical conclusion, which is Southern nationalism. Since when has the South been a "society"—which in this case would mean an autonomous political entity? For that matter, since when has the South been a democracy? To invoke democracy's good name in connection with the imposition of forced segregation by twenty million Southern whites against ten million Southern blacks is simply absurd.

The South, be it known to all, lost the Civil War, and with it the right to govern itself independently of the U. S. Constitution and U. S. Government. In alleging that the South's white majority has a "democratic" right to enforce segregation, Dr. Couch must realize that the "democracy of the South" functions within state boundaries, not within the Mason-Dixon Line. This means that, if we were to accept his definition of the unlimited rights of majorities over minorities, the Negro majorities which still exist in 180 Southern counties would have a "democratic" right to enact laws prohibiting the marriage of whites with whites. The idea is not one whit less democratic than the prevailing statutes of thirty states which prohibit the marriage of whites with Negroes.

Segregators who seek to justify compulsory segregation on grounds of "democratic" majority rule should also take into consideration those whites who live in colonial countries where colored majorities will shortly be coming into democracies of their own. Probably white folks would not be so enthusiastic about segregation if the other races were doing the segregating.

As an ultimate appeal to prejudice, Dr. Couch does not hesitate to repeat the lynch cry of the Klan: "Do you want your daughter to marry a nigger?" Only he does it with more finesse:

> The question says: One concession will lead to another, and ultimately to intermarriage. You and I and our people might not be involved, probably wouldn't. Most likely, for a long time, only a small number would be involved. But have we no duty to the remote future as well as to the present? And if you want to be fair, apply it to yourself. How would you like it . . . ?

Unless one believes with Dr. Couch that there are inferior races, and that a race in the majority in a body politic or otherwise possessed of power has a right to assert its superiority and legislate against interracial intermarriage, there can be no logical objection to one's own daughter or posterity's daughter marrying whomever she pleases. If democracy has its way, marriage will require *mutual* volition in the remote future, no less than at present. In the hope of reconciling those prejudiced persons who object to interracial intermarriage and social equality, it should also be pointed out that *the end of compulsory segregation is not going to usher in an era of compulsory association.*

TOTAL EQUALITY, AND HOW TO GET IT

The book *What the Negro Wants* brings together the answers of fourteen prominent Negro leaders who represent various viewpoints—Southern, Northern, conservative, liberal, radical—but who are unanimous in asserting that what the Negro wants is total equality: precisely the same rights, opportunities, privileges, and responsibilities as other Americans. But wanting total equality and getting it are two different things, especially in the South. What white Southerners, and Americans generally, think and do about the matter are necessarily the determining factors.

Inside and outside the South there are various groups which would severally force the Negro backward, hold him where he is, permit him to progress in certain fields and up to certain points, and those who would guarantee him total equality. Here we are concerned with ways and means of bringing about the latter. There are many reasons why we cannot simply cry, "Aiming point identified!" and shoot the works.

Standing in the way of total equality in the South is the formidable institution of white supremacy. At the moment the regime is slightly inclined to permit Negroes a measure of economic and political advancement, provided that segregation shall remain as a barrier against "social equality."

The administrators and press agents of white supremacy are brutally frank about this. For instance, Governor Chauncey Sparks of Alabama has not hesitated to inform the Negro students of Tuskegee Institute, face to face, that "absolute segregation" and "independent development" should govern the future of the races in the South. Similarly, Governor Broughton of North Carolina has scored "outside agitators, who . . . would flout established and mutually respected conventions and traditions—which cannot in this state, now or ever, be obliterated." He went on to say, "We are striving in North Carolina to give the Negro equal protection under the law, equal educational advantages, the full benefits of public health, agricultural advancement, decent housing conditions, and full and free economic opportunity . . . This is the assured path toward racial harmony and progress, not only in North Carolina, but in all America."

Such sentiments are seconded by virtually the entire white Southern press. For example, the Atlanta *Journal* recently said: "We have tried to outline four constructive ideas for promoting happy and mutually profitable race relationships and for serving the best interests of the South. Each and all of these proposals rest on the major premise that social segregation shall continue."

But perhaps the leading press agent for this school of thought is the columnist John Temple Graves. "Determined now and forever on segregation," Graves wrote in 1944: "Imagine a great Southwide move by middle-of-the-road governors, college presidents, editors, and economic leaders, with or without Negroes in attendance . . . imagine even that the movement or meeting be called a 'Segregation Conference' to emphasize the major premise on which advancement for the race would be not only proposed but put into practice . . ."

Later Graves went on to say, "Last spring this column proposed a meeting not of liberals but of Southerners of just plain decency and enlightenment plus power, to do something big for the Negro on his side of the segregation line. There is a vast and woefully untapped reservoir of good will for the Negro among millions of white Southerners who need only to be assured that they are not dealing with any proposition now or hereafter to eliminate segregation . . . The will of the Southern white against racial amalgamation is total. For that he is willing to filibuster, fight, play foul or fair, risk another Civil War."

Mark Etheridge, of the Louisville (Ky.) *Courier-Journal,* evidently thinks the white South would not only risk, but fight and win, a war to preserve segregation. Speaking in 1944, he said: "The Southern Negro cannot afford to drive from his side, in his march to a greater fulfillment of his rights, the Southern white men of good will. He must recognize that there is no power in the world—not even in all the mechanized armies of the earth, Allied and Axis—which could now force the Southern white people to the abandonment of the principle of social segregation. It is a cruel disillusionment, bearing the germs of strife and perhaps tragedy, for any of their [the Negroes'] leaders to tell them that they can expect it as the price of their participation in the war . . . If [the Southern white] is not willing to break down segregation—and he is not—he can at least see that it is not achieved on the brutal standards of a Ku Klux Klansman. He can see that it is made as painless as possible."

Etheridge grossly underestimates the potentialities of mechanized armies, but since the Axis armies would hardly have been inclined (not to say disinclined) to enforce total equality in the South, and since the U. S. Army is not likely to be given any such assignment, the gentleman is correct in so far as he suggests that the means for the forcible overthrow of segregation are not now in hand.

Obviously there is much to choose between the "separate-equality" brand of white supremacy manufactured by Couch, Graves, Etheridge & Co. and the lily-white product hawked by Bilbo, Rankin, Talmadge & Co. Fortunately, the former product is currently becoming the most popular; but the latter has many addicted customers, and its jobbers are ever on the alert for new openings. Lest we forget how distasteful archdemagoguery can be, let us bear briefly with "The Man" Bilbo, who declares:

> We, the people of the South, must draw the color line tighter and tighter, and the white man or woman who dares cross that color line should be promptly and forever ostracized. The white race is the custodian of the Gospel of Jesus Christ. Anyone who would in the name of Christianity make us a Negroid people betrays his religion and his race.

That is the way the demagogues and their followers are wont to speak in public. In private they are more apt to confide (as one did to me): "The only way we're willing to give the niggers equality is by fuckin' 'em white!"

And so it must be recognized that there are in the South two distinct breeds of white supremacists: (1) the "Southern liberals," some of whom will go so far as to promote "separate equality," and (2) the Southern slavocrats who would maintain the status quo or worse.

The thesis of the slavocrats is, "If you give a nigger $1.00, he'll take $1.25." Their assumption is that any economic or political concessions to Negroes will ultimately prove conducive to social equality. For once they are correct; but it would be impolitic for Negroes and their friends to proclaim as much from the housetops, for to do so would undoubtedly frighten all the liberalism out of the "Southern liberals," and thus deliver the South into the hands of the slavocrats.

When the slavocrats threaten that abolition of Jim Crow will bring on a resurgence of the Klan and mob violence, they are not just bluffing. But when I vouch for the fact, I do so not for the sake of intimidating Negroes and their friends, but to forewarn them so that their abolition movement need not be inadequate or premature.

It is this factor of kinetic violence that chiefly distinguishes the problem in the South from the problem elsewhere (Detroit and Los Angeles excepted). Local police, far from dealing appropriately with such violence, would very often be in the forefront of it. When the disorder reached major proportions, Southern governors would send in their lily-white, Klux-minded state guards. *Federal troops could not be sent in* without a legislature's or governor's request—and such requests would no more be forthcoming than they were in the wake of Reconstruction. In short, a massacre rather than a riot would ensue. (In Detroit, 85 per cent of those arrested were Negroes, 75 per cent of those killed were Negroes, and 60 per cent of the Negroes killed were shot by policemen; in the South Negroes would not escape so lightly.)

Any realistic strategy for achieving total equality must be based upon frank recognition of the basic facts of life in the South today. Outstanding among these is the fact that the case for economic and political equality can be argued on the street corner—yea, even in the klaverns—without necessarily making oneself a candidate for lynching. On the other hand, to loudly proclaim that total equality is the goal and that economic and political equality will be used toward that end, is sufficient to not only stop the clock but to turn it back.

In other words, upon the handling of Jim Crow depends all hope for total equality (and progress of all sorts) in the South. This is true because the entire system of white supremacy is predicated upon prefabricated prejudices against social equality, against which white Southerners have been conditioned to react emotionally instead of rationally.

It will be recalled that immediate, all-out, frontal assault has been recommended for storming the citadels of economic and political equality. Such tactics are proper and practical because the long arm of Uncle Sam exercises jurisdiction over the right to vote and the right to work as guaranteed by the FEPC. But in the matter of the right not to be segregated, there is as yet no established federal police power. Until there is, Southern Negroes and their friends must confine their attack against Jim Crow to co-ordinated flanking maneuvers.

What, then, are believers in total equality to do?

The Conference of Southern Negroes which convened at Durham, North Carolina, in 1942, took this stand in its epochal Durham Statement:

> We are fundamentally opposed to the principle and practice of compulsory segregation in our American society, whether of races or classes or creeds; however, we regard it as both sensible and timely to address ourselves now to the current problems of racial discrimination and neglect, and to ways in which we may co-operate in the advancement of programs aimed at the sound improvement of race relations within the democratic framework.

The Durham Statement practically demanded acknowledgment from the white South. It was forthcoming in a series of conferences which culminated in the formation of the Southern Regional Council, which absorbed the old Commission on Interracial Co-operation, and attracted to its fold one thousand white and Negro Southerners of varying shades of liberalism. Without exactly saying so, the SRC adopted in general the goals of the Durham Statement without specifically endorsing its condemnation of segregation—and outspoken opponents of Jim Crow were quick to make an issue of the fact.

Lillian Smith, author of *Strange Fruit,* in an article in *Common Ground* said: "Not much is going to be done to bring about racial democracy by this group [the SRC] until its leaders accept and acknowledge publicly the basic truth that segregation is injuring us on every level of our life and is so intolerable to the human spirit that we, all of us, black and white, must bend every effort to rid our minds, hearts, and culture of it." In the same issue, J. Saunders Redding, professor of English at Hampton Institute, charged that "The men who at present writing have policy-making powers in the new organization are pretty effectively enslaved by one big common thing: segregation. *Segregation is the sine qua non of race relations in the South.*"

No doubt there are some white members of the SRC who will go to their graves believing in segregation, but SRC director Guy B. Johnson, in a succeeding issue of *Common Ground,* had this to say: "Our goal is democracy and equality of opportunity. We are striving to improve the social, civic, and economic life of our region in spite of a deep-seated and undemocratic pattern of segregation . . . Personally, I should rather help capture the foothills which have to be captured sooner or later than merely to point out the distant peak and urge my comrades to storm it at once! I, too, can see the peak, but I can see no particular virtue in starting an association of peak gazers."

And so we have revolving in and about the SRC a controversy as to whether or not denunciation of segregation is essential to, or even advisable, in connection with an organized movement of Southern whites and Negroes "to do the most and best that can be done here and now."

Even among the Negro drafters of the Durham Statement there had been a difference of opinion on this. A minority argued that the statement, in the interests of diplomacy, could have refrained from mentioning segregation at all. The controversy again came to a head at the 1944 meeting of the SRC. There, two resolutions on segregation were introduced. One, introduced by a Negro editor, said:

> Legal racial segregation exists in the South. We recognize this fact. We shall center our efforts on gaining equal facilities

as provided by law and equal opportunities for all people of
the South.

The sponsor of this resolution said that it was dictated in the
interest of strategy and was not meant to imply any endorsement
of Jim Crow. Whether it did or not was warmly debated. A
substitute resolution was then offered by a Negro educator, as
follows:

> The Southern Regional Council opposes the principle and
> practice of segregation. We oppose segregation because it vio-
> lates democratic processes, it violates Christian principles, it
> develops friction and ill will between the races, it makes for
> gross discrimination, since there is seldom if ever equality in
> segregation; but as long as legal segregation exists the SRC
> shall work within the law to equalize all opportunities for
> Negroes within that framework as stated and implied in the
> laws of the several states.

It was felt that the first resolution implied an acceptance of
segregation, and that the second would ruin the SRC's hope of
ultimately being supported by Southern funds. And so it was
voted—45 to 25, and not at all along racial lines—to table both
resolutions.

Now who is right about this matter?

I would venture to say that the Durham Statement, coming
from Negroes, was morally obliged to include a condemnation
of segregation, and that it could not have been done in a more
statesmanlike manner. I would also say that the SRC, as an
organization of Southern whites and Negroes dedicated to the
task of asking for improvements from the incumbent system of
white supremacy, would needlessly frustrate itself by condemning
segregation at this time. And I would say further that Lillian
Smith has done and can do immense good by condemning segregation as an individual, but that she is not being realistic in
demanding the same of the SRC. On the other hand, the South
cannot get along without an organization of those Southerners
who carry the torch for total equality—and this it has in the
potent Southern Conference for Human Welfare.

There is an unfortunate propensity on the part of many
Southerners, white and Negro, to regard prejudice as the *sine*

qua non of race relations, and to overemphasize the role of education in combating it. For instance, Dr. Gordon B. Hancock of Virginia Union University, a director of the SRC, has written Miss Smith as follows:

> You who make the whole issue one of segregation are overlooking the matter of prejudice, the more fundamental issue that we of the SRC are trying to face. . . . You are primarily interested in denouncing the effects; we are primarily interested in attacking and destroying the cause . . .

Subsequently, in a letter to me, Dr. Hancock said:

> Race prejudice must be destroyed before discrimination can be taken out of segregation and the law itself is hopeless and helpless to accomplish this fact where prejudice is too strong. It is true that, here and there, discriminations are being eliminated as in the case of teachers' salaries; but it is also true that this is due to a relinquishment of prejudice in its most rabid form. In my releases to the Associated Negro Press I have been sloganizing as follows: *"Praejudicium generis delendum est* [race prejudice must be destroyed]!"

All of which is all very well, provided no one is given the impression that mere sloganizing—whether in Latin or any number of current languages—can under existing circumstances bring about the abolition of prejudice or segregation or discrimination or white supremacy. To argue whether prejudice or segregation came first is to carry on about the goose and the egg. *First* came the excess-profit motive which gave birth to the institution of white supremacy, and all its bastard offspring might be described as products of artificial insemination.

No one has exposed the economics of Southern racism more deftly than Lillian Smith in her study "Two Men and a Bargain." Unfortunately, this insight was lacking from her novel *Strange Fruit,* wherein the millowner appears as a kindly disposed gent who simply couldn't believe that his foremen were out lynching a Negro in order to insure a more stable supply of cheap labor.

In her rejection of the SRC, Miss Smith has observed that man is not just an economic and political unit, and that the South's major problems cannot be solved by trying to put a loaf of bread, a book, and a ballot in everyone's hand. She emphasizes the damaging psychological effects of segregation upon both whites and Negroes. Instead of a "Negro problem," she points out, what we actually have is a problem of white pathology. She would solve this problem, apparently, by first recognizing it for what it is and then prescribing the proper therapeutic treatment.

But Miss Smith can no more cure the white South's Jim Crow mania with therapy than Dr. Hancock can cure the white South's addiction to prejudice with Latin slogans or the SRC can cure the white South of discrimination by invoking the ideals of justice and brotherhood. For all of the white South's denials of racial democracy *arise out of* the denial of economic and political democracy to *all* people of the region.

It must be kept in mind that the Southern economy is based upon cheap labor which is in turn based upon white supremacy; consequently, all of the dominant political, educational, and social machinery of the region is prostituted to the maintenance of the interracial status quo or worse, which requires the perpetuation, rather than the elimination, of race prejudice. In competition with this machinery, unofficial attempts to educate prejudice out of existence haven't a chance.

So long as white supremacy remains an economic and political reality, no amount of education or agitation or mental therapy can bring about the abolition of segregation in the South by the South (any more than mere agitation could have abolished slavery). In other words, short of another civil war, *the Southern Negro must be emancipated economically and politically before he can be emancipated socially.* This means that he must first join democratic labor unions and beat a democratic path to the polls. Once those two things have been accomplished—gains in one will facilitate gains in the other—the abolition of Jim Crow will be as inevitable as was the abolition of chattel slavery after the Civil War broke out. Once the economic and political functions of Jim Crow have been negated, its social aspect will vanish as the subterfuge that it is.

At this point the strategy for achieving total equality in this country becomes clear.

In non-Southern areas (where Jim Crow enjoys a quasi-legal existence appreciably less rigorous than in Dixie), the campaign for total equality can and should be prosecuted by all-out frontal assault.

In the South, the economic and political serfdom of the Negro and the concomitant potential of uncontrolled violence requires that the case for social equality be presented *apart from* the case for economic and political equality.

If this strategy is not followed, there may be no Southern progress in any direction, but reaction in all directions. Hence this is not at all a strategy of appeasement, but the most radical of practical programs for achieving total equality without abortive violence.

The flanking movement in the South requires that a distinction be made pro tem between segregation and discrimination— that the two issues not be confused by indiscriminate application of the "Jim Crow" label to all manner of interracial inequities.

The several groups involved in the struggle for total equality should also assume specialized functions. The case against segregation per se should be left largely if not exclusively in the hands of the real Southern white liberals, who are in a position to present it most effectively. This they can do both individually, after the manner of Lillian Smith, and collectively, as in the Southern Conference for Human Welfare. Non-Southerners can help most by concentrating on the basic task of economic and political emancipation for the Southern Negro—by working for establishment of a permanent FEPC, by bringing suffrage cases before the Supreme Court, by insisting upon adequate federal protection of the economic and political rights thus secured, and by aiding the efforts to organize Southern Negroes into labor and farmers' unions.

Southern Negroes themselves should seek first to become union men and democratic voters. By also going to court and exercising every other legitimate form of demand, protest, and pressure, the Negro can have an appreciable amount of the physical injury taken out of Jim Crow. This is what he has been doing since Reconstruction, but the accelerator should be pressed to the floor. The reaction of a typical white Southerner to this assertion was, "Hold on a minute! This business of equal rights has got to be fed to us Southerners just so much at a time. It's like tryin' to feed beefsteak to a baby that's never done nothin' but suck titty. You got to wean it away." While there is some truth in that, there is considerably more truth, and justice too, in what the old Negro woman said to the judge who cautioned her that colored folks couldn't expect to get even breaks with white folks all in a minute: "God knows it's been a long minute!"

In going to court to demand equality under the law, Southern Negroes almost inevitably are confronted with the accusation that "What these niggers is really after is social equality!" When that happens, Southern Negroes can afford to reply that what they are actually demanding is *enforcement of the Jim Crow laws*—which in every case call for "separate-but-equal" provisions. The claimants should insist further that segregation is irrelevant to the economic or political matter at hand, and refuse to discuss it in the same connection.

It is, of course, true that Jim Crow has always meant injury added to insult. As colored folk say, it has always been a case of:

> *White folks in the dinin' room,*
> *Eatin' cake and cream;*
> *Niggers in the kitchen,*
> *Eatin' good old greasy greens.*

There is no need for anyone to be concerned over the prospect envisioned by the self-styled "Southern liberals" who would transform the Jim Crow fence from a discriminatory horizontal line into a vertical line of equal opportunity. Long before then, the preconditions for the abolition of Jim Crow altogether will have been established.

Confidentially (don't tell Talmadge & Co.), every step toward separate-but-equal provisions will prove to be a step toward free-and-equal status for all. Since the South is already spending almost all it can on public services, to actually provide equal facilities would require a lowering of white standards. This being the case, each time more equality is forced, more of the pinch of the Jim Crow shoe will be transferred to the white foot, and as soon as its intolerability becomes mutual, it will be cast aside.

Jim Crow is such a gross creature he has a way of rousing both
Jim Crowers and Jim Crowed to an equally blind frenzy. This
is forgivable among the latter, but not at all effective. To have
at Jim Crow like Don Quixote versus a windmill has often
proven less than unavailing.

It is past time Negroes and their friends stopped speaking
loosely about the "unconstitutionality" of Jim Crow. Jim Crow
may be un-American, unchristian, undemocratic, and unjust;
but under Supreme Court rulings to date, Jim Crow laws are
not themselves unconstitutional. At present, as Westbrook Pegler
so gleefully maintains, "it is still legal in the United States to
hold and express racial and religious prejudices"—even in the
form of Jim Crow laws.

The Fourteenth Amendment of the Constitution provides that
"No state shall make or enforce any law which shall abridge the
privileges or immunities of citizens of the United States . . . nor
deny to any person within its jurisdiction the equal protection
of the laws." Now the privileges and immunities of American
citizens are not at all nebulous—either they are specified in the
Constitution or federal laws, or they have no legal existence.
Freedom from Jim Crow—the right not to be segregated—is not
among the rights of citizens so specified—as those Negroes who
have traveled the hard road to the Supreme Court have learned.
In carrying out the Fourteenth Amendment guarantee of equal
protection of the laws, the Courts have merely granted *redress* in
cases where Negroes have complained of unequal Jim Crow
facilities; but the Jim Crow laws themselves have been left intact.

One ground for complaint against Jim Crow facilities which
has not been fully utilized is that the constitutional guarantee
of equal protection of the laws extends to equal *convenience* as
well as other aspects of equality. For example, Negroes might sue
for the right to attend the public school *nearest* them, regardless
of race. The supreme court of New Jersey upheld this particular
right in 1944.

But at best such court trials of Jim Crow can only bring about
a slow amelioration of the discrimination inherent in segregation
and bring to bear economic pressure for its abolition. The end
can and should be hastened by federal legislation. Congress has

the power, under its constitutional authority to enact laws to promote the public safety and welfare, to adopt an anti-segregation law (particularly in interstate commerce), or an even broader statute establishing the equal rights of races and outlawing the expression of racial and religious hatred.

Ideally and eventually, total equality should be guaranteed by an amendment to the Constitution. Such an organic law would not be without precedent. The Soviet Union, a land with 187 nationalities, has such a law and has found it eminently practicable and salutary. Article 123 of the Soviet Bill of Rights and Duties provides: "Equality of rights of citizens of the U.S.S.R., irrespective of their nationality or race, in all spheres of economic, state, social, and political life, is an indefeasible law. Any direct or indirect restriction of the rights of, or, conversely, any establishment of direct or indirect privileges for, citizens on account of their race or nationality, as well as any advocacy of racial or national exclusiveness or hatred or contempt, is punishable by law."

With reference to the working of this basic Russian law, Dr. Douglas Southall Freeman, the biographer of Robert E. Lee, has said in the Richmond (Va.) *News-Leader:*

"The Russian nation has for a generation shown what can be done to outlaw race prejudice in a country with many kinds of people. They did not wait for people's minds to change. They made racial discrimination and persecution illegal. . . . Ponder, please, these observations in a brief new study of what anthropology contributed to human understanding:

" 'They welcomed and honored the different races, different customs, different arts of the many tribes and countries that live as part of their nation. The more backward groups were given special aid to help them catch up with the more advanced. Each people was helped to develop its own cultural forms, its own written language, theater, music, dance, and so on. At the same time that each people was encouraged in its national self-development, the greatest possible interchange of customs was fostered, so that each group became more distinctively itself and at the same time more a part of the whole. The Russians have welcomed cultural *differences* and they have refused to treat them as *in-*

feriorities. No part of the Russian program has had greater success than their racial program.'

"How about applying that to America?"

The principal difficulty in applying that to America lies in the still present danger of maladministration of such a law—a danger which will continue to exist until American democracy has been strengthened and anti-democratic elements eliminated from the government. This is particularly true as regards the several proposals to outlaw or at least ban from the mails the expression of racial or religious hatred. To defend such expression in the name of freedom of speech is unwarranted, as the expression of racial and religious prejudice cannot possibly serve any legitimate purpose in a democracy. It is exactly equivalent to shouting "Fire!" in a crowded theater—a form of expression held to be illegal by the Supreme Court on the correct ground that it endangers the public safety and welfare.

However, the fact remains that a law banning the expression of racial and religious prejudice might now be perverted to such an extent that the Negro press, for example, would be banned rather than the anti-Negro press; and, as Jehovah's Witnesses have pointed out, certain religious minorities might be persecuted in like manner. Prejudiced administrators of the law might even go so far, theoretically, as to forbid the distribution of the Bible. Hence the enactment of such a law should await the strengthening of American democracy. Meanwhile, public exposure must be relied upon to mitigate the evil effects of racial and religious hate propaganda.

Unlike a congressional statute, a constitutional amendment establishing the equal rights of races would of course require ratification by three fourths of the states, which means that rejection by thirteen states could kill it. It will be recalled that refusal of the Southern states to ratify the Fourteenth Amendment following the Civil War led to military occupation. An amendment guaranteeing the equal rights of the races, including as it would a ban on segregation, would unquestionably get a hot reception in the South today. Unanimous ratification by all non-Southern states plus one or more borderline states would be necessary for its adoption.

Such a law or amendment would produce more rumors of civil war, but still no war. However, there would be mass violence, and the white supremacists would make good their threat to make life miserable for Negroes. White supremacy is going to die a hard death—almost as hard as slavery's. It will take the South approximately as long to get over the death of Jim Crow as it is taking to get over the passing of Old Black Joe, the slave.

Of course the Negro is entitled to total equality now. But by suffering segregation another decade (no more) before seeking to establish total equality as the *law* of the land, he can with the help of most Americans build the economic and political framework which will give it a concrete-and-steel substance without which the legal superstructure would be an empty stage setting.

TO MAKE THE SOUTH SAFE FOR DEMOCRACY

Because of its afore-mentioned poverty, prejudice, poor health, poor education, poll tax, white primary, and the relative weakness of its unions, the South is American democracy's Achilles' heel—its soft spot. Not only the Southern enemies of democracy are aware of this—many of the nation's most powerful antidemocratic elements are also concentrating their big guns on the South. Already they have succeeded in blasting into office a pack of prostitute Southern congressmen and senators who for decades have virtually controlled Congress and subverted democracy throughout America. Not satisfied with this, some among them are plotting to build up a reservoir of fascism in the South with which to flood the whole nation.

There is no intent here to oversimplify the problem of the South in terms of democracy versus fascism; on the contrary, this has been an attempt to sketch something of the complexity of the problem. Nevertheless, the struggle against fascism in the South is basic, just as the War Against Fascism was basic. A total democratic victory over fascism, inside and outside the South, is prerequisite to any and all forms of permanent Southern progress.

The War Against Fascism has not been completely won, either at home or abroad. While democracy-in-arms has proven itself more than a match for fascist aggression on the battle fronts of the world, it must fight on to total victory over fascism's continuing non-military machinations. There will be no draft to carry on this fight to the finish. The forces of democracy will be made up entirely of volunteer citizens, who must organize themselves

Dummy suspended by the Klan in Miami

Senator James Tunnell examines ballot boxes used in Arkansas in 1944

"Pass-the-Biscuits Pappy" O'Daniel, senator from Texas, serving Jesse Jones

Gerald L. K. Smith (right), the Reverend Arthur W. Terminiello (center), and Fred Kister in police station after warrants for their arrest had been issued

Bilbo   *Rankin*

Four filibustering champions of white supremacy

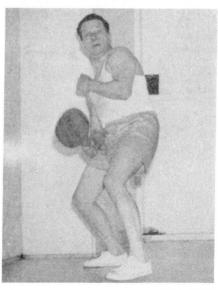

Eastland   *Ellender*

"His Majesty the Imperial Wizard"
James A. Colescott

Eugene Talmadge, governor of Geor
by the grace of the county unit sys

Tom Linder, commissioner of agricul-
ture for Georgia, economic isolationist,
champion of white supremacy, prophet
of Armageddon . . .

Tracy O'Neal, Atlanta Journal

into effective units, elect their own leaders, and decide what action is to be taken.

Just as democracy has defeated fascism in the field of military science, so must it finish the job with economico-political science. In this continuing phase of the struggle, economics and politics are as inextricably bound up as were the air, sea, and land forces during the armed conflict. This means that the forces of democracy, particularly the unions, must combine economic with political operations. The ever-increasing complexity of modern society, with its concomitant necessity for ever-increasing co-ordination, requires that democracy be both economic and political if it is to prevail.

The weapons of economic and political warfare are no less technical than those of military warfare, and they can be mastered only through training and experience. Primarily these weapons are the union card and the ballot. No one is going to issue these weapons. Citizens who enlist for democracy must take up these weapons themselves, learn to use them in concert, with self-discipline and eternal vigilance.

Fourscore and five years ago the American people took up arms to free the South from the curse of chattel slavery. Today the whole South is caught up in the bondage of wage slavery. But this time there need be no civil war or military occupation—for this time the bulk of the South's people stand ready to fight *for* freedom.

The late President Roosevelt was well aware of this. In his epochal speech at Gainesville, Georgia, in 1936, he said: "I speak to you of conditions in this, my other state. Most men and women who work for wages in this whole area get wages which are far too low . . . And let us remember well that buying power means many other kinds of better things—better schools, better health, better hospitals, better highways. These things will not come to us in the South if we oppose progress—if we believe in our hearts that the feudal system is the best system.

"One thing is certain—we are not going back to the old days. We are going forward to better days. We are calling for co-operation all along the line, and the co-operation is increasing because more and more people are coming to understand that abuses of the past which have been successfully eradicated are not going to be restored.

" . . . if the people . . . want definite action in the Congress of the United States, they must send to that Congress senators and representatives who are willing to stand up and fight night and day for federal statutes drawn to meet actual needs . . . which go to the root of the problems; which remove the inequalities, raise the standards, and, over a period of years, give constant improvement to the conditions of human life . . .

"I think the South is going to remain Democratic, but I think it is going to be a more intelligent form of democracy than has kept the South, for other reasons, in the Democratic column all these years. It will be intelligent thinking; and, in my judgment, because the South is learning, it is going to be a liberal democracy."

To achieve the liberal democratic South envisioned by Roosevelt requires—as has oft been said—the organization of Southern workers and farmers into democratic unions. But it also requires enlightened political action of the sort Roosevelt recommended. Through collective bargaining and co-operatives, Southern workers and farmers can achieve a rising standard of living; but to accelerate that rise and make it secure, Southern workers and farmers must also put political democracy to work.

This means that such roadblocks to democracy as the poll tax and white primary have got to go. . . .

But even after the road to the polls has been cleared, it cannot be expected that a perfect democracy will arise overnight. Nothing of the sort has as yet appeared in those Southern states where the poll tax and white primary have already been abolished. Not even a modicum of the improvements which are possible has been achieved—and all because the potential voters have not been duly informed, organized, and activated for democratic political action. This was only to be expected under the circumstances, past and present. Given freedom from want and fear, man is by nature democratically inclined; but it is too much to expect him to cast off the burden of an undemocratic past with a single gesture.

The South's undemocratic past hangs heavy over her head.

For generations great masses of Southerners have been denied a voice in governing themselves. Many of them have come to look upon politics as something completely rotten and beyond their power to set right. Their personal problems of securing food, clothing, shelter, and medical care have been so omnipresent as to virtually preclude their taking time to give due consideration to political means of improving their lot. Nor is their low literacy level conducive to informed political action. Consequently, Southern politics is based almost entirely upon personality and patronage, rather than issues.

In view of all this, some well-meaning Southern liberals have actually expressed doubt that the franchise should be further extended until such time as democratic forces are sufficiently organized and equipped to overcome the machinations of demagoguery. That this hesitancy is not entirely unfounded is borne out by what Talmadge recently told me. "Yeah, I'm a convert on the poll tax," he said. "I done decided that the best way to keep the niggers from votin' is to let all the white folks vote, and then pass the word around that Mr. Nigger is not wanted at the polls."

But if it is to ever come into its own, democracy must demonstrate that its faith and hope is in the people. Thomas Jefferson had the right idea when he said, "Let every man exercise his equal right to vote." Franklin D. Roosevelt was even more explicit when he said, "The right to vote must be open to all our citizens irrespective of race, color, or creed—without tax or artificial restriction of any kind. The sooner we get to that basis of political equality, the better it will be for the country as a whole."

One hazard encountered in doing this is that such modern opinion-forming media as the press and radio are largely dominated by anti-democratic elements. In other words, it is altogether possible for anti-democratic forces, through their control of propaganda instruments, to so pervert the public mind as to set up mental barriers to democracy which would be quite as effective as the poll tax, white primary, or other such formalized restrictions.

Even so, the democratic solution is not to be found in withholding suffrage even temporarily, but rather in universal extension of the suffrage *coupled with* an enormously intensified program of public political education and organized political action. The organizations of democracy—particularly the unions —have scarcely begun to make use of the press and radio facilities which are available to them. Such organizations have the two-headed job of informing their own members and informing the general public.

The decade-old AFL-CIO split in the American labor movement has weakened labor's political arm considerably, although in recent years the unions have succeeded in exerting a democratic political influence on the local, state, and national levels. But American labor still has a long way to go politically (not to mention the distance yet to be traveled by American farm folk).

In the elections of 1936 and 1940 the main branches of organized labor achieved a certain amount of political unity through such groups as Labor's Non-Partisan League. But since the Congress of Industrial Organizations established its Political Action Committee in 1944, the AFL executive board has laid down a policy of non-co-operation with any joint labor political committee which embraces the CIO.

I saw this AFL policy of non-co-operation at work in Atlanta early in 1946. A meeting had been called to discuss formation of a joint labor Georgia Legislative Committee. Attending in response to the call were the CIO, Railroad Brotherhoods, the independent telephone workers union, and several AFL unions. After representatives of all these had spoken in one voice of the urgent need for united political action by labor, the AFL's southeastern representative arose to remind AFL locals that if they participated in such a committee they would "doubtless hear from their internationals."

Fortunately, however, there is in the South an organization through which all branches of organized labor, as well as the farmers' unions, are co-operating with other community groups in a far-reaching program of political and educational action. This is the Southern Conference for Human Welfare, whose salutary influence has frequently been noted.

The Southern Conference arose in response to the urgent need for such an action group to cope with the problems presented by the President's *Report on the Economic Condition of the South*. In response to a call sent out "to everyone interested in a liberal honest effort to consider ways and means of lifting the level of life for all," some twelve hundred Southerners, white and Negro, convened for the SCHW organizational meeting in Birmingham in 1938. Among those present were many prominent leaders of labor, education, religion, agriculture, youth and Negro groups.

In a letter of greeting to the conference, President Roosevelt said: "The long struggle by liberal leaders of the South for human welfare in your region has been implemented on an unprecedented scale these past five and one half years by federal help. Yet we have recognized publicly this year that what has been done is only a beginning, and that the South's unbalance is a major concern not merely of the South, but of the whole nation.

"It is heartening, therefore, to face these human problems, not locally or individually, but in a united front from Fort Raleigh to the Alamo. You know, from years of trying, the difficulties of your task. I believe you will find it impossible in many instances to separate human from economic problems. But if you steer a true course and keep everlastingly at it, the South will long be thankful for this day."

Dr. Frank P. Graham, the distinguished liberal president of the University of North Carolina, was elected chairman of the conference; and he has faithfully served as its honorary chairman ever since. At the initial meeting he announced that, "The conference will be open to Southerners of all parties, races, and creeds, who, with good will and devotion, will work with the conference in its program to upbuild the South and to advance human freedom and human democracy in all our Southern states."

The manifold resolutions which this first conference adopted were indicative of the long-pent-up sentiments of decent Southerners, who, having at last established an organization of their own, did not hesitate to speak their minds. When a squad of policemen descended upon the city auditorium and threatened to arrest the entire assemblage if it did not segregate itself, the conference covered itself with glory by strongly resolving never again to convene where segregation would be imposed on its meetings.

Needless to say, such an uncompromising stand was enough to

incur the enmity of every agency of white supremacy in the South, and the conference has since been subjected to many a smear. But its good work continues to speak for itself, and to win it an ever-broadening mass membership, truly representative of the South's decent-thinking people.

Real progress was made during the two years which passed before the Southern Conference met in Chattanooga in 1940, when both the CIO and AFL urged their Southern unions to send delegates.

"We are here to celebrate a new South that is being born," Dr. Graham told the conference. "Here tonight we represent all walks of life in the South. We are not here to convert each other nor to quibble over differences. We are here to make the South safe for differences: to recognize the realities of our common life, and to join our strength together in working for our common goals of political and economic democracy, and for the kind of government that rests upon the dignity of the common man."

When the conference convened again in 1942, shortly after Pearl Harbor, it was to consider "the South's part in winning the war." The meeting was presided over by the Rev. John B. Thompson, and his remarks accurately reflect the program and nature of the conference.

"To most of us the problems we have discussed are old, old problems as ancient as our ancestors—and sometimes they have seemed as hopeless as our ancestors!" he declared. "But you and I are proud to be here because in this conference we have been developing new attitudes toward old problems, and new concerted action in our search for their solution.

"Tonight we are very solemn as we assemble again, for our unity is made even more real by our common danger and by the danger to democracy and freedom throughout the world. Tonight we Southerners have no sectional pride and no sectional blindness. Every newspaper and every radio reminds us that every problem we confront is now a world problem, and that every great world problem comes, uninvited, to our own doorsteps.

"That is why we have brought to this conference distinguished representatives of a national government which has tried to fulfill the promises of democracy, a government that is trying to make our own democracy more articulate at the very time we are fighting for the preservation of democratic ways throughout the world. That is why we have here representatives of labor who realize that the conditions of man's work may strengthen his soul or may destroy it; and that the unity of working men is absolutely essential both for their own well-being and for the nation's victory.

"That is why this conference includes many able scholars and intellectuals who know that education is not an ornament with which to adorn useless lives but a holy responsibility which must be related to fulfilling the needs of the people. Likewise we have here churchmen who know the teachings of the Jewish prophets and of Jesus well enough to realize that it is suicidal for religion to be used as an opiate for any class, and that the church will not be worthy to help save the world unless it pours out its own strength and moral passion on behalf of the most oppressed human beings in the commonwealth.

"We have here youth—students still in school and youngsters on way to camps—young men and women who love this Southland and this nation ardently but who do not want their lives to be spent in vain whether they are permitted to give long years of service or must go forth to sudden battle. We have here Negro people who have suffered untold indignities but who still give their patient and enthusiatic vote to the opportunities of our democracy in opposition to all forms of defeatism and disillusion.

"We know that thinking about our democratic goals and values is not irrelevant. It is necessary! For the things we believe in will determine the kind of struggle we make; its quality, its persistence, its success."

Yes, there are good people in the South—and the best of them belong to the conference.

There is in the South another organization with great potentialities for promoting progress. This is the Southern Regional Council, launched in 1944, with Dr. Howard Odum, of the University of North Carolina's school of sociology, as acting chairman and Dr. Guy S. Johnson as director. While the conference and the council have many aims and functions in common, there is both a quantitative and qualitative difference between them. The council's stated purpose is "to achieve, through research and action, the most and best that can be done here and now." But the council is not empowered to engage in political action, whereas the conference is.

This means that the council is eligible to receive donations from tax-exempt foundations and has neither a financial nor functional need for rank-and-file membership. The conference, on the other hand, must have mass membership, both for financial support and effective political action. With the conference specializing in political action, the council can help tend the non-political fields, seeking the widest possible audience for its research and educational services. These two organizations are, and of a right ought to be, complementary.

But whatever the organizational channels through which democracy comes to the South, the issue itself is clear. . . .

As it did after the Civil War, the South stands at the crossroads. It can continue down the path of prejudice, with poverty and privation for all but its exploiters. Or it can take the highroad to democracy—political, economic, racial; for democracy is indivisible—and proceed full speed ahead to the promised land of liberty and justice for all.

INDEX